Almon John

The Peerage of Scotland

A genealogical and historical account of all the peers of that ancient kingdom

Almon John

The Peerage of Scotland
A genealogical and historical account of all the peers of that ancient kingdom

ISBN/EAN: 9783337243203

Printed in Europe, USA, Canada, Australia, Japan

Cover: Foto ©ninafisch / pixelio.de

More available books at **www.hansebooks.com**

THE PEERAGE OF SCOTLAND:

A Genealogical and Historical Account

OF ALL THE

PEERS of that ANCIENT KINGDOM;

THEIR

DESCENTS, COLLATERAL BRANCHES, BIRTHS, MARRIAGES, and ISSUE.

TOGETHER WITH

A Like ACCOUNT of all the

ATTAINTED PEERS;

AND A

COMPLETE ALPHABETICAL LIST

OF THOSE

NOBLES OF SCOTLAND,

Whose TITLES are EXTINCT.

COLLECTED FROM

PARLIAMENT ROLLS, RECORDS, FAMILY DOCUMENTS, and the PERSONAL INFORMATION of MANY NOBLE PEERS.

ALSO THE

PATERNAL COATS of ARMS, CRESTS, SUPPORTERS, and MOTTOES, most elegantly engraved.

LONDON:

Printed for J. ALMON, opposite Burlington-House in Piccadilly; T. CADELL, in the Strand; R. BALDWIN, S. CROWDER, ROBINSON and ROBERTS, S. BLADON, and JOHNSON and DAVENPORT, in Pater-noster Row.

MDCCLXVII.

PREFACE.

THE nobility of Scotland yield to no other in Europe, for antiquity, illustrious actions in peace and war, and that patriotism they have displayed from the earliest ages. From the old form of their government, they were many of them a kind of sovereign lords, as well as from the nature of the country, its division into clans, the smallness of their number, and consequently the large extent of their possessions. They were so great a bar to, and so jealous of the encroachments of their monarchs, that even in peaceable times they had a watchful eye upon all their actions. In the frequent contests with England, we view them performing the most heroic exploits, and bringing into the field numerous armies of vassals, whom they directed even with an absolute sway. In proportion as the manners of their country were refined, arts and sciences flourished, and the feudal system was departed from; though their dangerous influence was abridged, yet we see them the support of the throne, and the protectors of the people; and the clearness of their pedigrees, few of them supported by fanciful descents, will prove the noble blood that fills the veins of the present illustrious nobility, to whom the united kingdom is so much indebted in politics, in arts and arms.

It is strange that so many years elapsed after the union, when they became a part of the second legislative order of Great Britain, before any thing like an authentic account of these illustrious families were offered for the gratification of the public curiosity, which is so naturally directed to such a subject. Those published in Scotland were prolix, confused and erroneous;
and

and the only piece of any reputation in England, so extremely defective and faulty, as even to scandalize the authors.

At length the Peerage of the indefatigable and judicious Douglas appeared, but with all the disadvantages of prolixity, and a large price, so that few, save persons of fortune, could purchase it. This rather increased than abated the desire of the editors of the present work, as it afforded them satisfaction in many particulars which otherwise they could not have obtained; and they therefore gratefully return thanks to the author for his truly valuable production, which nevertheless, in another edition, must undergo a thorough revisal.

They profess to have given, in the ensuing pages, the clearest, most authentic, and best digested account of the noble families of Scotland hitherto published in these kingdoms; and, by omitting unnecessary digressions and ostentatious quotations from histories and biographical memoirs, which only serve to increase the expence, without contributing to the purpose of such a work, have exhibited their genealogies clear and explicit; so that every collateral branch is seen with great facility and exactness, and few, even of the gentry of Scotland, who have intermarried with the nobility, but may here discover by what degree of consanguinity they are allied.

They have nothing further to offer by way of preface, but to wish the public may survey their labours with that candour and indulgence their industry and assiduity will be found to deserve.

Any mistakes (which must arise merely from the fallibility of human endeavours) that may be discovered by the purchasers, upon notice being sent of them to the publisher, Mr. Almon, in Piccadilly, will be rectified in the next edition.

THE

1

Hamilton Duke of Hamilton

2

Scott Duke of Buccleugh

Lenox Duke of Lenox

Gordon Duke of Gordon

5

Douglass Duke of Queensberry.

Campbell, Duke of Argyle.

Murray, Duke of Athol

Graham, Duke of Montrose.

Ker Duke of Roxburgh.

Hay Marquiss of Tweedale.

Kier Marquifs of Lothian?

Johnston Marquifs of Annandale

13

INDURE FURTH

Cranford Earl of Cranford

14

SERVA JUGUM

Hay Earl of Errol

15

Elizabeth Countess of Sutherland

16

Lesley Earl of Rothes

17

Douglass, Earl of Morton.

18

Erskine, Earl of Buchan.

Coningham, Earl of Glencairn.

Montgomery, Earl of Eglintoun.

21

Kennedy Earl of Cassils

22

Sinclair Earl of Caithness

Stewart Earl of Moray

Home Earl of Home

25

Fleming Earl of Wigton

26

Lyon Earl of Strathmore

Hamilton Earl of Abercorn

Erskine Earl of Kelly

29 Stuart, Earl of Galloway.

30 Hamilton, Earl of Haddington.

31 *Maitland*, Earl of *Lauderdale*.

82 *Campbell*, Earl of *Loudon*.

83 Hay, Earl of Kinnoul.

84 Crighton, Earl of Dumfries & Stair.

35 *Bruce*, Earl of *Elgin*.

36 *Ramsey*, Earl of *Dalhousie*.

37

37 Stewart Earl of Traquair

39 Lesley, Earl of Leven.

40 Talmash, Earl of Dysert.

41 Douglas, Earl of Selkirk.

42 Carnegy, Earl of Northesk.

43 Lindsay, Earl of Balcarras.

44 Alexander, Earl of Stirling.

45 Gordon, Earl of Abeyn.

46 Cochran, Earl of Dundonald.

47 *Campbell*, Earl of *Breadalbane*.

48 *Gordon*, Earl of *Aberdeen*.

19. Murray, Earl of Dunmore.

20. O'brien, Counts of Orkney.

51 Douglas, Earl of March.

52 Hume, Earl of Marchmont.

53 Carmichael, Earl of Hyndford.

54 Primrose, Earl of Roseberry.

55 Boyle, Earl of Glasgow.

56 Stuart, Earl of Bute.

57 Hope, Earl of Hopton.

58 Collier, Earl of Portmore.

59 Scot, Earl of Deloraine.

60 Carey, Visc.t Falkland.

Murray, Visc.^t Stormont.

Arbuthnot, Visc.^t Arbuthnot.

63 Macgill, Visc.t Oxenford.

64 Ingram, Visc.t Irwin.

65 Osborne, Visc.t Dumblain.

66 Borthwick, Lord Borthwick.

67. Forbes, Lord Forbes.

68. Fraser, Lord Saltoun.

69 Gray, Lord Gray.

70 Cathcart, Lord Cathcart.

71 Somerville, Lord Somerville.

72 Sempill, Lord Sempill.

73 Douglas, Lord Mordington.

75. Elphinston, Lord Elphinston.

76. Sandilands, Lord Torphichen.

77

Leslie Lord Lindores

78

Stewart Lord Blantyre

Cranstoun Lord Cranstoun

Napier Lord Napier

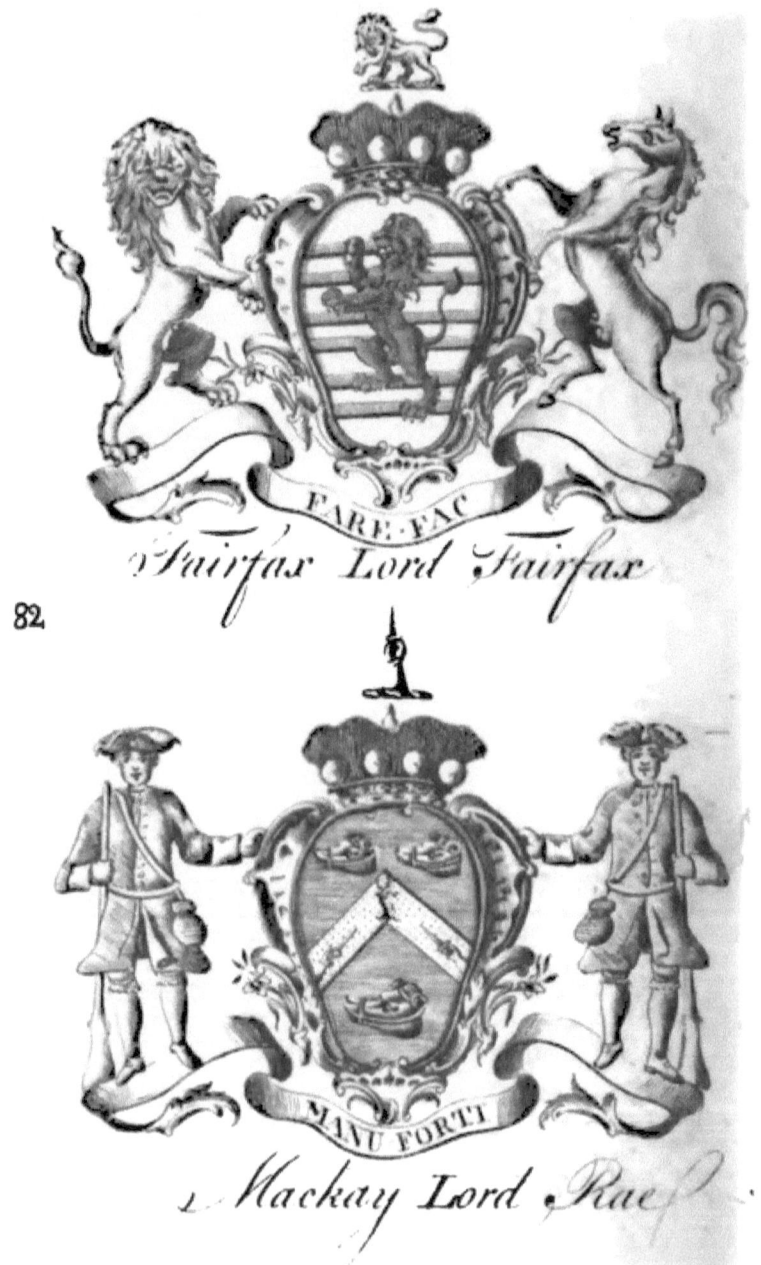

Fairfax Lord Fairfax

Mackay Lord Rae

Aston Lord Aston

Maclellan Lord Kircudbright

85

Ogilvy, Lord Banff.

86

Murray, Lord Elibank.

87

Falconer, Lord Halkertoun.

88

Hamilton, Lord Belhaven

89

Rollo. Lord Rollo.

90

Colvil Lord Colvile.

Ruthven, Lord Ruthven

Lesley, Lord Newark.

THE PEERAGE OF SCOTLAND.

DUKES.

HAMILTON, Duke of HAMILTON.

THIS antient and illustrious family is descended from the earls of Leicester, in England.

The first of this name on record is Sir William de Hambleden, or Hambleton, in the county of Bucks in England, of which manor he was possessed, who was third son of Robert third earl of Leicester, descended from the earl of Mellent in Normandy, who came into England with William the Conqueror; for Robert de Bellamont, after the death of his uncle, Hugh earl of Mellent, was by king Henry I. of England, created earl of Leicester in 1103, and was the first earl of Leicester after the conquest. He married Elizabeth, daughter of Hugh the Great, earl of Vermandois, a younger son of Henry I. king of France, and by her had, amongst other children,

Robert, second earl of Leicester, who in the year 1118 succeeded his father, and was also chief justiciary of England. He married Amicia, daughter of Ralph de Guader, earl of Norfolk, and by her had a son,

Robert Bellamont, who in the year 1168, became the third earl of Leicester; and marrying Petronella, daughter and heir of Hugh de Grandmesnil, with her had the honour of Hinkley in the county of Leicester, and was high steward of
England

England in succession to his father-in-law; they had issue Robert, the fourth earl of Leicester, whose issue is long since extinct,

Sir William de Hambleden above-mentioned, and Roger archbishop of St. Andrews; chancellor of Scotland.

This Sir William was born at the manor of Hambleton, in Buckinghamshire, from whence he assumed his sirname; and coming into Scotland, in the year 1215, was well received by king Alexander II. who conferred many favours upon him. He married Mary, daughter and heir of Gilbert, earl of Strathern, by whom he had a son,

Sir Gilbert, from whom all the Hamiltons, in Scotland, are descended. He was a man of valour and prowess, was in great favour with king Alexander III. and marrying Isabel, daughter of Sir James Randolph, sister of Thomas earl of Murray, governor of Scotland, by her had two sons, Walter his heir, and Sir John Hamilton of Rossaven, ancestor of the families of Fingaltom and Preston, from whom branched the Hamiltons of Mount-Hamilton, in Ireland.

Sir Walter, who succeeded, was a man of great fame and character; and in the 9th of Robert I. for his merit and service had a grant of the baronies of Hamilton, &c. &c. and was knighted. In 1324, king Robert bestowed on him the lands of Kenneil, &c. &c. He married Mary, daughter of Adam, lord Gordon, and had issue by her two sons Sir David and John, from whom are descended the Hamiltons of Innerwick, the earls of Haddington, and the Hamiltons of Priestfield, Redhouse, &c.

Sir David succeeded his father, served king David Bruce in his wars against the English, and was taken prisoner with him, at the battle of Durham, in the year 1346. He married Margaret, daughter of Walter Lesly, earl of Ross, by Euphemia his wife, daughter and heir of William earl of Ross, and by her had issue,

Sir David, who was knighted by Robert II. He married Janet, daughter and heir of Sir William Keith, of Galston, in Airshire, and by her had five sons, whereof Sir John the eldest continued the line; from Sir William, the second son, the Hamiltons of Bathgate descended; from Andrew, the third son, sprung the Hamiltons of Bruntwood, from whom branched the families of Burnclaugh, Roschaugh, Pancaitland, Bangour, and Wishaw. From George, the fourth, the Hamiltons of Boreland, and from David, the fifth, the Hamiltons of Bardowie. His daughter, Elizabeth, was married to Sir Alexander Frazer of Cowie and Dores, ancestor of the lord Salton. He died in 1395, and was succeeded by his eldest son Sir John lord of Cadzow, who married Janet, daughter of Sir James Douglas of Dalkeith, ancestor of the

earl

earl of Moreton, by whom he had Sir James, his succeſſor; David, anceſtor of the Hamiltons of Dalſerſe, Blackburn, Allerſhaw, Ladyland, Green, &c. and Thomas, from whom the earls of Clanbrazil, and the lords Limerick of Ireland, are deſcended.

Sir John, heir to his father, was ſent into England as an hoſtage for the ranſom of king James I. and was afterwards knighted by the ſaid king, and made one of his privy-council; and in 1445 all his lands were erected into a lordſhip called Hamilton, by king James II. In 1409, he was joined in commiſſion with John Biſhop of Dunkeld, Andrew Abbat of Melroſs, and Alexander Livingſton of Calender, to negociate with the Engliſh a peace between the two nations, which they concluded. Upon the rebellion of the earl of Douglas, he was ſent, with the earl of Angus, to command againſt the rebels, and intirely routed them, for which and other ſignal ſervices, he was rewarded with the lands of Drumſhargard and Carmonock, and made heritable ſheriff of Cliddeſdale.

He married firſt Janet, daughter of Sir Alexander Livingſton of Calendar, anceſtor of the earls of Linlithgow, by whom he had iſſue James ſecond lord Hamilton, and three other ſons; ſecondly, Euphemia, daughter of Patrick Graham, earl of Strathern, and widow of Archibald, earl of Douglas, by whom he had one daughter married to David earl of Crawford, afterwards duke of Montroſe.

James, ſecond lord Hamilton, was in high favour with king James II. and king James III. and in 1474, marrying the princeſs Mary, eldeſt ſiſter of that king, and widow of Thomas Boyd earl of Arran, by her had iſſue James his ſucceſſor, and a daughter Elizabeth; who being married to Matthew Stewart earl of Lenox, by him was grandmother of Henry lord Darnley, father of king James VI. the firſt monarch of Great Britain. He died in November 1479, and was ſucceeded by his ſaid ſon James, third lord Hamilton, who was one of the privy-council to king James IV. before he was of age; and was ſent into England to negotiate the marriage between that king and the princeſs Margaret, eldeſt daughter of king Henry VII. which having concluded, it was ſolemniſed in the moſt pompous manner; for which the king gave him the county or iſland of Arran, and created him earl thereof, by patent, dated Auguſt 10, 1503.

In 1512, he was ſent with a conſiderable force to the aſſiſtance of France, and had a penſion for life. In 1520, he was appointed warden of the South Marches, and was regent of Scotland in the minority of James V.

He married firſt, Beatrix, daughter of John lord Drummond, by whom he had a daughter, married to Andrew Stewart,

art, lord Ochiltree. His second wife was Janet, daughter of the lord Home, and sister of Alexander, first earl of Home, who also died without issue. His third wife was Janet, daughter of Sir David Beaton, comptroller of Scotland, by whom he had two sons, James his successor, and Sir John Hamilton of Cliddesdale, whose daughter Margaret married David earl of Douglas; also two daughters, lady Helen, the wife of Archibald the fourth earl of Argyll, and lady Jane, of Alexander, fifth earl of Glencairn. This first earl of Arran died in the year 1530, and was succeeded by James his eldest son; which James, second earl of Arran, was in 1543 declared by the three estates of the kingdom, tutor to the young queen Mary, and regent of the kingdom during her minority, as also declared next immediate heir to the crown, failing the queen, and her lawful issue.

On the 10th of September 1547, he commanded the Scots army at Pinkey-Cleugh, near Musselburgh, but was defeated by the duke of Somerset regent of England; the Scots losing 14,000 slain, and 1500 taken prisoners.

He was afterwards one of the knights of St. Michael, and by Henry II. of France, created duke of Chatelherault in Poitou, to him and his heirs, in the year 1552; but neither he nor his descendents ever enjoyed the duchy.

This earl, in that great and difficult office of regent, gained the esteem of all the Scots nation; for though he had been declared next heir to the crown, if the queen died without issue, and protector during her minority, yet he resigned the regency to the queen mother, at the desire of the young queen and parliament; so that it appeared he was not ambitious of power, except when his services might contribute to the prosperity of the kingdom, which he generously preferred to his own private interest: but in 1571, for his great adherence to queen Mary, and zeal for her cause, he suffered both imprisonment and forfeiture, and died January 22, 1573.

By his wife, the lady Margaret Douglas, daughter of James the third earl of Moreton, he left four sons and four daughters, whereof Barbara the eldest was the wife of James, lord Fleming, lord high chamberlain of Scotland. 2. Lady Anne, the wife of George fifth earl of Huntley. 3. Lady Margaret, of Alexander, lord Gordon. And, 4. Lady Jane, of Hugh, earl of Eglington.

Of the sons, 1. James, third earl, died without issue. 2. Lord John succeeded his brother. 3. Claud, lord Pasely, was ancestor to the earl of Abercorn viscount Strabane in Ireland. 4. Lord David died young.

John, fourth earl of Arran, whose estate and titles were forfeited by himself and his father, to avoid the storm that threatened him, fled into France; and notwithstanding the troubles he met

met with, he ever continued faithful to the queen, and her cause; of which her majesty was so sensible, that when sentence of death was past upon her in England, she took a ring off her finger, and giving it to one of her servants, ordered him to carry it to her cousin John lord Hamilton, and tell him, that was all she had to witness her great sense of his family's constant fidelity, and their sufferings for her interest; and desired it might be kept in the family, as a lasting evidence of her kindness; and the same is preserved to this day with a grateful regard.

In the reign of James VI. he was restored to all the titles and estates, lost either by the attainder of himself, or of James earl of Arran his father; and was also made one of his majesty's privy-council, governor of Dumbarton Castle; and in 1599 created marquis of Hamilton, being the first in Scotland who bore that title.

He deceased in the year 1604, leaving issue by Margaret, widow of Gilbert the fourth earl of Cassils, and daughter of John the ninth lord Glamis, ancestor of the earl of Strathmore, one son and one daughter, Margaret, married to John lord Maxwell, elder brother of Robert the first earl of Nithsdale. To him succeeded his son James, second marquis of Hamilton, who in June 1606, in a parliament held at Edinburgh, had Arbroath, on the coast of Forfarshire, erected into a lordship, with the dignity of a lord of parliament, to be held of his majesty in free barony; and on the 16th of June 1619, the seventeenth of James I. he was created baron of Innerdale in Cumberland, and earl of Cambridge in England; and was also lord steward of his majesty's houshold, high commissioner to the parliament in Scotland, and in 1623, knight of the garter. He married lady Ann Cuninghame, daughter of James earl of Glencairn, by whom he left issue three sons, the two eldest of whom were dukes of Hamilton, and the third, lord John, died unmarried. Also three daughters, whereof the lady Ann was married to Hugh earl of Eglington; lady Margaret to John earl of Crauford; and lady Mary to James the second earl of Queensberry.

His lordship deceased on March 3, 1624, and was succeeded by his eldest son James, third marquis of Hamilton, who assisted at the coronation of king Charles I. carrying the sword of state, and by that prince, for his fidelity to him and sufferings in his service, was created duke of Hamilton, April 12, 1643, to him and the heirs male of his body; and failing thereof, to those of his brother the earl of Lanerk, which failing, to the eldest heir female of his own body, &c. &c. He was in that reign, also, high commissioner to the general assembly of the church, master of the horse, gentleman of his majesty's bed-chamber, privy-counsellor in both kingdoms, and knight of the garter; and at the baptism of king Charles II. represented Frederick king of Bohemia, as one of the godfathers; but in 1643, he, and his brother, then earl of Lanerk, waiting upon the king at Oxford, the marquis of Montrose, and others, made complaint to his majesty against them, blaming their conduct in the king's cause in Scotland; and though the informations were groundless, yet the king was so far influenced by their enemies, that the earl was obliged to make his escape to Edinburgh; but the duke was sent prisoner to Bristol, then to Exeter, and after to Pendennis Castle, where he remained till April 1646; after which he was released, and very well received by the king, who excused his imprisonment caused by the advice and persuasion of those who were about his court.

In 1648, he prevailed so far with the Scotch parliament, that it was agreed to raise an army for the king's service, commanded by himself, with which he marched directly into England, was attacked by the parliament forces near Preston, defeated, and taken prisoner. After several months confinement, he was tried before the then high court of justice, and agreeable to their sentence, was beheaded in Palace-yard, Westminster, March 9, 1649, a few weeks after the king.

He married lady Mary Fielding, daughter of William earl of Denbigh, by Susannah his wife, sister of George Villiers the great duke of Buckingham; and by her had issue, three sons and three daughters. The sons, lords Charles, James, and William, died young; as did the eldest daughter lady Mary; lady Ann lived to be duchess of Hamilton, of whom hereafter; and lady Susannah married John the seventh earl of Cassils. He was succeeded by his brother

William earl of Lanerk, as second duke of Hamilton, who was born in December 1616. Which William had been created earl of Lanerk, lord Machanshire and Polmont; and was likewise secretary of state for Scotland. He married Elizabeth, daughter and coheir of James Maxwell, earl of Dirleton, and had issue a son, who died an infant, and four daughters; viz. 1. Lady Ann married to Robert earl of Southesk. 2. Lady Elizabeth first to James lord Kilmaurs, son of the earl of Glencairn, and secondly to Sir David Cuninghame, Bart. 3. Lady Mary, married first to Alexander, earl of Calendar; secondly to Sir James Livingston, Bart. and thirdly to James, earl of Finlater. 4. Lady Margaret, to William Blair, of that Ilk, in the shire of Air. His grace having raised a troop of horse at his own charge for the service of Charles II. in order to his restoration, in the fatal battle of Worcester on the 3d of September 1651, received a shot in his leg, of which he died, and was buried in the cathedral of Worcester.

Upon

Upon the death of this duke without surviving male issue, the estates and titles descending by the several patents to the heirs general, he was succeeded by his niece the lady Ann, duchess of Hamilton, eldest surviving daughter of his brother, James duke of Hamilton, who married William Douglas earl of Selkirk, eldest son of William first marquis of Douglas, by his second wife lady Mary Gordon, daughter of George the first marquis of Huntley; and in consequence of this marriage, upon a petition from his duchess, he was created duke of Hamilton in 1660, for life, and took that name, and soon after was made knight of the garter, and a privy counsellor.

In the reign of king James VII. (the IId of England) he was one of the privy council, lord of the treasury, an extraordinary lord of session, and also a privy counsellor in England; in which offices he continued till 1688, when king James abdicated the throne and government, and upon the prince of Orange's coming over to England, he was chosen by divers Scots nobility and gentry in London to be their president, when they addressed that prince to take upon him the administration of all affairs civil and military. He was chosen president of the convention of estates which settled the crown on that prince, who being crowned, the duke was continued president, and constituted extraordinary lord of session, and high admiral of Scotland. His grace deceased in the year 1694.

He had issue by the said Ann his duchess, seven sons and three daughters, *viz.* 1. James earl of Arran, his successor. 2. Lord William, who died in France without issue. 3. Charles earl of Selkirk. 4. John earl of Ruglen. 5. George earl of Orkney. 6. Lord Basil, who was drowned in the ford of Minnock, endeavouring to save his servant, who had an only daughter, married to Thomas earl of Dundonald. And, 7. Lord Archibald, who was governor of Jamaica, a lord of the admiralty, cofferer to the prince of Wales, surveyor general of the duchy of Cornwal, and a flag officer. He represented the shire of Lanerk in three parliaments, Queenborough in Kent in one, and in 1742, was elected for Dartmouth in Devonshire. He married the lady Jane Hamilton, youngest daughter of James earl of Abercorn; and dying April 6, 1754, left issue by her (who died in 1752, at Paris) two sons. Of the duke's three daughters, lady Katharine married John duke of Athol; lady Susanna, first, John earl of Dundonald, and, secondly, Charles marquis of Tweeddale; and lady Margaret, James Maul earl of Panmure. James earl of Arran succeeded his father, and was fourth duke of Hamilton. In the reign of Charles II. he was envoy extraordinary to the court of France, and gentleman of his majesty's bedchamber. When king James VII. came to the crown, he was made master of the wardrobe, knight of the thistle, and colonel of the royal regiment of horse. After the revolution

revolution he was twice sent to the Tower, on suspicion of corresponding with the abdicated king, but was never prosecuted. In the year 1698, he being then earl of Arran only, his mother the duchess made a surrender of her titles, and a patent was passed, creating him duke of Hamilton, with the same precedence as if he had succeeded thereto by his mother's death. In 1708, he was elected one of the sixteen peers for Scotland, made lord lieutenant and Custos Rotulorum of the county palatine of Lancaster, ranger of the forests therein, and one of her majesty's privy council.

On 10 September 1711, he was created baron of Dutton, and duke of Brandon in England. But the validity of these English titles was solemnly debated in the house of lords, December 20, 1711, together with that of duke of Dover, conferred on the duke of Queensberry, and the patents for them were declared illegal: As the prerogative could not operate when barred by an act of parliament; as the act of union had made all the peers of Scotland peers of Great Britain, with the same dignities and privileges (except sitting and voting in the house of peers, otherwise than by sixteen representatives) and as, therefore, to admit more than sixteen, was plainly absurd, and contrary to the words of that act or treaty.

In 1712, he was appointed master general of the ordnance, and soon after elected a knight of the garter, but was never installed; for during the treaty of peace in 1712, he was nominated ambassador to the French court; but fighting a duel with Charles lord Mohun, they were both killed on Sunday morning, the 15th of November that year. His grace's mother, Anne the duchess dowager, died at her seat in Lanerkshire, 17 October 1716, aged 80.

James duke of Hamilton, of whom we have been treating, married, first, lady Ann Spencer, daughter of Robert earl of Sunderland, by whom he had two daughters, ladies Ann and Mary, who both died young. His second wife was Elizabeth, daughter and heir of Digby lord Gerard of Bromley, by Elizabeth, youngest daughter of Charles Gerard the first earl of Macclesfield, by whom he had issue three sons and four daughters. 1. Lady Elizabeth, who died young. 2. Lady Katharine died in a week after her father. 3. James marquis of Cliddesdale, who succeeded as duke of Hamilton. 4. Lady Charlotte married to Charles Edwin, Esq; 5. Lord William, who in 1734 was chosen representative for the shire of Lanerk, and died the same year. He married Ann, daughter and heir of Francis Hawes, receiver general of the customs, and a South-sea director in 1720; after whose death, without issue, she married William late viscount Vane of Ireland. 6. Lady Susan married in August 1736, to Anthony Tracy Keck of Great Tew in Oxfordshire, Esq; and died June 3, 1755. 7. Lord Ann, so named

named from queen Ann, who was his godmother, who married Miss Pownel, an heiress, and died on Christmas day 1748, leaving issue by her.

James, the eldest son, who succeeded as 5th duke of Hamilton, was, in September 1726, elected a knight of the ancient order of the thistle, and installed at Holyrood house the following October. In May 1727, he was appointed a gentleman of the bedchamber to king George I. and so continued by king George II. He married first lady Anne, daughter of John Cochran, earl of Dundonald, by whom he had an only son, James, marquis of Cliddesdale. His second wife was Elizabeth, daughter and co-heir of Thomas Strangeways of Dorsetshire, Esq; a great fortune, by whom he had no issue. By his third, Elizabeth, daughter and heir of Edward Spencer of Rendilsham in Suffolk, Esq; he had issue a daughter Ann, born in 1739, and two sons, lord Archibald, born 27 July 1740, and lord Spencer in June 1742. His grace dying in March 1742, was succeeded by his eldest son

James, sixth duke of Hamilton, who married, Feb. 14, 1752, Elizabeth, second daughter of John Gunning, Esq; by Bridget, his wife, daughter of John viscount Mayo in Ireland, by whom he had issue a son James, marquis of Cliddesdale, born February 18, 1755, lord Douglas, born July the 25th, 1756; and a daughter, lady Elizabeth, born on January 26, 1753; and his grace dying the 17th of January 1758, was succeeded by his eldest son,

James-George, present and seventh duke of Hamilton, who upon the death of Archibald duke of Douglas, without issue, succeeded to the titles of marquis of Douglas, earl of Angus, &c. as heir male. His mother the duchess married, secondly, March the 3d, 1759, John marquis of Lorn, eldest son and heir apparent of the duke of Argyle, by whom she has issue.

TITLES.] The most noble James Hamilton, duke of Hamilton, Chetelherault and Brandon, marquis of Hamilton, Douglas, and Cliddesdale, earl of Arran, Angus and Lanerk, lord Machanshire, Polmont, and Aberbrothick, baron of Dutton, and hereditary keeper of the king's palace in Edinburgh, called Holyrood house.

CREATIONS.] Summoned to parliament in 1374, 4. Robert II. Earl of Arran in the county of Bute, 10 August 1503, 15 James IV. Duke of Chatelherault in Poitou in France in 1552. Marquis of Hamilton in the county of Lanerk, 19 April 1599; baron of Aberbrothick, June 1606, marquis of Douglas and earl of Angus, 17 June 1633, and April 18, 1703; earl of the county of Lanerk, lord Machanshire and Polmont, 3: March 1639, duke of Hamilton, 12 April 1643, and baron of Dutton in Cheshire, and duke of Brandon in Suffolk, 10 September 1711, 9 Ann.

ARMS.] Four grand quarters: First quarterly, 1st and 4th
ruby,

ruby, three cinquefoils pierced ermine, for Hamilton, being part of the arms of Robert de Bellamont; 2d and 3d pearl, a ship with its sails furled up, diamond, for the earldom of Arran. The 2d grand quarter is pearl, an human heart imperially crowned proper, on a chief sapphire, three mullets of the field, for the name of Douglas. 3d grand quarter as the 2d, 4th as the first.

CREST.] In a ducal coronet topaz, an oak fructed and penetrated tranfversly in the main stem, by a frame saw, proper.

SUPPORTERS.] Two antelopes pearl, their horns, ducal collars, chains and hoofs, topaz.

MOTTO.] Through.

CHIEF SEAT.] At Hamilton on Clyde in the county of Lanerk, nine miles from Lanerk, and 32 from Edinburgh, being a noble feat, with a fine park, the river Aven running through it.

SCOT, Duke of BUCCLEUGH.

THE firname *Scot* is of great antiquity in Scotland, as appears by many authentic records, traced as far back as the year 1107.

In the reigns of Alexander III. and Robert I. this family of Scot was very powerful on the borders toward England, of which they were often wardens; and in 1296,

Sir Richard Scot, knight, (who then fwore fealty to king Edward I. of England, as baron of Lanerkshire) marrying the heirefs of Murdifton in Cliddefdale, by her obtained that barony; and thereupon laid afide his paternal arms, which were argent, three lions heads erafed, gules; and took the arms of Murdifton, as borne by the prefent duke. He was fucceeded by Sir Michael Scot, who was of Murdifton and Ranelburn, in the reign of king David Bruce, and loft his life at the unfortunate battle of Durham, in the year 1346.

His fon Robert performed many actions of honour and courage in the fervice of the crown, and was nobly rewarded by king Robert II. To him fucceeded his fon, Sir Walter, alfo a faithful fervant of that prince, who gave him the barony of Kirkude, and made him a knight in 1390. He was killed at the battle of Homildon, in the year 1402, and was fucceeded by his fon Sir Robert Scot, who died in 1425, and was fucceeded by his fon Sir Walter Scot, who in 1426 obtained from the earl of Douglas a charter of the lands of Lempetlaw, for his fervice done to that earl; and afterwards, in 1446, exchanged his lands of Murdifton, with Thomas Inglis of Maner, for the lands of Broxholm. In the reign of James II. he was frequently employed in negotiations of peace between the two nations; and also exerted his valour to an eminent degree, in fuppreffing the rebellion of the earls of Douglas, Murray, and Ormond; for which

which he had a grant from the crown of the lands of Abington, Pharholm, Glendonory, &c. He left issue three sons, Sir David, his heir, Sir James and Sir Alexander; which Alexander in 1483 was director of the chancery, and was slain with king James III. in the battle of Bannockburn in 1488. In this reign, and that of James IV. Sir David the eldest son, who succeeded his father, made a great figure, and was often a commissioner to manage the several treaties between the two nations. He was one of the Scotch nobles that sat in the parliament held by that prince in 1487, and was then stiled *dominus de Buccleugh*, which is the first time we hear of that title in the family. He had a daughter Janet, married to Sir James Douglas of Drumlanrig, and one son who died before him; and dying in 1491, was succeeded by

Sir Walter his grandson, who was famous for his bravery in the reign of king James IV. whose great favourite he was. He accompanied that prince to the unfortunate field of Floddon, and in that battle distinguished himself greatly, but came off alive, and died in 1516. By his wife Elizabeth, daughter of Walter Ker of Cefsford, he had a son, Sir Walter Scot, who performed many great actions in the minority of James V. In 1544, the third of queen Mary, he greatly signalized himself against the forces of king Henry VIII. as likewise at the battle of Pinkey in 1547; and was made warden of the west marches.

He married first a daughter of the family of Carmichael, ancestor of the earl of Hyndford, and by her had Sir Walter Scot, and two other sons: and by Janet his second wife, daughter of John Bethune of Creich, he had three daughters, Grizel, married first to William lord Borthwick, and secondly to Walter Craincrofs, Esq; Jane married to John Cranston of that ilk, ancestor of lord Cranston, and Dorothy to James Crichton.

Sir Walter his heir married Grizel, another daughter of the said John Bethune; and dying before his father, by her left Sir Walter, successor to his grandfather, and three daughters; whereof Jane was married to Sir Thomas Ker of Fernyhirst, Margaret to Sir John Johnston of that ilk; and Elizabeth to John Carmichael of Meadowflat, captain of Crawford.

Sir Walter, who succeeded his grandfather in 1552, was a man of excellent parts and reputation; he married lady Margaret, daughter of David earl of Douglas and Angus, by whom he had Sir Walter his heir, and two daughters; Margaret, married to Robert Scot of Thirlefton, from whom the lords Napier, and Mary, to William Elliot of Lairifton.

Sir Walter his heir being in great favour with king James VI. was knighted, and made warden of the marches toward England; and being also a person of a warlike genius, carried

over

over a regiment to the Netherlands, where he served under the famous general, Maurice prince of Orange, and there gained such honour, that the aforesaid king, to reward his merit, advanced him to the dignity of lord Scot of Buccleugh, by patent, dated March 16, 1606. He married Mary, daughter of Sir William Ker of Cesford, sister of Robert first earl of Roxburgh, and had issue by her Walter his successor, and two daughters; Mary, married to James lord Rofs, and Elizabeth, to John master of Cranston. He died in 1611, and was succeeded by his said son,

Walter, second lord Scot, who was created earl of Buccleugh in 1619, and who being a nobleman of a warlike temper, had the command of a regiment under the states of Holland against the Spaniards, where he served with singular honour and reputation. He married lady Mary, daughter of Francis Hay earl of Errol; and by her had Francis second earl of Buccleugh, and two daughters; lady Mary married to John earl of Mar, and lady Jane to John marquis of Tweeddale. He deceased in 1633, and was succeeded by his son

Francis, second earl, who was a nobleman of great character and merit; and for his loyalty to king Charles II. Cromwell imposed a large fine (15000 l.) on his heir.

He married the lady Margaret Lesley, daughter of John earl of Rothes, and widow of the lord Balgony, and by her had two daughters, whereof

Lady Mary, the eldest, was countess of Buccleugh; and she marrying Walter Scot of Highchester, he was thereupon created earl of Terras for life; but she dying in 1662 without issue, her estate and honour came to her sister the

Lady Ann Scot, who in 1665 was married to James Fitzroy duke of Monmouth, eldest natural son of king Charles II. by Lucy daughter of Richard Walters of Haverford in the county of Pembroke, Esq; upon which marriage he took the name of Scot, and they were created duke and duchess of Buccleugh, by letters patent, to their heirs in general, dated April 20, 1673. The actions and sad catastrophe of this great man are too well known to make the mention of them necessary here. Suffice it then just to observe, that he was beheaded on Towerhill, July 15, 1685, leaving issue by his said duchess four sons, viz. 1. Charles earl of Doncaster, born in August 1672, died in February 1673. 2. James earl of Doncaster, born in May 1674, who after his father's attainder in England, was called earl of Dalkeith, by which title, on the 7th of February 1703, he was elected a knight of the ancient order of St. Andrew, or the Thistle. 3. Henry, who was born in the year 1676, and was created earl of Deloraine. 4. Francis, born in 1678, and died the next year: Also two daughters; 1. Lady Charlotte, who died young in 1683. And, 2. Lady Ann, who was born in

1675,

1675, but died within the Tower of London the next month after her father.

Ann the duchess dowager of Monmouth and Buccleugh, in May 1688, married Charles lord Cornwallis, and by him had a son named George, and two daughters, Ann and Isabel, who all died young. Their mother died in 1732, aged 81.

James earl of Dalkeith, second son, married the lady Henrietta, second daughter of Laurence Hyde earl of Rochester, by whom he had three sons and two daughters; Francis his heir, James and Henry, who both died young; ladies Ann and Charlotte, who died unmarried. And his lordship dying in March 1704, was buried at Westminster. To him succeeded Francis earl of Dalkeith, his only surviving son, who was made a knight of the thistle in 1724, and succeeded to the honours and title of duke of Buccleugh, upon the death of his grandmother the duchess in 1732; and in the next parliament was one of the sixteen peers. In 1743 he was restored to the titles of earl of Doncaster and baron Scot of Tyndale, the attainder for those titles being reversed by act of parliament, in consideration of his fidelity to the royal family, and zeal for the protestant cause. In the year 1720 he married the lady Jane Douglas, daughter of James duke of Queensberry; and by her, who died 31 August 1729, his grace had two sons and three daughters, viz. 1. Francis earl of Dalkeith, born in February 1720-21. 2. Lord Charles, who died a student at Oxford in 1747. 3. Lady Jane died in 1743. 4. Lady Ann in 1737. And 5. Lady Mary in 1739. His grace deceased April 22, 1751, and his eldest son,

Francis earl of Dalkeith, who was chosen member of parliament for Boroughbridge in Yorkshire in April 1746, and rechosen at the general election in 1747, married in 1742, lady Caroline Campbell, eldest daughter of John duke of Argyll; and by her (who married secondly, in September 1755, the right honourable Charles Townshend, second son of the late lord viscount Townshend) he had issue four sons and two daughters, viz. Lady Caroline Scot, born in 1743; John lord Whitechester in 1745, who died young; Henry, born in 1746; Campbell Scot, born in 1747; James in 1748, who died young; and lady Frances, born in July, 1750. His lordship deceasing in April 1750, before his father, was succeeded by Henry, his eldest surviving son, who also the next year succeeded his grandfather, and is the third and present duke of Buccleugh, &c. &c.

TITLES.] The most noble Henry Scot, duke of Buccleugh, earl of Dalkeith, baron Scot of Buccleugh and Eskdale: also an English peer, by the title of baron Scot of Tindale in Northumberland, and earl of Doncaster in Yorkshire.

CREATIONS.] Created lord Scot of Buccleugh, March 16, 1605;

1605; earl of Buccleugh, March 16, 1618; baron of Eskdale in Roxburghshire; earl of Dalkeith and duke of Buccleugh in the county of Edinburgh, April 20, 1673.

ARMS.] Topaz, on a bend sapphire, a star between two crescents of the field for Murdiston. His grace also bears the arms of king Charles II. surmounted with a battoon sinister.

CREST.] A stag passant, proper.

SUPPORTERS.] Two maidens richly attired in antique habits, their under robes sapphire, and the uppermost emerald, and on their heads a plume of three feathers pearl.

MOTTO.] Amo.

CHIEF SEATS.] At Dalkeith and East-Park, four miles south-east of Edinburgh; at Smeaton, one mile from Dalkeith; at Melrofs in Roxburghshire on the Twede, between Selkirk and Roxburgh; and at Hallplace in Berkshire.

LENNOX, Duke of LENNOX.

THE descent, &c. of this noble family being given in Collins's English Peerage, Vol. I. page 187, I shall not recapitulate them here; but rehearse his grace's titles, &c.

TITLES.] The most noble Charles Lenox, duke of Richmond, Lennox and Aubigny; earl of March and Darnly; and baron of Settrington and Torbolton.

CREATIONS.] Created baron of Torbolton and earl of Darnly, in the county of Air, and duke of Lennox or Dunbritonshire, 9 September 1675.

ARMS.] Quarterly, the 1st and 4th grand quarters, France and England quarterly, the 2d Scotland, and the 3d Ireland, the arms of king Charles II. within a border goboné or componed pearl and ruby, the pearl charged with roses of the 2d, barbed and seeded proper, being marks of illegitimacy.

CREST.] On a cap of maintenance, a lion of England, crowned with a ducal coronet ruby, and gorged with a collar goboné, as the border round the coat.

SUPPORTERS.] On the dexter side an unicorn pearl, his horn, mane, tufts, and hoofs, topaz; on the sinister an antelope pearl, attired and unguled of the second; each gorged with a collar, as the crest.

MOTTO.] En la rose je fleurie.

CHIEF SEAT.] At Goodwood in the county of Sussex, three miles from Chichester, and fifty from London.

GORDON, Duke of GORDON.

THIS antient and potent family took their sirname from the barony of Gordon in the county of Berwick, given by Malcolm Canmore, to a valiant knight, who came into Scotland with him, and made use of it to distinguish

his

his possessions. Ricardus de Gordon, his grandson, flourished in the reigns of Malcolm IV. and William the Lion, in 1160 and 1165. 'Tis plain the name was of great repute in France about these times; but I shall not puzzle my readers with dark and uncertain accounts.

In the reign of king Robert Bruce, Sir Adam de Gordon had from that king the lordship of Strathbogy in Aberdeenshire, which was then in the crown, by the forfeiture of David de Strathbogy, earl of Athol; upon which occasion he removed thither from Berwickshire, and gave these lands and lordships the name of Huntley. Sir Adam was killed at the battle of Halidon-Hill, in 1333, and was succeeded by his son Sir Alexander Gordon, who lost his life at the battle of Durham in 1346, in behalf of king David II. and was succeeded by Sir John Gordon his son, who, in the year 1358, obtained a confirmation of all his lands in Strathbogy. He was succeeded by his son Sir John, who was slain in the year 1388, at the battle of Otterburn. To him succeeded his son, Sir Adam Gordon, who by his wife Elizabeth, daughter of Sir William Keith, had an only daughter Elizabeth, who, on his being slain at the battle of Homildon, in 1402, became his heir: and she in the year 1408, marrying Alexander Seton, second son of Sir William Seton of that ilk, (to whom Robert duke of Albany, in the third year of his government, gave a charter and confirmation of the lands and baronies of Gordon, Huntley, Strathbogy, and several others) by him had issue Alexander Seton, who succeeded William Seton of Meldrum, and a daughter Elizabeth, the wife of Alexander earl of Ross.

Alexander their eldest son was one of the hostages for the ransom of king James I. and in 1431, was joined in commission with John Bishop of Glasgow, Sir Walter Ogilvy, and Sir John Forrester, Knts. to treat of a peace with England, which they happily concluded for nine years.

In the reign of James II. he was created earl of Huntley, and took the sirname of Gordon, to preserve the memory of the family. He placed the arms of that family in the first quarter; and had divers manors given him, particularly at Badenoch, which the family now enjoys.

This earl married first Jane, daughter and heir of Robert Keith, son of William Keith, first earl marshal of Scotland, but by her had no issue; secondly, Giles, daughter and heir of John Hay, of Tullibody, by whom he had issue Sir Alexander Seton, Knt. the first of the family of Touch; and by his third wife, Margaret, daughter of William lord Crichton, chancellor of Scotland, he had issue three sons, George, his heir; Sir Alexander, of Midmar, ancestor of the Gordons of Abergeldie, and Adam, dean of Caithness. Also three daughters,

Jane,

Jane, married to James Dunbar earl of Murray; Elizabeth to William Keith third earl marshal; and Christian to William lord Forbes. He died at a great age, in 1470, and was succeeded in his honours and possessions by his eldest son, by his third wife, George, second earl of Huntley. Which George was one of the privy-council to king James III. as he was to king James IV. by whom he was made lord chancellor of Scotland, and lieutenant of the north in 1498.

He married first lady Jane Stewart, daughter of king James I. and widow of James, earl of Angus, by whom he had four sons and six daughters, viz. Alexander, his heir; Sir Adam Gordon, lord of Aboyne, who by marriage with the countess became earl of Sutherland; Sir William, ancestor of the Gordons of Guight; Sir James, of Letterfary, admiral of the king's fleet in 1513. Of the daughters, Catharine was the wife of Perkin Warbeck, and secondly of Sir Matthew Badock, ancestor of the earl of Pembroke: Janet, of Alexander lord Lindsay, son and heir of David earl of Crawford; and secondly of Patrick, lord Grey: Mary, of Sir William Sinclair, of Westerhall: Sophia, of Sir Gilbert Hay, of Killmallock: Agnes, of Sir James Ogilvy, of Finlater; and Eleonora, of —— Crichton, of Innernytie. By his second wife, Elizabeth, daughter of William Hay, earl of Errol, he had no issue. He died in the year 1507, and was succeeded by his eldest son, Alexander third earl of Huntley, who was one of the privy-council to king James IV. which prince he accompanied to the battle of Flodden, and commanded the right wing of his army; and surviving that fatal day, was, in the minority of James V. made lord lieutenant of the north beyond the river Forth, and in the year 1517, one of the king's governors. He married Janet, daughter of John earl of Athol, and by her had three sons and four daughters. 1. John, who died before him, leaving issue by the lady Jane his wife, natural daughter of king James IV. by Margaret, daughter of John lord Drummond, two sons; whereof George succeeded his grandfather, and Alexander was bishop of Galloway. 2. Alexander, ancestor of the Gordons of Clunie. 3. William, bishop of Aberdeen. 4. Janet, the wife of Colin, earl of Argyll. 5. Jean, of Patrick, fourth lord Gray. 6. Isabel, of —— lord Innermeath. 7. ——, of —— Menzies of Weem. His lordship dying in the year 1523, was succeeded by George, his grandson, fourth earl of Huntley, who was a nobleman of great and eminent parts; and in 1535 became one of the privy-council, and lord lieutenant of Scotland, during king James V.'s being in France to espouse the princess Magdalen; and, upon the death of his master, was one of the peers who signed and sealed that association, to oppose the intended match between queen Mary and king Edward VI. of England.

In

In the fifth of queen Mary 1546, he was appointed lord chancellor of Scotland; and afterwards, in confideration of his extraordinary fervices at the unfortunate battle of Pinkey againft the Englifh, and other fervices to the crown, he had a grant of the earldom of Murray, which he enjoyed for divers years.

He married Elizabeth, daughter of Robert lord Keith, fon and heir of William third earl Marfhal, and by her had iffue feven fons and three daughters, viz. 1. George his heir; 2. James, a clergyman; 3. Sir John, of whom by-and-bye; 4. Sir Adam, who died *fine proles*; 5. Sir Patrick, flain at the battle of Glenlivet, in 1594; 6. Robert; 7. Thomas; 8. Margaret, the wife of John, eighth lord Forbes; 9. Jane, of James earl of Bothwell; fecondly of Alexander earl of Sutherland; and thirdly of Alexander Ogilvy, of Boyne; 10. Elizabeth, the wife of John, earl of Athol. Their father was flain in the fkirmifh at Correchie, in the year 1562, between the forces of queen Mary, and the earl of Murray; his fon Sir John Gordon was executed the next day at Aberdeen, and his eftate and honours forfeited. He was fucceeded by his eldeft fon,

George, fifth earl of Huntley, who was reftored to the eftates and honours of his anceftors, in the year 1567. Before his reftoration he was in great favour with queen Mary; for in 1565, he was one of her privy-council, lord high chancellor of Scotland, and lieutenant-general of all the forces in the north. He married Anne, daughter of the regent, James Hamilton the fecond earl of Arran, by whom he had iffue, George his fucceffor, and a daughter Jane, wife of George earl of Caithnefs; and his lordfhip dying in the year 1576, was fucceeded by his faid fon,

George, fixth earl of Huntley, who was a perfon of great accomplifhments, and, at length, much in favour with king James the VIth, by whom he was made lord lieutenant of the north, and created marquis of Huntley, on the 17th of April 1599, which title he lived to enjoy 35 years.

He married lady Henrietta, daughter of Efme Stewart, duke of Lennox, and by her had four fons and four daughters; lady Ann, married to James Stewart earl of Murray, lady Elizabeth to Alexander Livingfton earl of Linlithgow, lady Mary to William marquis of Douglas, and lady Jane to Claud Hamilton the fecond lord Strabane of the kingdom of Ireland. Of the fons, 1. George lord Gordon, the eldeft fucceeded his father; 2 Sir John, was created vifcount Meldrum, and lord Aboyne, by king Charles I. in 1627, and married lady Sophia Hay, daughter of Francis ninth earl of Errol, but was unfortunately burnt to death. 3. Lord Francis, who died in 1620; and 4. Lord Adam, laird of Auchindown.

down. The marquis deceased in the year 1636, and was succeeded by his eldest son,

George, second marquis of Huntley, who, while he was lord Gordon, was a captain in the Scots guards of Louis the XIIIth of France; and upon breaking out of the troubles in the reign of king Charles I. being very firm to that prince's interest, had a commission to be lieutenant of the north, during the height of the civil war, and was forfeited by parliament in 1645. At the end of the war, on the 30th of March 1649, he was executed at Edinburgh for his loyalty.

He married Ann, daughter of Archibald the seventh earl of Argyll, by whom he had five sons and five daughters, viz. 1. George lord Gordon, killed at the battle of Aldford in 1645, in his father's life-time 2. Lord Lewis, his successor. 3. Lord Charles, created earl of Aboyn. 4. Lord James, who after the fatal death of Charles I. retired to France and died there. 5. Lord Henry. Ann, the eldest daughter, married James the third earl of Perth; Henrietta, the second, first, George lord Seton, and secondly, John Stewart earl of Traquair; Jane, Thomas Hamilton earl of Hadington; ladies Mary and Catherine died unmarried.

He was succeeded by Lewis his second son, third marquis of Huntley, who married Isabel, daughter to Sir James Grant of that ilk, and by her had a son George, his heir, and three daughters; lady Ann married to the count de Crolly; lady Mary first to Adam Urquhart of Meldrum, and secondly, to James Drummond earl of Perth; and lady Jane to Charles Seton earl of Dumfermline; and the marquis not long surviving his father, was succeeded by his only son,

George, fourth marquis of Huntley, who was by king Charles II. created duke of Gordon, November 1, 1684; and by James the VIIth constituted one of the lords of the treasury, one of the privy-council, governor of Edinburgh Castle, and knight of the thistle; but at the revolution in 1688, holding out the said castle for his majesty's interest, and seeing no hopes of relief from his master, he surrendered it, at length, to the troops of king William, and lived retired at home till his death, in 1716.

He married lady Elizabeth Howard, second daughter of Henry duke of Norfolk, by lady Ann Somerset his wife, eldest daughter of Edward marquis of Worcester, and by her, who died in July 1732, had issue one son, Alexander marquis of Huntley, and one daughter, lady Jane, married to James Drummond earl of Perth.

He was succeeded by his son Alexander, second duke of Gordon, who, in 1706, married lady Henrietta Mordaunt, daughter of Charles earl of Peterborough and Monmouth, by whom he had issue four sons, Cosmo-George, marquis of Huntley, lord Charles,

Charles, lord Lewis who died in 1754, and lord Adam, a colonel in the army and member for Aberdeenshire. Also seven daughters, lady Henrietta, lady Mary, lady Ann, the third wife of William earl of Aberdeen; lady Betty, wife of the Rev. Mr. Skelly; lady Jane; lady Catherine, wife of Francis Charteris, of Ampsfield, Esq; and lady Charlotte.

His grace departing this life in the year 1728, was succeeded by his eldest son Cosmo-George, third duke of Gordon; he was then about nine years of age, being the first of the family who had been educated in the protestant religion, which he was, under the inspection of his mother. In regard of his loyalty during the rebellion in 1745, the king was pleased to honour him with the green ribbon of the order of St. Andrew: soon after which he was elected one of the sixteen peers for North Britain in the parliament of 1747. In 1741, he married lady Katharine Gordon, daughter of William earl of Aberdeen, by whom he had issue three sons, Alexander, marquis of Huntley; lord William, and lord George. Also three daughters, ladies Susan, Anne, and Catharine. His grace dying in France in August 1752, was succeeded by his eldest son,

Alexander, now fourth duke of Gordon. His grace's mother married secondly, colonel Morris.

TITLES.] The most noble Alexander Gordon, duke of Gordon, marquis and earl of Huntley, earl of Enzie, and baron Gordon of Strathbogy.

CREATIONS.] Created lord Gordon of Strathbogy, in the county of Aberdeen 16 June 1376, earl of Huntley, in the county of Berwick in 1449, marquis of the same place 17 April 1599, by James VI. and duke of Gordon, in the county of Bamff, 1 November 1684, by Charles II.

ARMS.] Quarterly, first sapphire, three boars heads erazed topaz, for Gordon; 2d, topaz, three lions heads erazed ruby, for Badenoch; 3d, topaz, three crescents within a double tressure ruby, for Seton; 4th, sapphire, three cinquefoils pearl, for Frazer.

CREST.] In a marquis's coronet topaz, a stag's head gardant proper.

SUPPORTERS.] On the dexter side a greyhound pearl, gorged with a collar ruby, and three buckles topaz. On the sinister a senator of the college of justice, proper.

MOTTO.] Bydand; that is, abiding or lasting; and animo non astutia.

CHIEF SEATS.] At Strathbogy, 26 miles northwest of Aberdeen; and at Gordon Castle in Bamffshire, one of the finest mansions in the north.

DOUGLAS, Duke of QUEENSBERRY.

THE barony of Drumlanrig, in the county of Dumfries, antiently belonged to the earls of Mar. Thomas earl of Mar gave these lands to William lord Douglas, who had married his sister lady Margaret, which king David the IId did by charter confirm to him, who was thereafter earl of Douglas, and was succeeded by his son James earl of Douglas and Mar, slain in the battle of Otterburn, in the year 1388, who gave the barony of Drumlanrig to his son,

Sir William, the first lord Drumlanrig, and the heirs of his body; and in case of failure, to Archibald, another son, and his lawful heirs. This Sir William, the first lord Drumlanrig, signalized himself in the wars against the English: In the year 1411, he retook the town of Roxburgh, then in their possession. In 1412, he was sent ambassador to England to solicit the release of king James the first, then prisoner in that realm, from whom he obtained a charter, all written with the king's own hand, on vellum, confirming to him and his heirs the several baronies of Drumlanrig, Hawick in Tiviotdale, and Selkirk, 30 November 1412. In all the public transactions during the king's absence, we find him a great sharer; and when the English carried over the said king James into France, to try if his presence would draw the Scots in the French service over to the English; he went there to wait on his master, and on the 25th of October 1415, lost his life in the famous battle of Agincourt. He married Elizabeth, daughter of Sir Robert Stewart of Durisdeer and Rosyth, and by her had William, second baron of Drumlanrig, who in 1427, was one of the hostages sent to England for the redemption of the aforesaid king; and being, like his father, a military man, signalized himself in most of the actions between the Scots and English, particularly at the battle of Sark near Solway, where the Scots, according to their account, gained a great victory under his cousin Hugh earl of Ormond, brother to the earl of Douglas. Dying in 1458, he left issue by Jane his wife, daughter of Sir Herbert Maxwell, lord of Calaverock, ancestor to the earl of Nithsdale,

William, third baron of Drumlanrig, who gave many signal proofs of his valour in several actions, as at the siege of Roxburgh in 1460, where king James the IId lost his life, and another at Alnwick, where, in 1462, the French garrison was relieved by his cousin the earl of Angus, in the sight of a numerous English army, double to that the earl had under his command. He married Margaret, daughter of Roger Carlile lord Torthorold, and dying in 1464, by her left issue,

William the fourth baron of Drumlanrig, who treading in the steps of his brave ancestors, was slain in the service of his master

master king James III. at the battle of Kirkconnel near Sanquhar, against Alexander duke of Albany, the king's brother. He married Elizabeth, daughter of Sir Robert Crichton of Sanquhar, ancestor of the earl of Dumfries, and by her had four sons; James, his heir; Archibald, ancestor of the Douglasses of Cashory and Dalony; George, ancestor of the Douglasses of Pinziere; and John, vicar of Kirkconnel. Also three daughters; Margaret, wife of John lord Cathcart, and secondly, of Sir Robert Dalziel, ancestor of the earl of Carnwarth; Janet, of William lord Somerville, and secondly, of Alexander Gordon, son and heir of John Gordon of Lochinvar, ancestor of the viscounts Kenmure; and Elizabeth, of John Campbell, son and heir of James of Loudoun, ancestor of the earl of Loudoun. He was succeeded by his eldest son,

James, fifth lord, who married Janet, daughter of David Scot of Buccleugh, ancestor of the duke of Buccleugh; and by her had a son,

William, sixth lord of Drumlanrig; and one daughter, Janet, wife of Roger Grierson of Lag. Which William, sixth lord, losing his life with king James the IVth at the battle of Flodden, 1513, left issue by Elizabeth his wife, daughter of Sir John Gordon of Lochinvar, ancestor of the viscount Kenmure, James his successor, and Robert, from whom, by a natural son, is descended the family of Douglas of Burford; and three daughters, Janet, married to Robert the fourth lord Maxwell; Agnes to Andrew Cunningham of Kirkshaw; and Margaret to John lord Cathcart.

Sir James, his eldest son, the seventh lord, was one of those loyal persons who in the year 1526 attempted to deliver the young king James the fifth from the nobility who kept him in the condition of a captive; for which, and his loyalty to queen Mary, the duke of Chatelherault, who was regent, made him a knight. In 1553, the queen made him warden of the east marches, which office he discharged with great conduct and reputation for many years, till in his old age he resigned it.

He married first Margaret, daughter of George Douglas, son and heir of Archibald earl of Angus, by whom he had two daughters; Janet, married first to Sir William Douglas of Cossogle, and secondly, to John Charteris of Ampsfield; and Margaret the wife of John Jardin of Applegirth. Being divorced from his said lady, he married secondly Christian Montgomery, daughter of John, son and heir of Hugh the first earl of Eglinton, and by her he had an only son, Sir William, and four daughters, *viz.* 1. Margaret, married first to Edward lord Sanquhar; secondly, to Sir William Graham, fifth earl of Mentieth; and thirdly, to Mr. Wauchop of Niddery. 2. Helen, married to Roger Grierson of Lag. 3. Janet, married first to James Tweedie of Drumelzier, and, secondly, to Sir William

22   DUKE OF QUEENSBERRY.

Ker of Cesford, ancestor of the duke of Roxburgh. 4. Christian, the wife of Sir Alexander Stewart of Gairlies, ancestor of the earl of Galloway.

William, his only son and heir, was seated at Hawick, and died before his father in 1572. He was one of the king's party in the minority of James VI. when queen Mary's forces were defeated. He married Margaret, daughter of Sir James Gordon of Lochinvar, by whom he had a son, Sir James, who succeeded his grandfather, and three daughters; Margaret, married to Sir Robert Montgomery of Skemorly; Janet, to Sir James Murray of Cockpool; and Christian, first, to Sir Robert Dalziel, second earl of Carnwath; and secondly, to Sir Alexander Stewart of Gairlies, father of the first earl of Galloway.

Sir James, the eighth lord, who succeeded his grandfather, was greatly instrumental in reconciling the parties at court, and other disorders in the nation which disturbed the reign of king James the V.th before he came to the crown of England. He married Mary, daughter of John lord Fleming, and sister of John earl of Wigton, by whom he had issue four sons and two daughters; Sir William, who succeeded him, Sir James, David, and George: Janet, married to William Livingston, ancestor of the viscount Teviot; and Helen, to John Menzies of Castlehill. His lordship deceasing in August 1615, was succeeded by his eldest son,

Sir William Douglas, who married lady Isabel, daughter of Mark Ker earl of Lothian, and by her had four sons; James Douglas, who succeeded him; Sir William Douglas of Kilhead, great grandfather of Sir John Douglas of Kilhead, baronet; Archibald Douglas of Dornick; and Robert, who died unmarried. Also two daughters; lady Margaret, married to James Johnson earl of Hartfield, grandfather to the first marquis of Anandale; and lady Janet, who married Thomas Maclellan lord Kirkcudbright. This lord was much in the favour of king James, whom he had the honour to entertain at his mansion of Drumlanrig in his majesty's return to England 1617. On 1 April 1628, by a patent dated at Whitehall, he was created lord Douglas of Hawick and Tibbers, and viscount Drumlanrig, by king Charles I. who, while he was in Scotland, on 13 June 1633, created him also earl of Queensberry by a patent past in that kingdom. He dying in 1639, was succeeded by his eldest son,

James second earl of Queensberry, who was a great sufferer in the royal cause of Charles I. and designing to join the marquis of Montrose before the battle of Philiphaw 1645, he was intercepted and taken prisoner; whereupon he was fined an hundred thousand marks, which he paid, and died at Drumlanrig in the sixty third year of his age, 1671. He married first the lady Mary, youngest daughter of James marquis of Hamilton,

ton, and earl of Cambridge, but by her had no issue: and, secondly, lady Margaret Stewart, daughter of John earl of Traquair, lord treasurer of Scotland, and by her had issue four sons and five daughters, viz. 1. William, who succeeded him. 2. James, lieutenant-general, who died at Namur, 1691. 3. John, killed at the siege of Treves, 1673. 4. Robert, slain at the siege of Maestricht, 1676. 5. Lady Mary, married to Alexander Stewart the third earl of Galloway. 6. Lady Katharine, married to Sir James Douglas of Kilhead, baronet. 7. Lady Henrietta, married to Sir Robert Grierson of Lag, baronet. 8. Lady Margaret, first, wife of Sir Alexander Jardin of Applegirth, baronet; and secondly, of Sir David Thoirs. And 9. Lady Isabel, wife to Sir William Lockhart of Carstairs, baronet. He was succeeded by his eldest son,

William, third earl of Queensberry, who having suffered much in his father's fortune during the civil wars, was, in 1667, sworn one of the privy council in Scotland to king Charles II. and by a commission under the great seal, dated at Windsor, 1 June 1680, was constituted justice general of that kingdom. On 11 February 1681, he was created lord Douglas of Kilmount, Middlebie, and Dornick, viscount of Nith, Torthorald and Ross, earl of Drumlanrig and Sanquhar, and marquis of Queensberry; and in April 1682, by the king's warrant to Sir Alexander Erskine lyon king of arms, he had an addition to his coat armorial, for him and his heirs for ever, of the double tressure, as it is in the royal atchievement.

On the 12th of May following he was constituted lord high treasurer of Scotland; and by two other commissions, dated 21 September 1682, he was made governor of Edinburgh castle, and one of the extraordinary lords of session. And that no honours might be wanting which his prince could bestow upon him, he was, on 3 February, 1683, created marquis of Dumfries and duke of Queensberry; and afterwards made privy counsellor in both kingdoms. In the beginning of the reign of king James VII. he was appointed high commissioner for Scotland; and, with his son James earl of Drumlanrig, was constituted his majesty's lieutenant in the counties of Dumfries, Wigton, and Kirkcudbright; but the measures which were soon after taken at court, not suiting with his principles, he was removed, and in 1686 made president of the privy council in Scotland; but in six months after, not complying with the project of taking away the penal laws and test, he was entirely laid aside. Amongst his other excellent qualities, he was a great master of œconomy; for having come to a fortune much impaired through the iniquity of the times, he not only retrieved it, but acquired an ample estate in Tweeddale, which he gave his second son William.

He likewise at a great expence rebuilt the castle of Drumlanrig, the seat of his family.

In 1657 he married lady Isabel, daughter of William marquis of Douglas, by whom he had issue, 1. James, his successor. 2. William, created earl of March. 3. Lord George, who died unmarried. And, 4. Lady Ann, who in 1697 was married to David earl of Wemys, and died in 1699. His grace dying in 1694, was succeeded by his eldest son,

James, second duke of Queensberry, who in 1684, was by king Charles II. made one of the privy council in Scotland, and lieutenant-colonel of a regiment of horse commanded by John Graham, viscount Dundee. He continued in these posts till the year 1688, about which time he quitted them on account of the arbitrary measures at court. After the revolution, which he appeared in very early, he was by the prince of Orange made colonel of the Scots guard of horse, which commission was renewed to him immediately after the prince was declared king of that realm; and at the same time he was made one of the lords of the privy council and exchequer, and one of the gentlemen of his majesty's bedchamber.

In 1690 king William sent him into Scotland, to command a separate body of troops under lieutenant-general Mackay. Two years after he was made one of the lords of the treasury; and in 1693 he had a patent to sit and vote in the parliament of Scotland, being lord high treasurer, though his father was alive, and himself no peer. When his father died he laid aside all thoughts of military employments, quitted his commission, and was by the same king made lord privy seal in Scotland, and one of the extraordinary lords of session.

In the year 1700 he was appointed lord high commissioner in two sessions of parliament; and on the 14th of June 1701, in a chapter held at Kensington, was elected a knight of the garter, and on the 10th of July following was installed at Windsor. Queen Ann made him secretary of state for Scotland; and appointed him her high commissioner in 1702. He was appointed first commissioner on the part of Scotland, to treat of the union, and was high commissioner in 1703.

On the 3d of September 1706, his grace was again appointed high commissioner, and was one of the commissioners who compleated the union between the two kingdoms, after which he was elected one of the sixteen peers for Scotland to serve in the first parliament of Great Britain. He soon after had an honourable pension of 3000 l. out of the post office; and in 1711 was created duke of Dover. He continued secretary of state for North Britain till his death, which happened at London in July 6, 1711, in the 49th year of his age.

In December 1685 he married Mary, second daughter of Charles lord Clifford, eldest son of Richard earl of Burlington
and

and Cork, by the lady Jane Seymour, daughter of William duke of Somerset, and by her had four sons and three daughters, viz. 1. William earl of Drumlanrig, who died an infant. 2. James, who also died young. 3. Lord Charles, born at Edinburgh 24 November 1698, and in 1707, for the great services of his father and ancestors, was created earl of Solway, and is now duke of Queensberry. 4. Lord George, born at London in February 1700, and died at Paris in 1724.

Of the daughters, 1. Lady Isabel, the eldest, died unmarried. 2. Lady Jane married Francis duke of Buccleugh, then earl of Dalkeith, and died of the small-pox in the year 1729. 3. Lady Ann married the right honourable William Finch, late his majesty's envoy at the Hague, member for the university of Cambridge, and brother of the earl of Winchelsea and Nottingham, but died in 1741. His grace departing this life, as before observed, was succeeded by his third son,

Charles, now third duke of Queensberry. He was gentleman of the bedchamber to king George I. in 1720; and to Frederick late prince of Wales in 1738. His grace, in 1719, married the lady Catharine Hyde, daughter of Henry earl of Clarendon and Rochester, by whom he had a daughter, Catharine, who died young; and two sons, Henry earl of Drumlanrig, born 30 October 1722, and married, July 10, 1754, lady Elizabeth Hope, daughter of John earl of Hopeton; but was killed by the accidental going off of his own pistol on his journey from Scotland to London, October 20 following; and lord Charles, earl of Drumlanrig, who was born 17 July 1726, and represented the county of Dumfries in parliament, but died in October 1756, in the 30th year of his age, unmarried.

TITLES.] The most noble Charles Douglas, duke of Queensberry and Dover; marquis of Queensberry, Dumfries, and Beverly; earl of Queensberry, Drumlanrig, Sanquhar, and Solway; viscount Drumlanrig, Nith, Torthorald, Tibbers, and Ross; baron Douglas of Hawick, Kilmount, Middleby, Tibbers, Dornick, and Rippon, one of his Majesty's privy council.

CREATIONS.] Created lord Douglas of Hawick and Tibbers, and viscount Drumlanrig, 1 April 1628; earl of Queensberry, 13 June 1633; lord Douglas of Kilmount, Middleby, and Dornick; viscount Nith, Drumlanrig, Torthorald, and Ross; earl of Drumlanrig and Sanquhar, and marquis of Queensberry, 11 February 1682; marquis of Dumfries, and duke of Queensberry, 3 February 1684; viscount Tibbers, and earl of Solway in 1707, all Scotch honours: baron of Rippon; and marquis of Beverly in the county of York, and duke of Dover in Kent, English honours, 26 May 1708; which English titles, duke of Dover and the rest, were disallowed by the house of lords in December 1711, and voted illegal.

ARMS.]

DUKE OF QUEENSBERRY.

'ARMS.] Quarterly, 1st and 4th pearl, a heart ruby imperially crowned proper, on a chief sapphire, three mullets of the first for Douglas. 2d and 3d sapphire, a bend between six cross croslets fitchy, topaz, for the earldom of Mar; the whole within a border of the latter, charged with a double tressure of Scotland, being an augmentation, as is also the heart in the 1st and 4th quarters, being used in memory of the pilgrimage made by Sir James Douglas, ancestor of his grace, to the holy land, with the heart of king Robert Bruce, which was there interred at the said king's request in the year 1330; and the double tressure ruby was added by king Charles II. when he honoured the family with the marquisate of Queensberry, before which the border was only plain.

CREST.] On a wreath, a heart as in the coat, between two wings expanded topaz.

SUPPORTERS] Two pegasus's, or flying horses, pearl, their manes, wings, tails, and hoofs topaz.

MOTTO.] Forward.

CHIEF SEATS.] At Drumlanrig in the county of Dumfries, a stately palace, with noble gardens, avenues, and terras walks, eighteen miles from Dumfries, and forty four from Edinburgh.

At Middleton Stoney in Oxfordshire, and at Amesbury in Wiltshire.

CAMPBELL, Duke of ARGYLL.

THE noble and illustrious name of Campbell is of very great antiquity in Scotland.

Camden derives their pedigree from the ancient kings of Argyll, in the sixth century. The first appellation they used, was O Dubhin, which, according to an early custom, they assumed from Diarmed O Dubhin, one of their ancestors, who was a brave and warlike man, and from him, in the Irish language, they are called to this time Siol Diarmed, that is, the posterity or offspring of Diarmed. From the aforesaid Diarmed O Dubhin, the bards have recorded a long series of the barons of Lochow, whose actions they tell us were very renowned both for conduct and courage; and to him succeeded Paul O Dubhin, who was lord of Lochow, and was denominated Paul Infpuran, from his being the king's treasurer; but he having no male issue, his estate went to his daughter Eva; who being married to Gilespick O Dubhin, a relation of her own, he got the name changed to Campbell, thereby to perpetuate the memory of a noble and heroic piece of service performed by him for the crown of France, in the reign of Malcolm Canmore. By Eva, the said Gilespick O Dubhin, or Campbell, had a son named Duncan, who was father of Colin, and he of Archibald, the father of another Duncan, whose
son

son Sir Gilespick Campbell, knight, and lord of Lochow, was father of Sir Colin-More Campbell, who was one of those great men summoned to Berwick in August 1292, on the part of Robert Bruce, when king Edward I. of England came there to decide the dispute between the said Robert and John Baliol, for the crown of Scotland.

He married a lady of the family of Sinclair, by whom he had two sons, Sir Donald Campbell of Redhouse, from whom is descended the family of Loudon. and Sir Neil his successor, who was honoured with knighthood by Alexander III. and assisted at the coronation of the aforesaid king Robert in 1306.

In 1315 he was one of the barons in the parliament held at Air, where they made an entail of the crown to king Robert and his heirs; and for that signal loyalty, and other his good services, the king made him a grant of several lands, then in the crown; and also gave him in marriage his own sister, the lady Mary Bruce.

By the said lady he had two sons, Colin and John, which John was dignified with the title of earl of Athol, and died without issue; and Sir Colin, who succeeded his father in 1316, being in the expedition made into Ireland, in behalf of Edward Bruce, king of that realm, who was routed and slain in battle by the English, he there behaving himself with great gallantry, was rewarded with a grant of divers lands in the county of Argyll.

In the minority of king David Bruce, raising 400 men for that prince, and taking therewith the castle of Dunoon, then in possession of the English, he rewarded him with the heretable government thereof, and gave him a yearly pension.

He married a daughter of the family of Lennox, and dying in 1340, by her left Archibald, who succeeded him; John, ancestor of the Campbells of Barbeck, of whom Succoth, &c. are descended; and Dougal, who lost his estate for joining with Baliol; which Sir Archibald also constantly adhering to king David's interest, during his captivity in England, his majesty bestowed on him sundry lands, which are still in the family; and he marrying Mary, daughter of Sir John Laumont, by her had issue,

Sir Colin his heir, who was employed by king Robert II. in restraining the incursions of the Highlanders, who had then infested the western parts of the realm; and reducing them to his majesty's obedience, had thereupon a grant of divers lands and lordships, still in the family's possession.

He married Margaret, daughter of Sir John Drummond of Stobhall, and by her had issue Colin, ancestor of the Campbells of Ardkinlas, &c. and Donald; beside,

Sir Duncan, his successor, who being a person of great parts,
arrived

arrived to high advancements, both in honour and eſtate; for in the reign of king James I. he was made his majeſty's juſtice general, one of his privy council, and lieutenant within the ſhire of Argyll; all which offices were confirmed to him by James II. whom he helped to ſettle on the throne, and was thereupon made high chancellor of Scotland, with the gift of ſeveral lands, and had ſummons to parliament by the title of lord Campbell in 1445. He married, firſt, the lady Margaret Stewart, daughter of Robert duke of Albany, governor of Scotland; and by her had three ſons; Celeſtine, who died young; Archibald, from whom is derived the male line of this noble family; and Sir Colin Campbell, anceſtor of the earl of Breadalbane. He married, ſecondly, Margaret, daughter of Sir John Stewart of Blackhill, by whom he had alſo three ſons, viz. Duncan, who was anceſtor of the family of Auchinbreck, &c. &c. Neil, anceſtor of the family of Elbongreg, Ormandle, &c. and Arthur, anceſtor of the Campbells of Otter, &c.

Archibald, who was the eldeſt ſurviving brother, dying in his father's life-time, left iſſue by Elizabeth, daughter of Sir John Somervile of Carnwath, anceſtor of the lord Somervile, a ſon,

Colin, ſecond lord, who ſucceeded his grandfather, and was created earl of Argyll in 1457. In the reign of James III. he was employed in the higheſt offices of ſtate, as lord privy ſeal, maſter of the houſhold, and lord high chancellor; and remained chancellor till he died, which was in the year 1493. He married Iſabel, daughter and coheir of John Stewart lord Lorn, by whom he had two ſons, Archibald his heir, and Thomas, anceſtor of the Campbells of Lundie in Angus: alſo ſeven daughters, whereof Margaret was married to George lord Seton, anceſtor of the earl of Winton; Iſabel to William, ſon and heir of John lord Drummond, anceſtor of the earls of Perth; Helen to Hugh Montgomery, earl of Eglinton; Elizabeth to John lord Oliphant; and Mary to Æneas Macdonald; —— to Alexander Mackenzie of Kintail, anceſtor of the earl of Seaforth; and Catharine to Torquil M'Leod of Lewis. On his deceaſe his eldeſt ſon

Archibald became the ſecond earl of Argyll, who was by king James IV. promoted to be chancellor and chamberlain of Scotland, and maſter of the king's houſhold; but on the 9th of September 1513, commanding the van of the army at the battle of Floddon, where he behaved with great valour, was killed with his royal maſter. He married Elizabeth, daughter of John Stewart earl of Lennox, and had iſſue by her four ſons and five daughters; Margaret married to John lord Erſkine, afterwards earl of Mar; Iſabel to Gilbert Kennedy, earl of Caſſils; Mary to John Stewart, earl of Athol; Jane to Sir John Lamont; Anne to Simon, maſter of Lovat. The ſons were, 1. Colin. 2. Archibald, who left only one daughter. 3. Sir John

John Campbell of Calder, whose daughter Jane married Alexander, the fourth lord Lovat. And 4. Donald, ancestor of the Campbells of Cythaik in Angus.

Colin, the eldest son, succeeded his father, and was the third earl, and one of the council to king James V. as also in his reign made lord lieutenant of the borders, warden of the marches, heretable sheriff of Argyllshire, justice general of Scotland, and master of the king's houshold. He married lady Janet Gordon, daughter of Alexander earl of Huntley, and by her had issue Archibald, John, and Alexander; and a daughter, Margaret, who was married to James Stewart earl of Murray; and secondly, to John earl of Sutherland. He died in 1542, and was succeeded by his eldest son,

Archibald, fourth earl of Argyll, who was lord chancellor of Scotland, and one of those peers who, upon the death of king James V. strongly opposed the intended match between queen Mary and king Edward VI. of England; upon which a war happening with that kingdom, he remarkably distinguished himself both at the unfortunate battle of Pinkie, and the siege of Haddington, for his queen and country. This noble lord was the first of his quality who embraced the protestant religion. He married Helen, daughter of James Hamilton the first earl of Arran, by whom he had issue, Archibald his heir; and by a second wife, Mary, daughter of William Graham earl of Menteith, he had Sir Colin Campbell of Buchan, of whom hereafter; and two daughters, Margaret, married to James Stewart, lord Down; and Janet, to Hector M'Lean of Dowart. His lordship dying in 1558, was succeeded by his eldest son,

Archibald, fifth earl, a person of singular accomplishments, who entered into an association with the earls of Glencairn, Moreton, and others, faithfully to assist one another in advancing the cause of the protestant religion, which in 1560 they happily established by act of parliament. In 1571 he was appointed high chancellor of Scotland, which office he held till 1575, the time of his death; and leaving no issue by his two wives, the lady Jane Stewart, natural daughter of king James V. and lady Jane Cunningham, daughter of Alexander earl of Glencairn, his estate and honour descended to his brother,

Colin, the sixth earl, who was also lord chancellor of Scotland, and one of the privy council of king James VI. and dying in 1584, left issue by Agnes his second wife, daughter of William Keith earl Marishal, Archibald his heir, and Sir Colin Campbell of Lundie, baronet.

Which Archibald, seventh earl, was commander of the forces sent against the earls of Huntley and Errol at the battle of Glenlivet, 1594. He reduced the Mac Gregors in 1603, and the Macdonalds in the Western Islands, in 1614; for which

great

great services he had a grant of all Kintyre, which was confirmed by parliament in 1617. He married first lady Anne Douglas, daughter of William earl of Moreton, by whom he had Archibald, who succeeded him; and four daughters, Ann, married to George second marquis of Huntley; Annabel to Robert Ker, second earl of Lothian; Jane to John Gordon, first viscount Kenmure; and Mary to Sir Robert Montgomery of Skemorly. By his second wife Ann, daughter of Sir William Cornwallis of Brome in the county of Suffolk, ancestor of the earl Cornwallis, by Lucy his wife, third daughter and coheir of John Nevil lord Latimer, he had issue a son, James, who in 1622 was created baron of Kintyre, and in 1642, earl of Irvine; but dying without heirs male, his titles became extinct; as also a daughter, Mary, married to James lord Rollo. His lordship deceasing in the year 1638, was succeeded by

Archibald, his eldest son, and eighth earl, who was of the privy council to king Charles I. into whose hands he resigned the justiciaryship of all Scotland in 1628, which had been in his family for two hundred years, reserving to himself and his heirs the jurisdiction of Argyll, and the western isles, and wherever else he had lands in Scotland; all which in 1633 was ratified by act of parliament; and in 1641 he was created marquis of Argyll.

He was one of the ablest statesmen of his time, and joined with the parliament of Scotland in the Presbyterian government then established. He contributed much to the reception and coronation of king Charles II. and on 1 January, 1650, put the crown on his head at Scoon; but after the restoration, 1661, he was accused by the earl of Middleton, then made high commissioner, of a multitude of crimes, especially in complying with Oliver as to the death of the late king; for which he was condemned in parliament, and 27 May 1661, beheaded at the market-cross of Edinburgh, being, more truly, sacrificed for his zeal in promoting the protestant interest and church government of Scotland.

He married lady Margaret, daughter of William Douglas earl of Moreton, and by her had issue two sons, lord Archibald his heir, and lord Neil: also three daughters, the ladies, Ann, who died unmarried; Jane, married to Robert Ker marquis of Lothian; and Mary, first to George Sinclair earl of Caithness, and afterwards to John Campbell earl of Breadalbane. He was succeeded by his eldest son,

Archibald, the ninth earl, who was, when lord Lorn, commander of king Charles II's foot guard, and signalized himself against Oliver, never capitulating till he was ordered by his majesty so to do, yet was forfeited by his father's misfortune; but in 1663 was restored by the said king to the honours and estate of his ancestors, as earl of Argyll only. He was also by
the

the said king appointed one of his privy council, and one of the commissioners of the treasury, which office for many years he discharged with great fidelity; but in 1681, opposing the duke of York, who promoted popery in Scotland, the duke was so enraged against him, that all methods imaginable were proposed to ruin him; which at last was effected, on pretence of putting his own meaning upon the test when he took it, (though others had done it as well as he) and because he declared he would take no oaths to bind himself up from making such amendments in church and state as were necessary for the public safety. His enemies thereupon accused him of disloyalty; and incensing the king against him, he was confined prisoner in the castle of Edinburgh; after which, being tried before the justice court, he was found guilty of high treason, and sentenced to suffer death. Some days after his estate was disposed of to others; and he getting out of prison in the dress of a lady's page, went into Holland, and so escaped his destiny at that time, though afterwards he fell a sacrifice to the same rage that first made him unhappy; for in 1685, having got together some officers and soldiers in Holland, he put them on board three ships, and landed in Argyllshire; and published two declarations; one in the name of all those who had taken up arms; the other in his own.

In June 1685, being defeated, and taken, he was sent prisoner to the castle of Edinburgh, and beheaded on the 30th at the market-cross on his former illegal sentence.

He married lady Mary Stewart, daughter of James earl of Murray, by whom he had four sons and two daughters; lady Ann, first married to Richard Maitland earl of Lauderdale, and secondly to Charles earl of Murray; and lady Jane to William Ker marquis of Lothian. Of the sons, Archibald, John, Charles and James: The youngest, who was a captain in the army, married Margaret Lesly, daughter of David lord Newark. Charles was a colonel in the army. John Campbell of Mammore, the second son, married a daughter of John lord Elphingston, of whom hereafter; and

Archibald, the eldest, first duke of Argyle, was one of those few Scots peers who came from Holland with the prince of Orange, and 5 November 1688, landed with him at Torbay, and very much promoted the revolution in Scotland; he was owned as earl of Argyll by the parliament before they took off the attainder against his father, which, by the claim of right, was declared to be a scandal on the justice of the nation. This earl was sent from the nobility to London, with Sir James Montgomery and Sir John Dalrymple, from the barons and boroughs, to offer the crown of Scotland, in the name of the convention of estates, to their majesties king William and queen Mary; for whose service he after sent over a regiment to Flanders,

ders, of which the officers were all of his own name and family.

On 11 April 1689, the day that their majesties were crowned king and queen of England, he, with the other commissioners, presented the act of settlement to their majesties, and taking their oath, they were the same day proclaimed king and queen of Scotland; and on the 11th of May following, the commissioners tendered them the coronation oath, which was distinctly pronounced by the earl, while their majesties repeated the sentences after him, holding up their right hands all the while, according to the custom of Scotland. On this their advancement to the throne, he was appointed one of the privy-council, one of the lords of the treasury, colonel of the Scots guard of horse, one of the extraordinary lords of session, and at length created duke of Argyll in June 1701. In the reign of queen Anne he was one of the commissioners for uniting the two nations; and marrying Elizabeth, daughter of Sir Lionel Talmash of Helingham in Suffolk, Bart. and sister of Lionel earl of Dysart, by Elizabeth his wife, daughter and heir of William Murray earl of Dysart, by her had issue two sons, John marquis of Lorn, and Archibald earl of Ila; also a daughter, lady Anne, married to James Stewart, second earl of Bute. His grace deceasing in the year 1703, was succeeded by his eldest son,

John, second duke of Argyll, who was born in 1680; and in 1701 had the command of a regiment of foot, and soon after was made an extraordinary lord of session, and a knight of the thistle. He distinguished himself through the whole course of the queen's war, by his bravery and intrepidity, particularly at the battles of Ramillies, Oudenarde, and Malplaquet, and at the sieges of Menin, Fort Plassendale, Ostend and Tournay.

In 1705 he was her majesty's high commissioner to the parliament of Scotland, and was afterwards general of her army in Spain, general and commander in chief in North Britain, governor of Minorca, and one of the privy-council in England.

In 1705 he was created baron of Chatham and earl of Greenwich, and in 1710 elected a knight of the most noble order of the garter.

On the death of queen Anne he was one of the lords justices till the arrival of king George I. pursuant to his majesty's former appointment; and on the 19th of the said month was appointed first gentleman of the bed-chamber, or groom of the stole, to his royal highness George prince of Wales; as on the 27th he was appointed commander in chief of his majesty's forces in Scotland, and soon after sworn of the privy-council. In 1715, a rebellion breaking out in Scotland,

land, his grace attacked and routed the enemy at Dumblain, on the 13th of November, with a force not half their number. In February 1718, he was declared lord steward of the king's houshold, and on the 30th of April created duke of Greenwich. He was several times one of the regency during the king's absence; was appointed governor of Portsmouth by king George II. was colonel of the queen's regiment of horse, and afterwards had the royal blue regiment of horseguards. At length he was master-general of the ordnance, and field-marshal of Great Britain. And was as conspicuous for his patriotism and eloquence in parliament, as he had been for bravery and conduct in the field.

He married first, Mary, daughter of John Brown, Esq; and niece of Sir Charles Duncombe, Knt. lord mayor of London; but she dying in 1716, without issue, his grace married secondly, Mrs. Jane Warburton, one of the maids of honour to queen Anne, as also to queen Caroline, when princess of Wales, and by her had five daughters, lady Caroline, married first to Francis earl of Dalkeith, eldest son of Francis duke of Buccleugh; and secondly, to the right hon. Charles Townshend, Esq; second son of the late lord viscount Townshend. Lady Ann married to William earl of Strafford. Lady Jane died in her twelfth year. Lady Betty married to James Stewart Mackenzie, brother of John earl of Bute. Lady Mary married to Edward viscount Coke, heir apparent of Thomas earl of Leicester, and to his mother Margaret baroness Clifford, who left her a widow without issue. His grace dying in October 1743, the titles of duke and earl of Greenwich, and baron of Chatham, expired with him; but he was succeeded in his other titles by his brother,

Archibald, third duke of Argyll, who was in 1705, at 23 years of age, constituted lord treasurer of Scotland, and the next year appointed one of the commissioners for the union treaty, during which he was created a peer of Scotland, by the titles of lord Ornsay, Dunoon, and Aros, also viscount and earl of Ila, 29 October 1706. On the happy conclusion of the said treaty, he was elected one of the sixteen peers to represent Scotland in the first British parliament, as he was in every one after except the fourth.

In October 1715, during the rebellion, he, by his great vigour and diligence, secured Inverary, the capital town of Argyllshire, when general Gordon came with near 3000 men to force or surprize it. He was then in the office of lord register in Scotland; and on the death of William marquis of Annandale in 1721, was appointed keeper of the privy seal, which office being renewed to him by king George II. he held it till 1733: After which his grace was in the several high posts of justice general of Scotland, an extraordinary lord of
session,

session, keeper of the great seal, and chancellor of the university of Aberdeen.

He married the daughter of Mr. Whitfield, Pay-master of the marines, but by her, who died in 1723, he had no issue, and his grace dying the 15th of April 1761, in the 79th year of his age, was succeeded, in his titles and estate, by

John Campbell, now fourth duke of Argyll, son of the hon. John Campbell of Mammore, second son of Archibald, ninth earl of Argyll. His grace is a general and colonel of the Scots Grays, governor of Milford-Haven and Limerick, one of the sixteen peers for Scotland, a lord of the privy-council, and a knight of the antient order of the thistle.

In the year 1720, he married the hon. Miss Bellenden, daughter of John, lord Bellenden, by whom he has issue, four sons and one daughter, viz. 1. John marquis of Lorn, a lieutenant-general and colonel of the first regiment of foot, who in March, 1759, married the duchess dowager of Hamilton, by whom he has issue three children. 2. Henry, killed at the battle of La Feldt. 3. Lord William, who in May 1763, married Miss Sarah Izard of Charles-Town in South-Carolina, and in January 1764, was chosen knight of the shire for the county of Argyll. He is a captain in the navy, and governor of Nova-Scotia. 4. Lord Frederick, member in the present parliament for Renfrew, and a counsellor at law. 5. Lady Mary, who was the third wife of Charles Bruce earl of Aylesbury, who dying in 1746, she married the right hon. Henry Seymour Conway, brother of Francis earl of Hertford, one of his majesty's principal secretaries of state, by whom she has two daughters.

TITLES.] The most noble John Campbell, duke, marquis, and earl of Argyll; marquis of Kintyre and Lorn; earl of Campbell and Cowal; viscount Lochow and Glenilla; lord of Inverary, Mull, Morvern, and Tyrie. Lord-lieutenant of Argyllshire, admiral of the Western Isles, hereditable master of the king's houshold, hereditable keeper of Dunstaffnage and Carrick.

CREATIONS.] Lord Campbell, by summons to parliament, in 1445, the 8th of James II. and by the same king in 1457, created earl of the county of Argyll; marquis of the same 15 November 1641, the 17th of Charles I. duke of Argyll, marquis of Kintyre and Lorn, earl of Campbell and Cowal, viscount Lochow and Glenilla, lord of Inverary, Mull, Morvern, and Tyrie, 23 June 1701, the 13th of William III.

ARMS.] Quarterly, 1st and 4th girony of eight pieces topaz and diamond, for Campbell; 2d and 3d pearl, a lymphad, or old fashioned ship with one mast, close sails, and oars in action, all diamond, with flag and penants flying ruby, for the lordship of Lorn.

CREST.]

CREST.] On a wreath, a boar's head couped proper, topaz.
SUPPPORTERS.] Two lions gardant ruby.
MOTTO.] Ne oblivifcaris.

Note, That behind the arms are two honourable badges in faltire, which his grace's anceftors have borne a long time as great mafters of the king's houfhold, and jufticiaries of Scotland. The firft is a batoon topaz, femee of thiftles emerald, enfigned with an imperial crown proper; and thereon the creft of Scotland, which is a lion fejant guardant ruby, crowned with the like crown he fits on; having in his dexter paw a fword proper, the pomel and hilt topaz; and in the finifter a fcepter of the laft. The other badge is a fword, as that in the lion's paw.

CHIEF SEATS.] At Inverary in Argyllfhire, feventy miles from Edinburgh; at Campbelton in Kintyre; and at Rofneath in the county of Dunbarton.

MURRAY, Duke of ATHOL.

THE firname of Murray is, undoubtedly, amongft the moft antient in Scotland, and the family of very remote fettlement in the county of Perth, and were defcended from Sir Malcolm Murray, whofe fon Sir William in the year 1282, marrying Adda, daughter of Malyfs Senefchal of Strathern, thereby became poffeffed of the barony of Tullibardin, as appears by a charter dated that year.

In 1292, he was one of the barons fummoned to Berwick by king Edward I. of England, when that prince was to determine the controverfy about the fucceffion to the crown of Scotland, then difputed between John Baliol and Robert Bruce. By the faid Adda his wife he had

Sir Andrew Murray, his heir, who having joined the intereft Baliol, againft David Bruce, was beheaded at Perth in 1332. To him fucceeded his fon, Sir William, third baron of Tullibardin, whofe fon John fucceeded him, and he was fucceeded by his fon, Sir Walter, who died in 1390, and to him fucceeded his fon, Sir David, fixth baron, who was knighted by king James I. and founded the collegiate church of Tullibardin; and he dying in 1446, was fucceeded by his fon Sir William. Which Sir William was knighted by king James III. made fteward of Strathern, and marrying Margaret, daughter of Sir John Colquhoun of Lufs, by her had many fons, from whom different families of the Murrays are defcended.

Sir William, his eldeft fon, fucceeded him, and married Katharine, daughter of Andrew, lord Gray, by whom he had four fons and two daughters, viz. Sir John, who died without iffue, Sir William his heir, Sir Andrew of Arngofk, anceftor of vifcount Stormount, and David: Chriftjan, married to George lord Seton; and Elizabeth to Thomas Stewart of Grantully.

Grantully. He died in 1509, and was succeeded by his second son,

William, ninth baron of Tullibardin, who married lady Margaret, daughter of John, earl of Athol, and had issue by her three sons and one daughter. He was succeeded by his eldest son,

William, tenth baron, who by his wife Catherine, daughter of Sir John Campbell, of Glenurchy, ancestor of the earl of Breadalbin, had issue four sons and four daughters, and dying in 1562, was succeeded by his eldest son,

Sir William Murray, eleventh baron, who was a great statesman, and deceased in 1583. He married Agnes, daughter of William Graham earl of Montrose, by whom he had three sons and two daughters, Sir John his successor, Sir William of Pitcairly, and Mungo Murray of Dornock; Margaret married to Sir Robert Bruce of Clackmanan, and Jane to Sir John Hepburn.

Sir John, who succeeded, was one of the privy-council to king James VI. in 1592, by whom he was created lord Murray, and earl of Tullibardin, July 20, 1606. He married Katharine, daughter of David lord Drummond, and by her had issue five sons and four daughters, viz. William his heir; captain John; Sir Patrick, knight of the Bath; and Sir Mungo, who succeeded pursuant to the limitation of the patent as viscount Stormont; and Robert. Of the four daughters, Ann, the eldest, was married to Patrick Lyon, earl of Kinghorn, ancestor of the earl of Strathmore; Lilias, to Sir John Grant; Margaret, to James Haldane; and Katharine, to David Ross. To him succeeded his eldest son,

William, second earl, who being the happy rescuer of his majesty from a tumult of the citizens of Perth in 1600, when John earl of Gowry their provost was killed, had thereupon a special grant of the sheriffship of Perthshire, which continued in his family till the suppression of all heritable jurisdictions, by act of parliament, in 1747. He married Dorothy, daughter and coheir of John Stewart, fifth earl of Athol, by Mary his wife, daughter of William Ruthven, the first earl of Gowry; and by her had a son, John, of whom hereafter, and one daughter, lady Anne, wife of Sir John Moncrief, of that ilk. Knowing that his said son was heir of line to the earldom of Athol, and being unwilling the two honours of Athol and Tullibardin, with the estates, should be conjoined in the same person, he surrendered his title of Tullibardin into the king's hands in favour of his brother Patrick, which was confirmed by a patent, in 1628, and the said Patrick, hereby, third earl of Tullibardin, married Elizabeth Dent, by whom he had issue James, fourth earl of Tullibardin, and William of Red-castle, a brave youth, executed for his adherence to

king

king Charles I. in 1646, at St. Andrews. Which James, fourth earl, had two fons, who both died unmarried, whereby the eftates and honours of Tullibardin devolved on his coufin, and nearest heir male, John, fifth earl, fon of William, fecond earl, and his lady Dorothea Stewart, as above.

Which John, who had alfo fucceeded to the title of earl of Athol, was by that match related to the royal family. He was a faithful friend to king Charles I. from the beginning of his troubles in 1640, when he raifed a body of near 2000 men for his fervice. He married Jane, daughter of Sir Duncan Campbell of Glenurchy; and dying in 1642, was fucceeded by his fon,

John, the fixth earl, who in the year 1653, when but eighteen years of age, loyally took up arms in defence of king Charles II. and had feveral encounters with the Englifh infurgents in the north of Scotland; for which his majefty, after the reftoration, made him juftice general, lord privy feal, captain of his guard, one of the extraordinary lords of feffion, and created him marquis of Athol, February 7, 1676. On the 11th of June 1685, the firft of James VII. he defeated a party of the earl of Argyll's men; after which he was conftituted lord lieutenant of the county of Argyll, and made knight of the thiftle. He dying in May 1703, left iffue by lady Amelia-Sophia, daughter of that loyal nobleman James Stanley earl of Derby, and baron Strange of Knockyn, who was beheaded in 1651, fix fons and one daughter; John, his heir; Charles, created earl of Dunmore; lord James, married to lady Lillie Drummond, daughter of John the fecond earl of Perth; and left two daughters, one married to Andrew lord Rollo; the other to Mr. Farquharfon of Invercauld; William, the fourth fon, was lord Nairn, by marrying the heirefs of Robert Nairn lord Nairn; lord Edward and lord Mungo; and the daughter, Amelia, was married to Hugh Frafer lord Lovat. His lordfhip was fucceeded by his eldeft fon,

John, fecond marquis, who was made fecretary of ftate in the reign of William III. high commiffioner to the parliament, chancellor of the univerfity of St. Andrews, and in 1697 created earl of Tullibardin, and vifcount Glenalmond.

On the 30th of June 1703, he was created marquis of Tullibardin and duke of Athol, and on the 7th of February following he was elected a knight of the thiftle: In 1706, when the twenty fecond article of the union came to be debated concerning the number of reprefentatives for Scotland in the parliament of Great Britain, his grace thought fit to proteft againft the number as infufficient and unreafonable.

He was elected one of the fixteen peers in the 3d and 4th Britifh parliaments; and in 1712 was fworn one of her Majefty's privy council; appointed privy feal in 1713, and the next year was high commiffioner to the general affembly of the church.

He married, first, lady Katharine Hamilton, daughter of William and Ann duke and duchess of Hamilton; and by her had issue six sons, and one daughter, Susanna, married to William Gordon earl of Aberdeen. Of the six sons, the first called marquis of Tullibardin, was a colonel in the Dutch service, and was slain at the battle of Mons in 1709. The second son, William, marquis of Tullibardin, was attainted in 1716 for being a party in the rebellion of that time; and being taken in the last rebellion in 1746, was sent to the Tower, where he died the year after. James the third son succeeded as duke of Athol. Lord Charles died without issue. Lord George married an heiress of his own name, by whom he left a daughter, Amelia, who in 1750 became the second wife of the Hon. John Sinclair, who would have succeeded his father as lord Sinclair, but was attainted in 1716: Also three sons, John, now duke of Athol, James and George. This lord George Murray presumptuously acted with the rebels in 1745 as a lieutenant general, and after the defeat at Culloden escaped into France, but was attainted in 1746, and died in November 1760. The sixth son, lord Basil, died unmarried.

He married secondly, Mary, daughter of William lord Ross, by whom he had three sons, lord John Murray, member in the late parliament for Perthshire, colonel of the Highland regiment, and a lieutenant general; lord Edward, who had issue a son, now an officer in the army, and a daughter; lord Frederick, a captain in the royal navy. He had also one daughter by this second wife, lady Mary, married to James lord Deskford. His grace dying in 1724, was succeeded by his third son James, above noticed, on whom the titles forfeited by his brother were settled by act of parliament.

Which James, second duke of Athol, was at his father's death a commoner for the county of Perth, and a colonel in the third regiment of guards. In 1726 he married dame Jane Lanoy, widow of Sir Timothy Lanoy of Hammersmith in Middlesex, Bart. and sister of Sir John Frederick of Westminster, baronet. By her he had a son in 1735, who died the same year; and two daughters, lady Jane, wife of John earl of Crawford, and died without issue; and lady Charlotte, the wife of her cousin, John Murray, Esq; knight of the shire for the county of Perth, and son of lord George, as above.

His grace became an English peer by the title of lord Strange, as also lord of the Isle of Man on the decease of James Stanley the 10th earl of Derby, who died without issue on the 1st of February 1735-6; which dignities he derived from his grandmother Amelia-Sophia, daughter of James earl of Derby, beheaded in 1651, as above recited. In April 1763 he resigned the privy seal of Scotland, and succeeded the duke of Queensberry as keeper of the great seal. He departed this life on January

nuary 8, 1764, and the titles of duke of Athol, &c. &c. devolved on his nephew, the honourable John Murray, Esq; it having been found, that the attainder of lord George his father could operate only against himself, and conveyed no corruption of blood to his children.

Which John, now third duke of Athol, having married his cousin lady Charlotte, now baroness Strange, the heirs male and of line of this illustrious family are conjoined. They have issue four sons and three daughters, viz. John marquis of Tullibardin, born on June 30, 1755; lords James, George and William; ladies Charlotte, Emilia and Rachael. In 1764, a contract was made with the government for the sale and surrender of the Isle of Man, together with its regalities, franchises and sea-ports; all which were annexed by act of parliament to the crown, on payment of 70,000 l. Reserving to his grace, his estate therein, manor-rights, patronage of the bishoprick, honorary service at the coronation, &c. And his majesty was further pleased, in consideration of the said surrender, to grant, by his letters bearing date July 10, 1765, a pension of 2000 l. per annum upon the Irish establishment, for the lives of the present duke and duchess.

TITLES.] The most noble James Murray, duke, marquis, and earl of Athol, marquis and earl of Tullibardin, viscount Glenalmond, and lord Murray; one of the sixteen peers for Scotland.

CREATIONS.] Lord Murray of Tullibardin in the county of Perth, 25 April 1604, 3 James VI. earl and marquis of Athol in the county of Perth, 17 February 1675, 28 Charles II. viscount Glenalmond, and earl of Tullibardin, 27 July 1697, 9 William III. and marquis of Tullibardin and duke of Athol, 30 April 1703, 2 Ann.

ARMS.] Quarterly, first sapphire, three mullets pearl, within a double tressure flowered and counterflowered with fleurs de lis topaz, for Murray. 2d grand quarter is quarterly, 1st and 4th topaz, a fess cheque, pearl and sapphire, for Stewart; 2d and 3d pally of six, topaz and diamond, for the title of Athol. In the third quarter ruby three legs armed proper, conjoined in the centre; at the upper part of the thighs, flext in triangle, garnished and spurred, topaz for lord of the Isle of Man. The 4th as the 1st.

CREST.] On a wreath, a demi savage, wreathed about the head and waist, emerald; holding in his right hand a dagger proper, the pomel and hilt topaz; and in his left a key of the latter.

SUPPORTERS.] On the dexter side, a lion ruby, gorged with a collar sapphire, and thereon three mullets pearl, being the supporter of Tullibardin. On the sinister, a savage wreathed about the head and waist as the crest, his feet in fetters of iron, and the chain over his right arm; which supporter and crest, with the motto, were obtained by John Stewart, earl of Athol, for his service in reducing the rebel Donald, lord of the isles, and bringing him to submission, in the reign of James III.

MOTTO.] Furth fortune and fill the fetters.

CHIEF SEATS.] At Dunkell near the river Tay; at Blair castle in Athol; at Huntingtowr; the castle of Tullibardin in Perthshire; and at Castleton in the Isle of Man.

GRAHAM, Duke of MONTROSE.

THIS noble and great family is descended from the renowned Græme, who, in the year 404, was general of king Fergus II's army; and in 420, making a breach upon the trench or wall, which the emperor Severus had made between the rivers Forth and Clyde, as the utmost bounds of the Roman empire, to keep out the Scots from molesting them in their possessions, the said trench has ever since been called Græme's dyke; and during the minority of Eugene II. the son of Fergus II. he was governor of Scotland, married a lady of the royal house of Denmark, and was progenitor of all the Grahams in Scotland.

In the year 1225, William de Græme, now spelt Graham, was one of the witnesses to the foundation of the abbey of Holyrood-house, by king David I. He had a son, John de Græme, who had a son William, and William a son, Sir David Graham, who obtaining from king William the lion a grant of the lands of Charleton and Barrowfield near Glasgow, and the lordship of Kinaber in the county of Kincardin in 1214, was therein succeeded by Sir David his son, who had also a grant from Maldwin earl of Lenos, of the lands of Strathblane in Stirlingshire, and Mugdok in Lenos, and from the earl of Dunbar got the lands of Dundaff. His son David succeeding, obtained particular charters of his whole lands, and had them ratified to him under the great seal of Alexander III. He married Annabel, sister of Malise earl of Strathern, with her had the barony of Kincarn, or Kincardin of Strathern, in the county of Perth, and by her had issue three sons, Sir Patrick his heir, who was sheriff of Stirling; Sir John, a constant companion and bosom friend of the brave Sir William Wallace, who was killed at the battle of Falkirk in 1298; and Sir David Græme.

In the year 1296, Sir Patrick his successor strenuously asserting the independence of his country against king Edward I. of England, was killed at the battle of Dunbar in 1296, and left issue two sons, Sir David his heir, and Sir John, who married the heir of Robert de Avenel, and with her had the lands of Eskdale in the south.

Sir David, who succeeded his father, being also a very great
[atriot,

patriot, and zealous loyalift in behalf of king Robert Bruce, he, upon that king's acceffion to the throne, had a grant of divers lands, for his good fervices before that time performed; and in the year 1320 was one of the barons who wrote that notable letter to the pope, afferting the independence of Scotland, and extolling the faid king as the nation's deliverer; to which record his feal now remains entire. His fon Sir David fucceeded, and in the year 1346, when king David was taken prifoner at the battle of Durham, he was one of the barons of Scotland, appointed to treat with the Englifh for the king's redemption: He had iffue a fon, Sir Patrick, and a daughter, married to William earl of Rofs.

Which Sir Patrick was lord of Dundaff, and one of the hoftages for the faid king's ranfom, 1357. By his firft wife he had William lord Graham; and a daughter, Matilda, the wife of Sir John Drummond of Concraig; and by his fecond, Euphemia, daughter of Sir John Stewart, brother of king Robert II. and fifter of Walter Stewart lord of Ralefton, he had Sir Patrick, from whom defcended the earls of Menteith; as alfo Robert, David and Alexander. He died before the year 1404, and was fucceeded by his eldeft fon,

Sir William Graham of Kincardin, who was joined in embaffy to king Henry IV. of England, with the earls of Crawford and Mar, to negociate and fettle a peace. He married, firft, Mariot, daughter of Sir John Oliphant, by whom he had two fons, Alexander, who died before him, and John. His fecond wife was lady Mariot Stewart, daughter of king Robert III. widow of James Kennedy of Denure, and of George earl of Angus; by her he had iffue five fons, Sir Robert, who was anceftor of the Grahams of Fintry; Patrick, bifhop of St. Andrews; William, from whom are defcended the Grahams of Garvock, Balgoun; Harry and Walter, anceftors of the Grahams of Knockdolien. Dying in 1424, he was fucceeded by Patrick, eldeft fon of Alexander his eldeft fon, who died in his life-time.

Which Patrick, lord Graham, was chofen one of the governors of the realm, during the minority of king James II. and died in 1465, leaving iffue,

William, his fon and heir, who married Ann, daughter of George Douglas fourth earl of Angus, by whom he had iffue two fons and two daughters; Jane, married to John the fecond lord Ogilvy; and Chriftian, married firft to James Haldane of Gleneagles; and fecondly, to Sir Thomas Maul, anceftor of the earl Panmure. Of the fons, William fucceeded him, and George was anceftor of the Grahams of Calender. He died in the year 1472, and was fucceeded by his faid eldeft fon,

William, who adhered to the party of king James III. againft that of the nobles, and was a commander for him at the battle of Bannockburn 1488, wherein the king loſt his life. In return for his loyalty, king James IV. was pleaſed to create him earl of Montroſe, March 3, 1504. He married firſt Annabel, daughter of John lord Drummond, by whom he had a ſon and heir, William, lord Graham; and ſecondly, Janet, daughter of Sir Archibald Edmondſon of Duntreath, by whom he had three daughters, Margaret, the wife of John Stewart maſter of Lennox; Elizabeth, married to Walter, the grandſon and heir of John the firſt lord Drummond; and Nicola, married to William Murray of Abercairny. His third wife was Chriſtian Wavane, by whom he had Patrick, anceſtor of the Grahams of Inſbraco and Gorthy, and Andrew, who became the firſt Proteſtant biſhop of Dunblain, 1575. This earl was killed at the battle of Floddon 1513. To him ſucceeded his eldeſt ſon,

William, ſecond earl of Montroſe. He was appointed governor to king James V. by the regent, John duke of Albany. He married lady Janet, daughter of William Keith the firſt earl Mariſhal, and by her had iſſue four ſons and five daughters; Robert, lord Graham, who was killed at the battle of Pinkie in 1547, leaving a poſthumous ſon, John, by his wife, daughter of Malcolm lord Fleming, who ſucceeded his grandfather; Alexander, penſioner of Cambuſkeneth; Mungo, anceſtor of the Grahams of Killen; and William, anceſtor of the Grahams of Orchil: Margaret, married to Robert maſter of Erſkine, who was alſo killed at the battle of Pinkey; Elizabeth, to George the third earl of Caithneſs; Agnes, to Sir William Murray of Tullibardin, anceſtor of the duke of Athol; Janet, to Andrew Murray of Balvaird; and Katharine, to John Graham of Knokdolan. His lordſhip died in 1571, and was ſucceeded by his grandſon,

John, third earl, who in 1584 was conſtituted lord high treaſurer, and in 1597 was lord chancellor till the year 1604; after which he was declared viceroy of Scotland during his life, and held that great office till his death. He married Lilias, daughter of David lord Drummond, by whom he had iſſue three ſons and one daughter, viz. John lord Graham, who ſucceeded him; Sir Robert Graham of Innermeath; Sir William Graham of Braco in Strathern; and his daughter Lilias married John Fleming, the firſt earl of Wigton. Dying in 1608, he was ſucceeded by

John lord Graham, fourth earl of Montroſe, who was ambaſſador from king James VI. to ſeveral foreign courts; and after the acceſſion of king Charles I. was preſident of the council in Scotland, but died in 1626; and by his wife, lady Margaret, daughter of William earl of Gowry, had iſſue James, who ſucceeded him; and four daughters; lady Lilias, married to Sir John Colquhoun, Bart. lady Margaret, to Archibald lord Napier; lady Dorothy, to James firſt lord Rollo; and lady Beatrix,

Beatrix, to David Drummond, lord Maderty, elder brother of William the first viscount Strathallan. On his decease, as above, he was succeeded by his said son,

James, fifth earl and first marquis of Montrose, born in 1612, who was but young when his father died; and the transactions of this great and unfortunate nobleman being faithfully recorded in our histories of the reign of Charles I. we shall not enter upon them here, but observe, that he was sentenced to be hanged, 21 May 1650, at the cross of Edinburgh, on a gibbet thirty feet high, for the space of three hours; then to be beheaded and quartered, and his head fixed on the tolbooth prison: If he repented, and was absolved of excommunication, his body might be buried in St. Giles's church, but otherwise it should be buried in the place where he was to suffer. He expected his fate with great calmness of mind, being satisfied in the justice of his own actions for the royal cause, and met death with uncommon resolution.

His body being interred at the place of execution, it there remained till the restoration, when by his majesty's own appointment all the parts were collected and laid together in the church of Holyrood house, from whence his corpse was with great solemnity carried to St. Giles's church, and there deposited near the remains of his grandfather.

While this nobleman was at the Hague with the king in the year 1649, he was nominated and designed for a knight of the garter; but his own tragical death prevented his obtaining the three requisites for a companion of that most noble order, namely, election, knighthood, and installation.

He married lady Magdalen Carnegie, daughter of David earl of Southesk, and by her left issue an only son and heir,

James, second marquis of Montrose, who immediately on the king's return being restored to his estate and honours, was admitted one of his majesty's privy council; but dying in 1669, with the title of a worthy honest man, by his wife lady Isabel, daughter of William Douglas earl of Moreton, had issue two sons, James, who succeeded him, and lord Charles, who died young; and three daughters: Lady Ann married to Alexander Livingston earl of Calender; lady Grizel to William, second son of William lord Cochran, ancestor of the earls of Dundonald; and lady Jane to Sir Jonathan Urquhart of Cromerty. He was succeeded by his eldest son,

James, third marquis, who was first made captain of his majesty's horse guard, and then president of the council; but died in 1684, in the prime of his years, to the general regret of the nation, leaving issue by the lady Christian, his wife, daughter of John Lesley duke of Rothes,

James, fourth marquis, who soon after he came of age, was by queen Ann made admiral of Scotland in 1705, and in the year following prefident of the council. On 24 April 1707, in regard of his inviolable zeal for the proteftant fucceffion, and his hearty concurrence in the union of the two kingdoms, her majefty was pleafed to create him duke of Montrofe, &c. which dignity was to defcend not only to his male iffue, but alfo to his heirs of entail. He was appointed lord privy feal in room of the duke of Queensberry 1709, and continued fo till 1713, when he was removed for not complying with the court meafures, under the miniftry of Robert earl of Oxford. His grace on the deceafe of queen Ann in 1714, made a fpeedy journey to Edinburgh, and affifted at the proclaiming king George I. and on his return to London, being one of the regency, concurred chearfully with the reft in fecuring the public tranquillity till his majefty's arrival: Upon which he was elected one of the fixteen peers for Scotland, in the firft parliament of that reign, and made fecretary of ftate in the room of John earl of Mar. He was foon after appointed keeper of the great feal for North Britain, which poft he held about fix years: He was alfo chancellor of the univerfity of Glafgow, and one of the reprefentatives for the peerage of Scotland in the firft, fecond, fifth, fixth and feventh parliaments of Great Britain, and died in 1741.

He married lady Chriftian Carnegie, daughter of David earl of Northefk, and by her, who died in 1744, he had iffue four fons, James marquis of Graham, who died in his infancy; David, William, now duke, and lord George, a brave officer in the navy, who died in 1746, without iffue; and one daughter, Margaret, who died unmarried.

In confideration of the fervice and conftant loyalty of this noble duke, his majefty king George I. was pleafed to advance his eldeft furviving fon, David marquis of Graham, to the dignity of a peer of South Britain, by the ftile and title of earl and baron Graham of Belford in the county of Northumberland, 23 May 1722, with remainder to his two brothers, William and George: But the aforefaid David dying in 1731 unmarried, and lord George as above, the third furviving fon,

William, fucceeded as fecond duke of Montrofe, and earl Graham of Belford, who in October 1742, married lady Lucy Manners, daughter of John the fecond duke of Rutland, by whom he has a fon and heir, ftiled marquis of Graham, born February 8, 1755, and a daughter lady Lucy, born in July 1751. His grace is chancellor of the univerfity of Glafgow, and governor of the bank of Scotland.

TITLES.] The moft noble William Graham, duke, marquis, and earl of Montrofe, marquis and baron of Graham, Dundaff, Kincarn, Mindoc, and Kinaber, chancellor of the univerfity of Glafgow, and governor of the royal bank.

CREATIONS.]

CREATIONS.] Earl of Montrose in the county of Forfar, 3 March 1504, 5 James IV. marquis 16 May 1644, 20 Charles I. and marquis Graham and duke of Montrose, 4 April 1707, 6 Ann. He is also an English peer, by the titles of earl and baron Graham of Belford in the county of Northumberland, so created by king George I. 23 May 1722.

ARMS.] Quarterly, 1st and 4th topaz, on a chief diamond, three escallop shells of the 1st, for the name of Graham; 2d and 3d pearl, three roses ruby, barbed and seeded proper, for the title of Montrose.

CREST.] On a wreath, an eagle topaz talloning a stork proper.

SUPPORTERS.] Two storks of the latter.

MOTTO.] Ne oublie.

CHIEF SEATS.] At Glasgow in the county of Lanerk; at Kincairn in the county of Perth; and at Myndock-castle in the county of Dunbarton.

KER, Duke of ROXBURGH.

THE firname of Ker or Car, is of great antiquity, and some think the founder of the family came originally from France, with William the Conqueror, who gave him great grants of lands in the north of England, and that from him all the Kers, in Great Britain, are descended. Of his descendants, was Ker of Ker-Hall in the county of Lancaster; from whom descended two brothers, Ralph and Robert, in the county of Roxburgh, who made the two branches of Cesford and Ferniherst, about the time of king David II. 1340; and Robert having obtained the lands of Smellholme, was ancestor to the house of Cesford, of whom we are treating. The other branch of Ferniherst, is the marquis of Lothian. Leaving their remoter ancestors, we shall begin with

Sir William Ker of Cesford, who married Janet, daughter of James Douglas of Drumlanrig, widow of James Twedie of Drumelzer, and had issue

Sir Robert Ker of Cesford, who was knighted at the coronation of queen Ann, consort of king James VI. in 1590, and was a gentleman of the bed-chamber to that king. He was also created lord Ker of Cesford, and was one of those barons, who in 1603, by his majesty's appointment, accompanied him into England; and in 1607, had a grant of the dissolved abbies of Kelso and Lesmehago, which were then erected into a barony by authority of king and parliament, for his service as warden of the Middle Marches, in well ordering and quieting the borders; after which he was created earl of Roxburgh in 1616. In the reign of Charles I. he was appointed lord privy seal, which office he held the space of twelve years. He married, first, Mary, daughter of Sir William Maitland, of Lethingten, thington, by whom he had issue a son William, master of Roxburgh, who died without issue in 1625. Also three daughters, Jane married to John Drummond, second earl of Perth, Mary to James viscount Dudhope, and Isabel to James Carnegie, second earl of Southesk: And secondly, Jane, daughter of Patrick lord Drummond, by whom he had a son,

Henry, lord Ker, who died before him; but having married lady Margaret, daughter of William Hay, tenth earl of Errol, by her left three daughters, Jane heir to her grandfather, Ann married to John Fleming the fourth earl of Wigton, and Margaret to Sir Harry Innes of Innes, Bart.

The lady Jane who was heir, by her grandfather's appointment, married her cousin german

Sir William Drummond, son of his eldest daughter lady Jane, before-mentioned, and thereupon became second earl of Roxburgh, and took the name and arms of Ker, and dying in 1675, left two sons, Robert who succeeded him, John who became lord Bellenden, and one daughter Jane, who was the second wife of Colin earl of Balcarras. He was succeeded by his eldest son,

Robert, third earl of Roxburgh, who was a privy-counsellor to king Charles II. but accompanying the duke of York from London to Scotland, in the ship Gloucester, he was lost on the coast of Yarmouth, with above a hundred persons more, the ship, after striking on the sands, foundering on the 5th of May 1682. He married lady Mary Hay, daughter of John marquis of Tweedale, and by her, who lived a widow seventy years, and died in January 1753, he left three sons, viz.

Robert, who succeeded as fourth earl of Roxburgh, but died abroad in his travels 1696; John who was created duke of Roxburgh, and William who was a colonel of dragoons, and groom of the bed-chamber to his majesty when prince of Wales. In the first and fifth parliaments after the union, he was elected for the burghs of Kinghorn, &c. In the sixth he was returned for the burghs of Aberdeen, &c. and was voted not duly elected, but was soon after chosen for the town of Berwick, and was a general officer, in the army.

The said earl Robert dying unmarried was succeeded by John, his next brother, as fifth earl of Roxburgh, who was by queen Ann made secretary of state for Scotland 1704; and being very faithful in promoting the union, was advanced to the dignity of marquis of Beaumont and Cesford, and duke of Roxbugh, 27 April 1707, and elected one of the sixteen peers in the first parliament of Great Britain. Being a hearty friend to the protestant succession he was previously nominated one of the regency, in supposition of the queen's death, till the next heir should arrive; and in the first year of king George I. he was sworn of the privy-council, lord-lieutenant

of

of Selkirk and Roxburghshires, and keeper of the privy seal for Scotland. He was also one of the sixteen peers in the second, fifth, and sixth parliaments of Great Britain, and three times one of the lords justices during the king's absence abroad. In October 1722, he was elected a knight of the most noble order of the garter, and in November following installed at Windsor. He was secretary of state for North Britain from 1716 to 1725, but after the death of king George I. his grace chose to retire from court for the remainder of his days, and died February 24, 1741.

He married lady Mary Finch, daughter of Daniel earl of Winchelsea and Nottingham, and widow of William Savil marquis of Halifax, by whom he had issue an only son

Robert, second duke of Roxburgh. On 24 May 1722, he was created an English peer by the stile and title of baron and earl Ker of Wakefield in the county of York. In 1739 he married Essex, eldest daughter of Sir Roger Mostyn, of Mostyn in Flintshire, Bart. by lady Essex Finch, his aunt, by whom he had issue John marquis of Beaumont, born in April 1740; lord Robert Ker, born in March 1745; lady Mary, born March 1741, and died in June 1758; and lady Essex. His grace dying August 20, 1755, was succeeded by his eldest son,

John, now third duke of Roxburgh.

TITLES.] The most noble John Ker, duke of Roxburgh, marquis of Beaumont and Cesford, earl of Roxburgh and Kelso, viscount Broxmouth, baron Ker of Roxburgh, Cesford and Caverton; also a peer of England by the stile and title of baron and earl Ker of Wakefield in the county of York.

CREATIONS.] Lord Ker of Cesford in 1603, earl of Roxburgh and Kelso 19 Sept. 1616, by James VI. and marquis of Beaumont and Cesford, and duke of Roxburgh, 27 April 1707.

ARMS.] Quarterly, 1st and 4th emerald, on a cheveron between three unicorns heads erazed pearl, horned and mained topaz; as many mullets diamond, for the name of Ker. 2d and 3d ruby, three macles topaz, for Weepont, as being descended from that family.

CREST.] On a wreath, a unicorn's head as those in the coat.

SUPPORTERS.] Two savages, wreathed about the waist with laurel, each holding a batoon over his shoulder, all proper.

MOTTO.] Pro Christo & Patria dulce periculum.

CHIEF SEATS.] At Floor in Roxburghshire; at Friers in the same county; at Broxmouth in the county of Hadington, near Dunbar on the sea-coast; and at Bray in the county of Bucks.

MARQUISSES.

HAY, Marquis of TWEEDDALE.

I HAVE undoubted authority for afserting, that the name of this illustrious family was derived from France. That there were lands and a lordship of that denomination in Normandy, long before the time of William the Conqueror, as is made appear by Mr. Douglas, in his Peerage of Scotland; and that the Hays in Normandy had the same armorial bearings with those in Scotland. And there is sufficient proof that William de la Haya, ancestor of the family of Tweeddale, was settled in Lothian, about the reigns of David I. and Malcolm IV. In the reign of William the Lion, about the year 1200, John the son of William Hay, marrying the heir of Robert de Lyne, with her had the barony of Lockhart; and from him descended Sir Gilbert Hay, who was a person much esteemed by king Robert Bruce; and marrying Mary, daughter and coheir of Simon Frafer, lord of Oliver Caftle, with her obtained a fair estate in the county of Tweeddale, and thereupon the family hath continued to quarter the arms of Frafer. He died about 1320, leaving by the said Mary his wife, Sir Thomas Hay, who on the 17th of October 1346, was taken prisoner with king David II. at the battle of Durham; and in 1357 his son Sir William Hay was one of the hostages for that king's ransom.

His son, Sir Thomas, who died in 1400, was succeeded by Sir William Hay of Lockhart, who married Joanna, eldest daughter and coheir of Sir Hugh Gifford, lord of Yester, with whom he got the lands and barony of Yester, which he assumed for his chief title, and added the arms of Gifford, to his former bearing, in 1421; by her he had issue Sir Thomas his heir, and other children; also by a second marriage, Edmund, ancestor of the Hays of Bara and Limplum in the North, of whom those of Adderston, Mordington, &c. in the South, are descended.

Sir Thomas, his heir, was one of the hostages for the ransom of king James I. in 1423, but he dying without issue, Sir David, a third son, became lord Yester, and was father of John, and he of another John, who was slain on the 9th of September 1513, at the battle of Floddon, with king James IV. and to him succeeded his son John, third lord Hay, of Yester, who married Elizabeth, daughter of George Douglas, son of Archibald earl of Angus, and by her had a son John, and a daughter Elizabeth, who was married to George lord Seton.

John

John who succeeded being taken prisoner at the battle of Pinkey, 1547, was carried to the Tower of London, where he continued till the pacification was concluded between the two nations; and dying in the year 1557, left issue by his wife Margaret, daughter of William lord Livingston, ancestor of the earl of Linlithgow, William his successor, and Thomas; and a daughter Mary, married to —— Congalton of that ilk.

William, his eldest son, fifth lord Yester, was one of the peers that joined with great zeal for the reformation in the reign of queen Mary; and marrying Margaret, daughter of Sir John Ker of Ferniherst, by her had two sons, whereof William the eldest was sixth lord Yester; but he dying in 1591, without male issue, his brother James became seventh lord Yester, and at the coronation of king James VI. was made knight of the Bath. He married lady Margaret, daughter of Mark Ker earl of Lothian; by whom he had John his heir, Sir William Hay of Linplum, and a daughter Margaret, who was first married to Alexander Seton earl of Dumferline, and afterwards to James Livingston earl of Calendar. He died in the year 1600, and was succeeded by his eldest son,

John, eighth lord Yester, who in the beginning of the troubles of king Charles I. had the command of a regiment in the royal army, for which and other his good services, he was created earl of Tweeddale on December 1, 1646; and dying in 1653, left issue by Jane his first wife, daughter of Alexander earl of Duraferline, John his heir and successor; and by his second wife Margaret, daughter of Alexander Montgomery earl of Eglington, he left William Hay of Drumelzer, whose daughter married and had issue. He died in 1653, and was succeeded by his said eldest son,

John, second earl, who was a nobleman of fine parts, and of great experience in affairs. King Charles II. on his restoration, appointed him to be one of the privy council, a commissioner of the treasury, and one of the extraordinary lords of session, in which posts he was continued by king James VII. till the revolution; and then having complied with the government under king William and queen Mary, their majesties had so great a regard for his wisdom and conduct, that they were pleased to make him one of the lords of the treasury, lord chancellor of Scotland, and in 1694 created him marquis of Tweeddale.

He married the lady Jane, daughter of Walter Scot, first earl of Buccleugh, and by her had issue seven sons and seven daughters, viz. John his successor; lord Francis, who died young; lord David, of Belton; lord Charles, who also died young; lord Alexander, of Spot; lord Gilbert, and lord William: Of the daughters, lady Margaret was married to Robert Ker, third

third earl of Roxburgh; and lady Jane, to William Douglas earl of March. The other daughters died young. He deceased in 1697, and was succeeded by his eldest son,

John, second marquis of Tweeddale; who was one of the privy council to king William III. in whose reign he was also high commissioner to the parliament of Scotland, and first commissioner of the treasury. In the reign of queen Ann he was made high chancellor of Scotland, and in 1704 was high commissioner to the parliament, when the act of security was confirmed and past into a law: after which, in 1707, he was elected one of the sixteen peers to the first parliament of Great Britain. He married lady Ann, only daughter of John Maitland, duke of Lauderdale; by whom he had issue three sons and two daughters; lady Ann, third wife of William lord Rofs; lady Jane, wife of John Lefley earl of Rothes; and of the sons, which were Charles lord Yefter, the lords John and William; the second was colonel of the royal regiment of Scots dragoons, and brigadier general in the army, and acquired great honour by his bravery under the duke of Marlborough at Schellenburg and Ramellies; but in 1706 he died of a fever at Courtray, much lamented, leaving issue by the lady Elizabeth, daughter of James fourth earl of Carnwath, a son John, who died December 10, 1755. And his lordship deceasing in 1713, was succeeded by his eldest son,

Charles, third marquis. In the first of king George I. he was made lord lieutenant of the county of East Lothian, and in March 1714 was elected one of the sixteen peers for Scotland; but dying on the 15th of December 1715, left issue by the lady Sufan, daughter of William and Ann duke and duchefs of Hamilton, and widow of John Cochran earl of Dundonald, four sons and three daughters, viz. John his successor; lord James, who died young; lord Charles, a volunteer at Gibraltar in 1727, as likewise with prince Eugene on the Rhine in the campaign 1735; he was afterwards a major general, and colonel of a regiment of foot, and died the first of May 1759; and lord George. The daughters were lady Sufan, who died unmarried; ladies Catharine and Anne.

John, lord Yefter, the eldest son, succeeded his father as fourth marquis, and was chosen one of the sixteen peers in the sixth, seventh, ninth, tenth, and eleventh parliaments of Great Britain. In 1742 he was appointed secretary of state for Scotland, which office he resigned in 1746. In 1761 he was appointed justice general of Scotland. He married lady Frances Carteret, youngest daughter of John earl Granville, in April 1748, and by her had one son, George, and two daughters, ladies Grace and Catharine. His lordship departing this life December the 9th, 1762, was succeeded by his son,

George, now fifth marquis of Tweeddale.

TITLES.]

MARQUIS OF LOTHIAN.

TITLES.] The most honourable John Hay, marquis and earl of Tweeddale, viscount Pebles, and lord Yester.

CREATIONS.] Earl of Tweeddale, 1 December 1646, 22 Charles I. and marquis, 26 December 1694, 7 William III.

ARMS.] Quarterly, 1st and 4th sapphire, three cinquefoils pearl for Frafer; 2d and 3d ruby, three bars ermine for Gifford of Yester; and over all, by way of surtout, pearl, three escutcheons ruby, being the paternal coat of Hay.

CREST.] On a wreath a stag's head erazed pearl, horned topaz.

SUPPORTERS.] Two bucks proper, attired and unguled topaz; each having a collar sapphire, charged with three cinquefoils as in the coat.

MOTTO.] Spare nought.

CHIEF SEATS.] At Pinkie in Mid-Lothian, and at Yester in East-Lothian.

KER, Marquis of LOTHIAN.

THE antiquity of the name of Ker has been already noticed under the duke of Roxburgh's pedigree. Sir George M'Kenzie, that learned antiquary, is of opinion, that the Kers settled in the south parts of Scotland about the year 1330; but it is certain they were numerous and flourishing long before that time; for many of that name swore fealty to Edward I. king of England, between the years 1291 and 1297. However, I shall not enter into these remote times, but deduce my account from Mark Ker, second son of Sir Andrew Ker of Cessford, who in the year 1564 was abbot of Newbottle, and in 1569 an extraordinary lord of session. He married lady Helen, daughter of George Lesley earl of Rothes, and by her had issue four sons and one daughter; Katharine, married to William Maxwell lord Herries. The sons were, Mark, who succeeded him; Andrew Ker of Fenton, George and William Ker, Esqrs. He died in 1584, and

Mark, the eldest son, succeeded, and was a judge in the court of session, and master of requests; and in his favour the abbacy of Newbottle was erected into a temporal barony, by authority of king and parliament, 1591.

On June 10, 1606, he was created earl of Lothian. He married Margaret, daughter of John lord Herries, by whom he had issue four sons, Robert, William, Mark, and James; and seven daughters, Jane married to Robert master of Boyd, Janet to William Coningham earl of Glencairn, Margaret to James Hay lord Yester, Isabel to William Douglas first earl of Queensberry, Lilias to John lord Bothwick, Mary to Sir James Richardson of Smeaton, and Elizabeth to Sir Alexander Hamilton of Innerwick.

Robert, his eldest son, succeeded him, and was second earl. He married lady Annabel, daughter of Archibald Campbell the seventh earl of Argyll, by whom he had two daughters, ladies Ann and Joanna, but leaving no male issue, he, with the king's approbation, made over his estate and titles to his said daughter lady Ann; and upon his decease in 1624, she succeeded thereto accordingly; and marrying Sir William Ker, son and heir of Robert first earl of Ancram, king Charles I. conferred those titles upon him. They had issue three sons and seven daughters; lady Ann married to Alexander Frafer master of Salton; lady Elizabeth to John lord Bothwick; lady Mary to James Brodie of that ilk; lady Margaret to Sir James Richardson of Smeaton; lady Vere to lord Neil Campbell, second son of the marquis of Argyll; and lady Henrietta to Sir Francis Scot of Thirlestane. The sons were, Robert, their heir; Sir William, director of the chancery in 1661; and Charles, ancestor of the Kers of Abbotrule. His lordship was succeeded by his eldest son,

Robert, fourth earl of Lothian. He was one of the privy council to king William, and by him made justice general of Scotland, and marquis of Lothian; and married lady Jane, daughter of Archibald Campbell marquis of Argyll, by whom he had issue four sons and one daughter, viz. William earl of Ancram; lord Charles Ker, director of the chancery, who left a numerous issue, and his eldest son, Robert Ker, Esq; is now director of the chancery; lord John, a colonel in the army; and lord Mark, general of foot, colonel of a regiment of dragoons, and governor of Edinburgh castle, who died unmarried February 2, 1752. The daughter, lady Mary, married James marquis of Douglas, and was mother of Archibald, late duke of Douglas.

His lordship departing this life in the year 1703, was succeeded by his eldest son,

William, second marquis of Lothian, who was by queen Ann appointed one of the commissioners to treat of the union between England and Scotland; in November 1705, he was elected a knight of the ancient order of the thistle, and one of the sixteen peers to sit in the first and second parliaments of Great Britain: he was afterwards made colonel of the third regiment of foot guards, and major general of the forces in Scotland; and in March 1714-15, he was again chosen one of the sixteen peers. He married lady Jane, daughter of Archibald Campbell, the unfortunate earl of Argyll, who was beheaded in 1685, and by her had issue William his heir, and four daughters; lady Jane, married to William lord Cranston; lady Ann, to Alexander the seventh earl of Hume; lady Elizabeth, to William lord Rofs; and lady Mary, to Alexander Hamilton of Innerwick, Esq; postmaster general of Scotland.

land. Deceasing March 1, 1721-2, he was succeeded by his only son,

William, third marquis of Lothian, who was elected one of the sixteen peers to the eighth, ninth, tenth, and eleventh British parliaments. He was elected a knight of the thistle in 1734, and soon after appointed his majesty's high commissioner to the general assembly of the church of Scotland; as also lord register in the court of session, which last he resigned in 1760. He married first, Margaret, daughter of Sir Thomas Nicolson, Bart. and by her, who died 27th of September 1759, had two sons; 1. William earl of Ancram, who was lieutenant colonel to his great uncle lord Mark Ker's dragoons, and is now colonel of a regiment of dragoons, and a lieutenant-general of his majesty's forces. He married lady Louisa-Carolina, only daughter of Robert Darcy earl of Holderness, by whom he hath a son, William lord Newbottle, born in 1737, who married, the 29th of July 1762, Miss Fortescue, niece of the earl of Mornington of the kingdom of Ireland; and two daughters, lady Louisa, wife of lord George Lennox, brother of the duke of Richmond, and lady Wilhelmina-Emilia. 2. Lord Robert, a captain in the army, slain at the battle of Culloden, April 16, 1746. He married, secondly, Jane, daughter of his cousin, lord Charles Ker of Cramond.

TITLES.] The most honourable William-Henry Ker, marquis and earl of Lothian, earl of Ancram, baron Ker of Newbottle and Jedburgh, and knight of the ancient order of the thistle.

CREATIONS.] Baron of Newbottle in the county of Edinburgh, 15 October 1587; baron of Jedburgh in the county of Roxburgh in February 1621; earl of Lothian, 10 July 1606; earl of Ancram in the same county, all by king James VI. and marquis of Lothian, 23 June 1701, by William III.

ARMS.] Quarterly, 1st and 4th sapphire, the sun in its splendor, as a coat of augmentation for Lothian; 2d and 3d ruby; on a chevron pearl, three mullets of the field for the name of Ker.

CREST.] On a wreath, the sun, as in the coat.

SUPPORTERS.] On the dexter side, an angel apparelled sapphire, its hair and wings topaz. On the sinister, a unicorn pearl, horned, mained, and unguled, topaz.

MOTTO.] Sero sed Serio.

CHIEF SEAT.] At Newbottle, in the shire of Edinburgh; and Monteviot lodge, in the shire of Roxburgh.

JOHNSTON, Marquis of ANNANDALE.

THE Johnstons are an ancient and warlike family, and derive their firname from the barony of Johnston, their patrimony in Annandale. This family were often wardens of the west borders before the union of the two crowns, and laid the foundation of their grandeur by their remarkable services against the English, the Douglasses, and other borderers. They also suppressed the thieves, who during the war between the two nations committed great ravages on the borders; and thereupon took for a device a winged spur, to denote their diligence; and for their motto, *Alight Thieves All*, signifying their authority in commanding them to surrender.

In the reign of Robert II. Sir John Johnston of that ilk, on the said king's accession to the crown in 1370, defeated the English who invaded Scotland from the marches. He was succeeded by his son Sir John Johnston, who died about the year 1420, and was succeeded by his son,

Sir Adam Johnston, who was also remarkable for his loyalty to his prince, and love to his country, and was particularly instrumental in suppressing the rebellion of William earl of Douglas; for which eminent service to the crown he had a gift of the lands of Pitenen in the county of Lanerk from king James II. and was succeeded by his son, by his first wife,

John, who in 1457 was one of the conservators of the peace with England. He married Mary, a daughter of the family of Maxwell, and by her had James his heir, and John. By a second wife he had Sir Gilbert Johnston, who obtained the lands and barony of Elphingston, by the daughter and heir of Sir Alexander Elphingston. James, eldest son of John, lived in the time of king James IV. and had one son, Adam, who died in 1488, and left issue James, who was in great favour with James IV. and V. He was succeeded by his eldest son John, who signalized himself at the battle of Pinkey, in 1547. He was succeeded about 1568, by his eldest son James, who was succeeded by his son John, who married Margaret, daughter of Sir William Scot of Buccleugh, by whom he had a son, James, and two daughters, Elizabeth, wife of Alexander Jardin; and Grizel, of Sir Robert Maxwell. He died in 1586, and was succeeded by his said son,

James, who was in great favour with king James VI. who made him warden of the marches, and knighted him; but in 1608, being in a family dispute with the lord Maxwell, he thereby lost his life, which was much regretted, being a gentleman of great wisdom, and very well inclined. He married Sarah, daughter of John lord Herries, and by her had

Sir James his heir, who, by king Charles I. was created lord Johnston, and earl of Hartfield, but afterwards, for his loyalty to the king, he suffered imprisonment and the sequestration of his estate. He had issue by Margaret his first wife, daughter of William Douglas the first earl of Queensberry, James his successor, and three daughters; Mary, married to Sir George Graham of Netherby, ancestor of the viscount Preston; Margaret, to Sir Robert Dalziel of Glenay, ancestor of the earl of Carnwath; and Janet, to Sir William Murray of Stanhope. He was succeeded by his said son,

James, second earl, who after the restoration changed his title of Hartfield to Annandale with the king's approbation, and was one of his majesty's privy council. He married lady Henrietta, daughter of William marquis of Douglas, by the lady Mary his second wife, daughter of George Gordon marquis of Huntley, and by her had issue William his heir, John, and three daughters; lady Mary, married to William Lindsay earl of Crawford; lady Margaret, to Sir James Montgomery; and lady Henrietta, to Sir John Carmichael, baronets. He died July 7, 1672, and was succeeded by his eldest son,

William, who was one of the privy council to king William III. by whom, in 1696, he was also made one of the commissioners of the treasury, and created marquis of Annandale in 1701. In the reign of queen Ann he was made secretary of state, president of the council, one of the extraordinary lords of session, knight of the thistle, and one of the commissioners for the treaty of union; but in the parliament 1706, his lordship opposed the union, and delivered several speeches and protestations containing the reasons of his dissent, which were all entered in the records of parliament: he was however elected one of the sixteen peers for Scotland, to sit in the third parliament of Great Britain. On the 12th of October 1714, he was sworn one of his majesty's privy council, and appointed keeper of the privy seal in Scotland; after which he was lord lieutenant of the counties of Dumfries, Peebles, and Kirkcudbright, was again elected in the fifth parliament one of the sixteen peers, and died January 14, 1721. He married first Sophia, daughter and sole heir of John Fairholm of Craigiehall in the county of Stirling, Esq; by whom he had issue two sons, James late marquis of Annandale, and lord William, who died in 1722 unmarried; and a daughter, Henrietta, who was married to Charles Hope, earl of Hopeton: and secondly, Charlotte, daughter of John Vanden Bempden of Westminster, Esq; by whom he had issue two sons, lord George, born in 1720, so named, the king being his godfather; and the lord John, who was elected to parliament for the burghs of Dumfries, &c. in 1741, and died unmarried in 1742; and the said marquis was succeeded by his eldest son,

James, second marquis of Annandale, who was returned to the second parliament of Great Britain for the shires of Dumfries

fries and Linlithgow; but being the eldeſt ſon of a peer, was declared incapable of ſitting for either of them by the laws of Scotland. The ſaid lord being a valetudinary man, travelled much abroad for his health, and died at Naples. He was ſucceeded by his only ſurviving brother,

George, now third marquis of Annandale, who has been declared a lunatick ever ſince the year 1745, by commiſſioners appointed for that purpoſe.

TITLES.] The moſt honourable George Johnſton, marquis and earl of Annandale, viſcount Annan, and lord Johnſton of Lockwood, Lochmaban and Moffat in Annandale, hereditary keeper of Lochmaban.

CREATIONS.] Lord Johnſton 20 June 1633, and earl of Hartfield in 1643, by Charles I. earl of Annandale in 1661, by Charles II. and marquis of Annandale 24 June 1701, by William III.

ARMS.] Quarterly, 1ſt and 4th pearl a ſaltire diamond; on a chief ruby three cuſhions topaz; 2d and 3d topaz, an anchor in pale ruby.

CREST.] On a wreath a ſpur erect topaz, winged pearl.

SUPPORTERS.] On the dexter ſide a lion pearl, armed and langued ſapphire, and imperially crowned topaz: on the ſiniſter a horſe pearl furniſhed ruby.

MOTTO.] Nunquam non paratus.

CHIEF SEAT.] At Lockwood of Annandale in Dumfries-ſhire, near the famous well of Moffat.

EARLS.

CRAWFURD, Earl of CRAWFURD and LINDSAY.

THE immediate anceſtor of the ancient and noble family of Lindſay, which came firſt to Scotland with Edgar Atheling and Margaret his ſiſter, queen of king Malcolm Canmore, was Sir David Lindſay, lord of Crawfurd and Glaneſk, who flouriſhed in the reign of king David Bruce, and was the eighth generation of the illuſtrious houſe of Crawfurd, in a direct male line. He was ſucceeded by his third ſon Sir William Lindſay of Crawfurd, who in the time of king David II. got a grant of the land and barony of Byres in Eaſt Lothian, to him and the heirs male of his body, &c. dated January 17, 1366, was created lord Lindſay of Byres, by king Robert II. about the year 1376, and raiſed further his fortune by marriage with Chriſtian, daughter and ſole heir of Sir William

liam Muir of Abercorn in the county of Linlithgow; and having with her that lordship, and several others, he thereupon added to his arms three mullets; and afterwards changed his lands of Dunotter in the county of Kincardin, with Sir William Keith marshal of Scotland, for his lands of Struthers in the county of Fife, which then became the principal seat of this noble family. He died in the year 1424, and was succeeded by his eldest son John, who in the 20th of James II. was constituted chief justiciary north of the river Forth, and one of his privy council, and was appointed to treat of a peace with the English in the year 1451. He married a daughter of Robert Stewart, lord Lorn, by whom he had nine sons and four daughters; whereof Christian was first married to Alexander Seton of Parbroath, Esq; and another Christian, married to John, son and heir of John lord Seton, and afterwards to Robert Coningham lord Kilmaurs! Of the sons, Walter, the fifth, was made lord St John; and in 1480 David, the eldest, succeeding his father assisted king James III. at the battle of Bannockburn; but in 1490, dying without issue, John his next brother became heir, who dying also without male issue in 1498, Patrick the third brother succeeded, and by James V. was made sheriff of the county of Fife; which office he had till 1531, when it was heretably conferred upon George Lesley earl of Rothes. He married Isabella, a daughter of —— Pitcairn of that ilk, by whom he had three sons, John, his heir; Patrick, lord of Kirkfothar, ancestor of the Lindsays of Kirkfothar, and others; and William of Pyotstown, of whom are descended the Lindsays of Pitscottie, Wilmerston, and others. He died in 1526, and his eldest son, Sir John Lindsay of Pitcruvie, marrying Elizabeth, daughter of Sir Robert Lundy of Balgony, by her had two sons, John who succeeded his grandfather, and David of Scotstoun; and a daughter Janet, wife of Sir David Murray, of Belvaird. John, his eldest son, was the sixth lord Lindsay, of Byres, and married lady Helen, daughter of John Stewart earl of Athol, by whom he had issue three sons and six daughters, Isabel married to Norman Lesley, son of George earl of Rothes; Catharine to Thomas Myreton of Cambo; Margaret to David Beaton of Meldrum, son of Cardinal Beaton; Janet to Henry master of Sinclair, and secondly to Sir George, son of Sir Robert Douglas of Lockleven; Helen to Thomas Fotheringhame of Pacorie; and Elizabeth to David Kinier of that ilk: Of the sons, Patrick was his heir, John died in France, and Norman was ancestor of the Lindsays of Newton of Nydie, now extinct. He died in the year 1563, and was succeeded by his eldest son Patrick, who was active for the reformation of religion, and on the king's side in the minority of James VI. He married Eupheme, daughter of Sir Robert

Douglas

Douglas of Lochleven, and by her had issue James his heir, and two daughters, Margaret married to James lord Lesley, eldest son of Andrew the fifth earl of Rothes, and Maulsie to William Ballingall of that ilk. He died on January 11, 1589, and was succeeded by his said son,

James, eighth lord, who married lady Eupheme, daughter of Andrew earl of Rothes, and by her had issue two sons and three daughters; Jane, wife of Robert Lundie, of Balgony; Catharine, of John Lundin, of that ilk; and Helen, of John, lord Cranstoun. He died in 1601, and his eldest son Robert succeeded him, and marrying Ann, daughter of Laurence lord Oliphant, by her had only a daughter married to Alexander Falconer the first lord Halkerton, and dying Nov. 9, 1609, his brother John, tenth lord, succeeded to the estate. He married lady Christian Hamilton, daughter of Thomas earl of Haddington, by whom he had issue John his heir, and a daughter, Helen, married to Sir William Scot of Ardross. Dying in 1616, he was succeeded by his said son,

John, eleventh lord, who by king Charles I. in 1633, was created earl of Lindsay, and succeeded to the title of earl of Crawfurd, in consequence of an intail made by Lodowic, the last earl, and became fourteenth earl of Crawfurd. In 1641, he was constituted lord high treasurer of Scotland, which office he held for eight years; but in 1649, was laid aside by the estates of parliament, for his vigorous appearance in raising the army, which was intended to relieve the king in the Isle of Wight. After the death of the king he adhered to king Charles II. at whose coronation at Scoon, on the first of January 1650, he carried the scepter; but the same year receiving a commission from his majesty to raise forces for his service, in order to his restoration, he, with several other lords, was surprized at Elliot in Angus by the English, and sent prisoner to the Tower of London, where he suffered a tedious imprisonment, till the restoration 1660, whereupon, in consideration of his loss and sufferings, his majesty was pleased to restore him to the treasurer's office, January 9, 1661, which he resigned in favour of his son-in-law, the earl of Rothes, in 1664.

He married lady Margaret, second daughter of James the second marquis of Hamilton, by whom he had issue two sons and four daughters; William his successor; Patrick, of whom hereafter, as ancestor of the present earl of Crawfurd; lady Ann married to John Lesley duke of Rothes; lady Christian to Thomas Hamilton earl of Haddington; lady Helen, to Sir Robert Sinclair of Stevenson, Bart. and lady Elizabeth to David earl of Northesk. He died in the year 1676, and was succeeded by his eldest son,

William,

William, fifteenth earl of Crawfurd, and second of Lindsay, who was president of the privy council, and one of the lords of the treasury 1689, having been a great promoter of the revolution. He married first lady Mary, daughter of James Johnston earl of Annandale, by whom he had issue three sons, John his heir; James who was a colonel, and unfortunately slain at the battle of Almanza in 1707, and Patrick; and a daughter, lady Henrietta, wife of William Baillie, of Lamington, Esq; and secondly, lady Henrietta, daughter of Charles Seton earl of Dumferline, by whom he had a son Thomas, and six daughters, ladies Anne, Christian, Margaret, Helen, Susan, and Catharine, married to Patrick Lindsay, Esq; descended of the family of Kirkforthar, who was governor of the Isle of Man, and provost of Edinburgh. His lordship died in 1698, and was succeeded by his eldest son,

John, sixteenth earl, who chusing a military life, had several considerable commands in the army; and in 1702 was one of the privy council to queen Ann. In 1707 he was made brigadier-general; and on the conclusion of the union, was elected one of the sixteen peers for Scotland, to sit in the first parliament of Great Britain; being likewise in April 1708, made major-general, and again chosen one of the sixteen peers for North Britain.

On the 5th of May 1710, he was made a lieutenant-general, and in 1713, was appointed colonel of the second troop of horse grenadier guards, and one of her majesty's privy council. He married Emilia, daughter of James Stewart lord Down, eldest son and heir apparent of Alexander the sixth earl of Murray, by whom he had issue two sons and two daughters, John and William, which last died in the post of a captain in the royal navy; lady Catharine married to John Wemyss, Esq; an officer in the army, and lady Mary to —— Campbell of Glenfaddel. He died in 1714, and was succeeded by his son,

John, seventeenth earl, who betook himself early to a military life, and was several years colonel of a company in the third regiment of foot guards. In 1733 he was a gentleman of the bed chamber to the prince of Wales, and the next year had the command of a regiment of foot. In 1734 he was a volunteer in the imperial army on the Rhine; and also in a battle against the Turks in 1739, when he received a dangerous wound in his thigh. In 1740 he had the command of the second troop of horse grenadier guards, after which he was colonel of the royal Scots dragoons. He was one of the sixteen peers for North Britain in three parliaments, the eighth, ninth, and tenth. After struggling some years with his wound, his lordship languished and died in the year 1749. He married in 1747 lady Jane Murray, daughter of James duke of
Athol,

Athol, who soon after died without issue at the baths of Aix in Germany; and leaving no issue, the several dignities of earl of Crawfurd and Lindsay, devolved on his cousin and heir male, George viscount Garnock, descended of Patrick, second son of John, first earl of Lindsay and fourteenth earl of Crawfurd, to whom we now return. Which Patrick married Margaret, daughter and coheir of Sir John Crawfurd, of Kilbirnie, in the shire of Air, upon whom Sir John settled his whole estate, to them and their heirs whatever, they being obliged to bear the name and arms of Crawfurd. By her he had issue three sons and three daughters; John his heir, Patrick, and Archibald; Margaret wife of David, earl of Glasgow; Anne of Mr. Henry Maule, brother and heir of James earl of Panmure; and Magdalen of George Dundas of Duddingstone, Esq; He was succeeded by his eldest son,

John, who was by queen Anne in 1703, made one of the privy council, and created viscount Garnock. He married lady Margaret Stewart, daughter of James earl of Bute, by whom he had issue five sons and three daughters; whereof Patrick, the second viscount, married Miss Home, daughter of George Home, of Kelly, Esq; by whom he had issue two sons and three daughters; John who died before his father; George his successor; Margaret and Janet, who died infants; and Christian-Graham, the wife of Patrick Bogle, Esq; He died in the year 1737, and was succeeded by his only surviving son,

George, third viscount, who on the decease of John Lindsay earl of Crawfurd, without issue, as before observed, succeeded also as eighteenth earl of Crawfurd and fifth of Lindsay. His lordship married December 26, 1755, Jane, daughter of Robert Hamilton of Bourtreehill, Esq; by whom he has three sons and two daughters; George lord Lindsay, born February 4, 1758; Robert and Bute; ladies Jane and Mary.

TITLES.] The right honourable George Lindsay Crawfurd, earl of Crawfurd and Lindsay, viscount and baron Garnock, baron Crawfurd and Spinzy.

CREATIONS.] Earl of Crawfurd in the county of Lanerk 1399, by Robert III. baron of Spinzy in 1590, by James VI. earl of Lindsay in the county aforesaid by Charles I. baron and viscount Garnock 10 April 1703, by queen Ann.

ARMS.] Quarterly, 1st and 4th ruby, a fess cheque pearl and sapphire; 2d and 3d topaz, a lion rampant ruby, suppress with a ribband diamond.

CREST.] On a wreath, an ostrich proper, holding in its beak a key, topaz.

SUPPORTERS.] Two lions sejant ruby.

MOTTO.] Indure furth.

CHIEF SEATS.] At Struthers in the county of Fife, and at Kilbirney in Airshire.

HAY,

HAY, Earl of ERROL.

IN the year 980, and the reign of Kenneth III. when the Danes had invaded Scotland, and prevailed in the battle of Loncarty near Perth, the Scots were worsted and gave way; and in their flight through a narrow pass were stopt by a countryman and his two sons, who encouraged them to rally and renew the fight; telling them, it was better and more honourable to die in the field fighting for their king and country, than to fly and be afterwards killed by the merciless Danes; and upbraided those who would fly like cowards, when all lay at stake: The more timorous stood still, and many of the stout men, who fled more by the desertion of their companions, than want of courage, joined with the old man and his sons to stop the rest, till there was a good number together: The countrymen, who were armed only with what their ploughs furnished, leading them on, and returning upon the Danes, made a furious onset, crying aloud, Help is at hand; the Danes believing that a fresh army was falling on them, the Scots thereby totally defeated them, and freed their own country from servitude.

The battle being over, the old man, afterwards known by the name of Hay, was brought to the king, who assembling a parliament at Scoon, gave to the said Hay and his sons, as a just reward of their valour, so much land on the river Tay in the district of Gowry, as a falcon from a man's hand flew over till it settled; which being six miles in length was afterwards called Errol, and is still possest by the family of Hay, which is lineally descended from the said valiant Hay: And the king being willing to promote the said Hay and his sons from the rank of plebeians to the order of nobility, he assigned them a coat of arms, which was argent three escutcheons gules, to intimate that the father and the two sons had been the three fortunate shields of Scotland. Thus all ancient Scotch authors and tradition speak; but it appears there were families of the name of Hay in Italy and France, before the battle of Loncarty; and it has been asserted, that the Hays, both of Scotland and Italy, came first from Armenia. Be this as it may, however, I shall begin my account of this noble family with the mention of William de Haya, who had a grant of the lands of Errol from William the Lion. In the charters of Malcolm IV. William, and Alexander II. frequent mention is made of Gulielmus de Haye, and Johannes de Haye, as witnesses; and at Berwick, in the dispute between John Baliol and Robert Bruce, before king Edward I. of England, Nicholas de Haye is one of the arbitrators. Since the beginning of king Robert Bruce's reign in 1306, the pedigree is very clear and uninterrupted.
Gilbert

Gilbert de Haye, lord of Errol, adhered to king Robert I. whom he assisted in retrieving the independence of his native country, then subject to the English; and in consideration of that his great loyalty and faithful services, he had a grant of divers crown lands: And the king, being further desirous to give him a lasting mark of esteem, was pleased, by a charter bearing date the 12th of November 1308, to grant unto him and his heirs for ever, the office of high constable of Scotland; which for several generations had been held by the family of Strathbogy, being then forfeited. He was killed at the fatal battle of Halidon-hill, July 19, 1333, and was succeeded by his son, Sir David, who was killed at the battle of Durham, Oct. 16, 1346, and was succeeded by his son, Sir Thomas, who married the princess Elizabeth Stewart, daughter of king Robert II. in whose reign he became possessed of the barony of Instuthill in the county of Perth, at which place he died in the year 1406, leaving issue two sons, Sir William his heir, and Sir Gilbert of Dronlaw; and two daughters of their mother's name, one married to Sir George Lesley, ancestor of the earl of Rothes; and the other to John Leslie, of that ilk.

His eldest son, Sir William, succeeded, and was one of the commissioners deputed by the estates of Scotland to treat with the English court touching the redemption of king James I. who was detained prisoner in that realm, for whom he was also one of the hostages, in 1424, and thereupon was knighted. He married Margaret, daughter of the lord Graham, and dying at Turriff in 1436, left two sons, Gilbert and William.

Gilbert, the eldest, died in his father's life-time, and having married Alicia, daughter of Sir William Hay of Yester, ancestor of the marquis of Tweeddale, by her had William his heir, and died in 1436.

Which William, being a person of singular merit, was by king James II. in 1452, in recompence of his faithful services, created earl of Errol, and died at Slanes in 1470. He married Beatrix, daughter of James Douglas lord Dalkeith, and by her had Nicholas his heir, William and Gilbert; and two daughters, lady Elizabeth, first the wife of Patrick, son and heir of Andrew lord Grey, and secondly of George lord Gordon, after earl of Huntley; and lady Margaret, married to William Fraser of Philorth, ancestor of lord Salton. His son,

Nicholas, second earl of Errol, was one of the privy council to king James III. and married lady Elizabeth Gordon, daughter of Alexander earl of Huntley, but died without issue, January 6, 1476, and was succeeded by his next brother,

William, third earl of Errol, and ninth high constable of Scotland. He married first lady Isabel Gordon, daughter of
George

George earl of Huntley, by whom he had issue three sons and one daughter, viz. William his successor; Thomas of Logyalmond, of whom hereafter; and John of Broganlish. The daughter, lady Beatrix, was the wife of Alexander Keith, son and heir of Sir William Keith of Innerugie. His second wife was lady Elizabeth Leslie, daughter of George earl of Rothes, by whom he had a daughter lady Mariana, wife of David Lindsay, son and heir of Sir Alexander Lindsay, of Auchtermonzie, afterwards earl of Crawfurd. He died in 1490, and was succeeded by his eldest son William, the fourth earl, who married lady Janet, daughter of John Stewart earl of Athol, by whom he had issue his successor, William fifth earl of Errol, who in the year 1510, was sheriff of Aberdeen; but on the 9th of September 1513, he was slain with king James IV. as were 87 gentlemen of his own family name, at the battle of Floddon. He married Elizabeth, daughter of the first lord Ruthven, by whom he had issue lady Marian, married to William earl of Crawfurd; lady Isabel, to Sir William Forbes of Tolquhoun, and a son, William, sixth earl of Errol, who was one of the privy council to king James V. and his particular favourite; and marrying lady Helen, daughter of John earl of Lennox, by her had issue William his heir, and Jane, of whom hereafter. Which William, seventh earl, dying without issue, about 1535, his estate and honour devolved upon George of Logie Almond, son and heir of Sir Thomas Hay of the said place, who was second son of William, the third earl of Errol, as before observed.

Which George, eighth earl of Errol, married first Margaret, daughter of Sir Alexander Robertson, laird of Strowan, and by her had issue four sons and two daughters, whereof Elizabeth was married to William lord Keith, son of William fifth earl Marshal, who died before his father, and lady Margaret to Laurence lord Oliphant; the sons were Andrew, John, George, and Thomas; the latter was parson of Turreff in the county of Aberdeen; the third dwelt at Ardlethan, the second succeeded to an ancient family of the Hays of Murchil: Secondly, Helen, daughter and coheir of Walter Bryson, of Pitcullen, by whom he had one daughter, lady Jane, married first to John Leslie of Balquhair, and secondly to Sir James Balfour, brother of Michael first lord Burleigh, and created lord Glenaly in Ireland, by James VI. He deceased in 1563, and was succeeded by his eldest son

Andrew, ninth earl of Errol, and one of the privy council to queen Mary. He married lady Jane, only daughter and heir of William sixth earl of Errol, before-mentioned, in whom the heirs male and of line of this noble family were united, and by her had issue three sons and one daughter, lady Eleanor, married to Alexander Livingston earl of Linlithgow; of the

sons,

sons, Alexander died before his father; Francis was his successor, and Thomas died without issue. He married secondly, lady Agnes, daughter of George third earl of Caithness, by whom he had Sir George Hay of Killour, in the county of Perth. He died in 1585, and was succeeded by his eldest surviving son,

Francis, tenth earl of Errol. He was a nobleman of great spirit, but in his religion a zealous Romanist, on which account he was a great sufferer in his estate and liberty. On the 3d of October 1594, he, with George the first marquis of Huntley, fought the battle of Glenlivet, and routed the forces of the earl of Argyll, who was sent against them. He was afterwards much in favour with king James VI. and was one of the Scots noblemen, who in the year 1604 were commissioners to treat of uniting the two kingdoms. He married first, lady Anne Stewart, daughter of John earl of Athol; and, secondly, lady Margaret Stewart, daughter and coheir of James earl of Murray, the regent, but had no issue by either: He married, thirdly, lady Elizabeth, daughter of William Douglas earl of Moreton, and by her had issue three sons and eight daughters, viz. William his successor, George, and Francis, who died without issue; lady Ann, married to George second earl of Winton; lady Christian, to John earl of Mar; lady Elizabeth, to Hugh lord Semple; lady Mary, to Walter Scot earl of Buccleugh; and lady Sophia, to John viscount Melgrum; ladies Elizabeth, Margaret and Helen. Dying at Bowness in Buchan in 1631, he was succeeded by his eldest son,

William, eleventh earl of Errol, who assisted at the coronation of king Charles I. and was in great favour with that prince. He married lady Ann Lyon, daughter of Patrick earl of Kinghorn, ancestor of the earl of Strathmore, and by her had issue Gilbert his heir, and a daughter, lady Margaret, first married to Henry lord Ker, son of Robert first earl of Roxburgh, and afterwards to John Kennedy earl of Cassils. He died in 1636, and was succeeded by his son,

Gilbert, twelfth earl, who was very active and serviceable in the restoration of king Charles II. and in the following parliament gave great proofs of his loyalty and moderation, and was afterwards one of that king's privy council. He married lady Katharine, daughter of James Carnegy earl of Southesk; but dying at Slanes in 1674 without issue, the male line of the first marriage of Andrew, ninth earl of Errol, thus ended, and the estate and honours devolved upon the next heir male, Sir John Hay of Killour, lineally descended from Sir George, before-mentioned, whose son, Sir Andrew Hay, married Margaret, daughter of Patrick Kinnaird of Inchture, sister of George first lord Kinnaird, and had issue, the said

Sir

Sir John Hay, who succeeding to the earldom, was the thirteenth earl of Errol, and the nineteenth high constable of Scotland of this family. He married the lady Ann Drummond, daughter of James earl of Perth, and by her had three sons, Charles his heir; James and Thomas, who both died without issue; and two daughters, lady Mary, who succeeded to the earldom of Errol; and lady Margaret, who continued the line. He died in 1705, and was succeeded by his eldest son,

Charles, fourteenth earl, who being one of the peers in the parliament 1706, dissented to every article of the union, and entered a protestation as follows:

' I Charles earl of Errol, lord high constable of Scotland, do hereby protest, That the office of high constable, with all
' the rights and privileges of the same belonging to me here-
' tably, and depending upon the monarchy, sovereignty, and
' antient constitutions of this kingdom, may not be prejudiced
' by the treaty of union between Scotland and England, nor
' any article, clause, or condition thereof; but that the said he-
' retable office, with all the rights and privileges thereof, may
' remain to me and my successors, entire and unhurt by any
' votes or acts of parliament whatever relating to the said uni-
' on; and I crave that this my protestation may be recorded in
' the registers and rolls of parliament.'

In April 1708 he was brought prisoner to London, with many other lords and commons, on account of the French invasion, and dying unmarried in 1717, was succeeded by

Lady Mary, his eldest sister, countess of Errol, who married Alexander, son of Sir David Falconer, lord president of the session in 1682, brother of Alexander lord Halkerton, who on his marriage with the countess of Errol took the name of Hay, but had no issue. The other sister,

Lady Margaret, having married James earl of Linlithgow and Callendar, had a daughter, lady Ann, who married William earl of Kilmarnock, and by her had issue three sons, James, lord Boyd, Charles and William; but the said earl was attainted and beheaded in 1746, upon which the title of Kilmarnock became extinct; and the countess of Errol dying in 1747, was succeeded by her grandson,

James lord Boyd, fifteenth earl of Errol, who took the sirname of Hay, and officiated as lord high constable of Scotland at the coronation of his present majesty. His lordship married Rebecca, daughter of Alexander Lockhart, Esq; brother of George Lockhart of Carnwath, Esq; by whom he hath one daughter, lady Mary Hay.

TITLES.] The right honourable James Hay earl of Errol, baron Hay of Slanes, and heretable high constable of Scotland.

CREATIONS.]

CREATIONS.] Baron Hay of Slanes, and earl of Errol in the county of Perth, 17 March, 1452, by James II.

ARMS.] Pearl, three efcutcheons ruby.

CREST.] On a wreath, a falcon proper.

SUPPORTERS.] Two men in country habits, each holding an ox yoke over his fhoulder.

MOTTO.] Serva jugum.

CHIEF SEATS.] At Dalgety and Slanes, both in the county of Aberdeen.

SUTHERLAND, Countefs of SUTHERLAND.

THIS illuftrious family yields to none in the kingdom for antiquity. Hiftorians mention thanes and earls of Sutherland, as foon as thofe dignities were known in Scotland. Allan, thane of Sutherland, gave a very fignal defeat to part of the Danifh army in 1031, who had invaded his country, and afterwards was treacheroufly murdered by the ufurper Macbeth, for adhering to his rightful fovereign Malcolm, the fon of king Duncan. He was fucceeded by his fon,

Walter, who by the faid king Malcolm was created earl of Sutherland in the year 1057, and was fucceeded by

Robert his fon, fecond earl, who built the caftle of Dunrobin, which he called after his own name, and is ftill the principal feat of this noble family. He was fucceeded by his fon, brother or coufin, 'tis uncertain which,

Hugh, third earl, who flew the Danifh general who had invaded his country of Sutherland, at Embo, and was fucceeded by

William his fon, fourth earl, who gained a remarkable victory over the Danes in the reign of Alexander II. He was fucceeded by his fon,

William, fifth earl, (but Mr. Douglas makes him only the third) who was one of thofe great men fummoned to Berwick on the part of Scotland, when the competition happened about the fucceffion to the crown, between John Baliol and Robert Bruce, which was then and there to be determined by king Edward I. of England. He was alfo one of thofe peers who in the year 1320 wrote that memorable letter to the pope, afferting the independency of Scotland, to which all of them put their feals: To him fucceeded his eldeft fon,

Kenneth, fixth earl, a perfon very faithful to kings Robert and David Bruce, in whofe fervice, and that of his country, he loft his life at the battle of Halidonhill, againft king Edward III. of England in 1333, leaving two fons, William his heir, and Nicol, from whom defcended the family of Sutherland lord Duffus. His eldeft fon,

William, feventh earl, fucceeded, and was one of thofe loyal peers who accompanied king David to the battle of Durham, where,

where, with that prince, he was taken prisoner, but afterwards being released, he sent his son John to England, as one of the hostages for the ransom of the said king. He married the princess Margaret, sister-german of king David, and by her had issue,

John, eighth earl, who in the reign of Robert II. signalized his courage during the war between the two nations. He married lady Mabilla Dunbar, daughter of Patrick tenth earl of March, by whom he had issue Robert and Nicholas, successively earls of Sutherland, and Hector, ancestor of the Sutherlands of Daldrid, of whom are descended most of the Sutherlands of the county of Sutherland. He died in 1389, and was succeeded by his eldest son, Robert, ninth earl, but he dying without issue, was succeeded by his brother,

Nicolas, tenth earl of Sutherland, who married Elizabeth, daughter of John M'Donald, lord of the isles, by whom he had issue, Robert his successor, John-Beg, ancestor of the Sutherlands of Berrisdale, &c. and Kenneth, ancestor of the Sutherlands of Torie. He died in 1399, and was succeeded by his eldest son,

Robert, eleventh earl, who signalized himself at the battle of Homildon, and on many other occasions. He married lady Mabilla, daughter of John Dunbar, second earl of Murray, of that sirname, by whom he had issue three sons, and deceasing in 1442, was succeeded by his eldest son,

John, twelfth earl of Sutherland, who married Margaret, daughter of Sir William Bailey of Lamington, and by her he had issue four sons and two daughters; Alexander, who died *vita patris*; John, his successor; Nicholas, and Thomas-Beg; lady Jane, wife of Sir James Dunbar of Cumnock; and lady Elizabeth, of —— Meldrum of that ilk. He died in 1460, and was succeeded by his said eldest surviving son,

John, thirteenth earl, who by his wife, lady Margaret Macdonald, daughter of Alexander earl of Ross, and lord of the isles, had issue John his heir, and Alexander, who died unmarried; also a daughter, Elizabeth, afterwards countess of Sutherland, of whom hereafter. He died in 1508, and was succeeded by his said son John, fourteenth earl, who dying without issue, his estate and honours devolved on his said sister Elizabeth, his undoubted heir of line; and she marrying Sir Adam Gordon, lord of Aboyne, second son of George second earl of Huntley, by lady Jane Stewart his wife, daughter of king James I. and widow of James earl of Angus, he, in his wife's right, became fifteenth earl of Sutherland; and by her had issue four sons and two daughters, viz. Alexander, John, Adam, and Gilbert; Beatrix and Eleanor, who both married. The countess dying in 1535, and the earl in 1537, and their eldest son, Alexander, who married lady Janet Stewart, daughter of

John,

John, second earl of Athol, dying before them, the honours and estates devolved on the eldest son of the said Alexander,

John, sixteenth earl, who was in the reign of queen Mary made governor and lieutenant of the kingdom, from the river Spey northward; and attending the said queen into France, was there, by king Henry III. of that realm, made a knight of the order of St. Michael, in 1550. He was likewise made governor of Murray and Ross, and supported queen Mary in her marriage with the lord Darnley, against the opposite party, especially the earl of Murray. He married lady Helen, sister of Matthew Stewart earl of Lenox, by whom he had issue two sons and four daughters, viz. John, who died an infant; Alexander, his successor; lady Margaret, who died unmarried; lady Janet, the wife, first, of —— Innes of that ilk; and secondly, of Thomas, a younger son of the earl of Huntley; lady Eleanora, who died unmarried; and lady Beatrix, the wife of William Sinclair of Dunbeath. He died in 1567, and was succeeded by his eldest surviving son,

Alexander, the seventeenth earl of Sutherland, who married first, Barbara, daughter of George Sinclair the third earl of Caithness, by whom he had no issue; secondly, lady Jane Gordon, daughter of George the fourth earl of Huntley, and countess dowager of Bothwell, by whom he had issue five sons and two daughters; one of whom, Jane, was married to Hutcheon Mackay, ancestor of lord Rae. The sons were, John, his successor; Alexander and Adam, who died infants; Sir Robert, created baronet, and Sir Alexander of Navisdale, knight. He died in 1594, and was succeeded by his eldest son,

John, eighteenth earl, who procured a new infeoftment of the said earldom, with several additional privileges. He married Ann, daughter of Alexander fourth lord Elphingston, lord high treasurer of Scotland, and by her had three sons and two daughters; lords John, Adam and George; lady Elizabeth, the wife of Sir James Crichton of Fendraught; and lady Anne, of Sir Gilbert Menzies of Pitfoddils. He died in 1615, and was succeeded by his eldest son,

John, nineteenth earl, who strenuously opposed the innovations king James VI. would have made in the church of Scotland in 1616. He was made lord privy seal in 1649, and married lady Jane Drummond, sole daughter and heir of James earl of Perth, and by her had issue,

George, twentieth earl, who was a nobleman of great goodness, and throughout his whole life was esteemed a person of singular integrity, continuing the zeal of his father for the protestant interest; and dying in 1703, left issue, by lady Jane his wife, daughter of David earl of Wemys, John his heir, and a daughter, lady Ann, married to Robert viscount Arbuthnot. He was succeeded by his son,

John,

John, twenty-first earl of Sutherland, who was one of the privy council to king William III. during whose reign he had the command of a regiment of foot; and in that of queen Ann, was one of the commissioners for the treaty of union, which, when concluded in 1707, he was one of the sixteen peers elected for Scotland, to the first parliament of Great Britain; and having at all times strenuously and boldly maintained the Protestant succession in the house of Hanover, his majesty king George I. upon his accession to the throne, made him president of the board of trade and manufactures; and in March 1714-15, the first of that reign, he was again chosen one of the sixteen peers for North Britain. He was also by that king made lord lieutenant of the counties of Inverness, Elgin, Nairn, Cromarty, Ross, Sutherland, and Caithness, with the isles of Orkney and Shetland; and in the year 1715, for his good services in the north, when the pretender invaded Scotland, his majesty wrote him a letter of thanks, signed with his own hand.

On the 22d of June, 1716, he was elected a knight of the ancient order of the thistle, and in September following the king settled on him a yearly pension of 1200 l. His lordship married, first, Helen, daughter of William lord Cochran, son of William the first earl of Dundonald, and had issue by her, William, his heir apparent, and two daughters; lady Jane, married to John lord Maitland, son of John earl of Lauderdale; and lady Helen, who died unmarried. His second wife was Katharine Talmash, sister of Lionel earl of Dysart, and widow of James Stewart lord Down, eldest son of James earl of Murray; and his third, the widow of Sir John Travel, a lady of great fortune; but by the two last he had no issue. He died in 1733, and his son and heir, William lord Strathnaver, having married Katharine, daughter of William Morrison of Preston Grange, Esq; had issue by her four sons and two daughters; George and John, who died young; William and Charles; Helen, the wife of Sir James Colquhoun of Luss, Bart. and Jane, of George Sinclair of Ulbster, Esq; and the said William lord Strathnaver dying in 1720, *vita patris*, his third son, William, succeeded his grandfather, and was the twenty-second earl. He was representative in the first parliament of king George II. for the county of Sutherland. In the eighth British parliament he was also one of the sixteen peers, and for some time the first commissioner of trade and manufactures at Edinburgh. His behaviour in the unnatural rebellion in 1745 will always be remembered to his honour. He married lady Elizabeth, daughter of David earl of Wemyss, by whom he had issue a son, William lord Strathnaver, and a daughter, lady Elizabeth, wife of James Wemyss, Esq; son of James earl of Wemyss. He deceased in France, in the year 1750, and was succeeded by his said son,

William,

William, twenty-third earl, who was made a captain in the fifty-sixth regiment of foot in January 1756, and was a lieutenant colonel and aid de camp to the king; and in 1763, was elected one of the sixteen peers for Scotland. In April 1761, his lordship married Mary, eldest daughter of William Maxwell of Reston, Esq; by whom he had issue a son, who died an infant, and a daughter, now countess of Sutherland, as undoubted heir of line. His lordship and his countess were illustrious patterns of conjugal worth and felicity, and seemed only to live for each other. The decease of their infant son had such an effect upon his lordship, that he was advised to repair to Bath, with a view that the waters might benefit his health, and the entertainments of the place divert his mind; but there he was seized with a fever, and his amiable consort, who could not be prevailed to leave his bed-side, by watching and anxiety of mind, quite overcome, sunk down, and expired of the same disorder, on June 2, 1766. The earl survived her only a fortnight, dying on the 16th of the same month. Their remains were carried to their seat in Scotland, for interment, and the honours and estates devolved upon their said infant daughter, who is now countess of Sutherland.

Note, The family of Sutherland chose the firname of Gordon, and quartered their arms ever since Adam Gordon married the heiress; but John the nineteenth earl quitted the name of Gordon, and resumed the old name of Sutherland.

TITLES.] The right honourable Elizabeth, countess of Sutherland, and baroness of Strathnaver, in the county of Sutherland.

CREATIONS.] Earl and baron, in 1057, by king Malcolm Canmore.

ARMS.] Ruby, three mullets topaz, within a border of the latter, charged with a double tressure, flowered and counter-flowered with fleurs de lis of the first.

CREST.] On a wreath, a cat sejant, proper.

SUPPORTERS] Two savages, wreathed about their heads and waists with laurel, each holding a batoon over his shoulder, all proper.

MOTTO.] Sans peur.

CHIEF SEATS.] At Dunrobin, Dornock castle, and the island of Brora, all in Sutherlandshire.

LESLEY, Earl of ROTHES.

NO Scottish firname (says Douglas) has made a greater figure in Europe, than that of Lesley. There are, at this time, several counts of the name in Germany, besides considerable families in France, Muscovy, Poland, &c.

There were at one time three general officers of this name, to three several crowned heads; count Walter Lesley to the emperor;

emperor; Alexander earl of Leven to king Charles I. of England; and David Lefley, afterwards lord Newark, to Guftavus Adolphus king of Sweden.

But to deduce the unqueftionable defcent of this family, I muft obferve, that Bartholomew de Leflyn was proprietor of the lands and barony of Leflyn, in Aberdeenfhire, in the reign of William the lion, who afcended the throne of Scotland in 1165, and died in 1214. He was fucceeded by his fon Malcolm, and Malcolm by his fon Norman, who by a daughter of a lord Lorn, had Sir Leonard de Lefley, who made a confiderable figure in the reign of Alexander III. He married Catharine More, heirefs of Taces in Fife, which barony continued long in the poffeffion of this family. By her he had iffue Sir Norman, who was fheriff of Aberdeen in 1305. He was fucceeded by his fon, Sir Andrew, who marrying Mary, daughter and coheir of Sir Alexander Abernethy of that ilk, with her got the baronies of Rothes and Ballinbreack, of which he had a charter from the faid king; and thereupon his defcendants have quartered the arms of Abernethy with their own. In the year 1320, he was one of thofe barons who figned that memorable letter to the pope, afferting the independency of Scotland. By his faid wife he had iffue, Norman his heir; Sir Walter, earl of Rofs, by marriage with Euphemia, countefs of Rofs; but their only fon, Alexander, earl of Rofs, died without iffue male. The third fon was Andrew, of whom hereafter; and the fourth George, anceftor of the Leflies of Balquhain. He was fucceeded by his eldeft fon, Norman, who married Margaret Lamberton, heir to her uncle Alexander de Lamberton, by whom he had iffue a fon, David, his fucceffor, who was one of the Scots nobles appointed hoftages for the ranfom of king James I. in 1424. He remained in England feven years, not returning to Scotland till 1431. But dying without iffue male, the lands and barony of Ballinbreich, &c. &c. devolved, according to entail, upon his coufin and heir male, Norman, grandfon of Andrew, third fon of Sir Andrew Lefley, above-mentioned; which Andrew obtained, in patrimony, the barony of Rothes, being a part of his mother's eftate; and dying before his father, left iffue Sir George Lefley of Fatekill, who was taken prifoner at the battle of Homildon in 1402. He married Elizabeth, eldeft daughter of Sir Thomas Hay of Errol, by the princefs Elizabeth, daughter of king Robert II. and by her had iffue,

Norman, lord Lefley of Rothes, who on the death of David lord Lefley, before-mentioned, fucceeded him. He married Chriftian, daughter of William lord Seton, anceftor of the earls of Winton, by whom he had iffue a fon,

George, firft earl of Rothes, fo created by James II. He married Margaret, daughter of —— Lundin of that ilk, by whom he had a daughter, lady Margaret, wife of George Lefley

ley of that ilk, in Garioch; his second wife was Christian, daughter of Sir William Haliburton, laird of Dirleton, and by her he had issue a son, Andrew, and a daughter, lady Elizabeth, married, first, to William lord Sinclair; and secondly, to William Hay, third earl of Errol; and his said son,

Andrew, dying before him, left by Marjory, daughter of William earl of Orkney, three sons; John, master of Rothes, who died without issue; George, successor to his grandfather; William, successor to his brother. The old earl was in great favour with kings James II. III. and IV. lived to a great age, and died in 1502. He was succeeded by his said grandson, George, second earl, who dying without issue,

William his brother succeeded as third earl, and on the 10th of September 1513, was slain at the battle of Floddon. He married Margaret, daughter of Michael Balfour of Montquhany, and by her left two sons, George and John Lesley of Parkhill, who died without male issue. He was succeeded by his eldest son, George, fourth earl, who being a nobleman of great wisdom and prudence, was much esteemed by king James V. who in 1537 took him over to France with the earl of Mar and others, when he espoused the princess Magdalen, a daughter of that crown; and afterwards he was sent ambassador to Denmark. In 1557 he was one of the commissioners sent to the court of Paris to conclude a marriage between Mary queen of Scots and the dauphin of that realm; and the next year died of a fever at Diep, in his return to Scotland. He married first Nicola, daughter of Sir John Somervil of Cambusnethan, and by her had issue a son, Andrew, and two daughters; lady Janet, the wife of —— Crichton, laird of Naughton; and lady Helen, of Mark, commendator of Newbottle. His second wife was Margaret Crichton, daughter of William lord Crichton, by whom he had a son, Robert, of Finrassie, and four daughters; lady Agnes, wife of Sir William Douglas of Lochleven, afterwards earl of Morton; lady Beatrix, of —— Beaton of Creich; lady Eupheme, of —— Learmont of Balcolmilie; and lady Margaret, of Archibald eighth earl of Angus. He was succeeded by his son,

Andrew, fifth earl, who was very faithful to queen Mary, to whom he was one of the privy council, and was much esteemed by her son king James VI. He married Jane, daughter of Sir John Hamilton of Evendale, and had issue three sons and two daughters, viz. James his heir, Patrick lord Lindores, and Andrew, who died without issue; lady Euphemia, wife of James, eighth lord Lindsay of Byres, ancestor of the earl of Crawfurd; and lady Margaret, first, of David, son and heir of Sir John Wemyfs of that ilk; and secondly, of James earl of Finlater. By his second wife, who was Jane, daughter of Patrick third lord Ruthven, he had two daughters, lady Elizabeth,

beth, wife of Sir William Cunningham of Caprington; and lady Mary, of Robert lord Melville. His third wife was Janet, daughter of David Durie of that ilk, by whom he had three sons and one daughter, viz. George, who died unmarried; Sir John Lesley of Newton, lineal ancestor of the lord Lindores; Robert, who died without issue; and Isabel, wife of James master of Sinclair.

James, his eldest son, dying before his father, left issue by Margaret his first wife, daughter of Patrick Lindsay, seventh lord Lindsay of Byres, ancestor of the earl of Crawfurd, four daughters, Margaret, wife of the Rev. John Murray of the family of Abercairny; Isabel, of the laird of Newhall; Agnes, of Andrew Wardlaw of Torrie; and Grizel, of Alexander earl of Dunfermline: and by Katharine his second wife, daughter of Patrick lord Drummond, he had a son, and a daughter, Jane, wife of Alexander Menzies of Weem.

John, his only son, succeeded his grandfather, and was sixth earl of Rothes. He was a nobleman of such excellent parts and address, that in the year 1637 he was the principal governing person in the nation, and at the treaty of Rippon was the first commissioner; in which treaty and others, he was so much for redressing his majesty's grievances, that dying at London in 1641, his death was a sensible loss to the king. He had a pension of 10,000 l. per annum, settled on him for life by parliament, in 1640. He married lady Anne, daughter of John Erskine the sixth earl of Mar, and by her had issue John his successor.

Which John, seventh earl, carried the sword of state when king Charles II. was crowned at Scoon, 1651; but on the 3d of September the same year, being in arms for his majesty, was taken prisoner at the battle of Worcester, and, by the powers then in authority, confined till the restoration; after which his majesty, to reward his merit and sufferings, was pleased to make him president of the council, and general of the forces in Scotland; and on the 2d of June 1663, he was appointed his majesty's high commissioner to the parliament.

He was also in that year made lord high treasurer of Scotland; and the year after lord keeper, and soon after lord high chancellor, which last post was during life: And in 1680, as a farther mark of his majesty's favour, he was honoured with the titles of duke of Rothes, marquis of Bambreigh, earl of Lesley, viscount Lugtoun, and baron of Achmuty and Caskieberry, and to the heirs male of his body for ever.

He married lady Ann, daughter of John Lindsay earl of Crawfurd, by whom he had only two daughters, ladies Margaret and Christian; of which the youngest was married to James Graham the third marquis of Montrose; and secondly, to Sir John Bruce of Kinross, Bart. Dying without male issue, in July 1681, the title of duke became extinct, but the earldom of Rothes devolved on his eldest daughter,

Lady Margaret, who married Charles Hamilton the fifth earl of Haddington, and by him had issue, besides Thomas earl of Haddington, a son John, who took the arms and firname of Lesley, and was the eighth earl of Rothes; and Charles, who died young.

Which John, eighth earl who succeeded, exercised many great offices in the kingdom; being in the reign of queen Ann lord privy seal, and one of the sixteen peers for North Britain, in the second, fifth, and sixth parliaments after the union. In November 1714, he was appointed vice admiral of Scotland; and in April 1717, was appointed his majesty's high commissioner to the general assembly of the church. He was also a colonel of foot, governor of Stirling castle, first commissioner of trade, and lord lieutenant of the shires of Fife, Kinross, and Aberdeen. He married lady Jane, second daughter of John Hay second marquis of Tweeddale, by whom he had issue eight sons and four daughters; ladies Jane, Mary, Margaret, and Anne. The sons were John, his successor; Charles, a colonel in the Dutch service; Thomas, his majesty's chamberlain of Strathern and Fife, and barrack master general of Scotland; James, an advocate, &c. who died September 4, 1761, without issue; David, who died young; William, major commandant of invalids in Ireland; Francis, who died young; and Andrew, equerry to the princess dowager of Wales. His lordship deceasing in 1723, was succeeded by his eldest son,

John, the present and ninth earl of Rothes, who is now colonel of the third regiment of foot guards, governor of Duncannon fort in Ireland, commander in chief and privy counsellor in that kingdom, a general of his majesty's forces, a knight of the ancient order of the thistle, and one of the sixteen peers elected for Scotland in the seventh, tenth, eleventh, and present parliaments. His lordship married in 1740, Miss Hannah Howard, second daughter and coheir of Matthew Howard of Thorpe in Norfolk, Esq; (who died in April 1761) and by her had issue two sons and two daughters, viz. John, lord Lesley, born in October 1744; and Charles Howard Lesley, who died in April 1762, aged fifteen; lady Jane-Elizabeth, born in 1741; and lady Mary, in May 1750. He married, secondly, in July 1763, Miss Lloyd, daughter of the countess of Haddington, by whom he has issue.

TITLES.] The right honourable John Lesley earl of Rothes, lord Lesley and Bambreigh, knight of the ancient order of the thistle, and general of his majesty's forces, colonel of the third regiment of foot guards, governor of Duncannon fort in Ireland, and commander in chief of the army in that kingdom; and also one of the sixteen peers for Scotland in parliament.

CREATIONS.]

CREATIONS.] Created earl of Rothes in the county of Elgin, in 1457, the 19th of James II.

ARMS.] Quarterly, 1st and 4th pearl, on a bend sapphire, three buckles topaz, for Lesley. 2d and 3d topaz, a lion rampant, ruby, suppressed by a ribband diamond, for Abernethy.

CREST.] On a wreath, a demi griphon, proper.

SUPPPORTERS.] Two griphons, party per fess, pearl and ruby.

MOTTO.] Grip fast.

CHIEF SEAT.] At Lesley in the county of Fife.

DOUGLAS, Earl of MORTON.

SIR James Douglas of Loudon was the first of this collateral branch of the great and illustrious family of Douglas. He obtained from the king a grant of the lands of Kincavel and Calderclear, to him and his heirs; and was succeeded by his son, Sir William, laird of Liddesdale, who for his bravery was called the Flower of Chivalry; but he dying without issue, his brother Sir John Douglas became heir, and was captain of the castle of Lochleven in Fife, the property of which was 300 years in the family. He married Agnes Monfode, by whom he had six sons and two daughters; Sir James his heir in his paternal estate; Sir William who died without issue; Sir Henry of Lugton; Thomas, John, Nicholas, ancestor of the Douglasses of Mains; Helen and Margaret.

Sir James, who succeeded his father, succeeded also his uncle the laird of Liddesdale in the baronies of Dalkeith and Aberdour. He married lady Agnes Dunbar, daughter of Patrick earl of March, and by her had issue two sons and four daughters; James lord Dalkeith; William lord of Mornington; Janet wife of Sir John Hamilton of Cadzow, ancestor of the duke of Hamilton; Margaret of Philip Arbuthnot, of that ilk; Agnes of Sir John Livingston; and —— of —— Tweedie of Drumelzier. His second wife was Giles, daughter of Walter, lord high steward of Scotland; by whom he had a son James Douglas of Roberton. He died in 1420, and was succeeded by his eldest son James, second lord Dalkeith, who married the princess Elizabeth, daughter of king Robert III. by whom he had issue three sons, William, James, and Archibald, ancestor of the Douglasses of Netherdale, of whom those of Tillywhilly, &c. are descended. His second wife was Janet, daughter of Sir William Borthwick, of that ilk, ancestor of lord Borthwick, and by her he had issue a son, Sir William de Douglas of Whittingame, from whom was descended Robert Douglas, who went into the service of Gustavus Adolphus king of Sweden, and commanded a regiment of horse in his service; in queen Christina's reign he was

crown

crown general of Sweden, and governor of Riga: His son, who was governor of East Gothland, married a sister of count Steinbock, by whom he had three sons; the eldest William was count Douglas in Sweden, aid de camp to Charles XII. and taken prisoner at the battle of Pultowa 1709; the second had a regiment at that battle and was taken prisoner, but not being ransomed, he entered into the Muscovite service, where he was a general officer; the third was a captain in the king of Sweden's guards. This lord dying in 1446, and his eldest son, William, dying in his life-time, without issue, he was succeeded by his second, James, third lord, who married, first, lady Margaret, daughter of James, earl of Douglas, by whom he had a daughter Beatrix, wife of William, first earl of Errol. His second wife was Elizabeth, daughter of —— Gifford, of Sheriffhall, by whom he had two sons, James, afterwards earl of Morton, and Henry, ancestor of the Douglasses of Core-head, Long Niddery, &c. of whom those of Harwood, Garvelsort, &c. &c. are descended. He died in 1457, and was succeeded by his eldest son, James, lord Dalkeith, who being in high favour with James II. was by him created earl of Morton, in the year 1458. He married the princess Jane, daughter of king James I. by whom he had a son and successor, and a daughter, lady Janet, wife, first, of Patrick Hepburn, first earl of Bothwell; and secondly, of Thomas lord Erskine, ancestor of the earl of Mar. He was succeeded by his son,

John, second earl, who married Janet, daughter of —— Crichton, of Cranston-Riddal, by whom he had issue two sons, James and Richard, and two daughters, Elizabeth married to Robert lord Keith, ancestor of the earl Marshal, and Agnes to Alexander lord Livingston, ancestor of the earl of Linlithgow. He was succeeded by his eldest son,

James, who married Katharine, natural daughter of king James IV. and by her had three daughters; lady Margaret, wife of James the second earl of Arran; lady Beatrix, of Robert lord Maxwell; and lady Elizabeth, of James Douglas, brother of David, earl of Angus, afterwards earl of Morton, and regent of Scotland. And the said earl, having no male issue, made an intail of his honour and estate in favour of his cousin, Sir Robert Douglas, of Lochleven; but afterwards made a conveyance of his estate and honour to his said son-in-law,

James, who thus became the fourth earl of Morton, in 1553, and dying without lawful issue, made an intail of the earldom in favour of his nephew Archibald earl of Angus, and in case of failure of male issue, to Sir William Douglas of Lochleven, before-mentioned, which settlement afterwards took place upon the death of the earl of Angus. This Sir William was

the

EARL OF MORTON.

the son of Sir Robert, before-mentioned, the son of Thomas, the son of Sir Robert, the son of another Sir Robert Douglas, of Lochleven, who was the son of Sir Henry, the son of Sir William, the eldest son of Sir Henry Douglas, of Lugton and Lochleven, third son of Sir John Douglas and Agnes Monfode, before-mentioned, Upon the death of Archibald, earl of Angus and Morton, those honours devolved upon the said Sir William.

But to return, in the reign of queen Mary the said James fourth earl of Morton, who succeeded his father-in-law, was one of the privy council, and by her majesty sent ambassador to England, and made lord high chancellor of Scotland; but in the same reign the earl of Bothwell having a design to murder Henry lord Darnley, the queen's husband, in order to marry the queen, and craving the earl of Morton's assistance therein, the earl, who abhorred such a detestable enterprize, left the court and retired into the country, during which time that scandalous and bloody tragedy was acted. When the earl of Bothwell had married the queen, it greatly alarmed the nation, as suspecting the earl to be the murderer of her former husband, and that by such an union the young prince was in great danger; whereupon the earl of Morton was one of the nobility who made an association to preserve him; and on the 29th of July 1567, which was the day of his coronation, took the oath to the infant king.

In this new turn of affairs the earl of Morton's share was very considerable; and he was soon after declared high chancellor of Scotland, then high admiral, sheriff of the county of Edinburgh, and on the 24th of November 1572, regent of the kingdom during the king's minority: but being disagreeable to the other party, who had the young king in their hands, they at length brought about his ruin; for by accusing him as accessary to the murder of the king's father, he was thereupon sent prisoner to Dunbarton Castle, from whence, on the 1st of June 1581, he was brought to his trial at Edinburgh, where he was found guilty by his peers, of being a party in the said murder, by not revealing it when the earl of Bothwell proposed it to him, and was sentenced to be hanged and quartered; but by the favour of the king he was the next day beheaded at the Market Cross of Edinburgh; and what was remarkable, the execution was performed by an engine of his own inventing for that use, called The Maiden, and he was the first who suffered by it.

Upon the death and forfeiture of the regent, the title of earl of Morton was soon after settled by parliament on the earl's nephew.

Archibald earl of Douglas and Angus, fifth earl of Morton; but he dying without issue, as before observed, Sir William

Douglas

Douglas of Lochleven, before noted, succeeded as heir of intail, and was the sixth earl of Morton; and marrying lady Agnes, daughter of George Lesley, earl of Rothes, by her had four sons and six daughters, viz. Robert, James, Sir Archibald, ancestor of the Douglasses of King-glaffie and Strathendrie, and Sir George of Keilor. Of the daughters, lady Margaret was married to Sir John Wemyss, ancestor of the earl of Wemyss; lady Christian first married to Laurence, master of Oliphant, and afterwards to Alexander earl of Hume; lady Mary to Walter Ogilvy lord Deskford, ancestor of the earl of Finlater; lady Euphemc to Sir Thomas Lyon of Auldbar, then lord treasurer of Scotland; lady Agnes to Archibald Campbell the seventh earl of Argyll; and lady Elizabeth to Francis Hay the ninth earl of Errol. Robert, the eldest son, dying before his father, left issue by Jane his wife, daughter of John Lyon lord Glamis, ancestor of the earl of Strathmore (who married to her second husband Archibald the fourteenth earl of Douglas, and to her third Alexander Lindsey lord Spinzy) a son

William, seventh earl, who in 1606, succeeded his grandfather, and being a nobleman of great reputation, was by Charles I. made lord treasurer of Scotland, one of his privy council, captain of his guards, and knight of the most noble order of the garter. He married lady Agnes, daughter of George Keith, fifth earl Marshal, by whom he had issue four sons and five daughters; lady Agnes was married to George Hay earl of Kinnoul; lady Margaret to Archibald Campbell marquis of Argyll; lady Mary to Charles Seton earl of Dumferling; lady Jane to James the third earl of Hume; lady Isabel to James Graham marquis of Montrose. The sons were, Robert, who succeeded him; Sir James of Snitfield, of whom afterwards; John killed at the battle of Carbardale, in 1650, and George was an officer in the Dutch service. The earl dying on October 7, 1648, was succeeded by his said eldest son,

Robert, eighth earl of Morton, who married Elizabeth, daughter of Sir Edward Villiers, sister of William the second viscount Grandison in Ireland, and niece of George the great duke of Buckingham in England, and by her had issue William his heir, and Robert who died without issue, in 1661; also two daughters, lady Ann married to William Keith earl marshal, and lady Margaret to Sir James Macdunald of Slate, Bt. He was succeeded by his eldest son,

William, ninth earl, who married Grisel, daughter of John Middleton earl of Middleton, by whom he had a son, who died before him, and therefore leaving no issue, his estate and honour devolved on his uncle

Sir James Douglas of Snitfield, before-mentioned, second
son

son of William the seventh earl, who married Anne, daughter and heir of Sir James Hay of Snitfield, by whom he had issue five sons and one daughter, viz. Charles lord Aberdour, who was drowned; James and Robert earls of Morton; William who died without issue; and George afterwards earl of Morton; the daughter died unmarried. He died in 1686, and was succeeded by his eldest surviving son,

James, eleventh earl, who having no issue, and dying in 1715, was succeeded by his brother

Robert, twelfth earl, who also dying unmarried, was succeeded by his brother

George, thirteenth earl, who was several times elected to parliament for the stewarty of Orkney and Zetland, and for the burghs of Selkirk, &c. and was also a colonel in the army. He died in the year 1737, being then one of the representatives for the peerage of Scotland, and by his second wife, Frances, daughter of William Adderley, of Halstow, had issue three sons, James who succeeded him, William who died young, and Robert Douglas, Esq; who was a captain of foot, and succeeded his brother as representative of the stewarty of Orkney and Zetland till his death; he served some time as a volunteer in the imperial army 1735; after which, being in the post of lieutenant colonel under his royal highness the duke of Cumberland, he was slain in the battle of Fontenoy, 11th of May 1745, N. S. This earl dying in January 1738, was succeeded by his eldest son

James, fourteenth earl, and ninth of the house of Lochleven, who was elected one of the sixteen peers for Scotland in 1739, in the room of Charles Hamilton earl of Selkirk deceased; and hath been chosen in every parliament since. In October 1760, his lordship was appointed lord register of Scotland, in the room of the late honourable Alexander Hume Campbell. His lordship married first, Agatha, daughter of James Haliburton of Pitcur, and by her had five sons and two daughters, viz. Charles who died young; Sholto-Charles lord Aberdour, commissioner of the police, who married Catharine, daughter of John Hamilton, Esq; by whom he has issue a son; James, George and Robert, who died young; lady Frances, who died in her infancy, and lady Mary. He married secondly, Bridget, daughter of Sir John Heathcote, of Normanton, Bart. in July 1755, by whom he hath a son John Douglas, Esq; born in July 1756, and a daughter, lady Bridget, born in April 1758. His lordship is president of the royal society, and knight of the antient order of the thistle.

TITLES.] The right honourable James Douglas earl of Morton, and lord Aberdour in Fife; hereditary steward and justice general of the Orkney Islands; knight of the order of
the

the thistle, lord register of Scotland, president of the royal society, and one of the commissioners for forfeited estates in Scotland.

CREATIONS.] Created earl of Morton in the county of Edinburgh, 14 March 1456, the 20th of James II.

ARMS.] Quarterly, 1st and 4th pearl, a man's heart ensigned with an imperial crown, all proper; on a chief sapphire three mullets of the field being his paternal coat. 2d and 3d pearl, three piles issuing from the chief ruby, the exteriors charged with a mullet topaz, for Douglas of Dalkeith and Lochleven.

CREST.] On a wreath, a wild boar sticking between two stems of oak, a chain and lock holding them together.

SUPPORTERS.] Two savages, wreathed about their heads and waists with oak leaves, each holding a batoon in his hand, the great end to the ground, all proper.

MOTTO.] Lock sicker, or securely.

CHIEF SEATS.] At Aberdour in the county of Fife; Dalmahoy and Belfield, in the Lothians.

ERSKINE, Earl of BUCHAN.

THE descent of the noble family of Erskine will be set forth under the title EARL OF MAR; therefore I shall in this place only observe, that Christian, daughter of John, master of Buchan, son of John Stewart, earl of Buchan, in 1551 succeeded her grandfather in the earldom; and marrying Robert Douglas, second son of Sir Robert Douglas, of Lochleven, and brother-german of William, sixth earl of Morton, he in her right became earl of Buchan, and by her had a son James, who succeeded; and married Margaret, daughter to Walter Ogilvy lord Deskford, ancestor of the earl of Finlater, and had an only daughter Mary; who marrying Sir James Erskine, eldest son of John earl of Mar, high treasurer of Scotland, by his second wife, lady Mary Stewart, daughter of Esme duke of Lennox, he in her right became earl of Buchan, which title was by patent under the great seal of Scotland limited to the said James Erskine her husband, and his lawful heirs male by her, or on failure, to his heirs male whatever.

Which James, first earl of Buchan, being a person of great accomplishments, was much in the favour of king Charles I. to whom he was a gentleman of the bed-chamber; and by the said Mary, countess of Buchan, his wife, had issue James his heir, and John who died without issue; and two daughters, lady Mary married to Alexander Forbes, the second lord Pitsligo; and lady Margaret married to Sir James Graham, son of John earl of Menteith. And their mother dying in England, the earl married, secondly, Elizabeth, daughter of Sir

Philip

Philip Knevill, of Bucknam-Castle in Norfolk, Bart. by whom he had a daughter, the wife of Mr. Walker, and other children, who died young. He died before 1630, and was succeeded by his eldest son,

James, second earl, who married lady Mary, daughter of William Ramsay, the first earl of Dalhousie, and by her had issue William his heir, and five daughters; lady Margery, married to Charles lord Fraser; lady Anne to James Canaries, M. D. lady Henrietta to Thomas Forbes of Tolquhoun; and lady Jane to George Gray of Halkerton, Esq; He was succeeded by his said son, William, the third earl, who was a man of great honour and integrity, and much in favour with James VII. (II. of England) in whose cause he suffered, and dying prisoner in Stirling-Castle, in 1695, without issue, the estate and title devolved on David Erskine, lord Cardross, his next heir male; which David was son of Henry, third lord Cardross, who was son of David, second lord, who was son of Henry, second son of John, earl of Mar, before-mentioned, by his second wife lady Mary Stewart.

Which David lord Cardross, fourth earl of Buchan, having upon all occasions, when employed in the public service, gained a general esteem, was by king William appointed one of his privy council, as he was to queen Ann; by whom he was also constituted one of the commissioners of the Exchequer, and governor of the castle of Blackness; but when the treaty of union was near concluded, he opposed it in parliament, being always of opinion, as he then declared, that several of the articles were inconsistent with the honour of his country. Upon the accession of king George I. to the crown, he was made one of the commissioners of trade, lord lieutenant of the shires of Stirling and Clackmannan, and elected one of the sixteen peers to the first parliament after his majesty's arrival, and in the two succeeding parliaments. In the year 1729, he was high commissioner to the church of Scotland. He married Frances, daughter, and at length sole heir, of Henry Fairfax of Hurst in the county of Berks, Esq; only son of Henry, second son of Thomas lord Fairfax in Ireland, by whom he had nine sons and seven daughters, Henry-David; David lord Auchterhouse, who both died young; Henry-David his successor; Fairfax-Erskine; George-Lewis; George-Augustus, and three more, who all died young. Lady Catharine, wife of William Fraser of Fraserfield, Esq; son of Alexander lord Salton; lady Frances of the brave colonel Gardner, slain at the battle of Preston-pans; lady Althea, lady Wilhelmina-Carolina, and three others, who died infants He married, secondly, Elizabeth, daughter of Sir William Blacket, Bart. who died in May 1763, by whom he had no issue. The earl dying October 14, 1745, was succeeded by his eldest son,

Henry-

Henry-David, now fifth earl of Buchan, born in 1699, who in March 1738, married Ann, daughter of Sir James Stewart of Goodtres, Bart. by whom he hath issue three sons and two daughters, viz. Stewart lord Cardross, born in March 1740, Henry, Thomas, lady Agnes, and lady Isabella.

TITLES.] The right honourable Henry-David Erskine earl of Buchan, and baron Cardross of Menteith in the county of Perth.

CREATION.] Created earl of Buchan, being part of Aberdeenshire, in 1469, by James III.

ARMS.] Quarterly, 1st sapphire, three garbs topaz, for the earldom of Buchan; 2d grand quarter, 1st and 4th sapphire, a bend between six cross croslets fitchy, topaz for the earldom of Mar; 2d and 3d pearl, a pale diamond, for the name of Erskine; 3d grand quarter, 1st and 4th topaz, a fess cheque pearl and sapphire for the name of Stewart; 2d and 3d Buchan; 4th pearl, three lions gemel ruby. Surmounted of a lion rampant diamond, for the name of Fairfax; and over all, by way of surtout, an escutcheon ruby, charged with an eagle displayed, topaz, looking towards the sun in his splendor, placed in the dexter chief point, for the title of Cardross.

CREST.] On a wreath, a dexter arm couped below the shoulder, and erect, grasping a batoon or ragged club, both proper.

SUPPORTERS.] Two ostriches of the latter.
MOTTO.] Judge nought.
CHIEF SEAT.] At Uphall, in West-Lothian.

CUNNINGHAME, Earl of GLENCAIRN.

THIS noble family, according to Sir George Mackenzie, took their firname from the land of Cunninghame, which is the north division of Airshire; and being by office, master of the king's stables and horses, took for their armorial figure the instrument whereby hay is thrown up to horses, which in blazon is called a shake-fork, with *over-fork, over*, for their motto.

But it is not my purpose to enter into these traditionary accounts, and I shall therefore observe, that in the year 1162, lived Robert de Cunninghame; who marrying Rescinda, daughter and heir of Sir Humphrey de Barclay, by her was father of Sir Robert Cunninghame, whose son Robert was succeeded by his son Henry, of Kilmaurs, a brave warrior, who behaved valiantly at the battle of Largo, under Alexander III. in 1263, who was succeeded by his eldest son, William, and his second Galfridus, was ancestor of the Cunninghames of Glengarnock, and others. The said William was succeeded by his son Edward, who died in 1290, and
whose

whose second son Richard was ancestor of the Cunninghames of Polmais, &c. His eldest, Gilbert, succeeded him, and left issue three sons, of whom the youngest, Sir Donald, was ancestor of the Cunninghames of Skuloch, Auchtermarker, Caddel, Quarrelton, Bellheartim, Newton, &c. The second Sir James, of those of Belton, and Hassenden, and whose son Nigel was the first of the family of Barns. The eldest Sir Robert succeeded his father, and swore fealty to Edward I. of England in 1296. He had two sons, Sir Andrew the youngest was ancestor of the Cunninghames of Drumwhistle, Ballindalloch, Balbougie, &c. and his eldest Sir William succeeded him in 1330. Which Sir William had four sons, Robert who died before him; Sir William his heir; Thomas ancestor of the Cunninghames of Caprington, from whence those of Enterkin, Legland, &c. are descended; and Sir Andrew. His second wife was Helen Bruce, countess of Carrick, in whose right he was earl of Carrick, but she dying without issue, that title fell to the crown. He died before 1384, and was succeeded by Sir William his eldest surviving son, who married Elizabeth, daughter and coheir of Sir Robert Deniston of that ilk, with whom he had the lands of Finlaston in the county of Renfrew, Kilmarnock in the county of Dunbarton, Redhall and Collington in Lothian; and in the year 1403 founded the collegiate church of Kilmaurs. He had three sons, Sir Robert his heir; William ancestor of the branch of Cunninghame-head, and Henry. Sir Robert his successor was one of the hostages for the ransom of king James I. when he was released from his confinement in England, by whom he was honoured with knighthood. He married Janet, daughter of Alexander lord Montgomery, and by her had two sons, Alexander and William, ancestor of the Cunninghames of Waterstoun, &c. His eldest, Alexander, lord of Kilmaurs, was one of the privy council to king James III. and by him created earl of Glencairn. He married Margaret, daughter of Patrick lord Hepburn of Hailes, by whom he had four sons, Robert his successor; William ancestor of the Cunninghames of Craigends, of whom those of Robertland, Camcarne, Bedlane, and Auchinturvy, Balquhain and Auchinyards, are descended; Alexander and Edward. He lost his life with king James III. at the battle of Bannockburn, June 11, 1488, and was succeeded by his eldest son,

Robert, second earl, who marrying Elizabeth, daughter of John lord Lindsay, of Byres, had issue his successor,

Cuthbert, third earl, who was one of the privy council to king James IV. He married lady Marjory Douglas, daughter of Archibald earl of Angus, ancestor of the dukes of Douglas, by whom he had issue,

William,

EARL OF GLENCAIRN.

William, fourth earl of Glencairn, who was of the privy council to king James V. and in 1542 was taken prisoner at the battle of Solway by the English. In 1543 he was one of the commissioners appointed to treat with the English about a marriage between queen Mary and king Edward VI. He married, first, Catharine, daughter of William lord Borthwick; and secondly, Margaret, daughter and heir of John Campbell, of West-Loudon, by whom he had issue five sons and one daughter, of whom William the youngest was bishop of Argyll, whose grandson dean Cunninghame settled in Ireland, and left a son Sir Halbert Cunninghame, who raised a regiment of dragoons at his own expence, with which he joined king William at the battle of Boyne, and was soon after killed near Killoony in the county of Sligoe. He married a daughter of Dr. Lesley, bishop of Raphoe, of the family of Rothes, by whom he had Henry his heir, who married a lady of the family of Sir John Williams, of the county of Carmarthen, Bart. widow of Charles lord Shelburne, and had issue a son Henry, created baron of Mount-Charles in Ireland, September 8, 1573. Robert, the fourth son, was ancestor of the Cunninghames of Montgrenan; Hugh, the third, of those of Curlung; Andrew, the second, of those of Corsehill; and Alexander lord Kilmaurs, the eldest succeeded him, and was fifth earl; commonly, for his great piety and benevolence, called *the good earl*. He married, first, lady Jane, daughter of James Hamilton, earl of Arran, by whom he had two sons and one daughter; William lord Kilmaurs, Andrew prior of Lesmahagoe, and lady Margaret, wife of John Wallace of Cragie; and secondly, Janet, daughter of Sir John Cunninghame of Caprington, by whom he had a son Archibald, and a daughter lady Jane, who married Archibald Campbell earl of Argyll; and secondly, Sir Humphrey Colquhoun of Luss. He died in 1574, and William the eldest succeeded in the earldom, and was sixth earl. He married Janet, daughter of Sir James Gordon of Lochinver, ancestor of the viscount Kenmure, and by her had two sons and four daughters; James his successor, John of Ross, ancestor of the Cunninghames of Aikenbar. Lady Jane, wife, first, of George Haldane, of Gleneagles; secondly, of —— Kilpatrick of Closeburn; and thirdly, of —— Ferguson, of Craigdarrock; lady Margaret, of Sir Hector Maclean, of Dowart, Bart. lady Elizabeth, first, of James Crawford, of Auchinames; and secondly, of Alexander Cunninghame, of Craigends; and lady Jane, of John Napier, of Kilmahew. He was succeeded by his eldest son,

James, the seventh earl, who was one of the privy council to king James VI. and in 1604 one of the commissioners for a treaty to unite England and Scotland; and by his first wife, Margaret,

EARL OF GLENCAIRN. 85

Margaret, daughter of Sir John Campbell, of Glenorchie, ancestor of the earl of Breadalbane, had issue two sons and six daughters, viz. William his heir; John of Camskeith; lady Jane died unmarried; lady Catharine, wife of Sir James Cunninghame, of Glencarnock; lady Margaret, first, of Sir James Hamilton, of Evandale; and secondly, of Sir James Maxwell, of Calderwood; lady Ann, of James the second marquis of Hamilton; lady Mary, of John Crawfurd, of Kilbirnie; and lady Susan, of Sir Alexander Lauder, of Hatton. He was succeeded by his eldest son,

William, eighth earl, who married lady Janet, daughter of Mark Ker the first earl of Lothian, by whom he had two sons and five daughters; William lord Kilmaurs; colonel Robert Cunninghame, usher to Charles II. Lady Margaret, wife of Sir Ludowic Stewart, of Minto; lady Elizabeth, first, of David Beaton, of Creich; and secondly, of ―――― Chisolm, of Cromlich; lady Jane, of ―――― Blair, of that ilk; lady Marian, of James, earl of Finlater, and lady Anne, who died unmarried. The earl died in 1631, and was succeeded by his eldest son,

William, ninth earl, who putting himself in arms on behalf of king Charles II. had a commission from his majesty to be general of all the forces he could raise for his service; and upon the restoration, the king made him lord high chancellor of Scotland, January 19, 1661, which post he held till his death. He married Ann, daughter of James Ogilvy, earl of Finlater, by the lady Elizabeth Lesley, by whom he had issue four sons and four daughters, viz. William, lord Kilmaurs, who died in the 18th year of his age; James, lord Kilmaurs, who also died before his father without issue; Alexander, his successor, and John who succeeded his brother. Lady Jane, wife of William, earl of Kilmarnock; lady Margaret, of John, lord Bargonie; lady Anne, who died unmarried; and lady Elizabeth, of William Hamilton, of Orbiston. His second wife was lady Margaret, daughter of Alexander, earl of Eglington, by whom he had no issue. He died in 1664, and was succeeded by his eldest surviving son,

Alexander, tenth earl of Glencairn; who married Nichola, daughter and coheir of Sir James Stewart of Strabrock, by whom he had a daughter lady Margaret, married to John Maitland, earl of Lauderdale, but died without male issue, and

John, his next brother, succeeded as eleventh earl, who, upon the accession of king William to the crown, was appointed one of his privy council, and colonel of a regiment of foot. In the first of queen Anne, he was appointed captain and governor of the castle of Dunbarton. He married, first, lady Jane, daughter of John, earl of Mar; and secondly, Margaret, daughter and heir of John Napier of Kilmahew.

G 3 By

By his first wife he had an only son, William, lord Kilmaurs, and dying in 1703, was succeeded by his said son,

William, twelfth earl, who was one of the privy council to queen Ann, and governor of the castle of Dunbarton. He married lady Henrietta, daughter of Alexander Stewart, earl of Galloway, (who died in October 1763) and by whom he had issue eight sons and four daughters; the eldest son died in infancy; William, lord Kilmaurs; John, James who died an infant, Malcolm Fleming; Alexander, a captain in the army, and died in 1739; Charles and James. Lady Margaret, married to Nicol Graham, of Gartmore, Esq; lady Henrietta, to John Campbell, of Shawfield, Esq; ladies Mary and Catharine. His lordship died in 1733, and was succeeded by his eldest surviving son,

William, thirteenth and present earl of Glencairn, who is a lieutenant-colonel in the army. In 1744, his lordship married Miss Macguire, by whom he hath issue four sons and two daughters, viz. William, lord Kilmaurs, born in June 1748, James in June 1749, John in May 1750, Alexander in June 28, 1754; ladies Henrietta and Elizabeth.

TITLES.] The right honourable William Cunninghame, earl of Glencairn, and baron Kilmaurs.

CREATION.] Created earl of Glencairn in the county of Dumfries, 28 May 1488, the 21st of James III.

ARMS.] Pearl, a shakefork, diamond.

CREST.] On a wreath, a unicorn's head couped pearl, horned and maned topaz.

SUPPORTERS.] Two rabbits sejant, proper.

MOTTO.] Over fork over.

CHIEF SEATS.] At Kilmaurs in Cunninghame, and at Finlayston in the county of Renfrew.

MONTGOMERY, Earl of EGLINGTON.

THIS noble family is originally French, of which was Hugh de Mungegumbrie, a near relation of Robert duke of Normandy. His son Roger de Montgomery accompanied William the Conqueror into England in 1066, and commanding the vanguard of his army, at the memorable battle of Hastings, where king Harold was slain, for that signal service the duke bestowed on him very large gifts, as the territory and honour of Arundel, with the earldom of Salisbury, where he founded the abbey of St. Peter's, and there died in 1094. He married Mabel, daughter of William de Talvaise, and had a son Roger, who had a son Philip, who came into Scotland with David I. and got a fair inheritance in the shire of Renfrew. His son Robert died betwixt 1177 and 1180, leaving a son and successor, Sir John, who was succeeded by

his

his son Sir Allan, who died in 1234, and was succeeded by Sir Robert, who dying without issue in 1260, was succeeded by his brother Sir John, who dying in 1285, was succeeded by his eldest son, another Sir John, who was one of the great barons of Scotland that swore fealty to Edward I. king of England, in the year 1296: but he afterwards joined king Robert Bruce; and dying in 1316, was succeeded by his son Sir Alexander, who was knighted by king Robert Bruce, and adhered to his son David II. His son and successor, Sir John, married a daughter and heir of Sir Hugh Eglington, by which marriage he became possest of the lordships of Eglington, Ardrossan, &c. in Cunninghame, and thereupon quartered the arms of Eglington with his own, and was afterwards called by that title. In 1388, being at the battle of Otterburn in Northumberland, he took prisoner with his own hand Henry lord Percy, named Hotspur, who after killing James earl of Douglas, and mortally wounding the earl of Murray, still prest on too boldly among his foes; with his ransom he built the castle of Punoon in the lordship of Eglesham. He had issue Sir John, who was one of the hostages sent into England for the ransom of king James in 1423, and was made a lord of parliament, by the title of lord Montgomery, in 1427; and marrying Margaret, daughter of Robert lord Maxwell, by her had issue,

Alexander, his heir, second lord Montgomery, who was one of the privy council to that king, and after his murder, to his son James II. He married Margaret, daughter of Sir Thomas Boyd of Kilmarnock, and by her had issue three sons and five daughters, viz. Andrew, his successor, (by Scotch authors called Alexander) George, ancestor of the Montgomeries of Skelmorly; and Thomas, parson of Eglesham; Margaret, married to John Stewart earl of Lennox; Janet, to Sir John Cunninghame of Kilmaurs, by whom she was mother of Alexander, created earl of Glencairn; Mary, to Sir Alexander Home of that ilk; Jane, to John lord Kennedy, ancestor of the earl of Cassils; and Agnes, to William Cunninghame of Glengarnock.

Andrew, third lord, succeeded his father, and married Elizabeth, daughter of Sir Patrick Hepburn of Hailes, by whom he had issue three sons, Alexander, his successor; Robert Montgomery of Breadstane, of whom the earl of Mount Alexander in Ireland is lineally descended; and Hugh Montgomery of Islot. He died before 1459, and was succeeded by his eldest son, Alexander, fourth lord, who married Catharine, daughter of Gilbert, lord Kennedy, by whom he had three sons, Hugh, his successor; James, of Smithston; and John. He deceased in 1487, and was succeeded by his eldest son,

Hugh, who was one of the privy council to king James IV. by whom he was created earl of Eglington in the year 1503; and marrying lady Helen, daughter of Colin Campbell the first earl of Argyll, by her had issue five sons and six daughters, viz: John master of Eglington; Sir Neil of Linshaw, ancestor of the Montgomeries of that place; William of Greenfield, ancestor of the Montgomeries of Auchenhood, &c. Hugh, who married Jane, daughter and heir of Robert lord Lyle; and Robert, bishop of Argyle: Margaret, wife of William lord Semple; Marjory, of William lord Somerville; Maud, of Colin Campbell of Ardkinlass, Mabel, of John Muir of Caldwall; Elizabeth, of John Blair of that ilk; and Agnes, of John Ker of Kersland.

John, his eldest son, being killed in a fray in 1520, in his father's life-time, left by Elizabeth his wife, daughter of Sir Archibald Edmondston of Duntreath, Hugh, successor to his grandfather, and a daughter, Christian, married to Sir William Douglas of Drumlanrig, ancestor of the duke of Queensberry. His son

Hugh, second earl, was one of the privy council to king James V. by whom, with the earl of Huntley, he was appointed governor of Scotland, while that prince went to France to espouse Magdalen the daughter of Francis I. king of France. He married Marian, daughter of George lord Seton, by whom he had issue,

Hugh, third earl, a firm friend to queen Mary in her greatest distress; but afterwards submitted to her son James VI. He married Agnes, daughter of Sir John Drummond of Innerpeffry, and had issue two sons and two daughters; lady Margaret, married to Robert Seton earl of Winton, of whom afterwards; and lady Agnes, to Robert lord Semple. The sons were, Hugh his heir; and Robert, who married Margaret, daughter of Sir Matthew Campbell of Loudon, by whom he had a daughter, Elizabeth, married to her cousin, Hugh earl of Eglington. He died in 1585, and was succeeded by his eldest son,

Hugh, fourth earl, who married Giles, daughter of Robert lord Boyd, and by her had issue, Hugh, the fifth earl, who, upon his father's being unfortunately murdered, in the flower of his age, by John Cunningham of Colneath and his accomplices, in 1589, succeeded him, and married his cousin Elizabeth, before-mentioned, and by her had issue one son, Robert, master of Eglington, who died before his father, leaving issue only a daughter, lady Margaret, the wife of Robert lord Boyd, but died without issue: And her grandfather dying in 1612, was succeeded, according to a resignation and entail he made of his honours, by Sir Alexander Seton, second son of lady Margaret, eldest daughter of Hugh third earl of Eglington, wife of the earl of Winton before-mentioned, who changed his name to Montgomery, and assumed the arms of Eglington.

Which Sir Alexander, sixth earl, being a nobleman of great valour, was called Greysteel; and in 1642 had the command of a regiment sent to Ireland, to suppress the rebellion of the native Irish; but in 1650, when he was raising forces in the

western

western parts for his majesty's service, he was surprised at Dunbarton by a party of English horse, and sent prisoner to Berwick upon Tweed, where he remained ten years, till the restoration, during which time his estate was sequestered, but upon that event, was restored. He married the lady Ann, daughter of Alexander Livingston the first earl of Linlithgow, and by her had issue five sons and two daughters; lady Margaret, married to John Hay the first earl of Tweeddale; and secondly, to William earl of Glencairn; and lady Anne, who died unmarried. Of his sons, Robert the youngest was major general in the king's army at the battle of Worcester, in 1651, and was taken prisoner and confined in Edinburgh castle, whence he escaped, got beyond sea to his master Charles II. and being made a gentleman of his bedchamber, returned with him at the restoration. He married a daughter of James viscount Kilsyth, by whom he had James Montgomery, Esq; his son and heir; James of Coalfield, the fourth son, was a colonel in the army, as was Alexander the third, who died in Ireland; Sir Henry of Giffen, the second, died without issue; and his eldest, Hugh, on the death of his father in 1661, succeeded as seventh earl. He married first, lady Ann, daughter of James the second marquis of Hamilton, by whom he had one daughter, lady Ann, married to James Ogilvy the third earl of Finlater; and by his second wife, lady Mary, daughter of John Lesley the sixth earl of Rothes, he had two sons, Alexander his successor, and Francis Montgomery of Giffen, who was of the privy council, and a commissioner of the treasury to king William and queen Ann; and married first, lady Margaret Lesley, daughter and sole heir of Alexander earl of Leven, by whom he had no issue; and secondly, Elizabeth, daughter of Sir Robert Sinclair of Longformacus, by whom he had two sons and one daughter, viz. John, member for the county of Ayr; and colonel Alexander, who died of the wounds he received at the battle of Almanza in 1711. His daughter Elizabeth was married to Patrick Ogilvy of Lonmay. Of the earl's five daughters, lady Mary was married to George earl of Winton; lady Margaret, to James earl of Loudoun; lady Christian, to John lord Balmerino; lady Eleanor, to Sir David Dunbar of Baldoon, Bart. and lady Anne, to Sir Andrew Ramsay of Abbotshall, Bart. The earl died in 1669, and was succeeded by his eldest son,

Alexander, eighth earl, who was one of the privy council to king William III. in the last year of whose reign he died, leaving by Elizabeth his wife, daughter of William Crichton earl of Dumfries, one daughter, lady Mary, wife of Sir James Agnew of Lochnow, Bart. and three sons, Alexander his successor; Hugh, a major in the army; and John, also a major. He was succeeded by his eldest son,

Alexander,

EARL OF EGLINGTON.

Alexander, ninth earl, who was likewise one of the privy council to the aforesaid king, and one of the commissioners of the treasury. He was elected one of the sixteen peers of Scotland in 1710 and 1713; was one of the privy council to queen Ann, and one of the commissioners of the chamberlain's court. He married first, Margaret, daughter of William lord Cochran son and heir of William earl of Dundonald, by whom he had two sons that died young, and four daughters, lady Katharine, married to James Stewart sixth earl of Galloway; lady Eupheme, to George Lockhart of Carnwath, Esq; lady Grace, to Robert Dalziel earl of Carnwath; and lady Jane, to Sir Alexander Maxwell of Monreith.

By his second wife, lady Ann, daughter of George Gordon the first earl of Aberdeen, he had an only daughter, lady Mary, wife of Sir David Cunningham of Milcraig; and by his third, Susanna, daughter of Sir Archibald Kennedy of Colzean, Bart. he had three sons, James, lord Montgomery; Alexander, now earl of Eglington; and Archibald Montgomery, Esq; colonel of a highland regiment of foot, which served bravely in America in the late war, and governor of Dunbarton castle; and seven daughters, lady Elizabeth, wife of Sir John Cunningham of Caprington, Bart. lady Helen, of the honourable Francis Stewart, son of the earl of Murray; lady Susan, of John Renton of Lamerton, Esq; lady Margaret, of Sir Alexander Macdonald of Macdonald, Bart. lady Frances; lady Christian, wife of James Murray of Abercairny, Esq; and lady Grace, of ―――― Boyne, Esq; Their father deceasing in the year 1729, was succeeded by his eldest surviving son,

Alexander, now earl of Eglington, who is a lord of the king's bedchamber, and was elected in the present parliament one of the sixteen peers for Scotland, and is unmarried.

TITLES.] The right honourable Alexander Montgomery, lord Montgomery, and earl of Eglington in the district of Cunningham in Ayrshire, a lord of the king's bedchamber, and one of the sixteen peers for Scotland.

CREATION.] Earl of Montgomery and Eglington in 1503, the 15th of James IV.

ARMS.] Quarterly, 1st and 4th sapphire, three fleurs de lis topaz, for the name of Montgomery; 2d and 3d ruby, three annulets topaz, stoned sapphire, for Eglington; all within a border topaz, flowered and counterflowered, ruby.

CREST.] On a wreath, a maid, holding in her dexter hand a man's head, and in her sinister an anchor.

SUPPORTERS.] Two wyverns emerald, vomiting fire, being the crest of the earl of Winton.

MOTTO.] Garde Bien.

CHIEF SEATS.] At Eglington in Ayrshire, and at Ardrossan in the same county.

KENNEDY, Earl of CASSILIS.

A FAMILY of rank and figure in Carrick were the undoubted ancestors of the Kennedies of Cassilis, who assumed their firname from their being head or chief of that family. All this is proved by Mr. Douglas, from authentic documents and charters. The term Kennedy comes from the Gallic or Celtic word Kean-na-ty, *head of the house*, or *chief of the clan*.

In the reign of David II. lived Sir John Kennedy of Dunnure, knight, who from that king got several lands, and added to his paternal inheritance of Dunnure, the barony of Cassilis, which he obtained by Marjory his wife, the daughter of Sir John Montgomery, and founded the church of Maybole in Carrick. He had three sons, of which Gilbert the eldest succeeding, was one of the hostages sent to England for the ransom of king David in 1357, and was knighted by king Robert III.

He married first, Mary, daughter of Sir James Sandilands of Calder, by whom he had Gilbert, who died without issue; and Thomas, ancestor of the Kennedies of Bargony. He married secondly, Marian, daughter of Sir Robert Maxwell of Calderwood, by whom he had a son, Sir James, his heir, who married the princess Mary Stewart, daughter of king Robert III. by whom he had issue Gilbert lord Kennedy, and James bishop of St. Andrews, who was lord chancellor of Scotland; and from this marriage they were authorised to bear their arms in a double tressure. He died on May 10, 1466, and was succeeded by his son,

Gilbert, who was by king James II. made heretable bailiff of the earldom of Carrick in the county of Ayr; and in 1460, was one of the six governors of the kingdom, during the minority of king James III. In 1450 he was dignified with the title of lord Kennedy. He married Agnes, daughter of Herbert lord Maxwell, by whom he had John, his successor in the honour, and two daughters, Katharine, married to Alexander lord Montgomery, ancestor of the earl of Eglington; and Marian, to Sir John Wallace of Craigie. He was succeeded by his son

John, second lord, who was one of the privy council to the aforesaid king, and died in 1508. He married Jane, daughter of Alexander lord Montgomery, by whom he had issue David, afterwards earl of Cassilis. By his second, lady Elizabeth, daughter of George lord Huntley, he had also a son, Alexander, ancestor of the Kennedies of Gervan Mains and Barquhanny; and a daughter, Jane, wife of Archibald earl of Angus. He was succeeded by his eldest son,

David, third lord Kennedy, who was one of the privy council to James IV. and by him created earl of Cassilis in 1509. He married first, Agnes, daughter of William lord Borthwick,

by

by whom he had a son, Gilbert; and secondly, lady Margaret, daughter of Thomas Boyd earl of Arran, by the princess Mary, eldest daughter of king James II. but by her had no issue, He was killed on the 9th of September 1513, with king James IV. at the battle of Floddon, and was succeeded by his son,

Gilbert, second earl, who was one of the privy council to king James V. by whom, in 1524, he was sent ambassador to England, to treat of a peace, but the next year he was murdered in attempting to rescue the king from the earl of Angus. He married lady Isabel, daughter of Archibald earl of Angus, by whom he had two sons, of which Quintin the youngest was abbot of Crosragwel, and was canonized for a saint; and the eldest,

Gilbert, succeeding his father, was third earl of Cassilis, and was by king James V. made lord treasurer of Scotland, and in 1588, was one of the peers sent over to France to assist at the marriage of queen Mary with Francis the dauphin, afterwards king Francis II. He married Elizabeth, daughter and heir of John Kennedy of Culzean, by whom he had issue two sons and two daughters; Gilbert, his successor; Sir Thomas of Culzean, ancestor of that family; lady Jane, wife of Robert Stewart earl of Orkney; and lady Catharine, of Patrick Vaus of Banburrow, knight. He died at Dieppe in France, November 28, 1558, supposed by poison, and was succeeded by his eldest son,

Gilbert, fourth earl, who was one of the privy council to queen Mary. He married Margaret, daughter of John Lyon lord Glamis, ancestor of the earl of Strathmore, and by her had two sons, John and Gilbert, of whom hereafter. He died in 1576, and was succeeded by his eldest son,

John, fifth earl, who was also appointed lord treasurer of Scotland in 1599, but dying without issue,

John, the son of his brother Gilbert, succeeded, and was the sixth earl. He married first, lady Jane, daughter of Thomas Hamilton the first earl of Haddington, and by her had issue a son, James, lord Kennedy, who died before his father; and two daughters, lady Margaret, wife of Dr. Gilbert Burnet, bishop of Salisbury; and lady Catharine, of William lord Cochran, son and heir of William earl of Dundonald. His second wife was lady Margaret, daughter of William Hay earl of Errol, and widow of Henry lord Ker, by whom he had issue John lord Kennedy, and two daughters, lady Mary and lady Elizabeth. He died in 1668, and was succeeded by his son,

John, seventh earl, who was one of the privy council to king William III. by whom he was also made one of the commissioners of the treasury. He married lady Susan, daughter of James duke of Hamilton, who was beheaded in 1648, and by her had issue John lord Kennedy, and a daughter, lady Ann, married to John Hamilton earl of Ruglen, (of whom the present

sent earl of March is the heir and representative) who succeeded also as earl of Selkirk. His second wife was Elizabeth, daughter of —— Foix, Esq; by whom he had a son, James, who died without issue; and a daughter, lady Elizabeth; and his eldest son, John lord Kennedy, dying in the year 1700, left issue by Elizabeth his wife, daughter of —— Hutcheson, Esq; who married to her second husband the said earl of Selkirk and Ruglen, a son,

John lord Kennedy, who, in 1702, succeeded his grandfather, and was the eighth earl. He married lady Susan, daughter of John earl of Selkirk and Ruglen, who died in March 1763; and his lordship dying in August 1759, was succeeded, by his own destination, in his estate, by Sir Thomas Kennedy of Culzean, his undoubted heir male, now earl of Cassilis, lineally descended of Sir Thomas Kennedy of Culzean, beforementioned. Which Sir Thomas, second son of Gilbert, third earl of Cassilis, by his wife Elizabeth, daughter of —— M'Gill of Cranston Riddle, had issue two sons, James and Sir Alexander. James, the eldest, had a son, James, who died without issue; but Sir Alexander's son and successor, John Kennedy of Culzean, was father of Sir Archibald Kennedy, a great favourite of Charles II. who created him a baronet in 1682. He left issue by his wife Elizabeth, daughter of David lord Newark, two sons and one daughter; Sir John and David Kennedy, Esqrs. His daughter Susan married Alexander earl of Eglington. He died in 1710, and was succeeded by his eldest son, Sir John, who by his wife, dame Jane Douglas, had three sons, Sir John, Sir Thomas, and David, an advocate. The eldest, Sir John, died without issue, and was succeeded by his brother, Sir Thomas, who, on the death of John eighth earl of Cassilis, as above, became the ninth earl of Cassilis, after a contest with the earl of March, &c. which was decided in his favour.

TITLES.] The right honourable Thomas Kennedy earl of Cassilis, and lord Kennedy, bailiff of Carrick, and governor of Dunbarton castle.

CREATION.] Earl of Cassilis in the county of Air, in 1509, the 21st of James IV.

ARMS.] Pearl, a chevron ruby, between three cross croslets fitchy, diamond, all within a double tressure, flowered and counterflowered with fleurs de lis of the 2d.

CREST.] On a wreath, a dolphin Naiant, sapphire.

SUPPORTERS.] Two swans proper.

MOTTO.] Avise la fin.

CHIEF SEAT.] At Cassilis in Airshire, &c.

SINCLAIR,

SINCLAIR, Earl of CAITHNESS.

William Sinclair, earl of Orkney, son of Henry earl of Orkney, by Ægidia, daughter of William Douglas, lord of Nithifdale, and the princefs Ægidia, daughter of king Robert II. was lord chancellor of Scotland in the reign of king James II. and got a grant of the earldom of Caithnefs. He married firft, lady Margaret, daughter of Archibald earl of Douglas and duke of Turenne in France, by whom he had iffue, William lord Newburgh, from whom is defcended the lord Sinclair; and a daughter, Catharine, wife of Alexander duke of Albany. His fecond wife was Elizabeth, daughter of Alexander Sutherland of Dunbeath, by whom he had iffue four fons; William, in whofe favour he refigned the earldom of Caithnefs; Sir Alexander, anceftor of the Sinclairs of Roflyn; Sir David; and John bifhop of Caithnefs. He died before the year 1480, and, according to the above-mentioned refignation, was fucceeded in the earldom of Caithnefs by his faid fon William, fecond earl, who married Mary, daughter of Sir William Keith of Innerugy near Buchanefs, by whom he had iffue John, his fucceffor; and Alexander, anceftor of the Sinclairs of Dunbeath. He was flain on the 9th of September 1513, at the battle of Floddon, and was fucceeded by his faid eldeft fon,

John, third earl, who married Elizabeth, daughter of Sir William Sutherland of Duffus, and by her had a fon,

George, fourth earl, who married lady Elizabeth, daughter of William Graham the fecond earl of Montrofe, by whom he had two fons, John, mafter of Caithnefs; and George, anceftor of the Sinclairs of May; and three daughters, lady Beatrix, married to Alexander earl of Sutherland; lady Elizabeth, to Hutchen Mackay of Far in Strathnavern, anceftor of lord Rae; and lady Barbara, to Sir Alexander Innes of that ilk. John, mafter of Caithnefs, dying in 1577, before his father, left iffue by lady Jane his wife, daughter of Patrick Hepburn earl of Bothwell, George, who fucceeded his grandfather; James Sinclair of Murchill, of whom hereafter; John, anceftor of the Sinclairs of Greenland, now of Ratter; and David: Alfo one daughter, Agnes, fecond wife of Andrew Hay, ninth earl of Errol.

George, the eldeft fon, fifth earl, fucceeded his grandfather in 1583, and married lady Jane, daughter of George Gordon earl of Huntley, by whom he had iffue William lord Berrendale, who married Mary, daughter of Henry lord Sinclair; and dying in his father's life-time, left iffue two fons, John lord Berrendale; and Francis, of whom by and bye. The faid John lord Berrendale dying alfo in 1639, left iffue by lady Margaret his wife, daughter of Colin Mackenzie earl of Seaforth, a fon, George,

George, who in 1643 succeeded his great grandfather, and was sixth earl of Caithness. He married lady Mary, daughter of Archibald Campbell marquis of Argyll; but dying without issue, she re-married with John earl of Breadalbane. Hereupon the honours devolved on George, second son of the fourth earl, before noticed, who became seventh earl of Caithness, by allowance of parliament; but he dying also without issue, the estate and honours devolved on John Sinclair of Murchill, lineally descended from Sir James Sinclair of Murchill, grandson of the fourth earl, and brother of George the fifth earl. Which Sir James, by his wife lady Elizabeth Stewart, third daughter of Robert earl of Orkney, had issue two sons, of whom the youngest, Francis, had a military command in Sweden, and the eldest, Sir James, succeeded his father; and by Jane, daughter of William Stewart of Mains and Burray, brother of Alexander first lord Garlies, had issue John who succeeded as seventh earl of Caithness, as above recited; and by Jane Carmichael, of the family of Hyndford, had issue three sons and one daughter, viz. Alexander, his successor; John Sinclair of Murchill, a senator of the college of justice; and Francis. Lady Janet, the daughter, was the wife of David Sinclair of South-Dun, Esq; He died in 1705, and was succeeded by his eldest son,

Alexander, ninth earl, who married lady Margaret Primrose, daughter of Archibald earl of Roseberry, and had a daughter, lady Dorothea, born in 1739, and married to James viscount M'Duff, eldest son and heir apparent of William earl of Fife, of the kingdom of Ireland.

TITLES.] The right honourable Alexander Sinclair, earl of Caithness and lord Berrendale.

CREATION.] Earl of the county of Caithness, the 29th of April 1556, the 14th of queen Mary.

ARMS.] Quarterly, 1st sapphire, a ship at anchor within a double tressure topaz, her oars erect in saltire, for Orkney; 2d and 3d topaz, a lion rampant ruby, for Far; 4th sapphire, a ship under sail topaz, for the title of Caithness; and over all a cross ingrailed dividing the four quarters diamond, for the name of Sinclair.

CREST.] On a wreath, a cock proper.

SUPPORTERS.] Two griphons of the latter, armed and beaked topaz.

MOTTO.] Commit thy work to God.

CHIEF SEATS.] At Castle-Sinclair and Thurso castle in the county of Caithness.

STEWART, Earl of MURRAY.

James Stewart, natural son of king James IV. by Jane, daughter of John lord Kennedy, was created earl of Murray by the said king, in 1501; and marrying lady Margaret, daughter of Colin third earl of Argyll, by her had a daughter, lady Mary, married to John Stewart master of Buchan; but having no male issue, the earldom reverted to the crown, and by queen Mary was bestowed, February 10, 1562, on

James Stewart, prior of St. Andrews, natural son of king James V. by Margaret, daughter of John lord Erskine, who by her was made one of the privy council.

He was also by the queen made lord lieutenant of the borders towards England; and after she was obliged to resign the government in favour of her son king James VI. he was chosen regent during the king's minority; but on the 23d of January 1570, as he was riding through the street of Linlithgow, he was shot from a window with a musket ball into the belly, of which wound he died the same evening. The assassin was one James Hamilton of Bothwel, incited thereto by the Romish party. He married lady Anne Keith, daughter of William Keith earl Marshal, and by her had two daughters, lady Elizabeth, wife of James lord Down; and lady Margaret, married to Francis Hay the ninth earl of Errol; and having no male issue,

Elizabeth, his eldest daughter, became countess of Murray; and marrying, as before observed, James Stewart lord Down, he was, by James VI. in 1581, created earl of Murray, being the third earl of the name of Stewart; but there happening a misunderstanding about some matters of interest between him and the earl of Huntley, he was murdered on the 17th of February 1592. He had issue by his said countess, two sons, James, and Sir Francis, knight of the bath; and three daughters, lady Margaret, married first to Charles Howard, earl of Nottingham in England; and secondly, to Sir William Monson, viscount Castlemain; lady Mary, to Alexander lord Salton; and lady Grizel, to Sir Robert Innes of that ilk.

James, the eldest son, succeeded as fourth earl; and, by the king's appointment, to remove the animosity between the families of Murray and Huntley, married lady Ann, daughter of George Gordon, sixth earl of Huntley, by whom he had a son, James, his successor, and a daughter, lady Mary, married to the laird of Grant. He died in 1633, and was succeeded by his son,

James, fifth earl, who married lady Margaret, daughter of Alexander earl of Home, by whom he had four sons and four daughters, James, lord Down, who died before his father, without issue; Alexander, lord Down, his successor; Francis, who died without issue; and Archibald, ancestor of the Stewarts of Duncarn: Lady Mary was married to Archibald Campbell, the ninth earl of Argyll; lady Margaret to Alexander Sutherland, the first lord Duffus; lady Henrietta, to Hugh Campbell of Calder; and lady Anne, to David Ross of Balnagowan. He died in 1653, and was succeeded by his eldest surviving son,

Alexander, sixth earl of Murray. He was made justice general

neral by king Charles II. also secretary of state; and by king James II. was appointed high commissioner to the parliament, and a knight of the thistle, in 1687. He married Amelia, daughter of Sir William Balfour of Pitcullo, and by her had issue four sons, James, Charles, John, who died without issue, and Francis; whereof the eldest died in his father's life-time. He married Katharine, sister of Lionel Talmash earl of Dysart, and by her, who afterwards married John the nineteenth earl of Sutherland, had two daughters, Elizabeth, married to Brigadier Alexander Grant, and Amelia, first, to Thomas Fraser of Strichen; and secondly, to John Lindsay earl of Crawfurd. Whereupon, in 1700, on the death of his father,

Charles, second son, succeeded, and was seventh earl, and elected a knight of the order of the thistle. He married the lady Anne Campbell, daughter of Archibald the ninth earl of Argyll, widow of Richard earl of Lauderdale, but dying without issue in 1735, was succeeded by his surviving brother,

See page 30.

Francis, eighth earl, who married Jane, daughter of John fourth lord Balmerino, by whom he had issue five sons, James lord Down; John, colonel of a regiment in the Dutch service; Francis, who married the lady Helen Montgomery, daughter of Alexander the ninth earl of Eglington, was a colonel in the army, and died in Germany; Archibald, captain of a ship of war; and Henry, major of dragoons, who died in Germany: Also two daughters, lady Anne, wife of John Stewart of Blairhall, Esq; son of Dougal Stewart, brother german of James first earl of Bute; and lady Amelia, of Sir Peter Halket of Pitfirren, Bart. colonel of a regiment of foot, killed in general Braddock's unfortunate engagement with the French near Fort Du Quesne, in North America, July 9, 1755. His lordship dying in 1739, was succeeded by his eldest son,

James, ninth and present earl of Murray, who was elected a knight of the thistle, and one of the sixteen peers for North Britain, in 1741, 1747, 1754, and 1761. He married first, Grace, countess dowager of Aboyn, daughter of George Lockhart of Carnwath, Esq; by whom he had issue Francis lord Down, who in June 1763, married Miss Grey, eldest daughter of lord Grey; and lady Euphemia: He married secondly, lady Margaret, daughter of David earl of Wemyss, by whom he hath two sons, James and David.

TITLES.] The right honourable James Stewart earl of Murray, and lord Down, of Down in Menteith, in the county of Perth, one of the sixteen peers for Scotland in the present parliament, and a knight of the ancient order of the thistle.

CREATION.] Earl of the county of Murray, 10 February 1561, the 20th of queen Mary.

ARMS.] Quarterly, 1st and 4th topaz, a lion rampant within a double tressure, (being the arms of Scotland) all within a border

border componé pearl and sapphire, for Stewart of the royal family; 2d topaz, a fess cheque pearl and sapphire, for Stewart of Down; 3d topaz, three escutcheons pendent by the corners, within a double treffure ruby, for Randolph earl of Murray.

CREST.] On a wreath, a pelican in her nest, feeding her young.

SUPPORTERS.] Two greyhounds proper.

MOTTO.] Salus per Christum redemptorem.

CHIEF SEATS.] At Dunibrisel on the coast of Fife; at Castle Stewart in the county of Inverness; and at the castle of Tarnaway in the county of Nairn.

HOME, Earl of HOME.

THIS family takes its surname from the castle of Home in the merse of Berwickshire, and derive their descent from William, a son of Patrick Home, earl of Dunbar; so that few families in Scotland can boast of so high and princely an origin, the house of Dunbar, earls of March, being undoubtedly sprung from the Saxon kings of England, and the princes and earls of Northumberland. Which William was succeeded by a son of his name, who lived in the reign of Alexander III. and the family, after several descents, became very eminent.

In the reign of Robert III. Sir Thomas Home of that ilk, taking to wife Nichola, heir of the family of Pepdie, in the county of Berwick, with her had the lordship of Dunglass, and thereby his fortune being much increased, he, in regard to that match, added to his paternal coat of arms, argent, three popinjays vert; and by the said Nicola his wife had Sir Alexander his successor; David Home, laird of Wederburn, and ancestor of that family; and Patrick, of whom hereafter.

Sir Alexander, who succeeded him, was taken prisoner by the English at the battle of Hamildon 1402, and had by his wife Jane, daughter of Sir William Hay, of Lockhart, three sons, Sir Alexander, Thomas, ancestor of the Homes of Tynninghame, Ninewells, &c. and George, ancestor of the Homes of Spot. His eldest son, Alexander, distinguished himself in the wars against the English. He married Mariota, daughter of Sir Robert Lauder, of Bass, by whom he had five sons, and dying in 1456, was succeeded by the eldest, Sir Alexander, who raised the grandeur of his family by the large estates he acquired, both by marriage and otherwise, and was created lord Home, Aug. 2, 1473. He married, first, Mariota, heiress of Landel in the county of Berwick, and by her had three sons, viz. Alexander, master of Home; George, ancestor of the Homes of Ayton; and Patrick, of the Homes of Fastcastle: Also one daughter, Helen, wife of Adam, son and

and heir of Sir Patrick Hepburn, laird of Hailes. His second wife was Elizabeth, daughter of Alexander lord Montgomery, by whom he had issue Thomas Home, of Langshaw in the county of Air, and Nicholas. This lord died in 1490, and his eldest son, Alexander, dying in his life-time, by Elizabeth, his wife, daughter of Adam, second lord Hailes, left issue two sons and four daughters, viz. Alexander, successor to his grandfather; John, ancestor of the Homes of Coldingnows, and the present earl of Home; Elizabeth, wife of James, earl of Arran; Helen, of Alexander, lord Erskine; ——, of Patrick, third earl of Bothwell; and Margaret, of John, earl of Crawfurd.

Alexander, second lord, son of Alexander, master of Home, succeeded his grandfather, and was one of the privy council to king James IV. by whom he was constituted lord chamberlain of Scotland for life, captain of Stirling-Castle, warden of the East Marches, governor of the young king, and of John earl of Mar the king's brother then in minority. He married Nicola, daughter and heir of George Ker, of Samuelton, by whom he had issue Alexander and George, lords Home; William and four other sons, who died without issue. He died before January 26, 1506, and was succeeded by his eldest son,

Alexander, third lord, who was a man of understanding, and in great favour with James IV. who appointed him lord high chamberlain of Scotland. But in the minority of James V. he was beheaded for high treason, with his brother William. He married Agnes Stewart, by whom he had only one daughter, Janet, wife of Sir John Hamilton. He was succeeded by his brother, George, fourth lord, who was a brave warrior, and remarkably distinguished himself on many occasions, against the enemies of his country, particularly at the battle of Haldinggrig, in the year 1541. He married Marian, daughter and coheir of Patrick lord Haliburton, and by her had issue Alexander his successor, and Andrew; and a daughter Margaret, married to Sir Alexander Erskine of Gogar in Midlothian, ancestor of the earl of Kelly. He was succeeded by his eldest son,

Alexander, fifth lord Home, who was loyal to queen Mary, in the time of the civil war; and marrying, first, Margaret, daughter of Sir Walter Ker of Cesford, ancestor of the duke of Roxburgh, by her had a daughter Margaret, married to George Keith the fifth earl Marshal: And secondly, Agnes, daughter of Patrick lord Grey, by whom he had a daughter, Isabel, wife of Sir James Home, of Eccles; and a son, Alexander, his successor, first earl of Home, who was in great favour with king James VI. by whom he was made one of the privy council, and created earl of Home. He married Mary, daughter of Edward Dudley, viscount L'Isle in England, by whom he had a son James, and two daughters; lady Margaret, married to James Stewart, earl of Murray, and lady Ann to John Maitland duke of Lauderdale, and he dying in 1619, was succeeded by his son,

James, second earl, who married two wives, Catharine, daughter of Henry, viscount Falkland, and lady Grace, eldest daughter of Francis the first earl of Westmorland, but dying in 1634, without issue, his honour, by reason of an intail on the heirs male, descended to Sir James Home of Coldingnows.

Which Sir James, third earl, was the son of Sir James, the son of another Sir James, the son of Sir John, the son of Mungo, the son of John, second son of Alexander master of Home, eldest son of Alexander, first lord Home, as before observed. He married lady Jane, daughter of William earl of Moreton, and had issue three sons, Alexander, James, and Charles. He died in 1666, and his eldest son,

Alexander, fourth earl, succeeded, and married lady Ann, daughter of Richard Sackvil, earl of Dorset in England; but dying without issue, in 1674, his brother,

James, became fifth earl. He married lady Anne Ramsay, daughter of George the second earl of Dalhousie; and dying without issue also, in 1688, was succeeded by the youngest brother,

Charles, sixth earl, who was a great opposer of the union. He married Ann, daughter of Sir William Purvis of that ilk, Bt. and dying in 1706, by her left issue Sir Alexander his heir, James and George, and three daughters; lady Jane married to Patrick Home lord Polwarth; lady Margaret to Alexander Bothwell, master of Holyrood house.

James, the second son, being taken in the rebellion in 1715, was sent prisoner to London, and secured with many others in Newgate; and on the 8th of May 1716, being tried, was found guilty of high treason; but happily received the benefit of his majesty's act of grace in 1717. The earl was succeeded by his eldest son,

Alexander, seventh earl, who was in 1711, made general of the Mint, being then one of the sixteen peers for Scotland; and marrying lady Ann Ker, daughter of William the second marquis of Lothian, by her had issue six sons and two daughters; William lord Dunglass, Alexander, Charles, James, Alexander and George, the last four of which died infants; lady Jane and lady Anne, who died in infancy. The earl died in 1720, and was succeeded by his eldest son,

William, eighth earl, who married Mrs. Laws in 1742, and the next year was made a captain and colonel in the third regiment of foot-guards. In the year 1750, his lordship was promoted to the command of a regiment of foot; and was elected one of the sixteen peers for North Britain in the ninth, tenth,

tenth, and eleventh parliaments. On the 8th of March 1755, he was conftituted a major-general of his majefty's forces; in Feb. 1759, promoted to the rank of lieutenant-general, and was appointed governor of Gibraltar, where dying on the 28th of April 1761, without iffue, he was fucceeded by his brother,

Alexander, the prefent earl, who married Primrofe, daughter of Charles, ninth lord Elphingfton, by whom he has a fon William, lord Dunglafs, and a daughter lady Elizabeth. His countefs deceafing, he married, fecondly, Marion, daughter of James Home, of Ayton, Efq;

TITLES.] The right honourable Alexander Home, earl of Home, and baron of Dunglafs.

CREATION.] Earl of Home and baron of Dunglafs in the county of Berwick, 4 March 1604, by James VI.

ARMS.] Quarterly, 1ft and 4th emerald, a lion rampant pearl, armed and tongued ruby, for Home; 2d and 3d pearl, three popinjays emerald, beaked and membered ruby, for Pepdies of Dunglafs, as being defcended from the heirefs of that family; and over all, by way of furtout, an efchutcheon topaz, charged with an orle fapphire, for the name of Landel.

CREST.] On a cap of dignity, a lion's head erazed, ruby.

SUPPORTERS.] Two lions, as thofe in the arms.

MOTTO.] True to the end.

CHIEF SEAT.] At Home Caftle and Hirfel, in the county of Berwick.

FLEMING, Earl of WIGTON.

ALL the Scotch hiftorians and antiquarians agree, that the firname of this family is derived from a perfon of diftinction, who in the time of king David I. about the year 1140, tranfplanted himfelf from Flanders into this realm, and took his firname Fleming from the country of his origin. It appears that, for fome time, they were promifcuoufly ftiled Flandrenfes, Flamang, le Flamang, and De Flamaticus, and after they had affumed Fleming for their firname, that, in Latin, was called *Flandrenfis*.

In the reigns of Malcolm IV. William I. Alexander II. and III. there are feveral of this name found witneffes to records of thofe kings, as Baldwin, Jordan, William, Duncan, and Simon le Fleming; and Sir Robert Fleming being one of thofe patriots, who in 1290, ftood up for the intereft of king Robert I. and the independence of Scotland, and never left his rightful fovereign, till he had fet the crown upon his head, in 1306, that prince, in recompence for that fignal fervice, and his other merits, rewarded him with the baronies of Lenzie and Cumbernauld in the county of Stirling, and with feveral other donations; in all which he was fucceeded by by his eldest son Sir Malcolm; and of Sir Patrick, the second son, we shall speak hereafter.

The eldest Sir Malcolm was in great favour with king Robert I. who, in memory of his father's services, and his own merit, made him a grant of divers lands in Dunbartonshire; as also sheriff of that county, and governor of Dunbarton Castle; in both which offices he was succeeded by his son Sir Malcolm, who had the tuition of the young king David and his royal consort committed to his charge in the aforesaid castle, and afterwards waited on his majesty into France, when Baliol's party became prevalent.

He had likewise the honour, after his return from France, in those evil times, to shelter and protect prince Robert Stewart of Scotland, afterwards king Robert II. from his great enemy Edward Baliol, who had usurped the crown from king David: But when the king's affairs took a more favourable turn, by Baliol's losing the sovereignty, he was sent again into France to attend king David home, in the year 1342. In reward of which faithful services, the king created him earl of Wigton, and bestowed upon him all the lands belonging to that earldom.

In 1346 he attended king David to the battle of Durham, where, with his royal master, he was taken prisoner; but being soon after released, was one of the commissioners, who in 1354, were appointed to treat with the English at Newcastle about the king's redemption; which being concluded, Thomas his grandson was one of the hostages for the ransom, and afterwards succeeded to the Fleming estates.

Which Thomas, second earl of Wigton, received a new charter of his lands from the aforesaid king; but having no issue, he in his old age sold to Archibald Douglas, lord of Galloway, for the sum of 00 l. the whole earldom of Wigton, and resigned to his cousin and heir male, Sir Malcolm Fleming of Biggar, the baronies of Lenzie, Cumbernauld, &c. which were ratified to him by a charter under the great seal.

Which Sir Malcolm was the son of Sir Patrick, second son of Sir Robert before-mentioned, by one of the daughters and coheirs of the brave Sir Simon Frafer, of Oliver-Castle, with whom he got the lands and barony of Biggar, and quartered the arms of Frafer with his own. Sir Malcolm his son having an opulent fortune, made no small figure in the time he lived. His brother Patrick was ancestor of the Flemings of Bord, &c. He was succeeded by his eldest son

Sir David, who at the battle of Otterburn, or Chevy-Chace, 1388, signalized his valour in a distinguishing manner; where the brave James earl of Douglas the general, and many other gallant men were slain. In the year 1405, he was knighted,

and

and sent ambassador to England; and afterwards, for his good services there, had a grant of divers lands in Carrick in the county of Air, with the barony of Cavers, and sheriffship of Roxburgh; and marrying first Jane, daughter of Sir David Barclay, lord of Brechin, by her had a daughter Marian, who was the wife of Sir William Maul of Panmure. By Isabel his second wife, who was heiress of the baron of Monycabo, he had two sons, Sir Malcolm and David, ancestor of the Flemings of Boghall, and their father being slain at Longhermilston-muir, on February 24, 1405, was succeeded by his eldest son,

Sir Malcolm, who was knighted by Robert III. He married lady Elizabeth, daughter of Robert Stewart duke of Albany, by whom he had issue a son, Sir Robert, and a daughter, Margaret, wife of Patrick, son and heir of Andrew, second lord Grey. He was barbarously murdered, with the earl of Douglas and his younger brother, by the contrivance of the lord chancellor Crichton, in the castle of Edinburgh, in 1441, and was succeeded by Sir Robert his heir, who was created lord Fleming of Cumbernauld; and marrying lady Jane, daughter of James seventh earl of Douglas, by her had Malcolm his heir apparent, and two daughters, Elizabeth and Beatrix, of which the eldest was married to John lord Livingston, and the youngest to Sir William Stirling of Keir. He lived to a great age, and dying in 1495, and his son and heir dying in his father's life-time, left by Eupheme his wife, daughter of James lord Livingston,

John, his son, second lord, who succeeded his grandfather; and being an accomplished gentleman, was by James V. sent ambassador to France, and after his return, made lord chamberlain of Scotland. He married Eupheme, daughter of John the first lord Drummond, and by her had issue Malcolm, and another Malcolm prior of Whittern. Also three daughters, Elizabeth wife of James lord Crichton; Margaret of John Cunningham of Glengarnock; and Jane, first of John, eldest son of Sir James Sandilands of Calder; and secondly, of David Crawfurd, of Kerse. He had two other wives, but no issue by either; and being barbarously murdered by John Tweedie, of Drumelzier, and his accomplices, in 1524, was succeeded by his eldest son,

Malcolm, third lord, who by king James V. was also constituted lord high chamberlain, which office he held to his death; and being slain at the battle of Pinkie or Musselburgh, on September 10, 1547, left issue by Janet his wife, natural daughter of king James IV. two sons, James and John, and four daughters; Janet married first, to John master of Livingston; and secondly to Andrew Brown, of Hartry, Esq; Agnes, to William, lord Livingston; Margaret, first to Robert, master of Montrose; secondly, to Thomas master of Erskine; and lastly, to John Stewart earl of Athole; and Mary, to Sir William Maitland, ancestor of the earl of Lauderdale.

James the eldest son, fourth lord, succeeded his father, and by queen Mary was constituted lord high chamberlain during life; and when the marriage was to be solemnized between her majesty and the dauphin of France, he was one of the peers whom the parliament sent over upon that solemn occasion; and dying soon after at Paris, in 1558, left by lady Barbara his wife, daughter of James Hamilton duke of Chattelherault, ancestor of the duke of Hamilton, a daughter Jane, married to John Scot, lord of Thirlestan; and secondly, to Gilbert earl of Cassilis; but leaving no male issue, his estate and honour came to

John his brother, fifth lord, who by the aforesaid queen was continued in the office of lord chamberlain, and made governor of Dunbarton Castle. He married Elizabeth, daughter and sole heir of Robert master of Ross; and dying in 1572, of a wound received by a musket ball in his knee, he left issue John his successor, and three daughters; Mary, wife of Sir James Douglas, of Drumlanrig; Elizabeth, of Sir Alexander Bruce of Airth; and Margaret, of Sir James Forrest, of Carden.

John his son, sixth lord, who succeeded, was by James VI. created earl of Wigton, March 19, 1606. He married lady Lilias, daughter of John Graham the third earl of Montrose, by whom he had issue two sons, John and James, and five daughters; lady Jane, married to George Campbell, son of Hugh lord Loudoun, by whom she had Margaret, baroness of Loudoun, the wife of John Campbell, created earl of Loudoun; lady Anne, married to Sir William Livingston, of Kilsyth; lady Margaret, to Sir John Charteris, of Amisfield; lady Lilias, to Sir David Murray, of Stanhope; and lady Mary to Sir Archibald Stewart, of Castlemilk. By a second wife, Sarah, daughter of William lord Herries, he had one daughter, lady Rachael, wife of John Lindsay, of Caventon, Esq; He deceased in 1619, and was succeeded by his eldest son.

John, seventh lord, and second earl, who married lady Margaret, daughter of Alexander the first earl of Linlithgow, and by her had John his heir, Sir William, who was gentleman-usher to king Charles I. and chamberlain of the houshold to king Charles II. and three daughters; lady Eleanor, married to David earl of Wemyss; lady Ann, first to Robert, second lord Boyd, and after to George Ramsay the second earl of Dalhousie; and lady Jane, to Sir John Grierson of Lag. His eldest son,

John,

John, third earl, in 1650, succeeded; and for his loyalty to king Charles I. was obliged to fly to the Highlands, where he lay concealed till his friends compounded for his delinquency; he dying in 1663, left issue by the lady Jane, daughter of John Drummond the second earl of Perth, six sons and two daughters, viz. John; Sir Robert, Henry and James, who died unmarried; William, and Charles, who died young: ladies Margaret and Jane, who died unmarried.

John, the eldest son, fourth earl, succeeded, and married Ann, daughter of Henry lord Ker, by whom he had a daughter, Jane, wife of George Maul, the third earl of Panmure; but having no male issue, his estate and honour devolved upon his brother,

William, the fifth earl, who was one of the privy council to king Charles II. by whom he was also made sheriff of the county of Dunbarton, and governor of that castle. He married lady Henrietta, daughter of Charles Seton earl of Dumferline, by whom he had issue, John his heir, Charles, and lady Mary, wife of Mr. Henry Maule of Kelly, father of the present earl of Panmure. He died in 1681, and was succeeded by his eldest son,

John, sixth earl, who married first lady Margaret, daughter of Colin Lindsay third earl of Balcarras, and by her had one daughter, lady Margaret, wife of Sir Archibald Primrose of Dunipace. He married secondly, lady Mary Keith, daughter of William earl Marshal, by whom he had one daughter, lady Clementina, married to Charles Elphingston, now lord Elphingston, by whom she hath issue three sons and four daughters, viz. John, married to Anne, eldest daughter of James lord Ruthven; William, George-Keith, Mary, Eleanor, Primrose and Clementina. His third wife was Eupheme, daughter of George Lockhart of Carnwath, Esq; who died in December 1762, but he had no issue by her. He was committed to Edinburgh castle at the beginning of the rebellion in 1715, but was soon after discharged without trial; and dying in 1743, was succeeded by his brother,

Charles, seventh earl, who dying unmarried in 1747, the title was claimed by Dr. Charles-Ross Fleming, physician of Dublin, and was determined in his favour by the lords of session in Scotland, in 1748; and in 1752 he voted as such at the election of a sixteenth peer. And the said

Charles-Ross Fleming is the eighth and present earl of Wigton.

TITLES.] The right honourable Charles-Ross Fleming earl of Wigton, and lord Fleming.

CREATIONS.] Lord Fleming by James II. and earl of Wigton in the county of Wigton, 19 March 1605, the 38th of James VI.

ARMS.] Quarterly, 1st and 4th pearl, a chevron within a double

double treffure, flowered and counterflowered with fleurs de lis ruby, for Fleming; 2d and 3d sapphire, three cinquefoils pearl, for Frafer.

CREST.] On a wreath, a goat's head erafed pearl, armed topaz.

SUPPORTERS.] Two stags proper, attired and unguled topaz; each gorged with a collar fapphire, charged with three cinquefoils pearl.

MOTTO.] Let deed shaw.

CHIEF SEATS] At Cumbernald, in the county of Stirling; and at Boighall, in Cliddefdale. But we believe they are now lord Elphingston's, in right of his wife.

LYON, Earl of STRATHMORE.

THIS illustrious family is defcended from that of Leonne in France, which derives its origin from the noble houfe of Leoni at Rome, a branch whereof came from France into England with William the conqueror in 1066, and from thence, in 1098, Sir Roger de Leonne came to Scotland with king Edgar, fon of Malcolm Canmore. This Sir Roger, for the good fervices he had done againft Donald Bane, the ufurper, had a grant of confiderable lands in Perthfhire, which from him were called Glen Lyon.

Afterwards Sir John Lyon obtained a grant from king David II. in 1343, of the baronies of Forteviot and Fergundeny, in the faid county, with Drumgoven, and others in the fhire of Aberdeen, and the grant was confirmed by king Robert II. Sir John Lyon, fon of the faid John, was commonly called The White Lyon, from his complexion, and was fecretary to the faid king Robert II. who in the year 1379, granted him the thanedom of Glamis in Forfarfhire, and not long after preferred him to be great chamberlain of Scotland.

He alfo advanced him to the degree of a lord of parliament, by the title of lord Glamis, and gave him in marriage the princefs Jane, his third and youngeft daughter, by Elizabeth Mure, his firft wife, together with the barony of Kinghorn in Fifefhire, and from that match his family had the honour to furround their arms with a double treffure.

He had likewife feveral grants of lands from the crown, to which he made a large addition by the purchafe of many baronies.

In 1382, he was fent ambaflador to England; but in his return, having the misfortune to quarrel with Sir James Lindfay of Crawfurd, was by him moft barbaroufly murdered at the mofs of Balhall, which was highly refented by the king, who ordered the corpfe to be buried in the abbey of Scoon, in 1383.

By his faid wife he had iffue an only fon, John, fecond lord Glamis, who being very young, the king his grandfather took him

him under his royal patronage, strictly forbidding any to harm him, under the highest penalty the law could inflict. He married lady Elizabeth, daughter of Patrick Graham earl of Strathern; and dying in 1435, was buried among the kings at Scoon, having had issue three sons, Patrick, his heir; Michael and David. He was succeeded by his eldest son,

Patrick, third lord, who was one of the hostages sent into England in 1424, for the return of king James I. and was one of the privy council to king James II. and master of his houshold; he married Isabel, daughter of Sir Alexander Ogilvy of Auchterhouse, by whom he had issue three sons, Alexander, John, and William, ancestor of the Lyons of Ogil, easter and wester; also a daughter, Elizabeth, wife of Alexander Robinson of Strowan. He died in 1459, and was succeeded by his eldest son,

Alexander, fourth lord, who married Agnes, daughter of William lord Crichton, chancellor of Scotland; but dying in 1485, without issue, his estate and honour descended to his brother,

John, fifth lord, who was one of the privy council to king James IV. by whom he was made justice general of Scotland. He married Margaret, daughter of Sir John Scrimgeor of Dudhope, constable of Dundee, by whom he had issue four sons and nine daughters; John, his successor; David, first of the family of Coffin; William and George; which three last were killed at the battle of Floddon in 1513. The eldest daughter, Christian, was the second wife of William earl of Errol; and the second, Margaret, of James Rind of Broxmouth. The names of the others I cannot find. He died in 1497, and was succeeded by his eldest son,

John, sixth lord Glamis, who married Elizabeth, daughter of Andrew, third lord Gray, by whom he had issue three sons, George, John, and Alexander; and a daughter, Elizabeth, first married to John master of Forbes; and secondly, to John Crichton of Strathurd.

George, the eldest son, seventh lord, succeeded his father in 1500; but dying in 1505, unmarried, the estate and honour came to his brother,

John, eighth lord, who married Janet Douglas, sister to Archibald the twelfth earl of Douglas, and had John, his heir; and a daughter, Elizabeth, wife of —— Ross of Craigy; and the said John, ninth lord, being a minor at his father's death, was, with his mother, wrongfully accused of treason, and the latter tried, condemned, and executed, in 1538. Himself, though but a minor, was also condemned, and his titles and estates forfeited to the crown; but his execution was suspended, on account of his youth; however, he continued in prison till queen Mary's accession to the crown; and in her first parliament,

ment, 1543, his forfeiture was repealed, and he was restored to his estates and honours. He married lady Jane Keith, daughter of William, third earl Marshal, by whom he had issue John, his successor; Sir Thomas Lyon of Auldbar, who was lord treasurer of Scotland, and died without issue: Also a daughter, Margaret, who was first married to Gilbert Kennedy, fourth earl of Cassilis; and secondly, to John, the first marquis of Hamilton. He was succeeded by his eldest son,

John, tenth lord, who for his great parts and learning, was in 1575 constituted lord high chancellor of Scotland. He married Elizabeth, daughter of Alexander, sixth lord Abernethy of Salton, by whom he had issue Patrick his heir; and two daughters, Jane, first married to Robert lord Douglas, heir apparent of William earl of Moreton; secondly, to Archibald, the eighth earl of Angus; and thirdly, to Alexander lord Spinzy, son of David earl of Crawfurd; and Elizabeth was the wife of Patrick lord Gray. Their father being unfortunately shot, in a squabble betwixt the earl of Crawfurd's servants and his own, in 1578, was succeeded by his son,

Patrick, eleventh lord, who was made captain of the guard, and one of the privy council to king James VI. and lord treasurer of Scotland, and in 1606, was created earl of Kinghorn, lord Lyon and Glamis. He married lady Ann, daughter of John Murray, first earl of Tullibardin; and dying at Edinburgh in 1615, left issue by her three sons, John, James, and Frederick, ancestor of the Lyons of Brigton; and a daughter, lady Ann, married to William, tenth earl of Errol.

John, his eldest son, succeeded as second earl; and marrying first, lady Martha, daughter of John seventh earl of Mar; and secondly, Elizabeth Maul, daughter of Patrick earl of Panmure; by the last had issue Patrick, his successor; and a daughter, lady Elizabeth, married to Charles earl of Aboyn. He was succeeded, in 1649, by his said son,

Patrick, third earl of Kinghorn, who, with the consent and approbation of king Charles II. changed his title from Kinghorn to Strathmore, and was one of the privy council in that reign, as also in that of king James VII. likewise one of the extraordinary lords of session. He married lady Helen, daughter of John earl of Middleton, and by her had issue two sons, John, and Patrick, who joined the earl of Mar in 1715, and was killed at the battle of Sheriffmuir, November 13, that year. Also two daughters; lady Grizel, married to David Ogilvy, the third earl of Airly; and lady Elizabeth, to Charles, second earl of Aboyn; and, after his decease, to Patrick lord Kinnaird. He died in 1695, and was succeeded by his eldest son,

John, fourth earl, who was one of the privy council to queen Ann. He married lady Elizabeth, daughter of Philip, second earl of Chesterfield, by whom he had issue six sons, Patrick and
Philip,

Philip, who died young; John, Charles, James, and Thomas; and two daughters, lady Helen, married to Robert Stewart lord Blantyre; and lady Mary. He died in 1712, and,

John, his eldest son, succeeded him; and being in the rebellion in 1715, under the command of John earl of Mar, was killed in the battle of Sheriffmuir. To him succeeded

Charles, his next brother, sixth earl, who married lady Susan Cochran, daughter of John the fourth earl of Dundonald; but being accidentally killed at Forfar in 1728, without issue, he was succeeded by his next brother,

James, seventh earl, who dying in 1735, without issue, was succeeded by

Thomas, the youngest brother, eighth earl, and then representative in parliament for the county of Forfar. In 1736, he married Jane, daughter and coheir of James Nicholson, of the county of Durham, Esq; by whom he had issue three sons and four daughters, viz. John, James, and Thomas; ladies Susan, Anne, Mary, and ——. His lordship deceased in 1755, and was succeeded by his eldest son, John, ninth and present earl of Strathmore, who is unmarried.

TITLES.] The right honourable Thomas Lyon, earl of Strathmore, lord Glamis, and Kinghorn.

CREATIONS.] Lord Glamis in the county of Forfar, and Kinghorn in the county of Fife, by Robert II. and earl of Kinghorn, 10 July, 1606, the 39th of James VI. which title was changed to Strathmore in Angus, soon after the restoration of Charles II.

ARMS.] Pearl, a lion rampant sapphire, armed and langued ruby, within a double tressure, flowered and counterflowered with fleurs de lis of the latter.

CREST.] On a wreath, a lady to the girdle, holding in her right hand the royal thistle, inclosed with a circle of laurel proper, in honour of the family's marriage with the daughter of king Robert II.

SUPPORTERS] On the dexter side a unicorn pearl, armed, mained, and unguled topaz; on the sinister a lion ruby.

MOTTO.] In te Domine speravi.

CHIEF SEATS.] At Glamis, in the county of Forfar; and at Castle Lyon, in the county of Perth.

HAMILTON, Earl of ABERCORN.

THE descent of this noble family will be found under the title of duke of Hamilton, where it is observed, that James, the second earl of Arran, was by king Henry II. of France created duke of Chatelherault; and marrying lady Margaret, daughter of James, third earl of Moreton, by her had issue four sons, lords, James, earl of Arran and duke of Chatelherault,

telherault, who died without issue; John, first marquis of Hamilton; Claud, and David. For the daughters, *see Duke of Hamilton*.

Claud, third son, in 1553 was promoted to be commendator of the abbey of Paisley, upon the resignation of John archbishop of St. Andrews, which was ratified and approved by pope Julius III. and upon the breaking out of the civil war, he, adhering to the interest of queen Mary, was by her constituted one of the principal commanders of her army at the battle of Langside, 1568, where he performed the part of a brave and valiant general; and resolutely persisting in her majesty's service, his estate was thereupon forfeited, and continued in other hands, till his majesty king James VI. in 1585, was pleased to restore the long injured family of Hamilton; and, in testimony of the great sense he had of that gentleman's sufferings for his loyalty to the said queen, created him lord Paisley in 1587. He married Margaret, daughter of George lord Seton, and by her had four sons, and a daughter, Margaret, married to William marquis of Douglas. The sons were, James; Sir Claud, ancestor of the Hamiltons of Eliefton, Monterlony, &c. Sir George, who behaved with great bravery in the service of king Charles I. and Sir Frederick, who acquired great honour under Gustavus Adolphus, king of Sweden, was colonel of a regiment in the service of Charles I. in Ireland, and was ancestor of the viscount Boyne of that kingdom. He was succeeded by

James, his eldest son, who being a man of great parts, and much in favour with king James VI. was by him made gentleman of his bedchamber, and created earl of Abercorn in 1606. He married Mariana, daughter of Thomas lord Boyd, and by her had issue five sons and three daughters; lady Anne, married to Hugh lord Semple; lady Margaret, to Sir William Cunninghame of Caprington; and lady Lucy, who died unmarried. Of the sons, James was his successor; Sir Claud was baron of Strabane; Sir William; Sir George, of whom hereafter; and Sir Alexander was father of count Hamilton, who settled first at the court of Philip-William, elector Palatine, who sent him envoy extraordinary to king James II. of England. He accompanied the elector's daughter, Eleanor-Magdalena, to Vienna, who married the emperor Leopold, and by the favour of the empress was created a count of the empire, with a grant of the county of Newburgh near Passaw, and other estates in Moravia and Hungary. He had issue a daughter, maid of honour to the empress Amelia, consort of the emperor Joseph; and a son, count Julius, chamberlain to the emperor, who married Maria Ernestina, born countess of Starenberg, who died in 1724, and had issue three sons and several daughters. The earl died in 1618, and was succeeded by his eldest son,

James, second earl, who was created lord Hamilton of Strabane

bane in 1616. He married Catharine, daughter and heir of Gervase Clifton of Leighton-Bromswold, (widow of Esme Stuart, duke of Richmond and Lennox, from whom the present lord Clifton and earl of Darnley is descended) by whom he had issue three sons, James lord Paisley, who died before him; and, by a daughter of William Lenthal, Esq; speaker of the house of commons in the long parliament, left issue an only daughter, Catharine, married first to William Lenthal of Burford in Oxfordshire, Esq; her cousin; and secondly, to her cousin Charles, the fifth earl of Abercorn. The second son, William, was colonel of a regiment, and killed in Germany. And

George, the third, succeeding to the title, was the third earl; but dying unmarried at Padua in Italy, we return to

Claud, second son of James the first earl, to whom his brother James, the second earl of Abercorn, resigned the barony of Strabane. He married, in 1630, lady Jane, youngest daughter of George, the first marquis of Huntley, and by her had issue two sons, James and George; and two daughters; Catharine, married first to James, eldest son of Sir Frederick Hamilton, fourth son of Claud, lord Paisley, before mentioned; secondly, to Owen Wynne of Lurganboy, in the county of Leitrim, Esq; and thirdly, to John Bingham of Castlebar, in the county of Mayo, Esq; Mariana, married to Richard Perkins of Lifford, in the county of Donegal, Esq; all in Ireland. He died in 1638, and was succeeded by his eldest son,

James; who dying without issue, June 16, 1655, was succeeded by his brother,

George, the fourth lord, who married Elizabeth, daughter of Christopher Fagan of Filtrim, in the county of Dublin, Esq; and dying April 14, 1668, left issue two sons, Claud and Charles; and two daughters; Anne, married to John Browne of Neale, in the county of Mayo, Esq; and Mary, to Gerard Dillon, Esq; recorder of Dublin, and prime serjeant to king James VII.

Claud succeeded to the titles of lord Strabane and earl of Abercorn, as heir male of George third earl, as before noticed; but attending king James II. from France, as colonel of a regiment in his army to Ireland, he was attainted, March 1, 1688-9. After the defeat at the Boyne, he embarked for France, and was killed in his voyage in 1690. He was outlawed, and forfeited his estate and title of Strabane, but the earldom devolved on his brother,

Charles, fifth earl of Abercorn, who obtaining a reversion of his brother's attainder, succeeded also to the title of Strabane. He married Catharine, only daughter of James lord Paisley, as before-mentioned; but having issue only a daughter, Elizabeth, who died young, the title of lord Hamilton of Strabane became extinct, and we return to

Sir

EARL OF ABERCORN.

Sir George, fourth son of James, the first earl of Abercorn; who during the rebellion performed good services in Ireland for king Charles I. and II. being a colonel of foot, and governor of the castle of Nenagh, in 1649. In 1651, he retired to France, where he continued till the restoration of king Charles II. who created him a baronet. He married Mary, daughter of Thomas viscount Thurles, eldest son of Walter earl of Ormond, and sister of James the first duke; and by her, who died in August 1680, had issue six sons and three daughters; 1. James; 2. Sir George, made a count in France, and marshal dù camp in that service, who married Frances, eldest daughter and coheir of Richard Jennings of Sandridge, in the county of Hertford, Esq; and sister of Sarah duchess of Marlborough; and dying in 1667, left issue by her, who re-married with Richard Talbot, duke of Tyrconnel, and died in Dublin, March 7, 1730-1, three daughters, Elizabeth viscountess Ross, Frances viscountess Dillon, and Mary viscountess Kingsland, all then in their infancy; 3. Anthony, who followed king James into France, and died a lieutenant general in that kingdom; 4. Thomas, a commander in the sea service, who died in New-England; 5. Richard, colonel of a regiment of horse in king James's army, and a brigadier general, fled also into France, where he died a lieutenant general; 6. John, a colonel in king James's service, lost his life at the battle of Aghrim; 7. Elizabeth, married to Philibert count of Gramont, by whom she had a daughter, Claude-Charlotte, married to Henry earl of Stafford; 8. Lucia, married to Sir Donogh O Brien of Lemineagh, Bart. 9. Margaret, to Matthew Ford of Coolgreny, in the county of Wexford, Esq; both in Ireland.

James, the eldest son, was groom of the bedchamber to king Charles II. and colonel of a regiment of foot; who being a volunteer on board the fleet with the duke of York, had one of his legs taken off by a cannon ball, of which wound he died, June 6, 1673, his father then living. He married Elizabeth, eldest daughter of John lord Colepeper, and by her, who died in 1709, had three sons; 1. James; 2. George, who lost his life at the battle of Steenkirk in 1692, commanding a regiment of foot; 3. William, who was one of the five Kentish petitioners, of which county he was deputy lieutenant, and colonel of a regiment of militia. He married Margaret, second daughter of Sir Thomas Colepeper of Hollingburne in Kent, knight, and was ancestor of the Hamiltons of Chilson. He was succeeded by his eldest son,

James, who was groom of the bedchamber to king Charles II. he also succeeding to the titles of baron Strabane and earl of Abercorn, was the sixth earl of Abercorn, and was created baron of Mountcastle and viscount Strabane. In 1706, to preserve

serve his Scotch peerage, he went over to that kingdom, and sat in the session of parliament which concluded the union.

In the reign of king James II. he had the command of a regiment of horse, and was one of that king's privy council, as he was to king William and queen Anne; and in September 1714, was appointed thereof to his majesty king George I. as he also was in 1727 to king George II. but died November 28, 1734. He married, in 1686, Elizabeth, daughter and heir of Sir Robert Reading of the city of Dublin, Bart. and by her had six sons and four daughters; 1. Lady Elizabeth, married first, to William Brownlow of Lurgan, Esq; and secondly, to the count de Kearney in France; 2. Lady Mary, married to Henry Coolley, Esq; 3. Lady Phillippa, married first, to Benjamin Pratt, dean of Down; and secondly, to Michael Connel of London, Esq; 4. Lady Jane, married to lord Archibald Hamilton, brother of James duke of Hamilton. The sons were, 1. James; 2. John, who died in 1714 unmarried; 3. George, who was deputy cofferer of Frederick prince of Wales's houshold. He married, in 1719, Bridget, daughter and heir of colonel William Coward of the city of Wells, and had by her six sons and six daughters. He was chosen representative for that city in 1734 and 1747; 4. Francis, a clergyman, who married Dorothy, daughter and coheir of James Forth of Redwood, in King's County in Ireland, Esq; and dying in May 1746, left issue; 5. William, cast away in the Royal Anne galley, with, the lord Belhaven, in November 1721; 6. Charles, in 1738, clerk of the green cloth to the prince of Wales; and in 1743, receiver general and collector of the revenues in the island of Minorca. He was chosen, in 1741, member of parliament for Truro in Cornwall, and re-chosen in 1743. The earl died in 1734, and was succeeded by his eldest son,

James, seventh earl. In 1737 he was appointed one of his majesty's privy council for the kingdom of Ireland, and in 1738, for Great Britain. He married Anne, daughter of co'onel John Plumer of Blakesware, in the county of Hertford; and by her, who died March 16, 1754, had issue six sons and one daughter; lady Anne, married August 16, 1746, to Sir Henry Mackworth, Bart. The sons were, 1. James; 2. John, who was drowned December 18, 1755, as he was going from the Lancaster man of war, of which he was captain, to Portsmouth, after having swam twenty minutes about his boat, which was overset, exhorting his men to resignation, and at the same time encouraging them to exert their strength to save their lives. He married, in November 1749, the widow of Richard Elliot, of Port-Elliot, in Cornwall, Esq; 3. William, who died young; 4. George, a clergyman; 5. Plumer, who died young; 6. William, lieutenant of the Victory man of war, in which he was unfortunately cast away, with Sir John

Balchen, in the year 1744. His lordship dying January 13, 1743-4, was succeeded by his eldest son,

James, the present and eighth earl of Abercorn. He was appointed one of his majesty's privy council for the kingdom of Ireland; and in 1761, was elected one of the sixteen peers to represent the Scots peerage in the present parliament.

TITLES.] The right honourable James Hamilton, earl and baron of Abercorn, and baron of Paisley; (viscount and baron of Strabane in Ireland) and baronet.

CREATIONS.] Baron of Paisley, in the county of Renfrew, in 1591; baron of Abercorn, in the county of Lanerk, in 1604; earl of the same place, baron of Hamilton, Mount-castle, and Kilpatrick, July 10, 1606, by king James VI. of Scotland, and I. of England; baronet by Charles I.

ARMS.] Quarterly, 1st and 4th ruby, three cinquefoils pierc'd, ermine, for Hamilton. 2d and 3d pearl, a ship with its sails furl'd up, diamond, for the earldom of Arran.

CREST.] In a ducal coronet, topaz, an oak fructed, and penetrated transversely in the main stem by a frame saw, proper, the frame topaz.

SUPPPORTERS.] Two antelopes, pearl, their horns, ducal collars, chains, and hoofs, topaz.

MOTTO.] Sola nobilitat virtus.

CHIEF SEATS.] At Stephen's-Green, in the city of Dublin; at Duddingston and Paisley, in the county of Renfrew; and at Witham, in the county of Essex, in England.

ERSKINE, Earl of KELLY.

THE descent of the illustrious family of Erskine, will be seen hereafter, under the title of earl of Mar.

Sir Alexander Erskine of Gogar in Midlothian, brother of John the fifth earl of Mar, who died in 1572, was intrusted with the custody of young king James VI. in the castle of Stirling. He married Margaret, daughter of George, 4th lord Home, and by her had issue three sons and three daughters, viz. Sir Alexander, killed at the surprize of Stirling, in 1578; Sir Thomas, and Sir George, of Innerteal, one of the senators of the college of justice; Margaret the wife of James Crichton, of Ruthven, Esq; Joan, of John Lesley, of Balquhain; and Mary, of Sir Dougal Campbell, of Auchinbreck. He was succeeded by his eldest surviving son,

Sir Thomas, who being educated with king James VI. from his childhood, thereby became a great favourite with that prince, who first made him a knight and gentleman of his bedchamber; and afterwards, in regard of his signal merit, having with Sir John Ramsay, in the year 1600, rescued the said king from the sons of William Ruthven, earl of Gowry, was thereupon honoured

noured with a coat of augmentation, and rewarded with the lordship of Dirleton, made captain of the English guards, groom of the stole, created viscount Fenton in 1606, and earl of Kelly, and in 1615 elected a knight of the most noble order of the garter. He married Ann, daughter of Gilbert Ogilvy of Pourie, and by her had two sons, viz. Thomas and Alexander; and a daughter, lady Ann, wife of Sir Robert Mowbray, of Barnbougle. He died in 1639, and was succeeded by his eldest son,

Thomas, second earl; but he dying unmarried, the estate and honour devolved on,

Alexander his brother, third earl, who suffered much for his loyalty during the usurpation, being in 1651 taken prisoner at the battle of Worcester; and dying in 1677, left issue, by his wife lady Ann Seton, daughter of Alexander, earl of Dumferlin, two sons and three daughters; lady Mary, married to Gavin Dalziel earl of Carnwath; lady Sophia, to Alexander Fraser lord Salton, and lady Margaret, to William lord Forbes. The sons were Alexander and Sir Charles, who was Lyon king at arms, and had issue Sir Alexander, late Lyon king at arms, father of Sir William, also Lyon king at arms. This earl died in 1677, and was succeeded by his eldest son,

Alexander, fourth earl. He married first, Mary, daughter of colonel Kilpatrick, governor of the Bosch, in Holland, by whom he had a daughter, lady Ann, wife of Sir Alexander Erskine, of Cambo, Bart. And secondly, Mary, daughter of Sir John Dalziel of Glenay, Bart. by whom he had a daughter, lady Elizabeth, wife of ———— Fraser, of Inneralachie, and a son,

Alexander, fifth earl, who married lady Ann Lindsay, daughter of Colin earl of Balcarras, and dying in 1710, by her left a son, Alexander his successor, and a daughter, lady Ann. He died in 1710, and was succeeded by his said son,

Alexander, sixth earl of Kelly. He married first Miss Murray, daughter of William Murray, of Abercairny, Esq; by whom he had no issue. His second lady was daughter of Dr. Archibald Pitcairn, of that ilk, by whom he had three sons and three daughters, Alexander, lord Fenton, born in 1732; Archibald, a captain in the army, and Andrew, also an officer in the army. And three daughters, lady Betty, wife of Walter Macfarlane, of that ilk; ladies Ann and Janet. His lordship being engaged in the rebellion 1745, his name stands first in the act of attainder 1746; but surrendering in due time, he prevented in part the penalties of that act. His lordship dying in March 1756, was succeeded by his eldest son,

Alexander, now seventh earl of Kelly, who is unmarried.

TITLES.] The right honourable Alexander Erskine earl of Kelly, viscount Fenton, and baron of Dirleton.

CREATIONS,

CREATIONS.] Baron of Dirleton in the county of Haddington 1603, viscount Fenton in 1606, and earl of Kelly in the county of Fife, 12 March 1619, all by king James VI.

ARMS.] Quarterly, 1st and 4th ruby, an imperial crown, within a double tressure flowered and counterflowered with fleurs de lis topaz, as a coat of augmentation before-mentioned; 2d and 3d pearl, a pale diamond for Erskine.

CREST.] On a wreath, a demi lion guardant ruby.

SUPPORTERS.] Two griphons topaz, charged on their breasts with a crescent diamond.

MOTTO.] Decori decus addit avito.

CHIEF SEAT.] At the castle of Kelly in the county of Fife.

HAMILTON, Earl of HADDINGTON.

ENOUGH has been said of the antiquity of the family of Hamilton, under the title *duke of Hamilton*, for the purpose of this work.

The immediate ancestor of the earl of Haddington, was Sir Thomas Hamilton of Byres in Haddingtonshire, descended from John Hamilton of Innerwick, second son of Sir Walter Hamilton, ancestor of the first duke of Hamilton; and his son, Sir Thomas Hamilton of Priestfield, marrying Elizabeth, daughter of James Heriot of Trabrown, by her had a son, Sir Thomas, who being bred to the law, was by king James VI. made one of the senators of the college of justice, secretary of state, lord advocate and register, baron of Binny and Byres in 1613, and earl of Melross in the county of Roxburgh in 1619; but he afterwards, with his majesty's approbation, changed the latter title to Haddington.

In 1627 he was constituted lord privy seal, which office he held for ten years. He married first, Margaret, daughter of James Borthwick of Newbyres, by whom he had issue, two daughters, lady Christian, first married to Robert lord Lindsay, by whom she had John the fourteenth earl of Crawfurd; and secondly, to Robert lord Boyd; and lady Isabel, to James, earl of Airly. He married secondly, Margaret, daughter of Sir John Foulis, of Collington, Bart. and by her had issue three sons and two daughters; lady Margaret, married, first, to David, lord Carnegie, and secondly to James, earl of Hartfield; and lady Jane, to John, sixth earl of Cassilis. The sons were Thomas, Sir James and Sir John. He married, thirdly, Juliana, daughter of Sir Thomas Ker, of Fernihurst, by whom he had a son, Robert, killed at the blowing up of the house of Dunglas. Dying in 1637, he was succeeded by his eldest son,

Thomas, second earl, who joining with the covenanters in the beginning of the civil war, was governor of the castle of Dunglas, seven miles below Dunbar, on the eastern coast of Haddingtonshire.

Haddingtonshire. His servant, one Parifs an Englishman, was the storekeeper, who in August 1640, treacherously set fire to the magazine, which blew up himself, the said earl, his brother Robert, the sheriff of Haddington, and nine other persons of quality, beside many that were wounded. He married first, lady Katherine, daughter of John the sixth earl of Mar, by whom he had issue two sons, Thomas lord Binny, and John; and secondly, lady Jane Gordon, daughter of George marquis of Huntley, by whom he had a daughter lady Margaret, married to John earl of Kintore. He was succeeded by his eldest son Thomas, above-mentioned, who was third earl, but dying without issue, was succeeded by his brother,

John, fourth earl, who was one of those peers, who in the parliament of Scotland 1706, zealously promoted the union. He married lady Christian Lindsay, daughter of John the fourteenth earl of Crawfurd, and by her had issue a son Charles, lord Binny, and three daughters; lady Margaret, married to John Hope, Esq; and was by him mother of Charles earl of Hopeton; lady Helen, to Sir William Anstruther, of that ilk, a senator of the college of justice; and lady Susan, to Adam Cockburn, of Ormiston, lord justice-clerk, in the reigns of king William III. queen Ann, and king George I. Dying in 1669, he was succeeded by his said son,

Charles, the fifth earl, who married Margaret countess of Rothes, eldest daughter of John duke of Rothes, and by her he had issue, John, who took the name of Lefley, and was the eighth earl of Rothes, Thomas, and Charles, who died young. His second son,

Thomas, succeeded as sixth earl, and was elected one of the sixteen peers for Scotland in the beginning of the year 1716, in the room of the marquis of Tweedale, deceased: he was also one of the sixteen peers in the two next parliaments, and on the first of March 1716, elected a knight of the antient order of the thistle: in April following he was made governor of Edinburgh castle; and in March 1727, was appointed one of the privy council to king George II. and died in 1735. He married Helen, sister of Charles Hope, earl of Hopeton, and had issue two sons, Charles lord Binny, and John, and two daughters, lady Margaret, and lady Christian, wife of Sir James Dalrymple, of Hailes, Bart. His eldest son, Charles, lord Binny, was elected a member of parliament for St. Germans in the county of Cornwall in the year 1722, and was a commissioner of trade in Scotland; and dying at Naples, in 1732, before his father, left issue, by his wife Rachael, daughter of George Baillie, of Jervifwood, three sons and two daughters, viz. Thomas; George, who has taken the name of Baillie, as representative of his grandfather, above; Charles-James, a captain of dragoons; Grifel, married to Philip Earl of Stanhope, and Rachael.

Thomas, the eldeſt ſon, ſucceeded his grandfather, as ſeventh earl of Haddington; and in 1750, married Mary, daughter of Rowland Holt, of Redgravehall in Suffolk, Eſq; nephew of lord chief juſtice Holt, by whom he hath iſſue two ſons, Charles, lord Binny, born July 5, 1753; and Thomas.

TITLES.] The right honourable Thomas Hamilton, earl of Haddington, and baron of Binny.

CREATIONS.] Baron of Binny, 30 November, 1613; and earl of Haddington, in Eaſt-Lothian, 20 March 1619, by king James VI.

ARMS.] Quarterly, 1ſt and 4th ruby, on a chevron between three cinquefoils pearl, two muchetors and a buckle ſapphire, all within a border topaz, charged with eight thiſtles emerald, for Hamilton of Innerwick; 2d and 3d pearl, a feſs wavey, between three roſes ruby, barbed and ſeeded proper, as a coat of augmentation, for the title of Melroſs.

CREST.] On a wreath, two dexter hands conjoined, iſſuing out of clouds proper, and holding between them a branch of laurel.

SUPPORTERS.] Two talbots pearl, each gorged with a plain collar ruby.

MOTTO.] Præſto et perſto.

CHIEF SEAT.] At Tyningham in Eaſt-Lothian.

STEWART, Earl of GALLOWAY.

ALEXANDER, ſixth lord high ſteward of Scotland, obtained from king Alexander III. in 1263, a grant of the lands of Gairlies and Glaſſerton, and therein was ſucceeded by Sir John his ſecond ſon, who after the death of Alexander III. joining Sir William Wallace againſt the Engliſh, was ſlain at the fatal battle of Falkirk, againſt king Edward I. in perſon, in the year 1298. By his wife Margaret, daughter and heir of Sir Alexander Bonkil, of that ilk, he became poſſeſt of the barony of Bonkil, and other lands, and had by her a numerous iſſue, viz. Alexander, of Bonkil, afterwards earl of Angus. Sir Alan, of Dreghorn, anceſtor of the Stewarts of Darnley, earls and dukes of Lennox. Sir Walter, of Dalſwinton, of whom hereafter. Sir John, of Jedburgh; Sir James, of Preſton, and Iſabel, wife of the brave Thomas Randolph, earl of Murray. Sir Walter Stewart, the third ſon, always adhered to king Robert Bruce: and his ſon and ſucceſſor, Sir John Stewart, of Dalſwinton, ſupported firmly the intereſt of king David Bruce. In 1357, he was one of the hoſtages for the ranſom of the ſaid king David, who was then a priſoner to king Edward III. of England. He had a ſon Sir Walter, who ſucceeded him, and

lived

lived in the reign of king Robert II. and III. but having no male issue, married his only daughter Marian to John Stewart, son of Sir William Stewart, sheriff of Tiviotdale; and they having a son Sir William, he had a son and successor Sir Alexander, Sir Thomas Stewart of Minto, ancestor of the lord Blantyre, and Sir Walter Stewart, of whom descended the branch of Tongrie.

Sir Alexander, who succeeded his father, married Elizabeth Stewart, by whom he had a son Alexander; and the said Alexander marrying Elizabeth, daughter of Sir Archibald Douglas, of Cavers, by her he had Sir Alexander, a great favourite of king James IV. and was killed with his royal master, at the battle of Floddon, in 1513. He was succeeded by his son, Sir Alexander, in 1513, who was one of the privy council to king James V. who sent him ambassador to Henry VIII. of England; but in 1571, was slain at Stirling, when the regent, Matthew earl of Lennox, was basely murdered. He married Margaret, daughter and heir of Patrick Dunbar of Clugston, and by her had issue two sons, Alexander and John, and a daughter Margaret, wife, first, of Patrick Agnew, of Lochnaw, and second, of Patrick Mackay, of Larg. By another wife, daughter of Walter Stewart of Barclay, he had three sons and a daughter; Robert, who died without issue; Anthony, and William: his daughter Helen, was first married to William Gordon, of Murefode, ancestor of the viscounts Kenmure, and secondly, to John Glendoning, of Drumraik. Alexander, the eldest son, was slain in his father's life-time at the surprise of the town of Stirling; but having married Katharine, daughter and coheir of William Maxwel lord Herries, by her left another Alexander, who succeeded his grandfather, and was knighted at the coronation of queen Ann, wife of king James VI. in 1590. He married Christian, daughter of Sir William Douglas, of Drumlanrig, ancestor of the duke of Queensberry, by whom he had two sons, Alexander and William, ancestor of the Stewarts of Burray, in Orkney, and three daughters; Helen, wife of John Douglas, of Stanhouse; Jane, of John Kennedy, of Culzean, and Nicola, of John Dunbar, of Mochrum. He died in 1596, and was succeeded by his eldest son, Sir Alexander, who was created lord Gairlies, and earl of Galloway, by James VI. and made one of the privy council to king Charles I. He married Grisel, daughter of John Gordon, of Lochinvar, ancestor of the viscount Kenmure; and by her had Alexander his heir, Sir James Stewart, who was created a baronet, and a daughter Ann, wife of Sir Andrew Agnew, of Locknaw, Bart. He was succeeded by his eldest son,

Alexander, the second earl, who in 1649 married lady Margaret, daughter of William Graham earl of Menteith, and by her had a son of his name; but he dying young, the estate and honour descended to his brother,

Sir James Stewart, Bart. aforesaid, third earl, who during the usurpation was very active for the royal cause, and a great sufferer in it; and dying in 1671, left issue by Nicola his wife, daughter of Sir Robert Grierson of Lag, three sons, Alexander, Robert, and William; and a daughter, lady Grisel, married to Alexander, viscount Kenmure.

Alexander, the eldest son, fourth earl, succeeded his father, and married lady Mary Douglas, daughter of James earl of Queensberry, by whom he had issue six sons and two daughters; Margaret, married to Sir John Clerk, of Penicuik, Bart. and lady Henrietta, to William earl of Glencairn. Of the sons, John, the third son, was representative in several parliaments of queen Anne and king George I. for the shires of Dumfries and Wigton, and brigadier general of his majesty's forces; and

Alexander, the eldest, succeeding his father, was fifth earl; but dying in 1694, unmarried, his next brother,

James, became sixth earl of Galloway, and married the lady Katharine Montgomery, daughter of Alexander earl of Eglington, and by her had issue Alexander lord Gairlies; James, lieutenant colonel of the third regiment of foot guards, twice elected to parliament for the shire of Wigton, and twice for the burghs of Wigton, &c. William, a captain of dragoons, and member for the burghs of Wigton, &c. in the ninth parliament of Great Britain, and George: also three daughters, lady Margaret, first married to James Carnegy, earl of Southesk; and secondly, to John lord Sinclair, who was attainted in 1716; lady Euphemia, married to Alexander Murray of Broughton, Esq; lady Ann, died March 12, 1755; and lady Catharine, who also died unmarried. Their father, the said earl, dying in 1747, was succeeded by his eldest son,

Alexander, now seventh earl of Galloway, who married first, lady Ann Keith, daughter of William earl Marshal, by whom he had issue two sons and a daughter; of the sons, James, the youngest, died of the small-pox, and Alexander, the eldest, died on his travels, in the year 1738. His daughter, lady Mary, was the wife of Kenneth, lord Fortrose, eldest son of the late earl of Seaforth. His lordship took to his second wife, lady Katharine, daughter of John Cochran, earl of Dundonald, and by her hath issue four sons and six daughters, viz. John, lord Garlies, member in the present parliament for Morpeth; George, a captain in the army, who was killed at Ticonderago, in America, in the year 1758; William, who died young; and Keith. Lady Catharine, the wife of James Murray of Broughton, Esq; member for Wigtonshire in the present parliament; lady Susanna; lady Margaret, wife of Charles earl of Aboyne; ladies Euphemia and Henrietta; and lady Charlotte, wife of William, earl of Dunmore. His lordship is a commissioner of the police in Scotland.

TITLES.]

TITLES.] The right honourable Alexander Stewart, earl of Galloway, and lord Gairlies, a lord of the police.

CREATIONS.] Baron of Gairlies, in the county of Wigton, 2 April 1607, and earl of the county or province of Galloway, 19 September 1623, by king James VI.

ARMS.] Topaz, a fess cheque pearl and sapphire, surmounted of a bend ingrailed, ruby, within a double tressure flowered and counterflowered with fleurs de lis of the last.

CREST.] On a wreath, a pelican feeding her young in the nest, all proper.

SUPPORTERS.] On the dexter side, a savage wreathed with laurel about the temples and middle, holding a batoon over his shoulder, all proper; and on the sinister, a lion rampant ruby.

MOTTO.] Virescit vulnere virtus.

CHIEF SEATS.] At Gairlies, Glanish, Glasserton and Clary, all in Wigtonshire.

MAITLAND, Earl of LAUDERDALE.

OF this family, who probably came from Normandy with William the conqueror, and from England with king David I. was Richard de Mautland of Thirlestan, who gave divers lands to the monastery of Dryburgh; all which were confirmed by his son William, who died about 1315, and whose heir was Sir Robert, who also was a benefactor to the said abbey.

In the reign of king David II. 1346, this Sir Robert obtained a grant from Sir John Gifford, lord of Yester, of the lands of Leithington in East Lothian, and therein was succeeded by John his son, and also in his lands of Thirlestan; and he marrying lady Agnes, daughter of Patrick Dunbar, earl of March, by her had Sir Robert his heir, who had issue another Sir Robert, one of the hostages for the ransom of king James, 1424; but he dying before his father, his brother William succeeded; which William was father of John, and he of another William, who being slain at the battle of Floddon, in his father's life-time, 1513, left issue by Martha his wife, daughter of George lord Seton, a son, Sir Richard, who succeeded his grandfather; and a daughter, Janet, married to Hugh lord Somerville. In the reign of queen Mary, Sir Richard was one of the judges in the court of session, and lord privy seal; and marrying Mary, daughter of Thomas Cranston of Crosby, by her had three sons, Sir William, his heir; Sir John, of whom hereafter; and Thomas: also four daughters, Helen, wife of Sir John Cockburn of Clerkington; Isabel, of James Herriot of Trabrown; Mary, of Alexander Lauder of Habton; and Elizabeth, of William Douglas of Whitinghame.

Sir William, who succeeded, was one of the privy council

to the said queen Mary, and in 1558, her secretary of state. He married Mary, daughter of Malcolm lord Fleming, and by her had issue a son, James; and a daughter, Mary, married to Robert, first earl of Roxburgh; but the son James dying without issue, his estate devolved on his uncle,

Sir John, who was also made lord privy seal, a judge in the court of session, secretary of state, and lord high chancellor of Scotland, and was soon after created baron of Thirlestan. He married Jane, daughter and heir of James, the fifth lord Fleming, by lady Barbara his wife, daughter of James Hamilton, duke of Chatelherault, and by her had John his successor; and a daughter, Ann, who was the wife of Robert lord Seton, son and heir of Robert the first earl of Winton. He died in 1595, and was succeeded by his said son,

John, second lord, who was created a viscount, and earl of Lauderdale; and dying in 1645, left issue by Isabel his wife, daughter of Alexander Seton, earl of Dumferling, three sons, John, his heir; Robert, and Charles, of whom hereafter. He was succeeded by

John, his eldest son, second earl of Lauderdale, who being taken prisoner at the battle of Worcester in 1651, and committed to the Tower of London, for his loyalty to king Charles II. he there underwent a severe confinement for the space of nine years, till the restoration of the king, when he was released; and then, as a recompence for his sufferings, he was made secretary of state, president of the council, one of the extraordinary lords of session, first commissioner of the treasury, one of the gentlemen of his majesty's bedchamber, and high commissioner to the parliament; and on the 2d of May 1672, was created marquis of March and duke of Lauderdale; and on the 3d of June following, was likewise installed at Windsor, a knight of the most noble order of the garter. He was also by that king, on the 25th of June 1674, created a peer of England, by the titles of baron of Petersham, and earl of Guilford; and made one of the privy council for the kingdoms of England, Scotland, and Ireland.

He married first, lady Ann, daughter and coheir of Alexander earl of Home, and by her had a daughter, lady Ann, married to John Hay, marquis of Tweeddale; and secondly, Elizabeth, daughter and heir of William Murray, earl of Dysart, widow of Sir Lionel Talmash of Heylingham, in the county of Suffolk, Bart. by whom he had no issue. Dying on the 24th of August, 1682, his English titles, and those of marquis and duke, became extinct; but that of earl descended to his brother

Charles, third earl, who was general of the mint, deputy treasurer, and one of the senators of the college of justice. He married Elizabeth, daughter and heir of Richard Lauder of Hatton, Esq; by whom he had issue six sons and two daughters,

viz.

viz. Richard and John, successively earls of Lauderdale; Charles, who married Lilias, daughter of Sir John Colquhoun of Luss, and relict of Sir John Stirling of Keir; Alexander, who married Janet, daughter of —— Campbell; William, who married Christian, daughter and heir of Robert viscount Oxenford, and father by her of Robert, the third viscount; Thomas; lady Isabel, wife of John lord Elphingston; and lady Mary, of Charles, earl of Southesk. His lordship deceasing in 1691, was succeeded by his eldest son,

Richard, fourth earl, who was a polite gentleman, a poet, and a favourite of Charles II. and being strongly attached to James VII. followed him to France, where he died. He married lady Ann Campbell, daughter of Archibald earl of Argyll; but dying without issue by her, who married, secondly, Charles earl of Murray, he was succeeded by his next brother,

John, fifth earl, who heartily joined in the revolution, and was a senator of the college of justice, till his death, in 1710. He married lady Margaret, daughter of Alexander, tenth earl of Glencairn, and by her had issue three sons, James, Charles, and John, a colonel in the guards; and a daughter, lady Elizabeth, married to James Carmichael, earl of Hyndford. James, the eldest son, married lady Jane, daughter of John earl of Sutherland, and leaving issue only a daughter, Jane, married to Sir James Ferguson of Kilkerran, Bart. one of the lords of session, his brother,

Charles, the second son, succeeeded to the estate and honour, in April 1739, and was sixth earl. He was one of the sixteen representatives for the peerage of Scotland, in the ninth parliament of Great Britain, 1741, and died in 1744. He was also president of the court of session, and general of the mint. He married lady Elizabeth Ogilvy, daughter of James earl of Finlater and Seafield, by whom he had issue eight sons and three daughters, viz. James, his successor; Charles, married to —— Barclay, heir of Towie; George, a dignitary in the church of Ireland; Richard, lieutenant colonel in the army; Alexander, colonel in the guards, and usher to the princess dowager of Wales, who married ——, daughter of colonel Maden; Frederick, a captain in the navy; Patrick, commander of an East-India ship; and John, a captain in the army: Lady Elizabeth, wife of James Ogilvy of Rothmay, Esq; lady Margaret, who died unmarried; and lady Janet, wife of Thomas Dundas of Fingask, Esq; His lordship died in 1744, and was succeeded by his eldest son,

James, the seventh and present earl of Lauderdale, who was promoted, in 1745, to the rank of lieutenant colonel in the sixteenth regiment of foot. In the two last parliaments, being the tenth and eleventh of Great Britain, he was returned one of the sixteen peers for Scotland. He married Mary, daughter
and

and coheir of Sir Thomas Lombe, alderman of London, by whom he had issue four sons and four daughters; Valdave-Charles, who died in infancy; James, now lord Maitland, born in June 1759; James, John; lady Hannah, who died young; ladies Elizabeth, Mary-Julian, and Hannah-Charlotte.

TITLES.] The right honourable James Maitland, earl of Lauderdale, viscount Maitland, baron of Thirlestan, Musselburgh and Bolton.

CREATIONS.] Baron of Thirlestan, in the county of Berwick, in 1590, and viscount Maitland, and earl of Lauderdale, in the aforesaid county, 24 March 1623, all by James VI.

ARMS.] Topaz, a lion rampant dechauffe, within a double tressure, flowered and counterflowered with fleurs de lis ruby.

CREST.] On a wreath, a lion sejant gardant ruby, crowned with a ducal crown, holding in his dexter paw a drawn sword, pomelled and hilted topaz; and in the sinister, a fleur de lis sapphire; which royal crest was allowed to John duke of Lauderdale by king Charles II.

SUPPORTERS.] Two eagles proper.

MOTTO.] Consilio et animis.

CHIEF SEATS.] At Lauder Forth, in the county of Berwick; also at Hatton, in the county of Edinburgh, or Mid Lothian.

CAMPBELL, Earl of LOUDOUN.

THE family of Loudoun seems to have taken its sirname from the lordship of Loudoun, in the shire of Air, where it hath long flourished; and thereof was James Loudoun, whose daughter and heir being married to Sir Reginald de Crawfurd, one of the branches of the noble family of Crawfurd, brought to him the said barony, with many other lands, and by him had Hugh their heir, whose son Hugh left issue Sir Reginald, and a daughter, Margaret, wife of Sir Malcolm Wallace, knight, and mother of the immortal Sir William Wallace. His son, Sir Reginald, swore fealty to Edward I. of England, in 1296, and was basely murdered at Air in 1297, leaving issue a son, another Sir Reginald, who had issue only a daughter, Susanna, his sole heir, who married Sir Duncan Campbell, who, with his said wife, got a charter in 1318, to erect the lands of Loudoun, Stevenston, &c. into one free barony, to them and their heirs, or failing, to the nearest heir of the said Susanna.

To Sir Duncan, and Susan his wife, succeeded Sir Andrew, their son, the father of Sir Hugh Campbell, who lived in the reign of James I. and had a son, Sir George, who was one of the hostages for the ransom of that king from his captivity in England, in 1424. To him succeeded another Sir George, his son, the father of a third Sir George, who marrying Agnes, daughter

daughter of Gilbert lord Kennedy, had two sons and two daughters; Elizabeth, married to Robert lord Erskine, ancestor of the earl of Mar; and Margaret, to Sir Allan Lockhart of Lee. The sons were, Sir Hugh, and George, ancestor of the Campbells of Killoch.

Sir Hugh, the eldest, succeeded. He married Isabel, daughter of Sir Thomas Wallace of Craigie, and dying in 1508, left issue Sir Hugh, his successor, and five daughters; Annabella, married to Sir Thomas Boswell of Auchinleck; and secondly, to Sir John Cunninghame of Caprington; Helen, to Laurence Crawfurd, ancestor of the earl of Crawfurd; Isabel, to Mungo Muir of Rowallan; Janet, to —— Campbell of Cesnock; and Margaret, to Thomas Kennedy of Bargony. He died in 1508, and was succeeded by his said son, Sir Hugh, who marrying lady Elizabeth Stewart, daughter of Matthew, earl of Lennox, had a daughter, Marian, wife of James Carmichael of Hyndford; and Sir Matthew, his heir, who married Isabel, daughter of Sir John Drummond of Innerpeffry, by Jane his wife, natural daughter to king James IV. and by her had issue two sons and seven daughters; Sir Hugh, his successor; and Matthew, who signalized himself in Germany, and from whom the famous marshal count Loudoun, or Laudohn, a chief general of the empress queen of Hungary, is descended: Margaret was wife of Robert Montgomery of Giffen; and secondly, of Lodowic, duke of Lenox; Marian, of Thomas lord Boyd; Jane, of Sir John Wallace of Craigie; Agnes, of Sir William Cunninghame of Caprington; Isabel, of William Crawfurd of Lochnorris; Anne, of Robert lord Kirkcudbright; and Annabella, of Daniel Ker of Kersland; and secondly, of David Dunbar of Enterkin. The eldest son, Hugh, succeeded, and was, by king James VI. created lord Loudoun, and made one of the privy council. He married Margaret, daughter of Sir John Gordon of Lochinvar, ancestor of viscount Kenmure, and by her had issue, George, his heir apparent, and three daughters; Juliana, married to Sir Colin Campbell of Glenorchy, bart. ancestor of the earl of Breadalbane; Isabel, to Sir John Maxwell of Pollock; and Margaret, to John Kennedy of Blairquhan. His second wife was lady Isabel, daughter of William earl of Gowrie, by whom he had two daughters, one of them the wife of Sir William Cunninghame of Cunninghame-head, and the other of David Crawfurd of Kerse, Esq; George, his heir-apparent, dying before his father, left by lady Jane Fleming, his wife, daughter of John, the first earl of Wigton, two daughters, Margaret, baroness of Loudoun; and Anne, wife of Sir Hugh Campbell of Cesnock. The eldest daughter succeeded her grandfather, and marrying

John Campbell, eldest son of Sir James Campbell of Lawers, son of Sir John, son of Archibald, son of James, son of Sir

John

John Campbell of Lawers, who was son of Sir Colin Campbell, first baron of Glenorchy, by his last wife, Margaret, daughter of Sir Luke Stirling of Keir; he was, by king Charles I. created earl of Loudoun, and in 1641, was appointed lord high chancellor of Scotland. In 1648, when the king was beheaded, and the parliament met again, he was chosen president of that session, which ordered the proclamation of king Charles II. but when his majesty was defeated at Worcester, his lordship was not only deprived of his office, but forced, for the security of his person, to fly into the Highlands, where he lay concealed, being by the powers then prevailing outlawed and forfeited: And afterwards, when Cromwell granted an indemnity to the people of Scotland, he and his son, lord Mauchlane, were particularly excepted. He lived, however, to be restored, at the coming of Charles II. and sat in the Scotch parliament in 1661. He had issue James, his heir, and two daughters, lady Jane, married to George Maul, the second earl of Panmure; and lady Ann, to John Elphingston, lord Balmerino.

James lord Mauchlane, second earl, who succeeded his father, married lady Margaret Montgomery, daughter of Hugh, seventh earl of Eglington; and dying in 1683, left issue three sons, Hugh, lord Mauchlane; colonel John Campbell of Skanstoun; and Sir James Campbell of Lawers, knight of the bath, groom of the bedchamber to king George II. governor of Edinburgh castle, a major general, and colonel of the Scots Greys, who was killed at the battle of Fontenoy, in 1745, leaving issue a son, by lady Jane his wife, daughter of David, earl of Glasgow, who took the name of Muir: also four daughters, lady Margaret, the third wife of Colin Lindsay, earl of Balcarras; lady Jane, married to Sir James Campbell of Aberuchil, Bart. lady Christian, to George Ross of Galston, Esq; and lady Eleanor, first, to James viscount Primrose, and secondly, to John earl of Stair. He died in 1683, and was succeeded by his eldest son,

Hugh, third earl of Loudoun, who was a privy counsellor to king William III. and by him made an extraordinary lord of session; and in August 1704, was elected a knight of the ancient order of the thistle, and appointed one of the principal secretaries of state. In March following, he was appointed one of the commissioners to treat of a union between the two kingdoms; which being concluded, he was elected one of the sixteen peers for Scotland, and so returned for the first seven parliaments of Great Britain. In November 1714, he was sworn of the privy council to king George I. and in 1722, appointed his majesty's high commissioner to the general assembly of the church of Scotland. In October 1727, king George II. was pleased to grant him a yearly pension of two thousand pounds for life. In March 1728, he was again appointed the king's high

high commissioner to the kirk of Scotland, and died in 1732. His lordship married lady Margaret Dalrymple, daughter of John earl of Stair, and by her had two daughters, lady Betty; and lady Margaret, wife of John Campbell of Shawfield, Esq; and a son,

John, the present and fourth earl, who hath been elected one of the peers for Scotland in the four last, as well as in the present parliament. He is also colonel of the thirtieth regiment of foot, and governor of Edinburgh castle, and was very active in his majesty's service during the rebellion 1745. On the eighth of March 1755, he was made a major general of his majesty's forces; in January 1756, governor of Virginia; and commander in chief of all his majesty's forces in America, in March following. In January 1758, he was made lieutenant general of his majesty's forces; and that year was, at his own request, recalled from his command in North America. His lordship is a fellow of the royal society.

TITLES.] The right honourable John Campbell, earl and baron of Loudoun, and lord Mauchlane, one of the sixteen peers for Scotland, governor of Edinburgh castle, a lieutenant general, colonel of the thirtieth regiment of foot, and F. R. S.

CREATIONS.] Baron of Loudoun in Cunninghame, in the county of Air, 1604, by James VI. and earl of the same place, 12 May 1633, the 9th of Charles I.

ARMS.] Gyrony of eight pieces, ruby and ermine, being the field of Crawfurd of Loudoun, who bore gules, a fess ermine.

CREST.] On a wreath, an eagle displayed, with two heads ruby, in a flame proper, looking towards a sun with the dexter head.

SUPPORTERS.] On the dexter side, a chevalier in armour, plumed on the head with three feathers ruby, and holding a spear in his right hand: on the sinister, a lady nobly drest, plumed on the head with three feathers pearl, and holding in her left hand a letter of challenge.

MOTTO.] I bide my time.

CHIEF SEAT.] At Loudoun castle, in Cunningham, in the shire of Air.

HAY, Earl of KINNOUL.

THIS noble family is a branch of the illustrious family of Errol, and is sprung from Sir William Hay, ancestor of the house of Leys, who was second son of Sir David, and brother german of Sir Gilbert Hay of Errol, who flourished in the reign of king Alexander III. From him was lineally descended Sir Edmund Hay of Melginch, who made a considerable figure in the reign of king James IV. He was father of Sir

Peter,

Peter, the father of Sir Patrick, who was in much estimation with king James VI. George, his second son, being, by the care of his father, well brought up, was, for the improvement of his education, sent to France, where he spent some years under the tuition of the learned Edmund Hay, his uncle: soon after his return, being about twenty-one years of age, he was introduced to the court of king James VI. (of England) by his kinsman James Hay, viscount Doncaster, and earl of Carlisle; and in a very short time raised to be one of the gentlemen of his majesty's bedchamber, and had a gift of the Carthusian priory at Perth.

He was by the said king preferred to the office of clerk register, in 1616, and in 1622, made lord high chancellor of Scotland; in which post he was continued by king Charles I. who esteeming him a wise and able servant, worthy of the trust reposed in him, was pleased to advance him to the dignity of viscount Dupplin, and earl of Kinnoul; and the chancellor's place he kept till his death, December 16, 1634, being the space of fourteen years. He married Margaret, daughter of Sir James Haliburton of Pitcur, and by her had issue Sir Peter, who died unmarried; and George, his successor; and a daughter, lady Margaret, married to Alexander Lindsay, lord Spinzy. He was succeeded by his only surviving son,

George, second earl, who was made captain of the yeomen of the guard to Charles I. and one of his privy council; and upon the breaking out of the war in that reign, he applied himself to the king's service with great courage and constancy; but lost most of his estate in the pursuit of his loyalty and duty to his majesty, in which he continued to the end of his life. He married lady Ann, eldest daughter of William, the seventh earl of Moreton, and had issue by her a son, William, and two daughters, lady Mary, married to William earl Marshal; and lady Catharine, to Sir James Baird of Auchmedden.

William, who succeeded his said father, and was third earl, marrying to his second wife, lady Elizabeth, daughter of James earl of Salisbury, by her had issue two sons, George his successor, and William; and dying in 1677, was succeeded by his eldest son,

George, fourth earl of Kinnoul, who died in Hungary, 1687, without issue, and was succeeded by his brother,

William, fifth earl, who dying a batchelor in 1709, the hohour descended to Thomas Hay of Balhusy, near Perth, the next male heir.

Which Thomas, sixth earl, was the brother and heir of George Hay of Balhusy, son of Peter Hay of the same place, third son of Sir Patrick Hay of Melginch, and brother of George, first earl of Kinnoul; and so succeeding, was elected one of the sixteen peers in the third and fourth British parliaments.

ments. In 1715, he was committed to Edinburgh castle, as a person concerned in the rebellion, but was soon after released without trial.

He married Elizabeth, daughter of William Drummond, viscount Strathallan, and had issue by her three sons and two daughters; lady Mary, married to John Erskine, the last earl of Mar; and lady Elizabeth, to James Ogilvy, earl of Finlater and Seafield. The youngest son, colonel John Hay of Cromlich, married Marjory, daughter of David Murray, viscount Stormont. In 1715, he followed the pretender from Scotland, who gave him the title of earl of Inverness: William, the second, died without issue; and

George-Henry, the eldest, viscount Dupplin, in 1711, and in his father's life-time, was one of the tellers of the exchequer, and created a peer of Great Britain by queen Anne, being then representative for Fowey in Cornwall.

In 1718, he succeeded his father as seventh earl of Kinnoul, and was appointed ambassador to Constantinople, where he resided till 1727. In 1709, he married lady Abigail Harley, youngest daughter of Robert earl of Oxford, and by her, who died July 15, 1750, had issue four sons and six daughters, ladies Margaret, Elizabeth, Ann, Abigail, and Henrietta, married July 30, 1754, to Robert Roper of Trimden, in the county of Durham, L.L.D. and lady Mary, the wife of Dr. John Hume, bishop of Salisbury. The sons were, Thomas, viscount Dupplin; Robert, the second son, who took the name and arms of Drummond, as heir of entail to his great grandfather, William Drummond, viscount Strathallan, and being a chaplain to his majesty, was in 1748 elected bishop of St. Asaph, and in the same year married Henrietta, daughter of Peter Auriol, merchant in London, and has issue six sons and one daughter. In 1761, he was elected bishop of Salisbury, and the same year archbishop of York, and sworn of the privy council; John, rector of Epworth in the county of Lincoln, died unmarried in 1751; and Henry-Edward was consul general in Portugal, in May 1754, and in 1762, plenipotentiary to the same king; who married Mary, daughter of Peter Flower, merchant in London, by whom he has three sons and three daughters. His lordship dying the 29th of June 1758, was succeeded by his eldest son,

Thomas, the eighth and present earl, who was a commissioner of the revenue in Ireland, after which he was a commissioner of the board of trade in England, one of the lords of the treasury, and a member in the three parliaments for the town of Cambridge, in the two last of which he had been chairman of the committee of privileges and elections. In December 1755, he was made joint pay-master of the forces with the earl of Darlington. His lordship is a privy counsellor,

lor, recorder of Cambridge, and chancellor of the university of St. Andrews. In 1757, he was appointed first lord of trade; and in 1759, ambassador to the king of Portugal. He was soon afterwards appointed chancellor of the dutchy of Lancaster; but resigned all his employments in November 1762. In June 1741, he married Constantia, daughter of John Kirle Ernle, of Whetham, in Wiltshire, Esq; she died June 29, 1753, without surviving issue.

TITLES.] The right honourable Thomas Hay, earl of Kinnoul, viscount Dupplin, and baron of Kinfauns, in Scotland; (and baron Hay of Pedwarden in England.)

CREATIONS.] Lord Hay of Kinfauns, and viscount Dupplin in Perthshire, 4 May 1627, earl of Kinnoul in the same county, 25 May 1633, by king Charles I. (and baron Hay of Pedwarden, in the county of Hereford, 31 December 1711, the 10th of queen Ann.)

ARMS.] Quarterly, 1st and 4th sapphire, a unicorn rampant pearl, armed, mained, and unguled topaz, within a border of the last, charged with eight half thistles emerald, and as many half roses ruby, joined together by way of party per pale, given to the family when created earl, as a coat of augmentation, the unicorn and border being part of the royal atchievement, and the thistles and roses conjoined, representing the union of the two kingdoms in the person of king James VI. The 2d and 3d pearl, three escutcheons ruby, for the name of Hay.

CREST.] On a wreath, a countryman couped at the knees, vested in grey, his waistcoat ruby, and bonnet sapphire, bearing on his right shoulder an ox yoke proper.

SUPPORTERS.] Two countrymen habited as the crest, the dexter holding over his shoulder the culter of a plough, and the sinister the paddle, both proper.

MOTTO.] Renovate animos.

CHIEF SEATS.] At Dupplin and Balhousie, adjoining, in Perthshire; and at Brodesworth in Yorkshire.

CRICHTON, Earl of DUMFRIES and STAIR.

THIS noble family is a branch of that of Mid-Lothian, who in the time of king Malcolm III. came, it is said, from Hungary, of which was Sir William Crichton, knight, who in the reign of king Robert I. marrying Isabel de Ross, daughter and coheir of Robert de Ross, lord of Sanquhar, with her had half that barony; and from that match descended Sir Robert Crichton, knight, so made by king James II. to whom he was one of the privy council; and he marrying Elizabeth, daughter and heir of Sir William Erskine of Kinnoul, in the
county

county of Perth, thereby greatly enriched himself, and by her had issue, amongst other children,

Robert, their heir, who signalized himself greatly in the wars against Alexander duke of Albany, and James earl of Douglas, in behalf of king James III. who thereupon rewarded him with several lands, and dignified him with the title of lord Crichton, or Crighton, about the year 1485. He married lady Marian Stewart, daughter of John earl of Lennox, by whom he had a son, Robert, and a daughter, Marian, married to Malcolm Crawfurd of Kilberny, ancestor of the earl of Crawfurd.

Robert, the son, second lord, marrying Elizabeth, daughter of Sir Cuthbert Murray of Cockpool, by her had a son and successor,

William, third lord, who married Elizabeth, daughter of Malcolm lord Fleming, and by her he had three sons, Robert, Edward, and John, of Rayhill, of whom hereafter; also a daughter, Agnes, wife of Sir Andrew Ker of Cessford, ancestor of the duke of Roxburgh.

Robert, the eldest, succeeding, was fourth lord; and dying without issue,

Edward, the second, became fifth lord Crichton. He married Margaret, daughter of Sir James Douglas of Drumlanrig, and by her had a son, Robert, sixth lord, who being executed for the murder of one Turner, a fencing master, June 29, 1612, and leaving no male issue, the title devolved on

William Crichton of Rayhill, the son of his uncle John before-mentioned, who was created viscount Ayr, and earl of Dumfries, by king Charles I. in 1623, and to the heirs male of his body for ever. He married Euphemie, daughter of James Seton of Touch; and dying in 1641, left issue by her, three sons and two daughters, viz. William, Sir James, and John, a colonel in Germany: lady Mary, wife of Edward, viscount Carlingford, of Ireland, and lady Catherine, of Sir John Charteris, of Amisfield. He was succeeded in 1641, by his eldest son,

William, second earl, who was one of the privy council to king Charles II. and married Penelope, daughter of Sir Robert Swift of the county of York, Knt. and by her had issue two sons, viz. Robert lord Crichton, who died young; and Charles lord Crichton. Also three daughters; lady Elizabeth, wife of Alexander, earl of Eglington; ladies Penelope and Mary, who died unmarried.

In the year 1690 the said William, resigning his honour into the king's hands, got a patent to his heirs male and female, with precedency according to the former creation; and

Charles lord Crichton, his surviving son, having married Sarah, daughter of James Dalrymple viscount Stair, and dying before him, by her left issue William successor to his grandfather, and four daughters, viz. Penelope, of whom hereafter; Margaret, Mary, and Elizabeth.

Which William, third earl, dying a minor in 1694,

Penelope, his eldest sister, became countess of Dumfries, and married colonel William Dalrymple, son of John earl of Stair, and brother of the late earl, and by him, who died in December 1744, had issue six sons and two daughters, viz. William now earl of Dumfries and Stair; John, captain of dragoons, who died unmarried; James, after earl of Stair, but died without issue in 1761; Charles, Hugh, and George. Lady Betty, wife of John Mac Dowal, of Freugh, Esq; and lady Penelope. Her ladyship died in 1742, and was succeeded by her eldest son,

William, fourth and present earl of Dumfries, who when a youth embraced the military profession, served in the earl of Stair's Inniskillin dragoons, and in the third regiment of guards twenty-six years. He was aid de camp to the said earl, at the battle of Dettingen, in 1741; was elected a knight of the antient order of the thistle in February 1752, and was appointed the king's high commissioner, for investing James, late duke of Hamilton, with the same order, in March 1755. Upon the death of his late brother James, earl of Stair (who succeeded his uncle the renowned John Dalrymple, earl of Stair, in 1747,) he succeeded to that honour also in the year 1761, and is the fourth earl of Stair. He married lady Ann Gordon, daughter of William late earl of Aberdeen, and sister of the present, (who died 15 April 1755,) and by her had issue a son, William, lord Crichton, who died in the 10th year of his age. His lordship is now a widower.

TITLES.] The right honourable William Crichton earl of Dumfries and Stair, viscount Air, and baron Crichton of Crichton in Midlothian, viscount and baron Stair, and baron Dalrymple and Stranrawer, and knight of the antient order of the thistle.

CREATIONS.] Viscount Air in the county of Air, 1622, by James VI. and earl of Dumfries 10 June 1633, by Charles I. earl and viscount of Stair, lord Glentuce and Stranrawer, April 1, 1690, 1 William III.

ARMS.] Quarterly, 1st and 4th topaz, on a saltire sapphire, nine lozenges of the first, for Dalrymple; 2d and 3d topaz, a chevron cheque pearl and diamond, between three water budgets of the last, for Rofs; and over all, by way of surtout, an escutcheon pearl, charged with a lion rampant sapphire, for Crichton.

CREST.] On a wreath, a dragon's head couped emerald, spouting fire.

SUPPORTERS.] Two lions sapphire, each crowned with an earl's coronet, topaz.

MOTTO.

MOTTO.] God send grace.
CHIEF SEAT.] At Sanquhar in the county of Dumfries, forty miles south-west of Edinburgh.

ALEXANDER, Earl of STIRLING.

THIS family, according to antiquaries, was a branch of that of Macdonald; for Alexander Macdonald, a younger son of the lord of the Isles, obtaining from the family of Argyll the lands of Menstrie in the county of Clackmanan, where he fixed his residence, his descendants thereafter took the firname of Alexander. In the reign of James V. Andrew Alexander of Menstrie, marrying Catharine, a daughter of the family of Graham, by her had Alexander his heir, who married Elizabeth, daughter of Sir Robert Douglas of Lochlevin; and was father of Andrew, who was father of another Alexander, whose son

Sir William travelled abroad as tutor to the earl of Argyll, and after his return betaking himself to the court of king James VI. his majesty was pleased to prefer him to be master of the requests, and honoured him with knighthood, in 1604; after which, having by his own expence and management begun to settle the colony of Nova Scotia in America, the king by his royal charter, dated Sept. 21, 1621, made him a grant thereof.

In 1625, the first of Charles I. he was made chief governor of Nova Scotia; where his majesty, to encourage the Scots gentry to settle, instituted an order of baronets, with a large track of land to each, for the advancement of that colony; gave Sir William the privilege of coining copper money, and created him a viscount and earl, in 1633.

He was also by that king made secretary of state, in which office he continued till his death, being fifteen years; and his lordship marrying Janet, daughter and heir of Sir William Erskine, Knt. a cousin-german of the earl of Mar, by her had seven sons, William; Sir Anthony, who died without issue; Henry, of whom hereafter; John, Charles, Ludowic, and James; and two daughters, lady Jane, married to Hugh viscount Montgomery, whose son Hugh was created earl of Mount-Alexander in Ireland, which title he assumed in honour of his mother's firname, and lady Mary, married to Sir William Murray, of Clermont, Bart. of whom is descended Robert Murray, Esq; receiver-general of the customs in Scotland. The eldest son, William, viscount Canada, being his majesty's resident in Nova Scotia, died there in his father's lifetime. He married lady Margaret, daughter of William first marquis of Douglas, and had a son William, and three daughters, Catharine, married to Walter lord Torpichen; Margaret,

EARL OF STIRLING.

to Sir Robert Sinclair, of Longformacus; and Lucy, to Edward Harrington, Esq; page of honour to the prince of Orange, in 1630.

William, their brother, succeeded his grandfather, and was second earl, and dying without issue, his estate and honour descended to his uncle Henry.

Which Henry Alexander, third earl, who married a daughter of Sir Peter Vanlore, alderman of London, had a son Henry, fourth earl, who married ―― Lee, by whom he had issue four sons and three daughters, viz. Henry, William, Robert, and Peter, who all died without issue; lady Mary, wife of ―― Phillips, Esq; by whom she had William-Phillips Lee, of Binfield in Berkshire, Esq; lady Judith, of Sir William Turnbull, of East-Hamstead-Park, in Berks, Bart. and lady Jane, who died without issue. The earl died in 1690, and was succeeded by his eldest son,

Henry, fifth earl, who dying without issue, was succeeded in his estates in England by his two sisters, ladies Mary and Judith; but the title devolved upon William Alexander, son of James, second son of David, son of Alexander, son of John, second son of Andrew, fourth baron of Menstrie, uncle of Alexander, first earl of Stirling.

Which William, sixth and present earl of Stirling, was one of his majesty's council in, and surveyor-general of, New Jersey, and married Sarah, daughter of Philip Livingston, Esq; by whom he has issue two daughters, ladies Mary, married to John, son and heir of Alexander Robertson, of Stralochy, and Catharine.

TITLES.] The right honourable William Alexander, viscount and earl of Stirling, lord Alexander and baronet.

CREATIONS.] Baronet of Nova Scotia 21 May 1625, baron Alexander and viscount Stirling in 1626, and earl of Stirling 14 June 1633, all by Charles I.

ARMS.] Quarterly, 1st and 4th party per pale, pearl and diamond a chevron, and in base a crescent, all counterchanged; 2d and 3d topaz, a ship with the sails furled up diamond, between three cross croslets fitchy, ruby; and over all, in surtout, the badge of a baronet of New Scotland, which is pearl, on a saltire sapphire, the royal arms of Scotland, ensigned on the top with an imperial crown proper.

CREST.] On a wreath, a bear sejant erect, proper.

SUPPORTERS.] On the dexter side, an Indian man, with long hair, and a dart in his right hand, having a plain circle or rim of gold on his head, beautified with a plume of seven feathers, topaz and sapphire; and round his waist a like circle and feathers. On the sinister, a mermaid with her comb and mirror, all proper.

MOTTO.] Per mare per terras.

CHIEF SEAT.] At New York.

BRUCE, Earl of ELGIN and KINCARDIN.

THE immediate anceftor of this noble family was Sir George Bruce, of Carnock, third fon of Sir Edward Bruce of Blairhall, and younger brother of Edward, lord Bruce, of Kinlofs, who was knighted by king James VI. and appointed one of the commiffioners to treat of an union with England, in 1604.

But as the Bruces are fuch an antient and noble family, and divided into fo many refpectable branches, I fhall go back to their origin, before I continue my account of this noble branch of the family.

The firft of this antient and illuftrious family was Robert de Brus, a noble Norman, who came to England with William the Conqueror, from whom he obtained no lefs than ninety-four lordfhips in the county of York, among which was the barony of Skelton, which he made his chief refidence. Robert de Brus his fon was alfo one of the commanders for king Stephen in the Englifh army, which defeated the Scots at the battle of Standard near Northallerton in Yorkfhire 1138.

He likewife obtained from David I. king of Scots, all the land of Annandale; and dying in 1141, left iffue by Agnes his firft wife, daughter of Fulco Poynell, a fon Adam, and his fecond wife was Agnes Annand, with whom he got the lordfhip of Annandale, and had iffue, William de Brus and Robert.

Adam, who was heir to his father, fucceeded him in the barony of Skelton, and the other large poffeffions thereunto belonging; but after the fourth generation, the male iffue of that line failing about the year 1300, the reprefentation of this illuftrious family fell to Robert earl of Carrick, afterwards king Robert Bruce, fon of Robert de Bruce, earl of Carrick, fon of Robert, fon of another Robert, fourth lord of Annandale, by the lady Ifabella his wife, fecond daughter of prince David, fon of Henry, prince of Scotland, eldeft fon of king David I. brother of Malcolm IV. and William the Lyon. Which Robert, fourth lord Annandale, was fon of Robert, third lord, who was fon of William, fecond fon of Robert, fecond lord of Skelton, above-mentioned. This title of earl of Carrick fell to the crown in 1344, and afterwards was given to the fons of the kings of Scotland, the laft of the poffeffors of it, being Henry prince of Wales, fon of king James VI. (1ft of England.) But the title is now claimed by John Peyto Verney, the prefent lord Willoughby de Broke, an englifh peer, as fon of the Hon. John Verney, fon of George, late lord Willoughby de Broke, by Margaret Heath, daughter of Margaret Mennes, wife of Sir John Heath, who was the only child of lady Margaret Stewart, daughter of John Stewart, created earl of

Carrick by Charles I. who was second son of Sir Robert Stewart, of Strathdon, a natural son of James V. But to return, the said Sir George Bruce of Carnock, by his wife Margaret, daughter of William Primrose, of Burnbrae, Esq; ancestor of the earl of Roseberry, had three sons and four daughters, viz. Sir George, Robert, of whom hereafter, and Alexander; Ann, the wife of Sir James Arnot, of Farnie; Magdalen, of Sir John Erskine, of Balgony; Margaret, of —— Mercer, of Aldie; and Nicola, first of Sir John Morrison, of Dairsie; and secondly, of John Dick, of Braid, son and heir of Sir William Dick, some time provost of Edinburgh. His eldest son Sir George, was succeeded by Sir Edward, who was created earl of Kincardin and lord Bruce of Torry, Dec. 26, 1647, and dying unmarried, was succeeded by his brother,

Alexander, second earl of Kincardin, who had issue by Veronica, daughter of the baron Somersdyke, in Holland, Charles, lord Bruce, who died before his father; Alexander, lord Bruce; lady Mary, wife of William Cochran of Ochiltree, ancestor of the earl of Dundonald; lady Ann, of Sir David Murray, of Stanhope, Bart. and lady Betty, of Mr. James Boswel, of Auchinleck. He was succeeded by his only surviving son Alexander, third earl, who died without issue, whereupon the dignity devolved upon the heir male, Sir Alexander Bruce, of Broomhall, son and heir of Robert, second son of Sir George, of Carnock, before-mentioned.

Which Sir Alexander, fourth earl, was a great opposer of the union, and married Christian, daughter of Robert Bruce, of Blairhall, by whom he had issue three sons and five daughters, four of whom died unmarried, and lady Veronica was the wife of Duncan Campbell, of Kaims. He was succeeded by his eldest son Robert, fifth earl; but he dying without issue, was succeeded by his next brother, Alexander, sixth earl, who married; but having issue only a daughter, lady Jane, wife of John Napier, jun. of Kilmahew, was succeeded by his youngest brother,

Thomas, seventh earl of Kincardin, who married Rachael, daughter of Robert Pauncefort, of Herefordshire, Esq; by whom he had issue two sons and three daughters, viz. William, lord Bruce; Thomas, who died without issue; ladies Sarah and Christian, and lady Rachael, wife of James Drummond, of Lundin, heir male and representative of the noble family of Perth. He died at Broomhall in 1739, and was succeeded by his eldest son,

William, eighth earl of Kincardin, who married Janet, daughter and sole heiress of Mr. James Roberton, advocate, one of the principal clerks of session, by whom he had issue three sons, Charles, his successor; James, a clergyman, and Thomas, an officer in the army. And two daughters, ladies Rachael

chael and Christian. He died at Brest, in France, in 1740, and was succeeded by his eldest son,

Charles, ninth and present earl of Kincardin, who, upon the death of Charles, the last earl of Aylesbury and Elgin, succeeded to the title of earl of Elgin, and in failure of issue of the Laird of Clackmannan, is the undoubted heir male and chief of all the Bruces in Scotland. His lordship married the only daughter and heir of Thomas White, Esq; banker in London, by whom he hath issue two daughters, ladies Martha and Janet.

For the pedigree of the branch of the Bruces, lords of Kinlofs, which failed in Charles the last earl of Aylesbury and Elgin, above-mentioned, see COLLINS's *Peerage of England*, from p. 325—p. 347.

TITLES.] The right honourable Charles Bruce, earl of Elgin and Kincardin, and baron Bruce of Kinlofs and Torry.

CREATIONS.] Baron Bruce of Kinlofs in the county of Elgin, 8 July 1604, and earl of Elgin 21 June 1611, by James VI. earl of Kincardin and baron Bruce of Torry, 26 December 1647.

ARMS.] Topaz, a saltire and chief ruby, on a canton pearl, a lion rampant sapphire, being the original arms of Bruce of Skelton; and the field topaz, saltire and chief ruby, were the arms of king Robert I. they altering the field, from pearl as he bore it, to topaz.

CREST.] On a wreath, a lion passant, sapphire.

SUPPORTERS.] Two savages regardant proper, wreathed about their temples and waists with laurel.

MOTTO.] Fuimus.

CHIEF SEATS.] At Broomhall, near Dunfermline; and Dairsie, near Coupar, in the county of Fife.

RAMSAY, Earl of DALHOTSIE.

OF this illustrious family, which is said to have come originally from Germany, but which more probably came from England, and that the name is local, and first assumed from the lands and abbacy of Ramsay, in Nottinghamshire, was Simon de Ramsay of Dalhotsie, in Lothian, or county of Edinburgh, who in the reign of David I. 1140, was a witness to a grant of the church of Livingston, in West Lothian; and from him descended Sir William Ramsay of the same place, who was one of those barons, who in 1320 wrote and sealed that noted letter to his holiness the pope, asserting the independency of their country.

To him succeeded Sir Alexander Ramsay, his son, who was also of Dalhotsie; and he signalizing his loyalty to David Bruce, against Edward Baliol, who then usurped the crown of Scotland,

Scotland, in confideration thereof, was conftituted warden of the middle marches; and in 1332, he was made conftable of the caftle of Roxburgh, which he had taken from the Englifh. To him fucceeded his fon, Sir William, who treading in the fteps of his father, and taking up arms for the fervice of his king and country, was rewarded with the lands of Nether Liberton, as appears by a charter ftill extant under the great feal, and therein was fucceeded by his fon Sir Patrick, who died in 1377, and was fucceeded by his grandfon, Sir Alexander, who in 1401, loft his life at the battle of Homildon-hill, againft the Percies. His fon Robert was fucceeded by his fon, Sir Alexander, whofe fon, another Alexander, died before his father, and left a fon, Sir Alexander, who lived in the time of king James IV. and loft his life at the fatal battle of Floddon, September 9, 1513. He was fucceeded by his fon, Nichol de Ramfay, who was a faithful and loyal fubject to king James V. and to his daughter, queen Mary. He died in 1554, and was fucceeded by his eldeft fon, George, who was in great favour with queen Mary, and firmly attached to her intereft. By his wife, Elizabeth, daughter of —— Hepburn of Waughton, he had four fons and two daughters; John; James, of whom hereafter; Alexander and William; Margaret, wife of Sir John Cranfton of that ilk; and ——, of Sir Walter Riddel of that ilk. He was fucceeded by his eldeft fon, John Ramfay, in 1579. He died without iffue, and was fucceeded by his nephew, George, eldeft fon of his brother James, who had a brother, Sir John, who was created vifcount Haddington.

Sir George Ramfay was knighted by king James VI. and created a baron, by the title of lord Ramfay of Melrofs, which title he after changed to that of Dalhotfie. He married Margaret, daughter and fole heir of Sir George Douglas of Ellenhill, brother of William, earl of Moreton, and by her had iffue, William, his heir, and a daughter, Margaret, who was married to Sir William Livingfton of Kilfyth. His fecond wife was Margaret Ker, by whom he had two fons, John and James. Dying in 1629, he was fucceeded by his eldeft fon,

William, who was by Charles I. created earl of Dalhotfie. He married lady Margaret, daughter of David Carnegie, the firft earl of Southefk, by whom he had iffue four fons; George; John, of whom hereafter; James and William: alfo three daughters; lady Marjory, wife of James, earl of Buchan; lady Margaret, firft, of John Scrimzeour, earl of Dundee; and fecondly, of Sir Henry Bruce of Clackmannan; and lady Magdalen, who died unmarried. He died in 1674, and was fucceeded by his eldeft fon,

George, fecond earl, who marrying lady Ann Fleming, daughter of John earl of Wigton, by her had iffue, William; George,

George, a brave officer, lieutenant general of the forces, and commander in chief in Scotland, in 1705; and Robert: also three daughters, lady Jane, married first, to George, lord Rofs, and secondly, to Robert Macgill, viscount Oxenford; lady Ann, to James, earl of Home; and lady Eupheme, to Mr. John Hay. He died in 1675, and was succeeded by his eldest son,

William, third earl, who married lady Mary, daughter of Henry Moor, earl of Drogheda, in the kingdom of Ireland, by Alice his wife, daughter of William lord Spenfer, and fifter of Henry, earl of Sutherland, and by her (who afterwards married, secondly, John, lord Bellenden, and thirdly, Samuel Collins, M. D.) had issue two sons, George and William; and a daughter, lady Elizabeth, married to Francis lord Hawley, in Ireland. He was succeeded by his son, George, fourth earl, and he by his brother, William, fifth earl, who, as well as his brother, died without issue, in 1710; whereupon the honour and estate devolved on colonel William Ramsay, son of John, the second son of William, the first earl of Dalhotsie, who was the sixth earl of Dalhotsie. He married Jane, daughter of George, lord Rofs, and by her had issue three sons and two daughters; George, lord Ramsay, the eldest, (who died in March 1739) married Jane, daughter of the right honourable Henry Maul of Kelly, brother-german of James, earl of Panmure, by whom he had three sons, Charles; George Ramsay, Esq; advocate, now earl; and two daughters, ladies Ann and Jane. He died in October, 1739, and was succeeded by his grandson,

Charles, seventh earl of Dalhotsie, who on the 5th of January, 1754, was appointed captain of a company in the first regiment of foot guards, and to rank as lieutenant colonel; but dying in January 1764, was succeeded by his brother,

George, eighth and present earl of Dalhotsie.

TITLES.] The right honourable George Ramsay, earl of Dalhotsie, and lord Ramsay.

CREATIONS.] Lord Ramsay, the 25th of August, 1618, by James VI. and earl of the castle of Dalhotsie, in Mid-Lothian, 19 June, 1633, by Charles I.

ARMS.] Pearl, an eagle displayed, diamond, beaked and membered ruby.

CREST.] On a wreath, a unicorn's head couped, pearl, horned and mained topaz.

SUPPORTERS.] Two griphons proper.

MOTTO.] Ora et labora.

CHIEF SEAT.] At the castle of Dalhotsie, near Dalkeith, in Mid-Lothian.

STEWART,

STEWART, Earl of TRAQUAIR.

THE immediate ancestor of this great branch of the illustrious family of Stewart, was James Stewart, earl of Buchan, whose father was Sir James Stewart, commonly called The Black Knight of Lorn, and his mother Jane, daughter of John Beaufort, duke of Somerset in England, and widow of king James I. so that the said James, earl of Buchan, being uterine brother of king James II. was by king James III. constituted lord chamberlain of Scotland, and obtaining from him the lands and barony of Traquair, then in the crown, and marrying to his second wife, Margaret, a daughter of the family of Murray of Philiphaugh, by her had a son,

James, upon whom he bestowed the said barony, which, on the 18th of May, 1491, was confirmed to him by the royal charter of king James IV. He marrying Christian, sister and coheir of Richard Rutherfoord of that ilk, with her had the baronies of Rutherfoord and Wells, in the county of Roxburgh; and losing his life with king James IV. at the battle of Floddon, in 1513, left a son,

William, second baron of Traquair, who married Christian, daughter of John Hay, lord Yester, ancestor of the marquis of Tweeddale, and had four sons, Robert, Sir John, Sir William, and James, all successively barons of Traquair, and all, except the youngest, died without issue, and he continued the line; and having three sons, John, who died before him; Sir Robert; and a daughter, Isabel, wife of William Rutherfoord of Quarrie Holes, father of Andrew, first lord Rutherfoord. He died in the year 1606, and his eldest son, John, by his wife Margaret, daughter of Andrew, master of Ochiltree, left issue a son, who succeeded his grandfather, and was knight of the shire for the county of Tweeddale. He was also one of the privy council to James VI. by whom he was knighted; and by king Charles I. made lord treasurer of Scotland, and created baron of Traquair, in 1628, and earl of Traquair, lord Linton, &c. in 1633. When the said king was confined in the Isle of Wight, this lord, at his own charge, levied a regiment of horse in order for his releasement; but marching at the head of it to the battle of Preston, in 1648, he and his son John, lord Linton, were taken prisoners, and sent to the castle of Warwick, where the old earl continued for the space of four years, and his estate was sequestered.

He married lady Katharine, daughter of David Carnegie, the first earl of Southesk, and dying in 1659, left issue John, the said lord Linton, and four daughters; lady Margaret, married to James Douglas, earl of Queensberry; lady Elizabeth, to Patrick Murray, lord Elibank; lady Anne, to Sir John Hamilton

milton of Reidhouse; and lady Catharine, to John Stewart, Esq; The earl died in 1659, and was succeeded by his said son,

John, second earl, who married lady Henrietta, daughter of George marquis of Huntley, by whom he had no issue; and secondly, lady Anne Seton, daughter of George earl of Winton, by whom he had four sons and three daughters; William, his successor; George, who died before his father, unmarried; Charles, earl of Traquair; and John, who died without issue: ladies Elizabeth, Isabel, and Lucy. He died in 1666, and was succeeded by his eldest son,

William, third earl, who dying unmarried, his brother,

Charles, succeeded, and was fourth earl. He married lady Mary Maxwell, daughter of Robert, the fourth earl of Nithsdale, by whom he had issue, Charles; John, who married Christian, daughter of Sir Philip Anstruther of Anstrutherfield, in the county of Fife, by whom he had a son, Charles; and three daughters, Christian, Mary and Lucy; and six daughters; ladies Lucy and Anne; Mary, wife of John lord Drummond, eldest son, by the second marriage, of James, fourth earl of Perth; lady Catharine, of William lord Maxwell, son and heir of Robert earl of Nithsdale, by whom she has a daughter, the wife of William Constable of Effringham, in England, Esq; and had issue, Marmaduke, William, and Catharine; ladies Barbara and Margaret. His lordship died in 1741, and was succeeded by his eldest son, Charles, fifth and present earl of Traquair, who married Teresa, daughter of Sir Baldwin Conyers of Horden, in the county of Durham, Bart.

In the last rebellion, 1745, this lord was apprehended and committed to the Tower of London for a treasonable correspondence, but was bailed out in the year 1747.

TITLES.] The right honourable Charles Stewart, earl and baron of Traquair, and lord Linton.

CREATIONS.] Baron Linton, and earl of Traquair, in the county of Peebles, 22d of June, 1633, by Charles I.

ARMS.] Quarterly, 1st topaz, a fess cheque pearl and sapphire, for Stewart, 2d sapphire, three garbs topaz, for Buchan; 3d diamond, a mullet pearl; 4th pearl, an orl ruby, and three martlets in chief diamond, for the name of Rutherfoord.

CREST.] On a wreath, a garb topaz, surmounted of a crow, proper.

SUPPORTERS] Two bears of the latter.

MOTTO.] Judge nought.

CHIEF SEAT.] At Traquair, in the county of Peebles.

OGILVIE,

OGILVIE, Earl of FINLATER and SEAFIELD.

SIR Walter Ogilvie, the eighth generation of the family of Ogilvie, marrying Isabel de Durward, heiress of Lintrethan, by her had Sir Walter Ogilvie of Auchleven, and Sir John, ancestor of the earls of Airly. Which Sir Walter marrying Margaret, only daughter and heir of Sir John Sinclair of Deskford and Finlater, in the county of Bamff, with her had both these baronies; and thereupon assumed his arms, argent, a cross ingrailed, sable, which is now borne by his posterity. In the 18th of James II. he got leave of the king to fortify his castle of Finlater, with an imbattled wall of lime and stone, and all other necessaries for a place of strength. He had two sons, Sir James, his heir; and Sir Walter, ancestor of the lord Bamff; and a daughter, Elizabeth, wife of Nicholas Dun of Rathey. His eldest son, Sir James, succeeded, and married Mary, daughter of Sir Robert Innes of that ilk, and by her had issue four sons and five daughters, viz. Sir James; Gilbert; Alexander, killed at the battle of Floddon, in 1513; George; Margaret, wife of James Abercrombie of Birkenbog; Marian, of Patrick Gordon of Haddo, ancestor of the earl of Aberdeen; Catharine, of William Crawfurd of Federat, in Aberdeenshire; Elizabeth, of John Grant of Freughie; and Mary, of Alexander Urquhart, sheriff of Cromarty. He died in 1490, and was succeeded by his eldest son,

Sir James, who married lady Agnes Gordon, daughter of George earl of Huntley, and by her had issue Alexander, his heir, James, John, Patrick, and George; and two daughters, Elizabeth, wife of Sir James Dunbar of Westfield; and ——, first, of the laird of M'Intosh; secondly, of —— Monro of Foulis; and thirdly, of a son of lord Lovat. He died in 1510, and was succeeded by his eldest son,

Alexander, who got a charter from king James V. for erecting his lands of Deskford, Finlater, and Cathmore, into one intire barony, called ever after the barony of Ogilvie. He married Janet, daughter of Alexander lord Salton, and by her had issue James, his only son, and a daughter, Elizabeth, wife of Alexander Irvine of Drum, Esq; and by a second wife, Elizabeth, sister of the earl of Huntley, had another daughter, Margaret, wife of John Gordon, third son of Alexander earl of Huntley, upon whom, by the evil council of his said wife, he settled his whole estate, in prejudice of his son; but the said John Gordon being beheaded and forfeited, in 1562, queen Mary restored the whole estate to the said son James, who married Janet, daughter of Sir Robert Gordon of Lochinvar; and secondly, dame Marian Livingston, by whom he had issue a son,

son, Alexander, who dying before him, left issue by Barbara, daughter of Sir William Ogilvie of Boyn, ancestor of the lord Bamff,

Sir Walter, who succeeded his grandfather, and was created a baron, by the title of lord Ogilvie of Deskford. He married first, Agnes, daughter of Robert lord Elphingston, by whom he had a daughter, Christian, married to Sir John Forbes of Pitsligo, and was mother of Alexander lord Pitsligo: And by his second wife, lady Mary, daughter of William earl of Morton, he had James, his heir, and two daughters; Margaret, first married to James Douglas, earl of Buchan, by whom she had a daughter, who married Sir James Erskine, son of the earl of Mar, who in her right became earl of Buchan; and secondly, to Andrew lord Gray; and Mary, married to Sir John Grant of that ilk. He was succeeded by his said son,

James, who was by king Charles I. created earl of Finlater. He married lady Elizabeth Lesley, daughter of Andrew earl of Rothes, and by her had two daughters; lady Elizabeth, of whom hereafter; and lady Anne, wife of William earl of Glencairn. And the said earl having no male issue, procured a patent from king Charles, on behalf of his daughter, lady Elizabeth, and her descendants, whereby the dignity and title of earl and countess of Finlater was conferred upon her and

Patrick Ogilvie of Inchmartin, her husband, second earl; which Patrick dying in 1658, left by the said countess his wife, one son,

James, third earl, who married lady Ann Montgomery, daughter of Hugh the seventh earl of Eglington, by lady Ann his wife, daughter of James the second marquis of Hamilton, and by her had three sons, and one daughter, lady Ann, the wife of George Allardice, Esq; and died in 1735. The sons were, Walter lord Deskford, who died before his father; James; and Patrick, a colonel in the army. He died in 1711, and was succeeded by his eldest surviving son,

James, fourth earl, who having in his youth accomplished himself by travels into foreign parts, and studying the law, on his return in 1685, was admitted advocate, and afterwards chosen burgess for the borough of Cullen, in the convention of states, where he made a remarkable speech in favour of king James VII. In 1701, he was created earl of Seafield, and made secretary of state, in which office he was continued by queen Ann, and in February 1703, made a knight of the ancient order of the thistle; and in March 1706, being then lord chancellor of Scotland, he was appointed one of the commissioners for the treaty of union, which being concluded, he was elected one of the sixteen peers for the first parliament of Great Britain, as he was also for several other parliaments.

He

He was one of her majesty's privy council, one of the extraordinary lords of session, lord of the exchequer and treasury; and in 1711, succeeded his father in the title of Finlater.

In March 1727, he was appointed by king George I. his majesty's high commissioner to the church of Scotland; and in October following, king George II. was pleased to grant him a yearly pension of two thousand pounds. His lordship married Ann, daughter of Sir William Dunbar of Durn, Bart. by whom he had issue two sons and two daughters; lady Elizabeth, married to Charles Maitland, earl of Lauderdale; and lady Janet, first, to Hugh Forbes, Esq; son and heir apparent of Sir William Forbes of Craigyvar, Bart. and secondly, to William Duff of Braco, Esq; now earl of Fife, of the kingdom of Ireland. The sons were, James, now earl of Finlater; and George, a very promising lawyer, who died without issue. His lordship died in 1730, and was succeeded by

James, his eldest son, fifth earl of Finlater, and second of Seafield, and was one of the sixteen peers in the four last parliaments, and vice admiral of Scotland. He married first, lady Elizabeth Hay, daughter of Thomas the sixth earl of Kinnoul, and had by her a son, James lord Deskford, who in July 1754, was made a commissioner of the revenue, is trustee for manufactures, fisheries, &c. and a commissioner for the forfeited estates. He married lady Mary, daughter of John duke of Athol, by whom he has issue James, master of Deskford; and John Ogilvie, Esq; and two daughters, lady Margaret, married to Sir Ludovick Grant of that ilk, Bart. representative in parliament for the shire of Elgin; and lady Anne, to John earl of Hopeton. His lordship married, secondly, lady Sophia Hope, daughter of Charles earl of Hopeton, who died the 26th of April, 1762, without issue.

TITLES.] The right honourable James Ogilvie, baron Deskford, and earl of Finlater, viscount Redhaven, and earl of Seafield, sheriff of the county of Bamff.

CREATIONS.] Baron of Deskford, 4 October, 1616, by James VI. earl of Finlater, 20 February, 1637, by king Charles I. both in the county of Bamff; viscount Redhaven, 28 June, 1698, by king William III. and earl of Seafield, in the county of Fife, 24 June, 1701, by the same king.

ARMS.] Quarterly, 1st and 4th pearl, a lion passant gardant, ruby, crowned with an imperial crown, proper, for Ogilvie: 2d and 3d pearl, a cross ingrailed diamond, for Sinclair.

CREST.] On a wreath, a lion rampant ruby, holding between his paws a plumb rule erect, proper.

SUPPORTERS.] Two lions gardant, ruby.

MOTTO.] Tout jour.

CHIEF SEATS.] At Cullen; and Deskford, in Bamffshire.

LESLY,

LESLY, Earl of LEVEN.

THE immediate anceſtor of this branch of the noble family of Leſly (*ſee earl of Rothes*) was William Leſly, deſcended of the houſe of Balquhain, which yields for antiquity, to few in Scotland; which William Leſly, who flouriſhed in the reigns of James II. and III. had a ſon, Alexander, whoſe eldeſt ſon Alexander ſucceeded him in the lands of Kininvie, and George, who by his wife, Mary Stewart, had a ſon George, who had the command of the caſtle of Blair, in the reign of king James VI. and by Ann, daughter of —— Stewart, of Ballechin, had Sir Alexander Leſly, who was the famous general under the great Guſtavus Adolphus, king of Sweden. He returned to Scotland when the troubles broke out there, and in 1638 took the command of the army of the covenanters, with which, in 1640, he invaded England, defeated lord Conway, at Newburn, and took poſſeſſion of Newcaſtle. For theſe ſervices he got an order from the parliament for 100,000 merks; and at the treaty at Rippon, being one of the Scots commiſſioners, ſo pleaſed king Charles I. by his conduct, that he created him lord Balgony, and ſoon thereafter earl of Leven, to him and his heirs whatſoever, in 1641. He afterwards commanded the Scots army of auxiliaries, and the victory at Marſton Moor in 1644, was principally aſcribed to his conduct. However, he was afterwards very ſerviceable in the reſtoration of king Charles II. He was a volunteer againſt Oliver Cromwell, at the battle of Dunbar, but, with others of the loyal party, having a meeting in Angus, they were ſurpriſed by general Monk at Alyth, and all ſent priſoners to London, where they were confined in the Tower. The old earl had his eſtate ſequeſtred, but was ſet at liberty through the mediation of the queen of Sweden, whoſe favours he went to acknowledge in perſon, and was received with great reſpect, according to his rank and the ſervices he had performed for that crown. At length he returned to Scotland, and died at his ſeat of Balgony, at a great age, in 1662. He married Agnes, daughter of —— Renton, of Billy, by whom he had iſſue two ſons and five daughters, viz. Guſtavus, who died before his father, and James lord Balgony: lady Ann, firſt, the wife of Hugh, maſter of Lovat, and ſecondly, of Sir Ralph de Vall; lady Margaret, of James Crichton, viſcount Fendraught; lady Mary, of William lord Cranſton; lady Barbara, of Sir John Ruthven, of Dunglas, and lady Chriſtian, of Walter Dunlaſs, jun. of that ilk. His ſon, James, lord Balgony, was a brave officer, and dying before his father, alſo, left iſſue by his wife, lady Margaret Leſlie, daughter of John earl of Rothes; Alexander, afterwards earl of Leven, and Catherine, married to George, firſt earl of

L   Melvil,

Melvil, of whom hereafter. Alexander his son succeeded his grandfather, and was the second earl, who by his wife Margaret, daughter of Sir William Howard, and sister of Charles earl of Carlisle, had two daughters, lady Margaret, and lady Catharine; and dying in 1663, without male issue, was succeeded in the honours and estate by his eldest daughter, who married Francis, second son of Hugh earl of Eglington, but dying in 1674, without issue, was succeeded by her sister, lady Catharine, countess of Leven, who dying unmarried, the estate and honours devolved on her cousin-german, David, son of her aunt Catharine, to whom we now return.

Which Catharine, by her aforesaid husband, George earl of Melvil, had issue three sons and one daughter, viz. Alexander lord Raith, who died without issue; David, and James; and lady Margaret, wife of Robert lord Burleigh. Which David, her second son, thus in his mother's right, became third earl of Leven, and succeeded his father as second earl of Melvil; therefore it may not be improper to say somewhat of his paternal family.

Of this noble family of Melvil, which is said to be Hungarian, and came to Scotland soon after the Norman settlement in England, was Walter Melvil of Raith, of whom descended Sir John Melvil of the county of Fife, who in the year 1296, was one of those barons who swore allegiance to king Edward I. of England; and from him descended another Sir John, who, in the time of king James II. marrying Margaret, daughter of Sir William Scot of Balweiry, had two sons, William Melvil of Raith, and Alexander, of Finally.

William, eldest son, married Margaret, daughter of Sir Robert Lundy of Balgony, and had a son, William, whose grandson, Sir John, left issue Sir Robert, who betook himself to the court of France, where he was placed in an honourable station by king Henry II. and therein continued many years. Upon his return to Scotland, the great character he had acquired soon inclined queen Mary to call him to her privy council, who afterwards sent him ambassador to London, as he was again by king James VI. who also made him vice-chancellor of Scotland, treasurer depute, and one of the lords of session; and at last, to reward his services and merit, created him lord Melvil. He married lady Mary Lesly, daughter of Andrew, the fifth earl of Rothes; and dying in 1621, left

Robert, his heir, second lord Melvil, who was one of the privy council to the aforesaid king; but he dying without issue, the honour, by reason of an intail, came to John Melvil of Raith, descended from John, who was eldest son of Sir John, brother of Robert first lord Melvil.

John, who thus became third lord Melvil, married Ann, daughter

daughter and coheir of Sir George Erskine of Innerdale, brother of Alexander earl of Kelly, and by her had

George, his heir, who in the reign of king Charles II. retired to Holland, and there remained till the revolution; at which time coming to England with the prince of Orange, afterwards king William, he was made secretary of state, lord privy seal, high commissioner to the parliament, and created earl of Melvil. He married Katharine, daughter of James lord Balgony, son of Alexander Lesly, the first earl of Leven, as before observed, and we now return to the said David, their son.

In the reign of king William he was made governor of Edinburgh castle, and one of his majesty's privy council; and was continued in his former posts by queen Anne, who made him master of the ordnance; and being one of the commissioners who concluded the union, was thereupon elected one of the sixteen peers for North Britain, as he was in the next parliament. In 1706, he was constituted lieutenant general and commander in chief of all her majesty's forces in Scotland, after which he chose a retired life, and died in June 1728. He married lady Ann Wemys, daughter of Margaret countess of Wemys, by whom he had two sons, George and Alexander; and a daughter, lady Mary, married to William Gordon, earl of Aberdeen. George lord Balgony, the eldest son, married lady Margaret, daughter of David Carnegie, earl of Northesk, and dying before his father, left a son, David, who succeeded his grandfather, and was fourth earl; but he dying young, was succeeded by his uncle,

Alexander, second son of David, the third earl, and was fifth earl of Leven, who before his accession to the peerage, was one of the ordinary lords of session, and was afterwards elected one of the sixteen peers in the parliaments of 1747 and 1754, and his majesty's high commissioner to the general assembly for thirteen years, viz. from 1741 to 1753, inclusive. He married first, Mary, daughter of colonel John Erskine of Carnock, by whom he had David, his heir; and secondly, Elizabeth, daughter of David Monnypeny of Pitmilly, by whom he had issue colonel Alexander Lesly, and three daughters, viz. lady Anne, married to George earl of Northesk; lady Elizabeth; and lady Mary, married to Dr. James Walker of Innerdivot. And his lordship dying September 2, 1754, was succeeded by his eldest son,

David, sixth earl of Leven, and fifth earl of Melvil, who married Wilhelmina, daughter of William Nisbet of Dirleton, Esq; by whom he has issue three sons and three daughters, viz. Alexander lord Balgony; William and David: ladies Jane, Mary-Elizabeth, and Charlotte.

TITLES.] The right honourable David Lesly, earl of Leven and Melvil, baron Melvil and Balgony.

CREATIONS.]

CREATIONS.] Lord Melvil, 30 April, 1616, by James VI. earl of Leven and lord Balgony, in the county of Fife, 15 November, 1641, by Charles I. and earl of Melvil, by William III.

ARMS.] Quarterly, 1st and 4th sapphire, a thistle proper, ensigned with an imperial crown of the last, as a coat of augmentation; 2d and 3d pearl, on a bend sapphire, three buckles topaz, for Lesly.

CREST.] On a wreath, a chevalier in complete armour, holding in his right hand a dagger erect, proper, the pomel and hilt topaz.

SUPPORTERS.] Two chevaliers as the crest, each holding in his exterior hand the banner of Scotland.

MOTTO.] Pro rege, et patria.

CHIEF SEATS.] At Balgony, and at Melvil, both in Fifeshire.

TALMASH, Earl of DYSART.

OF this noble family, whose extraction is English, there was, in the 25th of king Edward I. one Hugh de Talmash, who held of the crown the manor of Bentley, in the county of Suffolk, and in the 29th, had summons among the knights of the said county to attend the king at Berwick, for an expedition into Scotland.

Sir Lionel Talmash of Bentley, marrying Ann, daughter and heir of the family of Helmingham, of Helmingham-Hall, in the county of Suffolk, with her had that inheritance, and therein was succeeded by John their son, who married Ann, daughter and heir of Roger Louth of Santry, in the county of Huntington, by whom he had five sons and four daughters; Lionel, the eldest son, succeeding, he, in the 4th and 8th of Henry VIII. was sheriff of the counties of Norfolk and Suffolk. He married Edith, the heiress of Joice of Creeks-Hall, in the county of Suffolk, and dying in 1553, by her left a son, Lionel, who was knighted by queen Elizabeth; and marrying Dorothy, daughter of Richard Wentworth of Nettlested, in Suffolk, by her was father of another

Sir Lionel, who succeeded him, and in 1592, was sheriff of Norfolk and Suffolk. He married Susanna, daughter of Sir Ambrose Jermyn of Rushbrook, in Suffolk, and by her had

Sir Lionel Talmash, who was created a baronet in 1611, and marrying Katharine, daughter of Henry lord Cromwell of Ockham, by the lady Mary Powlet, daughter of John marquis of Winchester, by her had

Sir Lionel, his heir, the second baronet, who was a burgess in parliament for the town of Orford, in Suffolk. He married Elizabeth,

Elizabeth, daughter of John lord Stanhope of Harrington, in the county of Northampton, by whom he had a son,

Sir Lionel, the third baronet, who succeeded him, and seven daughters; and the said Sir Lionel marrying lady Elizabeth, eldest of the two daughters and coheirs of William Murray, earl of Dysart, in Scotland, a cadet of the illustrious house of Tullibardin; which lady procuring letters patent in the 3d of Charles II. whereby the honour was granted to herself and her heirs, he by her (who afterwards married John Maitland, duke of Lauderdale) had Sir Lionel Talmash, afterwards earl of Dysart; Thomas, the brave general in the reign of William III. and William; also two daughters, lady Elizabeth, married to Archibald Campbell, duke of Argyll; and lady Katharine, first, to James Stewart lord Down, son to the earl of Murray; and secondly, to John, the nineteenth earl of Sutherland. He was succeeded by his eldest son,

Sir Lionel, first earl of his family, who was elected knight of the shire in 1698, and the succeeding parliament for the county of Suffolk. When queen Anne ascended the throne, he was constituted lord lieutenant, custos rotulorum, and vice admiral of that county. He had also the offer of a baron's patent, the first her majesty would create; but he declining that honour, was again elected to serve in parliament for the said county, in which post he continued till the union of the two kingdoms, being then incapable of sitting as a commoner, having in his mother's right, by virtue of the patent aforesaid, become a peer of North Britain, by the titles of lord Huntingtowr and earl of Dysart. In the latter end of king William's reign, this noble lord, who had few equals in goodness to the poor and his tenants, married Grace, one of the two daughters and coheirs of Sir Thomas Wilbraham of Woodhey, in the county of Chester, Bart. and by her had an only son, Lionel, lord Huntingtowr, and four daughters, whereof ladies Mary and Grace died unmarried, but lady Elizabeth married Sir Robert Cotton of Cumbermere, in the county of Chester, Bart. and lady Katharine, John Bridges, marquis of Carnarvon, heir apparent of James duke of Chandos, and died in January 1754. Lionel lord Huntingtowr, who died in his father's lifetime, 1712, left a son,

Lionel, second earl, born in June 1707, who on the death of his grandfather in 1726, succeeded to the dignity, being now earl of Dysart, and a knight of the thistle. In 1713, he married lady Grace Carteret, eldest daughter of John earl Granville, and by her, who died July 23, 1755, he had a daughter, born in 1732, who died in 1744. Lady Harriot, who died 1733; lady Grace, born 1735, now living; and a fourth daughter, born in 1745. Also six sons, born severally in the years

years 1734, 39, 40, 43, 50, 51, whose names I could not procure; but the eldest, lord Huntingtowr, married, on October 3, 1760, the youngest natural daughter of the right honourable Sir Edward Walpole, by whom he has issue.

TITLES.] The right honourable Lionel Talmash, earl of Dysart, and lord Huntingtowr, and knight of the ancient order of the thistle.

CREATIONS.] Lord Huntingtowr, in the county of Perth, and earl of Dysart, in the county of Fife, by king Charles I. 1646.

ARMS.] Pearl, a fret diamond.

CREST.] On a wreath, a nag's head couped pearl, between two wings erect topaz.

SUPPORTERS.] Two antelopes proper, attired and unguled topaz.

MOTTO.] Confido conquiesco.

CHIEF SEATS.] At Ham, in the county of Surry; at Harrington, in the county of Northampton; at Helmingham, in the county of Suffolk; and at Woodhey, in the county of Chester.

DOUGLAS, Earl of SELKIRK.

THE descent of this noble peer being set forth under the family of the duke of Hamilton, which is derived paternally from the house of Douglas, we shall here only observe, that William duke of Hamilton having, in the year 1687, resigned the honour of earl of Selkirk into the hands of king James VII. his majesty was pleased to confer it, with the first precedency, on the duke's third son, Charles, in 1687. Which

Charles Hamilton, first earl, was gentleman of the bedchamber to king William III. as in 1714, he was to king George I. and in 1727, to king George II. being likewise appointed sheriff of Lanerkshire. He was also one of the representatives for the peerage of North Britain, in the fourth, sixth, seventh, and eighth parliaments, till his death. And dying a batchelor in 1739, was succeeded in the title by his next brother,

John Hamilton, earl of Ruglen, who was third earl, and married first, the lady Ann, daughter of John, the seventh earl of Cassilis, by whom he had William, lord Dair, and two daughters; lady Ann, married to William Douglas, earl of March; and lady Susanna, to John Kennedy, the eighth earl of Cassilis. By his second lady, the widow of lord Kennedy, he had no issue, and the said William lord Dair dying unmarried in the life-time of his father, the titles of earl of Selkirk, &c. descended to his great nephew, Dunbar, grandson of lord Basil, his youngest brother.

Which

Which lord Basil, by his wife Mary, daughter and heir of Sir David Dunbar of Baldoon, Bart. had issue a son, William, who died young; Basil, his heir; and two daughters; Mary, the wife of John Murray of Philiphaugh, Esq; and Catharine, of Thomas earl of Dundonald. Basil Hamilton of Baldoon, Esq; his heir, married Isabella, daughter of colonel Alexander Mackenzie, son of Kenneth, third earl of Seaforth, by whom he had issue Dunbar, now earl of Selkirk; Basil, who died young; Mary, the wife of Ronald Macdonald of Clanronald; and Elizabeth, who died young.

Which Dunbar, now fourth and present earl of Selkirk, married Helen, third daugter of the honourable John Hamilton, Esq; son of Thomas, sixth earl of Haddington, by whom he has issue two sons and two daughters, viz. Sholto-Basil, who died an infant; Basil-William, lord Dair; ladies Isabella and Helena. His lordship, upon his accession to his honours, resumed the name of Douglas, the paternal one of his family.

TITLES.] The right honourable Dunbar Hamilton, earl of Selkirk, and lord Dair.

CREATIONS.] Earl of Selkirk, in the county of Selkirk, 14 August, 1646, by Charles I.

ARMS.] Quarterly, 1st and 4th argent, an heart gules, ensigned with an imperial crown, or, on a chief azure, three mullets of the first, for Douglas; 2d gules, three cinquefoils, ermine, for Hamilton; 3d gules, a lion rampant, argent, within a border of the second, charged with ten roses of the first, for Dunbar of Baldoon.

CREST.] A salamander in flames.

SUPPORTERS.] On the dexter, a savage wreathed about the loins, with laurel; and on the sinister an antelope, both proper.

MOTTO.] Jamais arriere.

CHIEF SEATS.] At the castle of Crawfurd, in the county of Lanerk; at Baldoon, in the county of Galloway; and at St. Mary's Isle, in the stewartry of Kirkcudbright.

CARNEGIE, Earl of NORTHESK.

THE descent of this noble family will be taken proper notice of hereafter, under the forfeited title of Southesk. Their immediate ancestor, Sir David Carnegie of Colathie, was the tenth generation of that family. His second son, John, had a son and successor, Sir John, who was created lord Lour by king Charles I. in 1639, and in 1647, earl of Ethie, &c. which title, with the king's approbation, he afterwards changed to that of earl of Northesk, and lord Rosehill. He married Magdalen, daughter of Sir James Haliburton of Pitcur, and dying

EARL OF NORTHESK.

dying in 1667, left issue two sons, David, lord Rosehill; and Sir James, ancestor of the Carnegies of Boysack, &c. and four daughters, lady Anne, wife of Sir Henry Wood of Bonnytoun; lady Magdalen, first, of George Lindsay, lord Spinzey; and secondly, of John Lindsay of Edzel; lady Margery, of James, son and heir of John Scot of Scotstarvet; and lady Jane, first, of William Graham of Claverhouse; and secondly, of Sir John Preston of Airdrie, Bart. And

David, the eldest son, second earl, succeeding in the honour, married lady Jane Maul, daughter of Patrick earl of Panmure, by whom he had five sons and two daughters, lady Jane, married to Colin Lindsay, earl of Balcarras; 2nd lady Magdalen, to John Moodie of Airdbikie, Esq: The sons were, David, lord Rosehill; James, ancestor of the Carnegies of Finhaven, &c. Patrick, of those of Lour; Alexander, of those of Kinfauns; and Robert, who died without issue. He died in 1677, and was succeeded by his eldest son,

David, third earl, who married lady Elizabeth Lindsay, daughter of John earl of Crawfurd, by whom he had issue two sons and four daughters; lady Christian, married to James Graham, duke of Montrose; ladies Jane, Margaret, and Anne, died unmarried. The sons were, David, lord Rosehill; and John Carnegie, Esq; He died in 1688, and was succeeded by his eldest son,

David, fourth earl, who was one of the privy council to queen Ann, in whose reign he was also sheriff of the county of Forfar, and chosen one of the sixteen peers for Scotland in the second, third, and fourth parliaments of Great Britain, He married lady Margaret, daughter of James lord Bruntisland, and Margaret countess of Wemyss; and by her, who died in March 1763, had two sons, David lord Rosehill; and George: Also five daughters, lady Margaret, married to George lord Balgony, eldest son of David, first earl of Leven and Melvil; lady Betty, to James lord Balmerino; lady Anne, to Sir Alexander Hope of Carie, Bart. lady Christian, and lady Mary; and the earl their father dying in 1729, was succeeded by his eldest son, David, fifth earl, who dying unmarried, in 1741, was succeeded by his brother,

George, sixth and present earl, who was made a captain in the royal navy, August 25, 1741; and on the 25th of June, 1746, being commander of the Preston man of war, in commodore Peyton's squadron, he behaved with great bravery against the French squadron commanded by Monsieur Bourdonnais, in the East Indies, and is now vice admiral of the white. He married lady Ann Lesly, daughter of the earl of Leven, and by her has issue, David, lord Rosehill, born in May 1749; ladies Elizabeth and Margaret.

TITLES.]

EARL OF BALCARRAS. 153

TITLES.] The right honourable George Carnegie, earl of Northefk, and lord Rofehill, and vice admiral of the white.

CREATIONS.] Lord Rofehill, 20 April, 1639; and earl of Northefk, in the county of Forfar, firſt of November, 1647, by king Charles I.

ARMS.] Quarterly, 1ſt and 4th topaz, an eagle diſplayed ſapphire, armed and membered ruby, for Carnegie; 2d and 3d pearl, a pale ruby, for the title of Northeſk.

CREST.] On a wreath, a demi leopard proper.

SUPPORTERS.] Two leopards regardant proper.

MOTTO.] Tache ſans tache.

CHIEF SEAT.] At Ethie, in the county of Forfar.

LINDSAY, Earl of BALCARRAS.

THIS noble family is deſcended of the branch of the Lindſays of Edzell, deſcended from Alexander, ſecond earl of Crawfurd, (ſee that family) whoſe third ſon was Walter Lindſay of Edzell, whoſe ſon, Sir David, was ſucceeded by Walter, and he by another Sir David, his eldeſt ſon, who made a great figure in the reign of James V. to whom David earl of Crawfurd conveyed his eſtate and honour in 1541, occaſioned by the cruel uſage of his ſons; but he afterwards conveyed them back again to that earl's grandſon, reſerving to himſelf the title for life, &c. &c. He was ſucceeded by his eldeſt ſon, Sir David, one of the ſenators of the college of juſtice. To him ſucceeded his eldeſt ſon, another Sir David, in the year 1620, and he dying without iſſue in 1648, was ſucceeded by his nephew, ſon of Alexander Lindſay of Canterland, ſecond ſon of Sir David Lindſay of Edzell and Gleneſk. To him ſucceeded his eldeſt ſon, David, and to him his ſon David, who dying without iſſue, the eſtate devolved on Sir David Lindſay of Balcarras, ſon of John, ſecond ſon of Sir David, earl of Crawfurd, abovementioned. Which David was created lord Lindſay of Balcarras. He married lady Sophia, daughter of Alexander Seton, earl of Dumferlin, and left iſſue a ſon,

Alexander, lord Lindſay, who was created earl of Balcarras; and dying in 1659, left iſſue by his wife, lady Ann Mackenzie, daughter of Colin earl of Seaforth, two ſons and two daughters; lady Sophia, wife of colonel Charles Campbell, ſon of Archibald earl of Argyll; and lady Henrietta, of Sir James Campbell of Auchinbreck. Of his ſons, Charles, the eldeſt, ſucceeded in the earldom, and dying unmarried, was ſucceeded by his brother,

Colin, third earl, who was a privy counſellor to king Charles II. and James VII. by whom he was appointed one of the commiſſioners of the treaſury. He married three wives, and by the ſecond, lady Jane, daughter of David earl of Northesk, he had a daughter, lady Ann, married to Alexander Erskine, earl of Kelly. By his third, lady Jane Ker, daughter of William, the second earl of Roxburgh, he had issue a daughter, lady Margaret, married to John Fleming, sixth earl of Wigtoun; and a son Colin, lord Cumbernald, who died unmarried. And by his fourth wife, lady Margaret, daughter of James earl of Loudoun, he had issue two sons, Alexander and James; and two daughters, lady Eleanor, married to James Fraser of Lonmay, third son of William lord Salton; and lady Elizabeth, who died unmarried. He deceased in 1722, and was succeeded by his eldest son,

Alexander, fourth earl, who was elected one of the sixteen peers for North Britain in the parliament beginning 1734; but dying in 1746, without issue, was succeeded by his brother,

James, now fifth earl of Balcarras, who in 1749 married Anne, daughter of Sir Robert Dalrymple, son of Sir Hugh, lord president of the session, by whom he has issue six sons and two daughters, viz. Alexander lord Cumbernauld; Robert, Colin, James, William, and Charles; ladies Anne and Margaret.

TITLES.] The right honourable James Lindsay, earl of Balcarras, and lord Lindsay of Cumbernauld.

CREATIONS.] Lord Lindsay, 7 June, 1633, by Charles I. and earl of Balcarras, in the county of Fife, by Charles II. 1651.

ARMS.] Quarterly, 1st and 4th ruby, a fess cheque pearl and sapphire, for Lindsay; 2d and 3d topaz, a lion rampant ruby, debruised with a ribband diamond, for Abernethy; all within a border of the 3d, semée of stars topaz.

CREST.] On a wreath, a tent proper, semée of stars as the arms.

SUPPORTERS.] Two lions sejant gardant ruby, each having a collar sapphire, charged with three stars as the crest.

MOTTO.] Astra, castra, numen, lumen.

CHIEF SEAT.] At Balcarras, in Fifeshire.

GORDON, Earl of ABOYNE.

THE immediate ancestor of this noble family was Charles, the third and youngest son of George, second marquis of Huntley, who having highly manifested his loyalty to king Charles I. in the time of the civil war, as also to king Charles II. during the usurpation, was, in recompence of those services, raised to the dignity of earl of Aboyne, &c. and dying in 1680, left issue by his wife, lady Elizabeth, daughter of John earl of Strathmore, three sons, Charles, George, and John; and a daughter, lady Elizabeth, married to John, son and heir of George earl of Cromarty. He was succeeded by his eldest son,

Charles, second earl, who dying in 1705, left by lady Elizabeth his wife, daughter of Patrick earl of Strathmore, a son, John, his heir, and three daughters, lady Helen, wife of George Kinnaird, Esq; and mother of Charles lord Kinnaird; lady Elizabeth, who died unmarried; and lady Grace, wife of James Grant of Knockando, Esq; He was succeeded by his son,

John, third earl, who married Grace, daughter of George Lockhart of Carnwath, Esq; and by her, who married secondly, James earl of Murray, had three sons, Charles, John, and Lockhart; and his lordship dying in 1732, was succeeded by his eldest son,

Charles, now fourth earl of Aboyne, who married lady Margaret, daughter of Alexander earl of Galloway, by whom he has issue a son, George, lord Glenlivet; and two daughters, ladies Catharine and Margaret.

TITLES.] The right honourable Charles Gordon, earl of Aboyne, and baron Gordon of Glenlivet.

CREATION.] Earl of Aboyne, in the county of Aberdeen, 10 September, 1660, the 12th of Charles II.

ARMS.] Sapphire, a chevron between three boars heads couped topaz, for Gordon, within a double tressure, flowered with fleurs de lis within, and adorned with crescents without, of the last, for Seton.

CREST.] On a wreath, a demi lion ruby, armed and tongued sapphire.

SUPPORTERS.] Two chevaliers in complete armour, each holding an halbert proper.

MOTTO.] Stant cætera tigno.

CHIEF SEAT.] At Aboyne, in Aberdeenshire.

COCHRAN, Earl of DUNDONALD.

THE name of this family is undoubtedly local, and taken from the barony of Cochran, in the shire of Renfrew. It is of great antiquity; and though none of them arrived to the dignity of peerage till the reign of Charles I. yet they were barons of some distinction for many centuries before, and had large possessions in those parts.

Their immediate ancestor was Waldevus de Cochran, who in the reign of Alexander III. was witness to the grant made by Dungal, the son of Sweyn, to Walter Stewart, earl of Menteith, of the lands of Skipnish, in the shire of Argyll; and his successor, William de Cochran, performed homage to king Edward I. in England, in 1296.

In the reign of king Robert II. Goseline de Cochran was witness to several grants made by that king; and to him succeeded

ceeded his son William, father of Robert, whose son Robert was father of another William, and he of another Robert, who was father of Allan, and he of John, whose son, John, marrying a daughter of the family of Lindsay of Dunrod, had issue a son,

William, of that ilk, who erected from the foundation the ancient seat of Cochran, and adorned it with large plantations. He married Margaret, daughter of Robert Montgomery of Skelmorly, in the shire of Air, by Mary his wife, daughter of Robert lord Semple, and had three daughters; whereof

Elizabeth, marrying her cousin Alexander, a younger son of John Blair of that ilk, the said Alexander, by the entail, changed his name to Cochran, and had issue seven sons and two daughters, viz. John, the eldest, who died without issue; Sir William, of Cowden; Alexander, colonel in the army of Charles I. whose son was laird of Manshiell; Hugh, ancestor of the Cochrans of Ferguslee, also a colonel in the army of Charles I. Sir Bryce, likewise a colonel in that army, who lost his life in the service, in 1650; Arthur, a captain in the army; and Gavin, ancestor of the Cochrans of Craigmuir. Elizabeth, the eldest daughter, was wife of John Lennox of Woodhead, Esq; and Grizel, of Thomas Dunlop of Househill. Sir William, the second son, succeeded, on the death of his brother, who was created a baron, and earl of Dundonald. He married Eupheme, daughter of Sir William Scot of Ardros, near Ely in Fifeshire, and had issue two sons, William, lord Cochran; and Sir John, of Ochiltree, ancestor of the present earl, of whom hereafter: And a daughter, lady Grizel, married to George lord Ross. William lord Cochran dying before his father, left by his wife, lady Katharine Kennedy, daughter of John earl of Cassilis, John, who succeeded his grandfather; William Cochran of Kilmarnock, married to lady Grizel, daughter of James Graham, the second marquis of Montrose; Thomas, of Pollskelly, and Alexander, of Bonshaw, both which families are extinct; and three daughters, Margaret, married to Alexander Montgomery, earl of Eglington; Helen, to Hugh earl of Sutherland; and Jane, first, to John viscount Dundee; and secondly, to William Livingston, viscount Kilsyth. He was succeeded by his eldest son,

John, second earl, who married lady Susan, daughter of William and Anne, duke and duchess of Hamilton, and by her, (who married, secondly, Charles, marquis of Tweeddale) had two sons, William and John; and dying in 1691, was succeeded by his eldest son,

William, third earl; but he dying unmarried, in 1705, the honour devolved upon his brother,

John, fourth earl, who in 1713 was elected one of the sixteen peers for North Britain. In the first of king George I.

he

EARL OF DUNDONALD.

he was made colonel of the fourth troop of horse guards. He married first, lady Ann, daughter of Charles earl of Dunmore, by whom he had issue William, the fifth earl, and three daughters; lady Ann, married to James duke of Hamilton; lady Susan, to Charles Lyon, earl of Strathmore; and lady Catharine, to Alexander Stewart, earl of Galloway. He married in 1715, to his second wife, the lady Mary Osborn, second daughter of Peregrine duke of Leeds, and widow of Henry duke of Beaufort, but by her had no issue; and dying in 1720, was succeeded by

William, his only son, fifth earl, who dying in 1724, in the seventeenth year of his age, the honour descended to

Thomas Cochran of Kilmarnock, sixth earl, son of William, second son of William lord Cochran, before-mentioned, by the lady Grizel Graham, daughter of James, marquis of Montrose, by whom he also had five daughters, Catharine, the wife of David Smith of Methven, Esq; Isabella, of John Ogilvy of Balbegno; Anne; Christian; and Grizel, the wife of John Cochran of Ferguslee.

Which Thomas, his son, sixth earl, married Catharine, daughter of lord Basil Hamilton, sixth son of William and Anne, duke and duchess of Hamilton; and dying in 1737, left two daughters, lady Mary, and lady Catharine, wife of captain Wood; and one son,

William, lord Cochran, seventh earl of Dundonald, who having been killed at the taking of Cape Breton, in July 1758, was succeeded by Thomas Cochran, son of William, son of Sir John Cochran of Ochiltree, second son of William, first earl of Dundonald.

Which Thomas, the present and eighth earl of Dundonald, in his younger years was a major in the army, and represented in parliament the shire of Renfrew, in 1722, and in 1730, was appointed one of the commissioners of excise in Scotland, which office he enjoyed for several years. He married first, Elizabeth, daughter of James Ker of Morriston, Esq; by whom he had issue a son, William, who died young; and a daughter, lady Grizel. His second wife was Jane, daughter of Archibald Stewart of Torrence, Esq; by whom he has issue six sons and one daughter, viz. Archibald, lord Cochran; Charles, John, James, Basil, Alexander, and lady Betty.

TITLES.] The right honourable Thomas Cochran, earl of Dundonald, and lord Cochran.

CREATIONS.] Lord Cochran, in Renfrew, 17 December, 1647, by Charles I. and earl of Dundonald, near Irwin in Airshire, 12 May, 1669, by Charles II.

ARMS.] Pearl, a chevron ruby, between three boars heads erazed, sapphire.

CREST.] On a wreath, a horse passant, pearl.

SUPPORTERS.]

SUPPORTERS.] Two greyhounds of the last, collared and leished topaz.

MOTTO.] Virtute et labore.

CHIEF SEATS.] At Paisley Abby, in Renfrewshire; at Kilmarnock, in Lenos; and at the castle of Dundonald, in Airshire.

KEITH, Earl of KINTORE.

THE descent of this noble family will be shewn hereafter, under the title of Keith, earl Marshal. We shall only observe here, that William, the sixth earl Marshal, marrying lady Mary Erskine, daughter of John earl of Mar, had issue, William, his successor; George, who succeeded his brother William; and Sir John Keith, who being instrumental in preserving the regalia of the kingdom from falling into the hands of the English during the usurpation of Oliver Cromwell, was after the restoration created knight Marshal, and earl of Kintore, by king Charles II. and made one of his privy council, and treasurer depute. He married lady Margaret Hamilton, daughter of Thomas the second earl of Haddington, and had issue a son, William lord Keith, and two daughters, lady Jane, wife of Sir William Forbes of Monymusk; and lady Margaret, of Gavin Hamilton of Raploch, Esq; He was succeeded by his son,

William, second earl, who marrying Katharine, daughter of David Murray, viscount Stormont, had issue John, his heir, William, and two daughters, lady Katharine, married to David lord Halkerton; and lady Jane. He was succeeded by his eldest son,

John, third earl, who married Miss Erskine, daughter of James Erskine of Grange, Esq; but dying without issue, was succeeded by his brother,

William, fourth earl of Kintore, who dying without issue in 1761, the honours are supposed to lie dormant; but the estate descended to George, late earl Marishal, as heir of entail, who being forfeited for his concern in the rebellion of 1715, in the year 1759, had a pardon granted him by king George II. and was thereby enabled to succeed to the said estate, and is governor of Neufchatel for the king of Prussia.

TITLES.] The right honourable George Keith, earl of Kintore, lord Keith of Inverury.

CREATIONS.] Lord Keith, and earl of Kintore, in the county of Aberdeen, 26 June, 1677, by Charles II.

ARMS.] Quarterly, 1st and 4th ruby, a scepter and sword in saltire, with an imperial crown in chief, topaz, all within an orle of eight thistles of the 2d, as a coat of augmentation

for

for preserving the regalia of the kingdom; 2d and 3d pearl, on a chief ruby, three pallets topaz, for the paternal coat of Keith.

CREST.] On a wreath, an aged lady, from the middle upwards———, holding in her right hand a garland of laurel, proper.

SUPPORTERS.] Two chevaliers in armour, each holding a pike in a centinel's posture, proper.

MOTTO.] Quæ amissa salva.

CHIEF SEAT.] At Kirk Hall, near Inverury, in the county of Aberdeen.

CAMPBELL, Earl of BREADALBINE.

THE immediate ancestor of this great branch of the family of Argyll, was Sir Colin Campbell, third son of Sir Duncan of Lochow, by king James II. created lord Campbell of Argyll, by his wife, lady Margaret, or Marjory, daughter of Robert duke of Albany. Which Sir Colin, by his wife Margaret, daughter and coheir of John lord Lorn, had issue a son, Sir Duncan Campbell of Glenorchy, who married lady Margaret Douglas, daughter of George earl of Douglas and Angus, by whom he had Sir Colin, Archibald, ancestor of the Campbells of Glenlyon; Patrick, and a daughter. He lost his life in the battle of Floddon, in 1513, and was succeeded by his eldest son, Sir Colin, who was succeeded by his eldest son, Sir Duncan, and he by his brother, Sir John, in 1534; and he by another brother, Sir Colin, and Sir Colin, in 1584, by his eldest son, Sir Duncan, and he, in 1631, by his eldest son, Sir Colin, who married lady Juliana Campbell, daughter of Hugh earl of Loudoun, but dying without issue in 1640, was succeeded by his brother, Sir Robert Campbell of Glenorchy, who married Isabel, daughter of Sir Lauchlan Mackintosh of Forecastle, by whom he had five sons and nine daughters, and was succeeded by his eldest son, Sir John, who by his wife, lady Mary, daughter of William earl of Menteith, had issue Sir John, and a daughter, wife of Sir Alexander Menzies of Weem; and by a second wife, Christian, daughter of John Muschet of Craighead, he had issue several daughters, of whom are descended, Campbell of Stonefield, Macnaughton of that ilk, Campbell of Airds, and Campbell of Ardchattan, &c. He was succeeded by his son, Sir John. Which Sir John, in consideration of the loyalty of his ancestors, and his own personal merit, was created earl of Caithness; but in 1681, that title, on a claim and petition, being allowed by parliament to be vested in George Sinclair, who was the sixth earl of Caithness, was instead thereof created earl of Breadalbine, with precedence according to the former patent. In 1692, he was appointed a commissioner of the treasury, and one of the privy council to king William III. and died in March 1716, in the eighty first year of his age. He married first, lady Mary, daughter of Henry Rich, earl of Holland, who was beheaded, and had issue by her two sons, Duncan and John; and secondly, Mary, countess dowager of Caithness, daughter of Archibald marquis of Argyll, by whom he had a son, Colin, who died in his youth; and lady Mary, wife of Archibald Cockburn of Langton, Esq; Duncan, the eldest son, dying before his father, without issue,

John, the second son, succeeded him, and was the second earl; and in 1725, was made lord lieutenant of Perthshire. In 1737, he was elected one of the sixteen peers, in the room of the earl of Orkney deceased, and was re-elected in the succeeding parliament. By his second wife, Henrietta, daughter of Sir Edward Villiers, and sister of Edward the first earl of Jersey, he had two daughters, lady Charlotte, who died unmarried; and lady Harriot, who was lady of the bedchamber to the princesses Amelia and Carolina. Also a son,

John, viscount Glenorchy, who succeeded his father in February 1752, and was third earl. He was installed a knight of the Bath, 17 June, 1725, was master of the horse to the three eldest princesses, and a member for the borough of Saltash, in Cornwall, in the parliaments of 1727 and 1734. He was also ambassador to the court of Denmark in 1726, and so continued by king George II. for some years, at whose coronation he carried the princess Amelia's coronet. In 1741, he was again elected to parliament for Orford, in Suffolk; but vacated his seat in 1745, by accepting the place of master of the jewel office. His lordship was afterwards chief justice in eyre of his majesty's forests south of Trent. In 1752, he was elected one of the sixteen peers for Scotland, and has been also so elected to the last and present parliaments. He is a doctor of laws.

His lordship, in 1721, married first, lady Amabell Grey, eldest daughter of Henry duke of Kent, and by her, who died at Copenhagen, March 2, 1726-7, had one son, Henry, and one daughter, who were born in Denmark; but the son died ten weeks after his mother. The daughter, lady Jemima, married, in 1740, Philip Yorke, now earl of Hardwick; and succeeded her grandfather, the duke of Kent, in 1740, as marchioness Grey, the title being so granted and settled that year. His lordship married secondly, in 1730, Arabella, granddaughter and heir of Sir Thomas Pershall, of Great Sugnall, in Staffordshire, Bart. with whom he got a very considerable estate, and had issue two sons, George, who died an infant; and John, lord Glenorchy, who married Wilhelmina, second daughter of William Maxwell of Preston, Esq; sister of the late amiable countess of Sutherland, and aunt of the present countess. In 1765, his lordship was appointed keeper of the privy seal for Scotland, but resigned it in 1766.

TITLES.]

EARL OF ABERDEEN.   161

TITLES.] The right honourable John Campbell, earl of Breadalbine, viscount Glenorchy, lord Campbell, and baronet; one of the sixteen peers in the present parliament for Scotland, &c.

CREATIONS.] Baronet of New Scotland, 29 May, 1625, by king Charles I. lord Campbell, viscount Glenorchy, and earl of Breadalbine, in the county of Perth, 28 January, 1677, by Charles II.

ARMS.] Quarterly, 1st and 4th, gyrony of eight pieces topaz and diamond, for Campbell; 2d topaz, a fess cheque pearl and sapphire, for Stewart; 3d pearl, a galley diamond, her oars in action, and sails furled close, for the lordship of Lorn.

CREST.] On a wreath, a boar's head erazed, proper.

SUPPORTERS.] Two stags of the latter, attired and unguled, topaz.

MOTTO.] Follow me.

CHIEF SEATS.] At Kelchurn castle and Glenorchy, in the county of Argyll, near the Loch Aw; at Finlarig and Taymouth, in Breadalbine, near Loch Tay; and at Great Sugnal, Staffordshire.

GORDON, Earl of ABERDEEN.

THIS antient family, who, it is probable, sprung from the noble house of Gordon; three hundred years ago, and for many centuries possessed a large estate in the county of Aberdeen: of which was Patrick Gordon of Haddo, who married Marian, daughter of Sir James Ogilvie, ancestor of the earls of Finlater and Seafield, who was succeeded by his son, George, and he by a son, James, who married Marjory, daughter of Sir Thomas Menzies of Pitfodils, by whom he had issue Patrick, Robert, of Faach, James, and David, ancestor of the Gordons of Nethermuir; John and Alexander. He died in 1582, and Patrick, his eldest son, dying before him, left issue by his wife, Agnes, daughter of Alexander Fraser of Muchil, one son, James, who succeeded his grandfather. By his wife Jane, daughter of William lord Keith, he had issue two sons, George and William, and died in 1624. His eldest son, George, died before his father, leaving issue by his wife, Margaret, daughter of Alexander Bannerman of Elsick, a son,

Sir John, who succeeded his grandfather. Which Sir John Gordon of Haddo, in 1642, was created a baronet; but two years after, for his adherence to king Charles I. and holding out his castle of Haddo against the parliament army, was taken prisoner, condemned, and executed at Edinburgh. He married Mary, daughter of William Forbes of Tolquhoun, and had issue by her two sons and one daughter; Sir John, and Sir
M   George;

George; and his daughter, ——, was the wife of Sir John Forbes of Waterston. Sir John, his eldest son, recovered the title and estate after the restoration, and died in 1665, leaving issue only a daughter, wife of Sir James Gordon of Lesmore, whereupon he was succeeded by his brother,

Sir George, who was by king Charles II. in 1682, made one of the lords of session, and president of the council, afterwards lord chancellor of Scotland, and created earl of Aberdeen, &c. He married Ann, daughter and heir of George Lockhart of Torbrecks, by whom he had issue George, lord Haddo, who died before his father; and William; and four daughters, lady Ann, second wife of Alexander Montgomery, earl of Eglington; lady Martha, of John Udney, of Udney; lady Mary, of Alexander Fraser, lord Salton; and lady Margaret.

William, their brother, who succeeded as second earl of Aberdeen, in 1720, was, in June 1721, elected one of the sixteen peers, in the room of William Johnston, marquis of Annandale, deceased, and was re-elected to the next parliament. He married first, lady Mary, daughter of David earl of Leven and Melvil, and by her had one daughter, lady Ann, wife of William earl of Dumfries, and died in 1755. His second wife was lady Susan, eldest daughter of John duke of Athol, by whom he had issue George lord Haddo, and lady Catharine, married first, to Cosmo duke of Gordon, and by him mother of the present duke, &c. and secondly, to colonel Staats Long Morris. His third wife was lady Ann, third daughter of Alexander duke of Gordon, by whom he had four sons and one daughter, viz. William Gordon of Fyvie, Esq; captain of a troop of dragoons; Cosmo, an officer in the guards; Alexander, an advocate; and Charles. The daughter, lady Henrietta, married Robert Gordon of Haugh-head. Esq; The earl, their father, dying in 1745, was succeeded by his eldest son,

George, now third earl of Aberdeen, who was one of the sixteen peers in the two last parliaments, being the tenth and eleventh of Great Britain. He married Catharine, daughter of Mr. Oswald Hanson of Wakefield, in Yorkshire, by whom he has issue two sons and four daughters, viz. George, lord Haddo, and William; ladies Catharine, Anne, Susanna, and Mary.

TITLES.] The right honourable George Gordon, earl of Aberdeen, and lord Haddo.

CREATIONS.] Earl and baron, on 30 November, 1682, by king Charles II.

ARMS.] Sapphire, three boars heads couped, within a double tressure, flowered and counterflowered with thistles, roses, and fleurs de lis, topaz.

CREST.] On a wreath, two naked arms, holding a bow to let fly an arrow,

SUPPORTERS.]

SUPPORTERS.]· On the dexter side, a senator of the college of justice in robes, proper; and on the sinister, a minister of state in his robes, proper.

MOTTO.] Fortuna sequatur.

CHIEF SEAT.] Haddo house, &c. in Aberdeenshire.

MURRAY, Earl of DUNMORE.

LORD Charles Murray, second son of John marquis of Athol, and brother of John, the first duke of Athol, was master of the horse to the princess Anne of Denmark, and to queen Mary, the second wife of king James VII. and was by that king created earl of Dunmore, &c. &c. In the reign of queen Ann, he was one of the privy council, and governor of Blackness castle, near Linlithgow; and dying in 1710, left issue by his wife Catharine, daughter of Robert Watts, of the county of Hereford, Esq; five sons and three daughters, viz. James, John, William, of whom hereafter; Robert, member for Wotton-Basset, in the last parliament of George I. and for Bedwin, in the second of George II. and was colonel of a regiment, a brigadier general, and died in 1738; Thomas, colonel of a regiment of foot: Lady Henrietta, married to Patrick lord Kinnaird; lady Ann, to John Cochran, earl of Dundonald; and lady Katharine, to John lord Nairn. He was succeeded by his eldest son,

James, second earl, who dying without issue, was succeeded by his brother,

John, third earl of Dunmore, who in 1713 was elected one of the sixteen peers for North Britain, and at the same time appointed colonel of the third regiment of foot guards. In 1727, he was again elected one of the sixteen peers, and continued so till his death, April 18, 1752. He was also a lord of his majesty's bedchamber, general of foot, and governor of Plymouth. He was succeeded by his next brother,

William, fourth earl, who married his cousin, Catharine, daughter of William lord Nairn, by whom he had issue three sons and four daughters, viz. John, his successor; Charles; William, an officer in the army; Lady Margaret; lady Catharine, wife of John Drummond of Logyalmond, Esq; ladies Jane and Elizabeth. His lordship dying in 1756, was succeeded by his eldest son,

John, the present and fifth earl, who in February 1759, married lady Charlotte, daughter of Alexander earl of Galloway, by whom he has issue two daughters, ladies Catharine and Augusta. In 1761, his lordship was elected one of the sixteen peers for Scotland.

TITLES.] The right honourable William Murray, earl of Dunmore, viscount Fincastle, and baron Murray of Blair,

EARL OF DUNMORE.

Mouillin and Tilimet, and one of the sixteen peers for Scotland to the present parliament.

CREATION.] Earl of Dunmore, in the county of Perth, 16 August, 1686, by James VII. and II. of England.

ARMS.] Quarterly, 1st sapphire, three stars pearl, within a double tressure, with fleurs de lis, topaz, for the name of Murray; 2d quarterly, 1st and 4th topaz, a fess cheque pearl and sapphire, for Stewart; 2d and 3d pally of six, topaz and diamond, for Athol; 3d grand quarter as the 2d, the 4th as the 1st; and over all, as a surtout, an escutcheon ruby, charged with three legs in triangle, conjoined in fess at the upper part of the thigh, and garnished proper, for the Isle of Man, as related to the earls of Derby.

CREST.] On a wreath, a demi savage, wreathed about the middle with a laurel, holding in his right hand a sword erect, proper, the pomel and hilt topaz; and in the left a key of the latter.

SUPPORTERS.] On the dexter, a savage wreathed as the crest, his feet in fetters, and the chain over his right arm. On the sinister, a lion ruby, with a collar sapphire, charged with three stars pearl.

MOTTO.] Furth fortune.

CHIEF SEAT.] At Dunmore and Fincastle, of Athol, in the county of Perth.

OBRIEN, Countess of ORKNEY.

GEORGE, fifth son of William, first duke Hamilton of the Douglas family, chusing a military life, and distinguishing himself by his bravery and conduct in the battles of Boyne, Aghrim, Steenkirk, Landen, Oudenarde, Ramillies, Hochstet, Schelenberg, Mons, &c. and in the several sieges of Athlone, Limerick, and Namur; at the attack of the last place, was made a brigadier general by king William, and on March 1, 1689, appointed colonel of a regiment, and afterwards created earl of Orkney, &c. in recompence of his merit. In the first year of queen Ann he was constituted major general, and soon after a lieutenant general; soon after which, in Feb. 1703, he was elected a knight of the order of the thistle. In 1708, he was elected one of the sixteen peers for Scotland, in the second parliament of Great Britain, as he was in every other parliament till he died. In 1710, he was appointed one of the privy council, and general of the foot in Flanders, where, in 1712, he served under James Butler, duke of Ormond. In 1714, he was appointed a lord of the bedchamber to king George I. and likewise governor of Virginia. In the beginning of the next reign, he was promoted to the rank of field marshal, and governor of Edinburgh castle. He married Elizabeth, eldest

daughter

daughter of Sir Edward Villiers, and sister of Edward earl of Jersey, and had issue by her three daughters, lady Ann; lady Frances, married to Sir Thomas Lumley Sanderson, knight of the Bath, afterwards earl of Scarborough; and lady Harriot, to John lord Boyle in England, and earl of Orrery and Cork in Ireland. The earl dying January 29, 1736-7, aged seventy-two years, his eldest daughter,

Anne, who was married to William Obrien, earl of Inchiquin, in Ireland, by whom she had two surviving daughters, succeeded him both in honours and estate. Her daughters are, lady Mary, married in 1753, to captain Obrien of the foot guards, by whom she has issue; and lady Ann. And her ladyship dying in December 1756, was succeeded by her eldest daughter,

Mary, now countess of Orkney.

TITLES.] The right honourable Mary Obrien, countess of the islands of Orkney, viscountess Kirkwall, and baroness Dechmont.

CREATIONS.] Earl, viscount, and baron, January 3, 1695-6, by king William III.

ARMS.] Quarterly, 1st sapphire, a ship at anchor, within a double tressure, with fleurs de lis, topaz, for Orkney; 2d and 3d, the quartered arms of Hamilton; and in the 4th, the arms of Douglas.

CREST.] In a ducal coronet topaz, an oak fructed and penetrated transversly in the main stem by a frame saw, proper, the frame of the first.

SUPPORTERS.] On the dexter side, an antelope pearl, his horns, ducal collar, chain and hoofs, topaz. On the sinister, a stag proper, attired, collared, chained, and hoofed, as the dexter.

MOTTO.] Thorough.

CHIEF SEATS.] At Cliefden, in the county of Buckingham; and at Taplow Court, near Maidenhead bridge, in the same county.

DOUGLAS, Earl of MARCH and RUGLEN.

LORD William Douglas, second son of William duke of Queensberry, by his wife lady Isabel, daughter of William marquis of Douglas, was created earl of March by king William, with whom he was in great favour. He married lady Jane Hay, daughter of John marquis of Tweeddale, and had issue three sons and three daughters, viz. William; John Douglas of Broughton, Esq; who died without issue; as did the third son, James, of Stow; ladies Isabel, Mary, and Jane. He died in 1705, and was succeeded by his eldest son,

William, second earl, who married lady Ann, countess of Ruglen,

Ruglen, as heir general of her father, John Hamilton, earl of Selkirk and Ruglen, or Rutherglen, who died in 1746; and had issue by her, who in 1746, married, secondly, Anthony Sawyer, Esq; paymaster of his majesty's forces in Scotland,

James, the third and present earl of March, who also succeeded his mother in the earldom of Ruglen. He is one of the lords of his majesty's bedchamber, a knight of the ancient order of the thistle, and was elected, in the year 1761, one of the sixteen peers for Scotland.

TITLES.] The right honourable James Douglas, earl of March, and baron Douglas of Niedpath, Lymn, and Manerhead.

CREATION.] Earl and baron, 20 April 1697, by king William III.

ARMS.] Quarterly, 1st and 4th, the whole arms of the duke of Queensberry; 2d and 3d ruby, a lion rampant pearl, within a border of the last, charged with eight cinquefoils of the first, for the title of March.

CREST.] On a wreath, a man's heart ruby, ensigned with an imperial crown proper, between two wings erect, topaz.

SUPPORTERS.] On the dexter side, a pegasus pearl, the same as Queensberry: On the sinister, a lion, as in the arms.

MOTTO.] Forward.

CHIEF SEAT.] At Niedpath castle, in the county of Tweeddale.

HUME, Earl of MARCHMONT.

ENough has been said, for the purpose of this work, of the antiquity, &c. of the noble family of Hume, under that of the earl of Home. Sir Thomas Hume, the seventh generation of that family, in a direct male line, flourished in the reigns of Robert II. and III. and was the immediate ancestor of the earls of Marchmont. Sir David, his second son, of whom this illustrious family is lineally descended, had two sons, Sir David and Alexander; Sir David had issue, by Elizabeth Carmichael, George and Sir Patrick, of whom hereafter. George succeeded his grandfather, and marrying Marian, eldest daughter and coheir of John Sinclair of Herdmanston, by her had issue a son, David, ancestor of the family of Wedderburn. Sir Patrick, his brother, married Margaret, one of the daughters and coheirs of John Sinclair of Herdmanston, with whom he got the barony and lands of Polwarth, which anciently belonged to an honourable family of that sirname, who flourished in the shire of Berwick for several centuries, till Sir Patrick Polwarth, knight, died without issue male, in the reign of Robert II. whose only daughter and heir, Elizabeth, married Sir John Sinclair of Herdmanston, by whom

whom she had a son, William, whose son, John, having a son, John, and he a son, John, who married Katharine Hume, daughter of Sir Thomas Hume of that ilk, he, in 1444, obtained a charter from king James II. of the barony of Polwarth, to himself, and Katharine his wife, and to their heirs; and leaving only two daughters, Mary, married to the said George Home of Wedderburn, in Berwickshire; and Margaret, to the said Sir Patrick, the son of Sir David Hume, laird of Wedderburn, who bore a cross ingrailed, sable, the coat of Sinclair; and three piles ingrailed gules, for Polwarth, which, he quartered with his own arms. Being a military man, he gave many proofs of his valour on several occasions, and particularly at the siege of Roxburgh, where king James II. was slain; and having a son,

Sir Patrick, second lord, who inherited his courage as well as fortune, he had many lands bestowed on him, for his good services, by James III. He likewise obtained from king James IV. divers lands in the counties of Stirling and Perth, and in 1499, was made comptroller of Scotland. He married, first, Margaret, daughter of Sir John Edmondston of that ilk, and had issue by her, Alexander, his heir; and secondly, Eleanor, daughter of Sir James Shaw of Sauchy, by whom he had one son and four daughters, viz. George, ancestor of the Humes of Argathy, in Stirlingshire; Alison, wife of Sir James Shaw of Sauchie; Janet, of Sir Andrew Ker of Ferniherst, ancestor of the marquis of Lothian; Mary, of Sir William Baillie of Lamington; and Margaret, lady abbess of North Berwick. He died in 1504, and was succeeded by his eldest son,

Alexander, third lord, who married first, Margaret, daughter of Robert lord Crichton, ancestor of the earl of Dumfries; and secondly, Margaret, daughter of Sir Robert Lauder of Bass. By his said first wife, he had issue, Patrick, and Alexander, ancestor of the Humes of Heugh and Rhodes; and by his second, three daughters, Margaret, wife of Patrick Hepburn of Craig; Catharine, of Robert Pringle of that ilk; and Isabel, who became abbess of North Berwick. He died in 1532, and was succeeded by his eldest son,

Patrick, fourth baron, who marrying Elizabeth, daughter of Sir Patrick Hepburn of Waughton, had issue, Patrick, the fifth baron; Sir Alexander Hume of North Berwick, and Adam Hume, rector of the church of Polwarth; and two daughters, Margaret, wife of John Baillie of John's Kirk; and Anne, of —— French of Thorndyke.

Patrick the eldest, fifth baron, who succeeded, married Agnes, daughter of Sir Alexander Hume of Manderston, and by her had six sons and three daughters, viz. Patrick; Alexander, rector of Logie; Gavin, ancestor of the Humes of Cleugh;

Cleugh; Sir John, of North Berwick, who was provost of Edinburgh in 1591, and ambassador at the court of England in 1593, and was ancestor of the Humes of Castle Hume, in the county of Fermanagh, in Ireland; David, of Rowiestoun, and George, of Belyhose: Margaret, wife of David Hume of Law; Agnes, of —— Edmonston of Woolmet, and Margaret, of Sir Thomas Cranston, of Crosbie. He died in 1592, and was succeeded by his eldest son,

Sir Patrick, sixth baron, who was by king James VI. made master of the houshold, gentleman of the bedchamber, and warden of the marches towards England. He married Juliana, daughter of Sir Thomas Ker, of Ferniherst; and dying in 1609, left three sons and three daughters; Elizabeth, married to Sir James Carmichael of that ilk; Jane, to Christopher Cockburn, of Chausly; and Sophia, to Joseph Johnston, of Hilton. The sons were, Sir Patrick; Thomas, of Coldstream; and George, of Kimmergham.

Patrick the eldest son succeeding, was by king Charles I. created a baronet. He married Christian, daughter of Sir Alexander Hamilton, of Innerwick, and had issue by her two sons and two daughters; Sir Patrick; Alexander, a brave colonel in the army; Juliana, wife of Richard Newton, of that ilk, and Anne, of Alexander, son of John Hume of Manderston. He died in 1648, and was succeeded by his eldest son,

Sir Patrick, who, in 1665, was knight of the shire for the county of Berwick; but after travelling abroad, and being obliged to leave Scotland after his return, and at length going to Holland, was received with great kindness and generosity by the prince of Orange, whom he attended into England in 1688; and being instrumental in the success of the revolution, he was made one of the privy council, and created lord Polwarth, and had an orange proper, ensigned with an imperial crown, given him for a surtout in his arms, as a lasting mark of their majesties royal favour for his great fidelity and zeal. He was likewise by king William appointed sheriff of the county of Berwick; in 1692, high commissioner to the parliament, one of the extraordinary lords of session in 1693, lord chancellor of Scotland in 1696, a commissioner of the treasury and admiralty, and created earl of Marchmont. In 1702, he was appointed by queen Anne, her majesty's high commissioner to the general assembly of the church, and one of her privy council. Upon the accession of king George I. he was restored to the sheriffalty of Berwick, and made a lord of the police. He married Grisel, daughter of Sir Thomas Ker of Cavers, and had issue three sons, Patrick, Alexander, and Sir Andrew; and four daughters; lady Jane, married to James Sandilands, lord Torphichen; lady Grisel, to George Baillie of Jerviswood, Esq; who was knight of the shire for the county of Berwick in several parliaments; lady Anne, to

Sir

Sir John Hall, of Dunglafs, Bart. and lady Juliana, to Charles Billingham, Efq; The eldeft fon, Patrick, lord Polwarth, who in 1698 had the honour to fit and vote in parliament as lord treafurer of Scotland, married the lady Jane Home, daughter of Charles earl of Home, and died before his father without iffue. Alexander the fecond fucceeded, and Sir Andrew was a fenator of the college of juftice. He died in 1724, aged 84, and was fucceeded by his faid fecond fon,

Alexander, fecond earl, who was then one of the judges of feffion, but refigned his office as a judge, and was fucceeded therein by his brother Sir Andrew Home, above-mentioned.

In March 1715, he was appointed envoy extraordinary to the courts of Denmark and Pruffia, and in December following made lord regifter of Scotland.

In January 1721, he was appointed firft ambaffador in the congrefs to be held at Cambray; and in March following made his public entry into that city; being likewife, by commiffion from his majefty, invefted at Cambray with the green ribband of the antient order of the thiftle. In 1726, he was fworn one of the privy council, and in the following year was by king George II. appointed lord regifter of the feffion and exchequer in Scotland; which places he refigned in 1733, and died in 1740. He married Margaret, daughter and heir of Sir George Campbell of Cefnock, by whom he had iffue four fons and four daughters; George, and Patrick, who died in 1724, Hugh lord Polwarth, and Alexander, who ufed the firname of Campbell, as reprefenting his mother's family: being bred to the law he was one of his majefty's council, and knight of the fhire for the county of Berwick, when he died, in 1760, as he was in the three preceding parliaments. He was for fome time folicitor-general to Frederic prince of Wales, but refigned in 1745. In December 1755, he was made lord regifter of Scotland. He married Mifs Parris of Saville Row; and died in July 1760, without iffue. The daughters were, lady Anne, wife of Sir William Purves, Bart. lady Grifel, who died unmarried; lady Jane, wife of James Nimmo, Efq; and lady Margaret, who died unmarried. He was fucceeded by his eldeft fon,

Hugh, third earl of Marchmont, who was elected one of the parliamentary peers for Scotland, in the room of John earl of Crawfurd, who died in 1749, and was re-chofen in 1754, and in 1761. His lordfhip is one of his majefty's moft honourable privy council, and was many years firft lord of the police in Scotland; and upon the death of the late duke of Athol, in 1764, he was appointed keeper of the great feal of Scotland. He married firft, Mifs Anne Weftern, by whom he had a fon, who died young, and three daughters; lady Anne, married October 23, 1755, to John Paterfon, Efq; eldeft fon of Sir

John

John Paterson of Eccles, Bart. lady Margaret, and lady Diana married to Walter Scott, of Harden, Esq; and a son Patrick, who died young; but the countess dying in 1747, his lordship the year following married Miss Elizabeth Crompton of London, by whom he has issue a son, Alexander, lord Polwarth, born in July 1750. His lordship is a fellow of the royal society.

TITLES.] The right honourable Hugh Hume, earl of Marchmont, viscount Blassonbury, lord Polwarth of Polwarth Redbraes, and Greenlaw, in the county of Berwick, and baronet.

CREATIONS.] Lord Polwarth 26 December 1690, by king William and queen Mary: the other titles were granted on the 23d of April 1697, by king William III.

ARMS.] Quarterly, 1st grand quarter counter quartered; 1st and 4th emerald, a lion rampant pearl, for Hume; 2d and 3d pearl, three swallows of the first for Pepdie; 2d pearl, three piles issuing from the chief ingrailed ruby, for Polwarth; 3d pearl, a cross ingrailed diamond for Sinclair; the 4th grand quarter as the first; and over all as a surtout, an escutcheon pearl, charged with an orange, ensigned with an imperial crown, all proper, as a coat of augmentation, given by king William III.

CREST.] On a wreath a man's heart, out of which issues a dexter arm erect, grasping a scymitar, all proper.

SUPPORTERS.] Two lions regardant pearl, armed and tongued ruby.

MOTTO.] Fides probata coronat.

CHIEF SEATS.] In the town of Berwick upon Tweed; and at Redbraes, in the county of Berwick.

CARMICHAEL, Earl of HYNDFORD.

THIS antient firname is local, and was assumed, according to Douglas, by the proprietors of the lands and barony of Carmichael in the shire of Lanerk, where they still have their chief seat. The first upon record is William de Carmychel, who flourished about the middle of the fourteenth century: he had a son John, first baron of Carmichael. He was succeeded by his son William, and he by his son Sir John Carmichael, who accompanied Archibald earl of Douglas to the assistance of Charles VI. of France against the English; and signalizing his valour at the battle of Baugey in April 1421, and breaking his spear, when the French and Scots got the victory, had thereupon added to his paternal arms, a dexter hand and arm armed, holding a broken spear, which is now the crest of the family. He married lady Mary Douglas, a daughter of George, earl of Angus; by whom he had issue, William, Robert, ancestor of the Carmichaels of Balmedie, Meadowflat,

Meadowflat, &c. and John, provost of St. Andrew's. William his heir, was the father of Sir John, who, in consideration of his good services to king James III. had divers lands given him by that prince, and therein was succeeded by William his heir; and had also a son, Walter, of whom hereafter: William had a son John, who marrying Elizabeth, daughter of Hugh lord Somerville, had a son Sir John, who was knighted by queen Mary, and made warden of the middle marches towards England. In 1588, he was joined with Sir John Vaus and Peter Young, in an embassy to the court of Denmark, to propose a match between king James VI. and the princess Ann, a daughter of that crown; after the finishing whereof he was made captain of his majesty's guard, and sent ambassador to queen Elizabeth; and being murdered upon the borders, in the execution of his office of warden of the middle marches, in the year 1600, left by Margaret Douglas his wife, sister of David earl of Douglas, and of James earl of Moreton, regent of Scotland, John, who died in his life-time, Sir Hugh his successor, William, and four daughters; Elizabeth, wife of John Home, of Kelton-hill, Esq; Mary, of John lord Holyrood-house; Abigail, of Hugh Wair, of Crawfurd; and Anne, of Dr. Whiteford, bishop of Brechin. He was succeeded by his son,

Sir Hugh, who was one of the privy council to king James, by whom he was also made master of the horse, and sent ambassador to Denmark; and married Abigail, daughter of William Baillie of Lamington, by whom he had issue a son, John, and a daughter Margaret, wife of James Lockhart of Cleghorn; but John his son, dying without issue, the estate descended to his cousin, Sir James Carmichael of Hyndford, lineally descended of Walter, before-mentioned, son of William, sixth baron of Carmichael. Sir James, being the son of Walter, son of Gavin, son of the said Walter.

Sir James was a great favourite of king James VI. who made him his cup-bearer, and chamberlain of Scotland. By Charles I. he was created a baronet, and in 1634 was appointed chief justice clerk, and in 1639, a senator of the college of justice. Dec. 27, 1647, he was created lord Carmichael. He married Agnes, sister-german of John Wilkie, of Fowlden, Esq; by whom he had issue three sons and four daughters, viz. William, master of Carmichael, colonel of a regiment in the parliament's service; Sir David, of Maudsley, deputy treasurer to Charles II. Sir James, of Bonnytoun, colonel in the service of Charles II. at the battle of Dunbar, in 1650, whose granddaughter, Henrietta, became at length heir to the estates of Bonnytoun, &c. and was married to Robert Dundas, of Arniston, Esq; president of the session at this time, whose eldest daughter Elizabeth, wife of Capt Ross Lockhart, of Balnagowan,

gowan, is heiress of those estates. The daughters were, Mary, first, the wife of Sir William Lockhart, of Carstairs, and secondly, of Sir Walter Weir, of Stonebyres; Agnes, of Sir John Wilkie, of Fowlden; Anne, of Sir David Carmichael, of Balmedie; and Martha, of John Kennedy, of Kirkmichael. His eldest son, the master, married Grisel, daughter of William, marquis of Douglas, by whom he had issue a son, John, and two daughters, Mary, wife of Sir Archibald Stewart of Castlemilk; and Rachael, of James Weir of Stonebyres, Esq; He died before his father in 1658, and the old lord deceasing in 1672, was succeeded by his grandson,

John, second lord, who being one of the Scots peers who joined most early in the revolution, was by king William, in recompence of his good services, made a commissioner of the privy seal, colonel of a regiment of dragoons, one of the privy council, high commissioner to the general assembly, one of the secretaries of state, and created earl of Hyndford, &c. on June 25, 1701. In 1702, the first of queen Ann, he was made a privy counsellor, and in 1706, appointed one of the commissioners for the union with England. He married Beatrix Drummond, daughter of David lord Maderty, by Beatrix his wife, daughter of John earl of Montrose; and by her had six sons and three daughters; lady Beatrix, married to John Cockburn of Ormeston; lady Mary, to John Montgomery, of Giffen, and lady Anne, to Sir John Maxwell, of Nether Pollock, Bart. lord justice clerk, and the two last had issue. The sons were, James, William, an advocate, Daniel, who all had issue; David, John and Charles, who died without issue. He died in 1710, and was succeeded by his eldest son,

James lord Carmichael, second earl, who was one of the lords of the police, colonel of a regiment of dragoons, and a brigadier general. He married lady Elizabeth Maitland, daughter of John earl of Lauderdale, by whom he had issue five sons and six daughters, viz. John, lord Carmichael; William, late bishop of Meath, in Ireland; James, member in three parliaments for the burghs of Selkirk, &c. Archibald, a captain of foot, and Charles, who was in the service of the East India Company, which last four died without issue. The daughters were, lady Margaret, wife of Sir John Anstruther, of that ilk, and mother of Sir John, the present baronet; lady Mary, of Charles O'Hara, Esq; lady Anne, of —— Duscina, Esq; ladies Elizabeth, Rachael, and Grace, who died young. The earl deceased Aug. 16, 1737, and was succeeded by his eldest son,

John, third earl, who was colonel of a company in the third regiment of foot-guards in 1732. In 1739 and 1740, he was appointed his majesty's high commissioner to the general assembly of the church of Scotland. In 1742, he was elected a knight of the thistle, and appointed envoy extraordinary to the

king

king of Pruffia; from whofe court, in 1744, he went in the fame character to the emprefs of Ruffia, and returned in about fix years. Upon the conclufion of the treaty of Breflaw, he received a royal grant from the king of Pruffia, dated Sept. 30, 1742, for adding the eagle of Silefia to his paternal arms, with this motto, *Ex bene merito.* Which was alfo ratified by a diploma from her Hungarian and Bohemian majefty, dated Nov. 29, 1742. On his return from Ruffia in 1750, he was appointed a lord of the king's bed-chamber, and in 1752, was fent upon a fpecial commiffion to the court of Vienna. His lordfhip is a privy counfellor, commiffioner of the police in Scotland, and vice-admiral of that kingdom. He married, firft, Elizabeth, eldeft daughter of the famous Sir Cloudefley Shovel, and widow of Robert lord Romney, without iffue, and fecondly, Jane, daughter of Benjamin Vigor, of Fulham, in Middlefex, Efq; His lordfhip is one of the fixteen peers for Scotland in the prefent, or 12th, parliament of Great-Britain; as he was alfo in the 8th, 9th, 10th, and 11th parliaments.

TITLES.] The right honourable John Carmichael earl of Hyndford, lord Carmichael, and baronet.

CREATIONS.] Baronet by king Charles I. baron of Carmichael in the county of Lanerk, 27 December 1647, by the fame king; and earl of Hyndford in the fame county, 25 June 1701, by William III.

ARMS.] Pearl, a fefs wreathy, fapphire and ruby.

CREST.] On a wreath, an armed arm erect, holding a broken fpear.

SUPPORTERS] On the dexter fide, a chevalier in complete armour, plumed on the head with three feathers pearl, and holding in his right hand a batoon royal. On the finifter, a horfe of the latter, furnifh'd ruby.

MOTTO.] Toujours prefte.

N. B. The Silefia arms, granted as above, according to the titles of heraldry.

CHIEF SEATS.] At Carmichael Houfe, and at Weftraw, in the county of Lanerk.

PRIMROSE, Earl of ROSEBERRY.

THIS family took their firname from the lands and village of Primrofe, in the county of Fife. Duncan Primrofe, of an antient ftock of that name in Perthfhire, by Mary his wife, a daughter of the family of Main of Auchterhoufe, had Gilbert and Archibald, who marrying Janet, daughter of the family of Bleau of Caftlehill, in the county of Perth, had two fons, David and James, and a daughter Eupheme, married to Sir George Bruce of Carnock, anceftor of the earl of Kincardin. David fucceeded, and had a fon James, who dying without iffue, was fucceeded by his uncle, James,

James, who being bred to the law, was by king James VI. in 1602, made clerk of the council, which post he held near forty years; and by Katharine his wife, daughter of Richard Lawson of Boghill, he had Gilbert, his heir; Sir Archibald; and James, clerk of the council; ———, wife of George Herriot, founder of Herriot's hospital in Edinburgh; and Margaret, of Thomas Young of Lainie, Esq; Gilbert, married a daughter of the family of Foulis of Ravelston, and had a son, James, who died before him; and his brother,

Sir Archibald, succeeded, who was by king Charles I. appointed clerk of the council, as his father and grandfather had been, and by king Charles II. was created a baronet. At the time of the restoration, he was for his loyalty and merit made one of the judges in the court of session, and lord register, which offices he discharged many years with integrity and judgment; and in 1678, he was constituted justice general of Scotland.

This eminent and loyal person married first, Elizabeth, daughter of James Keith, of Benholm, son of George earl Marshal, and by her had issue Sir James, of Barnbougle, who died before his father, leaving by Elizabeth his wife, daughter of Sir Robert Sinclair, of Longformacus, an only daughter, the wife of George Hume, of Kimmergham; Sir William Primrose, of Carrington; major general Gilbert Primrose; and two daughters, Margaret, wife of Sir John Foulis, of Ravelston, to whom her father gave the estate of Dunipace, on condition his heir should carry the name and arms of Primrose, which his son Sir John did, who was grandfather of the late Sir Archibald Primrose, of Dunipace; and Catharine, wife of Sir John Carnegie, of Pitarrow. His second wife was Agnes, daughter of Sir William Gray, of Pittendrum, by whom he had a son, Archibald Primrose, of Dalmenie, ancestor of the present earl; and a daughter, Grizel, wife of Francis lord Semple. He died November 27, 1679, and was succeeded by his second son, Sir William Primrose, of Carrington, who by Mary his wife, daughter of Patrick Scot, of Thirlestane, had issue, Sir James; captain William Primrose, killed in foreign service; Mary, wife of William Hamilton, of Bargenie; Jane, of Hugh Montgomery, of Coalsfield; and Elizabeth, of Charles, master of Elphingston. He died September 23, 1687, and was succeeded by his eldest son,

Sir James, who was member for Edinburghshire in the first parliament of queen Anne, who created him viscount Primrose, by letters patent, bearing date November 30, 1703. He married lady Eleanor, daughter of James earl of Loudoun, by whom he had issue, Archibald, Hugh, and William, who died in 1724; and a daughter, Margaret. He died in 1706, and was succeeded by his eldest son,

Archibald,

Archibald, second viscount, who dying unmarried in 1716, was succeeded by his brother, Hugh, third viscount, a brave officer in the army, who dying without issue, was succeeded, in 1741, by Archibald Primrose, of Dalmenie, only son of the second marriage of Sir Archibald Primrose, of Carrington, before-mentioned. Which Archibald having completed his college education, travelled abroad for improvement; and after his return, disposed himself to a country life, till in 1695, when he was chosen member in parliament for the county of Edinburgh, and in 1700, was created viscount Roseberry by king William. Soon after the accession of queen Ann, he was made one of the privy council, one of the gentlemen of the bedchamber to prince George of Denmark; and on April 10, 1703, created earl of Roseberry, &c. to his heirs male and female. He was one of the commissioners in the treaty of union; which being concluded, he was elected one of the sixteen peers from Scotland to the four first parliaments of Great Britain. He married Dorothy, daughter and heir of Everingham Cressy, of Birkin, in the county of York, by whom he had issue James, his heir; Richard and John; and four daughters, lady Mary, wife of Sir Archibald Primrose, of Dunipace; lady Margaret, of Alexander Sinclair, earl of Caithness; and ladies Dorothy and Elizabeth, who died young. He was succeeded by his eldest son,

James, second earl, who marrying in his father's life-time Mary, daughter of lieutenant general John Campbell of Mammore, and sister of the duke of Argyll, by her had a son, Archibald, lord Dalmeny, who died in August 1755; and John, lord Dalmenie, who also died before his father; James, who died young; and Neil, the present earl: Ladies Mary and Dorothea, who died young. The earl died in 1755, and was succeeded by his only surviving son,

Neil, now third earl of Roseberry.

TITLES.] The right honourable Neil Primrose, earl of Roseberry, viscount Primrose and Roseberry, lord Dalmenie, and baronet.

CREATIONS.] Baronet by king Charles II. viscount Roseberry, in Mid Lothian, the 1st of April 1700, and earl of the same place, the 10th of April 1703.

ARMS.] Quarterly, 1st and 4th topaz, a lion rampant, emerald, for the title of Roseberry; 2d and 3d emerald, three primroses in a double tressure counterflory, topaz, for the name of Primrose.

CREST.] On a wreath, a demi lion ruby, holding in his dexter paw a primrose, as in the arms.

SUPPORTERS.] Two lions emerald.

MOTTO.] Fide et fiducia.

CHIEF SEATS.]

CHIEF SEATS.] At Barnbougle and Dalmenie, in the county of Linlithgow; and at Roseberry, in the county of Edinburgh.

BOYLE, Earl of GLASGOW.

THIS family is of very great antiquity in the west of Scotland, and had large possessions in Airshire, as appears from several old writs still preserved in the family.

In the reign of Alexander III. Richard Boyle of Kelburn marrying Margery, daughter of Sir Walter Cumming, had Richard his heir, who in 1296 was one of the barons of Scotland that swore allegiance to king Edward I. of England; and from him descended Hugo de Boyle, who in 1399, gave his lands to the monks of Paisley for the welfare of his soul. From the said Hugo descended John Boyle of Kelburn, who lost his life at the battle of Bannockburn with king James III. 1488, and his son John succeeding, obtained from king James V. a grant of divers lands in the isle of Cumra, near Bute; and marrying Agnes, a daughter of the family of Rofs, by her had two sons, John and Robert; John, the eldest, was of Halkhill, in Renfrew; which John had a son, David, father of another John, who succeeded his grandfather, and was a most zealous loyalist in the service of queen Mary; and by his wife Marian, daughter of Hugh Crawfurd, of Kilberny, ancestor of the viscounts Garnock, and the present earl of Crawfurd, had a son, John, and several daughters. He was succeeded by his said son,

John, who was banished his country about ten years, for his adherence to king Charles I. He married Agnes, daughter of Sir John Maxwell, of Pollock, in the county of Renfrew, by whom he had an only daughter, Grizel, who being an heiress, was married to her cousin, David Boyle, of Halkhill, Esq; descended from John Boyle of the same place, aforesaid, brother-german of her great grandfather, John Boyle, second son of John Boyle, of Kilburn, father of David, father of James, father of another David, father of John, father of the said David, who was created lord Boyle, Jan. 31, 1699, and having been returned a member in the convention of estates for the county of Bute, which declared the prince of Orange king of Scotland, was made one of his majesty's privy council. In the third year of queen Ann, he was created viscount and earl, made treasurer depute, one of the privy council, lord register, and one of the commissioners for concluding the union, in which year he had the honour to represent her majesty's person in the general assembly of the church. He married first, Margaret, sister of John viscount Garnock, ancestor of the present earl of Crawfurd, by whom he had three sons, John; Patrick, a senator of the college of justice; and Charles; and secondly,

condly, Jane, daughter and sole heir of William Muir of Rowallan, in Coningham, by whom he had two daughters, lady Jane, married to major general Sir James Campbell, knight of the bath, brother of Hugh earl of Loudoun, by whom he had a son, who took the name of Muir, as representing his mother, who was an heiress; and lady Anne. The earl died in 1733, and was succeeded by his eldest son,

John, second earl, who married Helen, daughter of William Morrison of Preston Grange, Esq; representative in several parliaments for the shires of Cromarty and Peebles, by whom he had issue two sons and six daughters, viz. John, now earl of Glasgow; and Patrick, who married Miss Mure of Caldwall, without issue; ladies Janet, Margaret, Jane; Marian deceased; Catharine and Helen. The earl died in 1740, and was succeeded by his eldest son,

John, third earl, at that time captain of a company at Minorca, who in 1754 was chosen rector of the university of Glasgow, and in June 1755, married Elizabeth, daughter of George lord Ross, by whom he has issue a son, John, lord Boyle, born March 26, 1756; and two daughters, ladies Betty and Jane.

TITLES.] The right honourable David Boyle, earl of Glasgow, viscount Kelburn, and lord Boyle of Stewarton.

CREATIONS.] Lord Boyle of Stewarton, 13 January 1699, by William III. and viscount Kelburn, both in Coningham; and earl of Glasgow, in the county of Lanerk, 10 April 1703, by queen Anne.

ARMS.] Quarterly, 1st and 4th topaz, an imperial eagle, ruby, for the title of Glasgow, being formerly the crest of the family; 2d and 3d party per bend, crenelle, pearl and ruby, for the name of Boyle in England, (as a coat of affection) and over all, by way of surtout, an escutcheon of the first, charged with three stags horns of the second, the paternal coat of Boyle of Kelburn.

CREST.] On a wreath, an eagle with two heads, party per pale crenelle, topaz and ruby.

SUPPORTERS.] On the dexter side, a savage proper, wreathed about his temples and middle with laurel, a branch of which he holds in his right hand. On the sinister, a lion, party per pale crenelle, pearl and ruby.

MOTTO.] Dominus providebit.

CHIEF SEATS.] At Kelburn and Rowallan, in Airshire.

STUART, Earl of BUTE.

THIS noble family is descended from Sir John Stuart, a son of king Robert II. who by his father's grant had a fair possession in the island of Bute, with the heretable jurisdiction of that county, wherein he was confirmed by the charter of his brother, Robert III. He married Jane, daughter of Sir John Semple of Elietson, ancestor of the lord Semple; and had three sons, Robert, William, and Andrew; Robert, the eldest, succeeding, was one of the privy council to king James II. His son, James Stuart of Bute, dying without issue in 1497, was succeeded by his cousin and heir male, James, son of his uncle William, who was succeeded by his son, Ninian, who married Janet Dunlop, and dying in 1508, left James his heir, who marrying to his second wife, Marian, daughter of John Fairly of Kyle, had two sons, John and Robert, and was succeeded by his eldest,

John, who was made chamberlain of Arran, captain of the castle of Brodick, in that island, and one of the gentlemen of the bedchamber to king James VI. and dying in 1602, left issue by his first wife, Mary, daughter of John Campbell of Skipnish, a son and heir,

Sir John, who was knighted by the said king, and married Elizabeth, daughter and coheir of Robert Hepburn of Ford, in the county of Haddington, with whom he had divers lands in that county; and had a son, Sir James, his successor; and colonel Thomas, who died in France. His eldest son,

Sir James, succeeded him, and was created a baronet by Charles I. in 1627; and by Isabel his wife, daughter of Sir Dougal Campbell of Auchinbreck, had issue two sons and three daughters, viz. Sir Dougal; Sir Robert, of Tillicoultry, a senator of the college of justice, who married, and had issue; Elizabeth, wife of Ninian Bannatyne of Keams; Anne, of Alexander Macdonald of Sana; and Jane, of Angus Campbell, jun. of Skipnish. He was succeeded, in 1662, by his eldest son,

Sir Dougal, who married Elizabeth, daughter of Sir Thomas Ruthven of Dunglas, by his wife lady Mary Lesley, daughter of Alexander earl of Leven, and by her had two sons and three daughters, Sir James; and Dougal, a senator of the college of justice, who married Mary, daughter and heir of Alexander Bruce of Blairhall, by whom he had a numerous issue: Barbara, wife of Alexander Campbell of Barbreck; Margaret, of Dougal Lawmond of that ilk; and ———, of ——— Stuart of Auchinskeoch. He died in 1672, and was succeeded by his eldest son,

Sir James, who was one of the privy council to queen Ann, by whom he was created earl of Bute, &c. He was a great opposer of the union, and married first, Agnes, daughter of Sir George Mackenzie of Rosehaugh, lord advocate or attorney general to king James VII. by whom he had issue James, lord Mountstewart, his heir; and a daughter, lady Margaret, married to John Crawfurd, viscount Garnock, ancestor of the present earl of Crawfurd: and secondly, Christian, daughter of William

William Dundas of Kincavil, by whom he had a son, John, who died without issue. The earl deceased in 1710, and was succeeded by his eldest son,

James, second earl, who was a gentleman of the bedchamber to king George I. one of the commissioners of trade in Scotland, lord lieutenant of Buteshire, and one of the sixteen peers for North Britain in the two parliaments of that king. He married lady Ann, daughter of Archibald duke of Argyll, and by her, who died 28 January 1723, had issue two sons, John, now earl; and James Stuart M'Kenzie, who by the entail of his great grandfather, succeeded to the estate at Roschaugh, and bears the name and arms of M'Kenzie. He is lord privy seal for Scotland, member in the present parliament for Ross-shire, and a privy counsellor. He married lady Betty Campbell, one of the daughters and coheirs of John, late duke of Argyll. And four daughters, lady Mary, married to Sir Robert Menzies of Weem, Bart. lady Anne, to James Ruthven, lord Ruthven; lady Jane, to William Courtenay, Esq; and lady Grace, to John Campbell of Stonefield, Esq; The earl died in 1722, and was succeeded by his eldest son,

John, third earl of Bute, who was elected one of the sixteen peers for Scotland in February 1736-7, on the death of the earl of Orkney. In September following he was made a lord of the police; and in August 1738, was invested with the ensigns of the antient order of the thistle, at Holyrood-house; and was one of the lords of the bedchamber to Frederick, late prince of Wales. He was groom of the stole to his present majesty, while prince of Wales; and upon his majesty's accession to the crown, he was sworn one of the privy council, and appointed groom of the stole to his majesty. In March 1761, his lordship was appointed one of his majesty's principal secretaries of state; and in June following, ranger of Richmond Park. In August following, having been elected one of the sixteen peers of Scotland, he was also elected chancellor of the university of Aberdeen, and one of the governors of the charter-house. In May 1762, his lordship was appointed first lord of the treasury, which he resigned in April 1763; and upon the 22d of September, 1762, he was installed a knight of the garter at Windsor. He married Mary, only daughter of the honourable Edward Wortley Montague, by the lady Mary Pierpont, daughter of Evelyn, the first duke of Kingston, who died in August 1762, by which lady, who, upon the death of her father in January 1761, succeeded to a very large estate, and in April following was created baroness Mount Stewart of Wortly, in Yorkshire, he has issue five sons, John, lord Mount Stewart, member for Bossiney, in Cornwall, to the present parliament, who married, on November 12, 1766, Miss Windsor, one of the daughters and coheirs of the late viscount Windsor; James, who, upon the death of his mother, will succeed to his grandfather's vast estate, taking the firname of Wortley Montague, Frederick, Charles, and William; and six daughters, lady Mary, who, in September 1761, was married to Sir James Lowther, Bart. lady Jane, lady Anne, married on July 2, 1764, to Hugh, now earl Percy, son and heir apparent of Hugh duke of Northumberland; ladies Augusta, Caroline, and Louisa.

TITLES.] The right honourable John Stuart earl of Bute, baron Mount Stewart, knight of the most noble order of the garter, and of the antient order of the thistle, and baronet; one of his majesty's most honourable privy council, a governor of the charter-house, ranger of Richmond Park, chancellor of the university of Aberdeen, and one of the sixteen peers for Scotland.

CREATIONS.] Baronet 28 March 1627, by Charles I. baron Mount Stewart in the isle of Bute, and earl of Bute 14 April 1703, by queen Anne.

ARMS.] Topaz, a fess cheque pearl and sapphire, within a double tressure, counterflory with fleurs de lis ruby, as being of the royal family.

CREST.] On a wreath, a demi lion ruby.

SUPPORTERS.] On the dexter side, a horse pearl, bridled ruby. On the sinister, a stag proper.

MOTTO.] Avito viret honore.

CHIEF SEATS.] At Mount-stewart in the Isle of Bute; Montague-House, Yorkshire; Luton-Hoe, Bedfordshire, and Kew in Surry.

HOPE, Earl of HOPETON.

THE firname of Hope is of great antiquity in Scotland; but the ancestor of this family was undoubtedly,

Henry Hope, merchant in Edinburgh, who had issue by his wife Jacque de Tott, a French lady, Sir Thomas Hope of Craigiehall; who being bred to the law, was by king James VI. preferred to be joint lord advocate, and sole advocate to Charles I. and marrying Elizabeth, daughter of John Bennet of Willingford, had issue four sons and two daughters, viz. Sir John, of Craigiehall, his successor, ancestor of the Hopes of Kinross and Rankailor; Sir Thomas, ancestor of the Hopes of Kerse; Sir Alexander, cup-bearer to Charles I. Sir James, of Hopeton, ancestor of the earls of Hopeton, of whom we are treating. Mary, wife of Sir Charles Erskine of Alva, and Anne, of David, lord Cardross, ancestor of the earl of Buchan.

James, fourth and youngest son, was advanced to be a judge in the court of session 1649. He married Anne, daughter

ter of John Foulis of Leadhills in the county of Lanerk, and by her had many children, none of whom survived but a daughter Rachael, wife of David Bethune of Balfour, and John his successor. He married, secondly, lady Mary, daughter of William, seventh earl marshal, by whom he had Sir William Hope of Balconrie, Bart. deputy-governor of the castle of Edinburgh. He died in 1661, and was succeeded by his eldest son,

John, who, in 1682, accompanying the duke of York from London to Scotland, was drowned at sea, leaving by lady Margaret Hamilton his wife, daughter of John earl of Haddington, Charles his only son, and a daughter Eleanor, married to Thomas Hamilton earl of Haddington. He was succeeded by his said son,

Charles, who being knight of the shire for the county of Linlithgow, was one of the privy council to queen Anne, and created earl of Hopeton: he was one of the sixteen peers for Scotland from 1722, till his death in March 1741-2. In August 1738, he was invested with the ensigns of the order of the thistle at Holyrood House. He married lady Henrietta Johnston, daughter of William marquis of Annandale, and by her, who died in 1750, had issue two sons and six daughters, viz. John, his successor, and Charles, knight of the shire for Linlithgow from 1743 to the present time. In November 1744, he was made commissary-general of the musters in Scotland, and is governor of Blackness castle, and fellow of the royal society: he takes the name of Weir by marrying the heiress of Sir William Weir of Blackwood, Bart. by whom he had two sons and one daughter; but that lady dying, he married secondly, the lady Anne Vane, daughter of Henry late earl of Darlington, by whom he has two sons. His lordship's daughters were, lady Sophia, second wife of James earl of Finlater and Seafield; lady Henrietta, wife of Francis lord Napier; lady Margaret, of John Dundas of Duddingston, Esq; lady Christian, of Thomas Graham of Balgowan, Esq; lady Helen, of James Watson of Saughton, Esq; and lady Charlotte, of Thomas lord Erskine. He died in 1741, and was succeeded by his eldest son,

John, lord Hope, second and present earl of Hopeton, who was his majesty's high commissioner to the church of Scotland in 1754, and married lady Anne Ogilvie, eldest daughter of James earl of Finlater and Seafield, by which lady, who died in February 1759, he had issue, Charles lord Hope, James, John, who died in September 1759, Henry, and three daughters, lady Betty, married July 10, 1754, to Henry earl of Drumlanrig, eldest son of the duke of Queensberry, and died in April 1756; the earl, her husband, having been unfortunately killed October 20, 1754, by the accidental going off of his piftol on his journey from Scotland to London; ladies Henrietta and Sophia. His lordship is a commiſſioner of the police, and of forfeited eſtates.

TITLES.] The right honourable John Hope earl of Hopeton, and lord Hope.

CREATION.] Earl of Hopeton in the county of Stirling, 15 April 1703, the 2d of queen Anne.

ARMS.] Sapphire, on a chevron topaz, between three befants a bay leaf emerald.

CREST.} On a wreath, a globe ſplit on the top, and above it a rainbow with a cloud at each end, all proper.

SUPPORTERS.] Two women in loofe garments, the hair of their heads hanging down, each holding an anchor in the outer hand.

MOTTO.] At ſpes non fracta.

CHIEF SEATS.] At Hopeton Houfe in Weſt Lothian, and at Ormiſton-hall and Byres in Eaſt Lothian.

COLLIER, Earl of PORTMORE.

THE family of Collier are originally defcended from the antient houfe of Robertfon of Strowan, the chief of that numerous clan in Scotland.

Sir Alexander Robertfon, Bart. fettled in Holland, and affumed the name of Collier.

Sir David his fon was in great favour with king William III. and in 1691 affifting in the reduction of Ireland to the king's obedience, was afterwards created lord Portmore. In the firſt of queen Anne he was promoted to the rank of a major-general, and in 1703 created earl of Portmore, &c.

In May 1710 he was conftituted commander in chief of her majefty's forces in Portugal, in the room of the earl of Galway: in January 1710, he was promoted to the rank of a general of foot, and in 1712 commanded part of the army in Flanders, under James Butler duke of Ormond. In 1712 he was one of the queen's privy council, and in January that year elected a knight of the thiftle. In Auguſt 1713, he was appointed governor of Gibraltar, and in October that year chofen one of the fixteen peers for North Britain. In April 1714, he was appointed commander of the royal regiment of Scots dragoons, in the room of John earl of Stair; and marrying Catharine, daughter of Sir Charles Sidley of Great-Chart in the county of Kent, Bart. who by king James VII. was created countefs of Dorcheſter for life, by her had iſſue two fons, David lord Milfington, who married Bridget, daughter of John Noel of Walcot in the county of Northampton, Efq; third fon of Baptiſt Noel the fecond viſcount Campden, by his fourth wife, by whom he had feveral children; but he and all his children

children dying before the earl who died in 1729, his brother Charles became second earl of Portmore.

Which Charles, in 1722, was twice chosen member of parliament for Wicomb in the county of Bucks; but his election was declared void. In 1727, he was elected for Andover in Hampshire. In 1734 and 1741, he was elected one of the sixteen peers for Scotland, and is a knight companion of the antient order of the thistle.

His lordship, in 1732, married Juliana duchess dowager of Leeds, daughter of Roger Hele of the county of Devon, Esq; by whom he has issue lady Catharine, born December 1733, who in 1750 married Nathaniel Curzon, Esq; (son and heir of Sir Nathaniel Curzon of Kedleston in Derbyshire, Bart.) now lord Scarsdale; a daughter born 1735; a son lord Milsington, who died January 16, 1756, and other children.

TITLES.] The right honourable Charles Collier, earl and baron of Portmore, viscount Milsington, and knight of the antient order of the thistle.

CREATIONS.] Baron of Portmore 1 June 1699, by king William III. viscount Milsington in Tiviotdale and county of Roxburgh, and earl of Portmore 16 April 1703, by queen Anne.

ARMS.] Ruby, on a chevron, between three wolves heads couped pearl, three trees emerald, fructed of the first.

CREST.] On a wreath, a unicorn rampant pearl, horned and unguled topaz.

SUPPORTERS.] Two wolves pearl.

MOTTO.] Avance.

CHIEF SEAT.] At Weybridge, in the county of Surry.

SCOT, Earl of DELORAINE.

THE family, of which this is a branch, has been already treated of under the title of duke of Buccleugh. I must therefore only observe, that lord Henry Scot, third son of the unfortunate James duke of Monmouth, born in 1676, was by queen Anne dignified with the titles of earl of Deloraine, viscount Hermitage, and lord Scot, of Goldieland, in the shire of Roxburgh. He was one of the sixteen peers for Scotland in the fifth, sixth, and seventh parliaments of Great-Britain. In 1715, he was appointed colonel of the second troop of grenadier guards; and in 1723, made a knight of the most honourable order of the Bath; after which he was colonel of a regiment of foot, a major-general, and a gentleman of his majesty's bedchamber, in which appointments he died in December 1730.

He married Anne, daughter and heir of William Duncomb of Battlesden in Bedfordshire, Esq; one of the lords justices of Ire-

EARL OF DELORAINE.

land in 1693, and comptroller of the army accounts to queen Anne: by her he had one daughter lady Anne, who died an infant in the first month, and two sons, Francis and Henry. He was succeeded by his eldest son,

Francis viscount Hermitage, second earl, who was twice married; but dying in April 1739, and leaving no issue, was succeeded by his brother,

Henry, third earl, who being disposed in his youth to a maritime life, was promoted to be a captain in the royal navy, and died in his 27th year, nine months after his brother, in January 1739-40. He married Elizabeth, daughter of John Fenwick, Esq; and left two sons, Henry, born in January 1736, and John in October 1738. He was succeeded by

Henry the eldest son, fourth and present earl of Deloraine.

TITLE.] The right honourable Henry Scot earl of Deloraine, viscount Hermitage, and baron Scot of Goldieland, all in the county of Roxburgh.

CREATIONS.] Earl, baron, and viscount, 29 March 1706, 5 Anne.

ARMS.] Topaz, on a bend sapphire, a star between two crescents of the field, a crescent for difference.

CREST.] On a wreath, a stag trippant, proper.

SUPPORTERS.] Two maidens richly attired in antique habits, their under robe emerald, the middle one sapphire, and the uppermost ruby, and each plumed on her head with feathers pearl.

MOTTO.] Amo.

CHIEF SEAT.] At Battlesden, in Bedfordshire, &c.

VISCOUNTS.

CAREY, Viscount FALKLAND.

THE family of Carey was anciently seated at Cockington, in the county of Devon, of which was Sir John Carey, knight of the shire for that county, and chief baron of the exchequer in 1387, who died in 1404. From him descended Sir Edward Carey of Berkhampsted, in Hertfordshire, the immediate ancestor of this noble family, who was master of the jewel office to king James VI. He had a son and successor, Sir Henry; and two daughters, Anne, married to Francis Leak, earl of Scarsdale; and Frances, to George Manners, earl of Rutland.

Sir Henry succeeded his father, and was made knight of the Bath in 1616, at the creation of Charles prince of Wales; and having been the first who brought the news into Scotland of the death of queen Elizabeth, he was thereupon made one of the
gentlemen

gentlemen of the king's bedchamber, and comptroller of his houshold. He was also by that king appointed lord deputy of Ireland, and was elected knight of the shire for the county of Hertford in 1621; but being created a peer of Scotland, it was, after debate, resolved by the house of Commons, to stay to be farther advised upon the question, which being never determined, noblemen of Scotland continued to be chosen till the union. Dying in 1633, he left issue by Elizabeth his wife, daughter of Sir Laurence Tanfield, chief baron of the exchequer, Lucius, his heir; and a daughter, Ann, married to James earl of Home. Which Lucius was in 1640 chosen a member in parliament for Newport, in the Isle of Wight, and advanced to be secretary of state; but on the 20th of September 1643, lost his life at the battle of Newbery, in the 34th year of his age, to the extreme regret of all good men. By his death, learning had the greatest loss in that age, he being thereof a complete master, and a glorious benefactor to it. He married Letitia, daughter of Richard Morrison of Tooley Park, in the county of Leicester, Esq; and had issue one son, his successor,

Henry, third viscount, who was a great patron of the muses, to whom he was a votary. He wrote a play, called The Marriage Night, which was well received. About the time of the restoration, he was elected a burgess to serve in the house of commons, for Arundel, in the county of Sussex, and appointed lord lieutenant of the county of Oxford; but four years after, was cut off in the prime of life, in 1664, greatly lamented. He was succeeded as viscount Falkland by his son,

Anthony, fourth viscount, who in the latter end of Charles II. and the succeeding reign, was paymaster of the forces; and in the reign of William III. was one of the privy council, and twice a commissioner of the admiralty. He dying in 1694, left issue one son,

Lucius Henry, fifth viscount, who married first, Dorothy, daughter of Francis Molineux, of the city of London, Esq; and had by her four sons, the eldest named Lucius-Charles. His second wife was Miss Dillon, daughter of the lord Dillon, in the kingdom of Ireland, a lieutenant general in the French service. His lordship dying in France, was succeeded by his eldest son,

Lucius-Charles, now viscount Falkland, who married, in April 1734, first, Jane, daughter and heir of Richard Butler, Esq; an eminent conveyancer in London, widow of the lord Villiers, son of the earl Grandison of Ireland, by whom he had two sons and four daughters, viz. ———, master of Falkland; Lucius Ferdinand Carey, Esq; governor of Goree, in Africa; Jane, Frances, Mary, and Charlotte. He married secondly, in October 1752, Sarah, daughter and heir of Thomas Inwen,

Esq; member of parliament for Southwark, and widow of Henry earl of Suffolk.

TITLES.] The right honourable Lucius Carey, baron Carey, and viscount Falkland.

CREATION.] Baron and viscount Falkland, in the county of Fife, 10 November 1620, by king James VI.

ARMS.] Quarterly, 1st and 4th pearl, on a bend diamond, three roses of the field, barbed and seeded proper, for Carey; 2d pearl, a fess between six annulets ruby, for Lucas; 3d, the arms of France and England quarterly, within a border compone, pearl and sapphire, as allied to the Plantagenet family, from that of Beaufort.

CREST.] On a wreath, a swan, proper.

SUPPORTERS.] On the dexter side, a unicorn pearl, his horn, mane, tufts, and hoofs, topaz. On the sinister, a lion gardant, proper; his ducal crown and plain collar topaz.

MOTTO.] In utroque fidelis.

MURRAY, Viscount STORMONT.

THE descent of this family has been recited under the title, *Duke of Athol*.

Their immediate ancestor was Sir William Murray of Tullibardin, whose youngest son, Sir Andrew, was progenitor of the present viscount Stormont. He married Margaret, daughter and sole heir to James Barclay of Arngosk and Kippo, with whom he had those lands; and was succeeded therein by

Sir David, his eldest son, who married Janet, daughter of the lord Lindsay of Pyrer, and left issue, Sir Andrew, Sir William, and David. Sir Andrew, the eldest, married lady Janet Graham, daughter of William earl of Montrose, and had issue, Sir Andrew Murray of Balvaird, Sir David, Robert, and Sir Patrick. The male issue of the eldest brother failing, the estate devolved on

Sir David Murray of Gosparty, who being bred from his youth at the court of king James VI. was first made cup-bearer to his majesty, and then master of the horse, captain of the guard, comptroller of Scotland, one of the privy council, and created baron of Scoon, and viscount Stormont. He married Elizabeth, daughter of Sir David Beton of Creich; but dying without issue, was succeeded, pursuant to the entail, by

Sir Mungo Murray, second viscount, brother of John, the first earl of Tullibardin, and son of Anne, daughter of Sir Andrew Murray of Arngosk and Balvaird, neice of the first viscount. Which Sir Mungo dying also without issue, the honour of Stormont, by virtue also of the entail, descended to

James Murray, earl of Annandale, third viscount; and he also dying without issue, we return to Sir Andrew Murray of Balvaird, the elder brother to the first lord Stormont, who being

ing created lord Balvaird in 1641; and marrying lady Elizabeth Carnegy, daughter of David earl of Southesk, had five sons, a daughter, Barbara, married to Patrick, the tenth lord Grey, and others.

David, the eldest son, succeeding, he also, by the death of James earl of Annandale, became fourth viscount Stormont. He married lady Elizabeth Carnegy, daughter of James earl of Southesk, and widow of the aforesaid James earl of Annandale, and by her had issue David, his heir; and two daughters, Katharine, married to William Keith, earl of Kintore; and Amelia, who died unmarried. His son,

David, fifth viscount, succeeded; and marrying Marjory, daughter of David Scot of Scotstarvet, in Fifeshire, had issue six sons and eight daughters, of whom Marjory was married to colonel John Hay of Cromlix, who had the title of earl of Invernefs from the Pretender, and forfeited in the rebellion 1715; he was second son of Thomas earl of Kinnoul; and Amelia, to Sir Alexander Lindsay of Evelick, in Perthshire, Bart.

The second son, James, was knight of the shire for Dumfries in 1710; in the fourth parliament was elected for the boroughs of Elgin, &c. and was one of her majesty's commissaries for settling the trade with France. In 1715, he was returned for the same burghs, but voted not duly elected. He soon after went abroad, and lived at the court of the Pretender, whom he served in divers capacities, and from him had the title of earl of Dunbar.

Of William, the fourth son, the reader will see a full account, under the title of lord Mansfield, in Collins's Peerage, vol. VII. page 397.

David, the eldest, sixth viscount, succeeded his father, and married the daughter and sole heir of John Stewart of Innernytie, Esq; by whom he had two sons and two daughters, David, James, Anne and Marjory. He died in 1748, and was succeeded by his eldest son,

David, seventh and present viscount Stormont, who at the two last elections was chosen one of the sixteen peers; in December 1755, he was appointed his majesty's ambassador to the king of Poland, and in May 1763, his majesty's ambassador extraordinary and plenipotentiary to the emperor and empress of Germany, and is a lord of the privy council. He married Henrietta-Frederica, daughter of Henry, count Bunau, and by her has issue a daughter, Elizabeth-Mary.

TITLES.] The right honourable David Murray, viscount Stormont, baron of Scoon and Balvaird, and heretable keeper of the palace of Scoon.

CREATIONS.] Baron of Scoon, 7 April 1604, and viscount Stormont, being a barony in the county of Perth, 26 April 1612,

1612, both by James VI. and lord Balvaird, in Fifeshire, by Charles I. 1641.

ARMS.] Quarterly, 1st and 4th sapphire, three stars pearl, within a double tressure, counterflory with fleurs de lis, topaz, for Murray; 2d and 3d ruby, three crosses pattee pearl, for Barclay of Balvaird.

CREST.] On a wreath, a buck's head couped, proper, with a cross pattee between his antlers, as in the arms.

SUPPORTERS.] Two lions ruby.

MOTTO.] Meliora spero.

CHIEF SEATS.] At Cumlingum castle, in Annandale; and at Scoon, in Perthshire.

ARBUTHNOT, Viscount ARBUTHNOT.

THE sirname of this family is local, and was assumed by the proprietors of the lands and barony of Arbuthnot, in the Mearns, as early as the first use of sirnames in Scotland.

In the year 1160, Hugo, the first of this family, marrying a daughter of the family of Oliphard, sheriff of the county of Mearns, with her he had the lands of Arbuthnot in that county, and was succeeded by Duncan de Arbuthnot, and he by his son Hugo, who had a son Hugo, whose son Duncan died in 1314, and had issue another Duncan, who had a son Hugo, and he a son Philippus, whose son Hugh was succeeded by his son Robert, who died in 1450. He was succeeded by his eldest son, David, who was succeeded by his eldest son, James, whose eldest son, Robert, was succeeded, in 1379, by his eldest son Andrew, whose eldest son, Sir Robert, dying without male issue, was succeeded by his nephew, whose eldest son,

Sir Robert Arbuthnot of that ilk, for his loyalty to king Charles I. was dignified with the title of baron of Inverbervie, and viscount Arbuthnot. He married lady Marjory Carnegie, daughter of David earl of Southesk, and had a son,

Robert, second viscount, who married first, the lady Elizabeth Keith, daughter of William earl Marshal, and had by her Robert, who succeeded him: and by Katharine his second wife, daughter of John Gordon of Pitburgh, Esq; he had John Arbuthnot of Fordon; Alexander, who took the sirname of Maitland, upon his marrying the heiress of Pitrichie; and Thomas Arbuthnot: also three daughters, Catharine. married to Mr. Robert Gordon of Clunie; Anne, to Mr. John Horn of Westerhall; and Helen, to John Macfarlane of that ilk; and secondly, to Mr. John Spotiwood of that ilk, who all had issue. He died in 1684, and was succeeded by his eldest son,

Robert, third viscount Arbuthnot, who married the lady Ann Sutherland, daughter of George earl of Sutherland, by whom he had two sons, Robert and John; and four daughters,

Jane,

Jane, married to captain Crawfurd of Camlurg; Anne, Mary, and Margaret, who all three died unmarried. Dying in 1692, he was succeeded by his eldest son,

Robert, fourth viscount, who dying unmarried in 1710, was succeeded by his brother,

John, fifth viscount Arbuthnot, who married Jane, daughter of William Morrison of Preston Grange, Esq; but dying without issue, May 1756, aged 64, the title descended to his cousin, son of John Arbuthnot of Fordun, before noticed, eldest son, by the second marriage, of Robert the second viscount. Which John is the sixth and present viscount Arbuthnot; and married first, May, daughter of —— Douglas of Bridgeford, by whom he had no issue; and secondly, Jane, daughter of Alexander Arbuthnot of Findourie, by whom he has issue three sons and two daughters, viz. Robert, master of Arbuthnot; John, Hugh, Charlotte, and Margaret.

TITLES.] The right honourable John Arbuthnot, viscount and baron Arbuthnot, in the county of Kincardin.

CREATION.] Viscount and baron, 16 November, 1641.

ARMS.] Sapphire, a crescent between three stars, pearl.

CREST.] On a wreath, a peacock's head couped, proper.

SUPPORTERS.] Two wyverns emerald, spouting fire.

MOTTO.] Laus Deo.

CHIEF SEAT.] At Arbuthnot, in Kincardinshire.

INGRAM, Viscount IRVINE.

ARTHUR Ingram, a wealthy citizen of London, purchased the manor of Temple Newsom, and other lands in Yorkshire, and was high sheriff of that county in 1619. He had a son Arthur, high sheriff of the same county in 1630, whose eldest son, Sir Thomas Ingram, was chancellor of the dutchy of Lancaster, and of the privy council to king Charles II. He married Frances, daughter of Thomas viscount Falconberg; but dying without issue, was succeeded by his brother Sir Arthur, and he by his eldest son Henry, who having manifested his loyalty to king Charles I. and II. was by the latter created lord Ingram and viscount Irvine. He married lady Essex, eldest daughter of Edward the second earl of Manchester, and had issue two sons, Arthur his heir, and Edward, and a daughter Essex, who died unmarried.

Arthur, the eldest son, who succeeded as second viscount Irvine, married Isabel, daughter of John Matchell, of Horsham in Sussex, Esq; by whom he had issue seven sons, Richard, Edward, Arthur, Henry, and Charles, successively viscounts Irvine; George, canon of Windsor, and chaplain to the house of Commons; and William, an eminent merchant in Holland. He died in 1702, and was succeeded by his eldest son,

Richard,

Richard, third viscount, who was governor of Hull, a colonel in the guards, and appointed governor of Barbadoes; but died in 1721, before he could embark for his government. He married lady Anne Howard, second daughter of Charles earl of Carlisle, but having no issue, was succeeded by his next surviving brother,

Arthur, fourth viscount, who dying in 1736, was succeeded by his brother,

Henry, fifth viscount, who was elected to parliament for Horsham in 1722; and being made commissary of stores at Gibraltar, was re-elected in May 1727, and again at the general election the same year. He was again elected in the parliament of 1734, and being made commissary of the stores in Minorca, in May 1730, he was re-chosen. He was appointed lord lieutenant of Yorkshire, in the room of his brother; but dying in 1736, without issue, was succeeded by his brother,

Charles, sixth viscount, who was a colonel in the guards, and adjutant general of the forces, was elected member for Horsham in 1737, and continued in parliament till his death, in 1748. He was succeeded by his son,

Charles, the present and seventh viscount, who was chosen member in parliament for Horsham, when he succeeded to the peerage. He married Miss Shepherd, a great fortune, by whom he has issue.

TITLES.] The right honourable Charles Ingram, baron Ingram of Irvine, and viscount Irvine, in the county of Air.

CREATIONS.] Viscount and baron, 3 May 1661, by king Charles II.

ARMS.] Ermine, on a fess, ruby, three escallopshells, topaz.

CREST.] On a wreath, a cock, proper.

SUPPORTERS.] On the dexter side, a griffin, quarterly, ruby, and pearl. On the sinister, an antelope of the last, horned, mained, tailed, and hoofed, topaz, and gorged with a ducal crown, ruby.

CHIEF SEATS.] At Hills, in the county of Sussex; and at Temple Newsom, near Leeds, in the county of York.

OSBORNE, Viscount DUNBLAINE.

SEE an account of this noble family under *Duke of Leeds*, (who is viscount Dunblaine) in Collins's Peerage, vol. I. page 237.

BARONS.

BORTHWICK, Lord BORTHWICK.

SOME writers deduce the origin of this family from one Andreas, a son of the lord of the castle of Burtick, in Livonia, who accompanied queen Margaret from Hungary to Scotland in the year 1057. They have been long a great and numerous family in Scotland, however, and Thomas de Borthwick obtained some lands near Lauder, in Berwickshire, from Robert Lauder of Quarrelwood, in the reign of king David II. who ascended the throne of Scotland in 1329. He left issue a son, Sir William, who possessed the lands of Catkune in 1378. His son Sir William was one of the guarantees of the treaty of peace with the English, in the year 1398, and had issue another Sir William, of Borthwick, who was one of the commissioners appointed to treat with the English in December 1400, and also in 1404 and 1405, and got a charter from Robert duke of Albany, governor of Scotland, of the lands and barony of Borthwick, which formerly belonged to Robert Scot, dated June 4, 1410. He was employed in many other affairs of state, and was created lord Borthwick before the year 1430, in which title he was succeeded by his son William, the second lord, who had been one of the hostages for king James I's ransom, in 1424, was ambassador to Rome in 1425, and was knighted in 1430. He was also three times ambassador to the court of England. He was succeeded about 1461, by his eldest son, William, third lord, who married Maryote-de Hope-Pringle, by whom he had issue two sons and four daughters; William, his heir; Alexander of Nenthorn, of whom hereafter; Agnes, wife of David, earl of Cassilis; Catharine, of William, earl of Glencairn; Mary, of James Hope-Pringle of Gallashiels; and Margaret, of Sir Oliver Sinclair of Roslin. He was slain, with his royal master, James IV. at the fatal battle of Floddon, in 1513, and was succeeded by his eldest son,

William, fourth lord, who by his wife Margaret, daughter of John Hay, lord Yester, had issue a son, John, fifth lord, and two daughters, Catharine, wife of Sir James Crichton, lord Fendraught; and Janet, of Alexander Lauder, son and heir of Alexander Lauder of Hatton. He died in 1542.

John, fifth lord, was a great loyalist, and firm friend to queen Mary, and married Elizabeth, daughter of David earl of Crawfurd, by whom he had issue one daughter, Maryota, wife of Andrew Hope-Pringle of Gallashiels; and

William, sixth lord, who by his wife Grizel, daughter of Sir Walter Scot, ancestor of the duke of Buccleugh, had issue a son,

James,

James, seventh lord, who left issue by Margaret his wife, daughter of William Hay, lord Yester,

John, eighth lord, who was a faithful and loyal subject of king Charles I. and by lady Elizabeth, daughter of William earl of Lothian, his wife, had issue,

John, ninth lord, who died without issue, in 1672; whereupon the title devolved upon Henry, son of captain Henry Borthwick, by his wife Mary, daughter of Sir Robert Pringle of Stitchel; which captain Henry was son of William, son of Alexander, second son of William, son of William, son of Alexander, second son of William, third lord Borthwick, before-mentioned.

Which Henry, tenth and present lord, having proved his descent, as above, has voted at every election of peers to serve for Scotland, since 1734.

TITLES.] Henry Borthwick, lord Borthwick.
CREATION.] Lord Borthwick, anno 1424.
ARMS.] Pearl, three cinquefoils, topaz.
CREST.] A negro's head, couped, proper.
SUPPORTERS.] Two angels, proper, winged, topaz.
MOTTO.] Qui conducit.
CHIEF SEAT.] Borthwick castle, in Lothian.

FORBES, Lord FORBES.

THE first of this name on record, was John de Forbes, who flourished in the reign of William the lion, and possessed the lands and barony of Forbes. His son, Fergus de Forbes, had a son and successor, Alexander Forbes, who in 1303 resolutely defended his castle of Urquhart, near Elgin, against king Edward I. which being taken by storm, he and the whole garrison were put to the sword; and by that fatal stroke his family had been extinct, if his wife had not preserved it by Alexander, a posthumous son; which Alexander, in compensation of what his father had lost in the service of his country, had a grant from king Robert I. of divers lands; but he inheriting the principles of his father, and loyally adhering to king David Bruce against Edward Baliol, was slain at the great battle of Duplin, in the year 1332.

In the reign of Robert II. Sir John Forbes of that ilk, the son of the aforesaid Alexander, acquiring from Thomas earl of Mar, several lands in the county of Aberdeen, was therein confirmed by the charter of that king; and in the fifth of Robert III. was constituted justice and coroner of that county. He had four sons, three of whom were knighted; Sir John, the third, was founder of the family of Tolquhon, from whom descended those of Culloden, Waterton, and Foveran: Sir William, the second, was ancestor of the lord Pitsligo; Alexander,

ander, the youngest, was ancestor of the Forbes's of Brux, &c. and Sir Alexander, the eldest, succeeded his father, and was created lord Forbes. He married lady Elizabeth, daughter of George earl of Angus, and obtained a grant from John earl of Buchan, to himself, and the said Elizabeth his wife, of the lands of Milkie, Fintry, Blackton, and Balcrofs. He had issue a son, James, second lord,

Which James, second lord, was knighted by king James II. and by lady Egidia his wife, daughter of William, first earl Marshal, had three sons, William, his heir; Duncan, ancestor of the Forbes's of Corsindal, Monimusk, &c. &c. and Patrick, from whom descended Sir Arthur Forbes, Knt. and Bart. father of Arthur, the first earl of Granard, in Ireland. He was succeeded by his eldest son,

William, third lord, who marrying Christian, daughter of Alexander first earl of Huntley, had three sons, viz.

Alexander, fourth lord, who dying without issue, was succeeded by

Arthur, his brother, fifth lord, who also dying without issue, the honour devolved on his youngest brother,

John, sixth lord Forbes, who married first, lady Catharine Stewart, daughter of John earl of Athol, by whom he had a son, James, who died young; and a daughter, Elizabeth, wife of —— Grant of that ilk; and secondly, Christian, daughter of Sir John Lundy of that ilk, by whom he had issue one son, William; and four daughters, Margaret, wife of Andrew Fraser of Muchil, ancestor of lord Fraser; Elizabeth, first, of Gilbert Keith of Troup; and secondly, of Alexander Innes of that ilk; Marjory, of Gilbert Forbes of Brux; and Christian, of William lord Ruthven. His third wife was Elizabeth, widow of Alexander lord Elphingstone, by whom he had a son, Arthur, of Putachie; and a daughter, Janet, first, the wife of John earl of Athol; secondly, of Alexander Hay of Dalgity; and thirdly, of William Leslie of Balquhain. He died in 1547, and was succeeded by his eldest son,

William, seventh lord, who was one of the gentlemen of the bedchamber to king James V. and marrying Elizabeth, daughter and coheir of Sir William Keith of Innerrugy, by her had six sons and eight daughters, viz. John, master of Forbes; William, of Fodderhouse; James, of Lethinty; Robert, prior of Monimusk; Arthur, of Logie; and Abraham, of Blackstoun; Jane, married to James, lord Ogilvy of Airly; Elizabeth, to Henry lord Sinclair; Christian, to George Johnston of Caskieben; Isabel, to John Gordon of Pitlurg; Catharine, to —— Barclay of Gartly, in Aberdeenshire; Margaret, to George Sinclair of May; Barbara, to Alexander Allardice of that ilk; and Anne, to Sir John Seton of Bains. He died in 1593, and was succeeded by his eldest son,

O John,

John, eighth lord, who married firſt, lady Margaret, daughter of Alexander earl of Huntley, by whom he had a ſon, John, who entered into holy orders abroad, and died without iſſue; and two daughters, Jane, wife of William Cummin of Earnſide; and Margaret, of George Sinclair of Dunbeath: And ſecondly, Janet, daughter of James Seton of Touch, by whom he had a daughter, Catharine, wife of —— Gordon of Rothmay; and a ſon,

Arthur, ninth lord, who married Jane, daughter of Alexander lord Elphingſton, and by her had five ſons and three daughters; Alexander; colonel John; colonel William; captain Arthur, and captain James Forbes; which two laſt were killed in the wars in Germany: Barbara, wife of George earl of Seaforth; Anne, of —— Forbes of Echt; and Elizabeth, of —— Skeen of that ilk. He was ſucceeded by his eldeſt ſon,

Alexander, tenth lord, who ſerved under the great Guſtavus Adolphus, king of Sweden, againſt the Imperialiſts, where he attained the degree of a lieutenant general; and at the beginning of the civil war in Great Britain, returning to his native country, was one of the commanders in the army ſent from Scotland into Ireland, to ſuppreſs the Iriſh rebellion, in 1643. He married firſt, Ann, daughter of Sir John Forbes of Pitſligo, and had iſſue by her, William, maſter of Forbes, and ſeveral other children, who died young: And ſecondly, Elizabeth, daughter of —— Forbes of Rires, by whom he had two ſons and three daughters; colonel James; captain Arthur: Chriſtian, wife of John Forbes of Balflug; Mary, firſt, of Hugh Roſe of Kilravock; and ſecondly, of —— Kinnaird of Cowberie; and Anne, who died unmarried; alſo eight other children, who died young. He was ſucceeded by his eldeſt ſon,

William, eleventh lord, who married Jane, daughter of John Campbell of Calder, by whom he had three ſons, William, Arthur, and Archibald; and two daughters, Mary, firſt married to William Sutherland, ſon of James, the ſecond lord Duffus; and ſecondly, to Sir Robert Gordon of Gordonſton; and Elizabeth, to —— Leith of Whitehaugh. Dying in 1691, he was ſucceeded by his eldeſt ſon,

William, twelfth lord, who was made one of the privy council by king William III. and colonel of a regiment of dragoons. In the beginning of queen Ann's reign, he was lieutenant colonel of the horſe guards in Scotland, commanded by Archibald duke of Argyll, and continued a privy counſellor. He married Ann, daughter of James Brodie of that ilk, and had two ſons, William and James; and one daughter, Mary, wife of John Ogilvie of Balbegno; and dying in 1716, was ſucceeded by

William, his eldeſt ſon, thirteenth lord, who married Dorethy, daughter of William Dale of Covent Garden, Weſtminſter,

minster, Esq; by whom he had one son and three daughters; Francis, his successor; Mary, who died young; Jane, wife of captain James Dundas, jun. of Dundas; and Elizabeth, of Dr. John Gregory, professor of medicine in the university of Aberdeen. He deceased in the year 1730, and was succeeded by his son,

Francis, fourteenth lord Forbes, who dying a minor, was succeeded by his uncle,

James, fifteenth lord, second son of William the twelfth lord, who married first, Mary, sister of Alexander Forbes, lord Pitsligo, by whom he had issue James, the present lord; and three daughters, Sophia, married to Charles Cummin of Kinninmount; Mary, to James Gordon of Cowbardie; and Anne, to Thomas Erskine of Pittodrie. By his second wife, Elizabeth, daughter of Sir James Gordon of Park, Bart. he had no issue. He died in 1761, and was succeeded by his son,

James, now sixteenth lord Forbes, who married Catharine, daughter of Sir Robert Innes of Orton, Bart. by whom he has a daughter. His lordship is lieutenant governor of Fort William, in Scotland.

TITLES.] The right honourable James Forbes, lord Forbes.

CREATION.] Lord Forbes, by king James II.

ARMS.] Sapphire, three bears heads couped, pearl, muzzled, ruby.

CREST.] On a wreath, a stag's head erazed, proper.

SUPPORTERS.] Two greyhounds pearl, each having a plain collar, ruby.

MOTTO.] Grace me guide.

CHIEF SEATS.] At Castle Forbes, and Putachie, in Aberdeenshire.

FRASER, Lord SALTON.

THE original of the illustrious name of Fraser, I shall take notice of under the attainted title of Fraser, lord Lovat.

Sir William Fraser, second son of Sir Alexander, second son of Sir Simon, of Oliver castle, who was one of the greatest heroes of his time, was the immediate ancestor of this noble family.

Which Sir William was succeeded by his eldest son, Sir Alexander, who was a man of great parts and merit, and highly in favour with king Robert II. He was succeeded, about 1408, by his eldest son, Sir William, and he by his son, Sir Alexander, in 1441. His eldest son, Alexander, baron of Philorth, was succeeded by his eldest son, Alexander, and he by his brother, Sir William, whose son, Alexander, was succeeded by his eldest son, another Alexander, whose son, Sir Alexander Fraser of Philorth and Frasersburg, went twice ambassador

bassador from king James VI. to the court of Denmark, and conveyed him into England on his accession to that crown: after which he obtained from that king a charter of regality, and freedom to build a castle at his town of Frasersburg, which town, harbour, and castle, he erected at his own charge. He married Magdalen, daughter of Sir Walter Ogilvy of Dunlugas, ancestor of lord Bamff, by whom he had issue Sir Alexander; Walter, who died unmarried; James, ancestor of the Frasers of Tyrie; Thomas, an ingenious antiquary, who wrote memoirs of his family, &c. Isabel, the wife of Patrick Cheyne of Estemont; Margaret, of —— Hay of Urie; and Elizabeth, of William Crawfurd of Federet. He died at his castle of Frasersburgh, April 12, 1623, and was succeeded by his eldest son,

Sir Alexander, who married Margaret, daughter of George lord Salton, who proved the heiress of that antient and noble family. By her he had issue two sons and two daughters, Sir Alexander; Sir John, who had no issue; ——, wife of —— Forbes of Blacktoun; and ——, of —— Baird of Auchmeddin. He was succeeded by his eldest son,

Sir Alexander Fraser of Philorth, who, in right of his mother, became heir of his grandfather, George Abernethy, lord Salton, and accordingly had the honours and dignities of lord Salton and Abernethy granted to him and his heirs by king Charles I. and ratified by the parliament in 1670. He was very zealous in the service of king Charles I. and II. and carried a regiment to Worcester at his own charge; after the royal party was defeated, he was obliged to travel home on foot. He was also an eminent speaker in parliament and church assemblies, had the honour of some share in bringing about the king's restoration, and lived to the age of ninety years. He married first, ——, daughter of William Forbes of Tolquhoun, by whom he had one daughter, the wife of Alexander Fraser of Teckmurray; and secondly, Elizabeth, daughter of Alexander Seton, laird of Meldrum, by whom he had issue,

Alexander Fraser, master of Salton, who died before his father, in 1682. He was frequently a member of the privy council in Scotland, and married three wives, first, lady Ann, eldest daughter of William third earl of Lothian, by whom he had Alexander, who died unmarried; and William lord Salton: secondly, lady Marian Coningham, daughter of William earl of Glencairn, widow of James, the first earl of Finlater; and lastly, lady Sophia Erskine, daughter of Alexander earl of Kelly, by neither of whom he had issue; whereupon his second son,

William, second lord, succeeded his grandfather, and married Margaret, daughter of Dr. James Sharp, archbishop of St. Andrews, by whom he had issue two sons and four daughters; Alexander, lord Salton; William Fraser of Frasersfield, married

LORD SALTON.

ried to lady Katharine, daughter of the earl of Buchan, and by her, who died in 1732, had issue, James Fraser of Lonmay, married to lady Eleanor, daughter of Colin, earl of Balcarras, and left one son. The daughters were, Helen, married to Sir James Gordon of Park; Henrietta, to John Gordon of Kinedder, Esq; Mary, to William Dalmahoy of Ravelrig, Esq; and Isabel. He died in 1716, and was succeeded by his eldest son,

Alexander, third lord Salton, who married lady Mary, daughter of George earl of Aberdeen, sometime chancellor of Scotland; and by her, who died in February 1753, had issue,

Alexander, who succeeded his father, and was fourth lord, but died without issue; William, who died also without issue; George, the present lord; Anne and Sophia.

Which George, fifth lord Salton, married his cousin-german, Helen, daughter of John Gordon of Kinnedder, Esq; by whom he has issue two sons and two daughters, viz. Alexander, master of Salton; John Fraser, Esq; Henrietta and Mary.

TITLE.] The right honourable George Fraser, lord Salton and Abernethy.

CREATION.] Baron Salton, in East Lothian, by king James II. and so granted and confirmed by king Charles I.

ARMS.] Quarterly, 1st sapphire, three cinquefoils, pearl, for Fraser; 2d topaz, a lion rampant, ruby, debruised with a ribband, diamond, for Abernethy; 3d ruby, a lion rampant, pearl, for Ross; 4th as the first.

CREST.] On a wreath, an ostrich, with a horse-shoe in its beak.

SUPPORTERS.] Two angels.

MOTTO.] In God is all.

CHIEF SEAT.] At Philorth and Fraserburgh, in Aberdeenshire.

GRAY, Lord GRAY.

THIS noble and antient family took their sirname from the castle of Croy, in Picardy, of which was Anschetil de Croy, who coming into England with William the Norman, obtained divers lands in the county of Oxford, and elsewhere; and from him sprang many great and illustrious families in England, as the dukes of Suffolk and Kent, the marquis of Dorset, the earls of Tankerville and Stamford, the barons, Grey of Codnor, Ruthin, Wilton, Rolefton, Wark, &c. also of Chillingham, from which last is descended the lord Gray of Scotland.

Sir Andrew de Gray of Chillingham, in the county of Northumberland, for his good and faithful services to Robert Bruce, obtained from that king, in 1315, the manor of Longforgan,

forgan, in the county of Perth, with others in the county of Forfar, and had also a grant of the lands of Browfield and Broxmouth. His son, Sir David, had a son, Sir John, who was one of the hostages for the ransom of king David II. when a prisoner in England.

To him succeeded his second son, Sir Patrick, whose wife was named Margaret, but of what family is not said, and by her he had

Sir Andrew, his heir, who married Janet, daughter and heir of Roger Mortimer, lord of Foulis, with whom he had that barony. He was succeeded by his only son,

Sir Andrew, who was one of those great persons who were hostages for the ransom of king James I. and in the reign of king James II. were confirmed hereditary lords. By Elizabeth his wife, daughter of Sir John Wemyss of Rires, ancestor of the earl of Wemyss, he had Andrew, his heir, and three daughters: and by his second wife, Elizabeth, daughter of Sir Walter Buchanan, Knt. had issue four sons. He died before the year 1449, and was succeeded by his eldest son,

Andrew, second lord, who had issue by Elizabeth his wife, (of what family is not recorded) Patrick, master of Gray, and Andrew. He died in 1469, and his eldest son, Patrick, dying before him, and leaving, by his wife Annabella, daughter of Alexander lord Forbes, a son, Sir Andrew, he, on the death of his grandfather, became third lord Gray, and was one of the privy council to king James IV. and justice general of Scotland. By his first wife, Janet, daughter of John lord Keith, son of William earl Marshal, he had Patrick, his heir; and by his second, who was the lady Elizabeth Stewart, daughter of John earl of Athol, he had Robert Gray; Gilbert, of Buttergask; Andrew Gray of Mureton; and Sir Edward; and four daughters. He died in 1514, and was succeeded by his eldest son,

Patrick, fourth lord, who dying without male issue, was succeeded by Patrick, his nephew, son of his brother Gilbert, who became fifth lord; and the said Patrick accompanying king James V. to the battle of Solway, 1542, was there taken prisoner, and paid several hundred pounds for his ransom. He married Marian, daughter of James lord Ogilvy, ancestor of the earl of Finlater, and by her had Patrick, his heir, Andrew, James, Robert, and Patrick; and several daughters. He died in 1582, and was succeeded by his eldest son,

Patrick, sixth lord, who married Barbara, daughter of Patrick lord Ruthven, and by her was father of five sons and five daughters. Dying in 1609, he was succeeded by his eldest son,

Patrick, seventh lord, who was gentleman of the bedchamber, master of the wardrobe, and one of the privy council to king James VI. and marrying lady Mary Sinclair, daughter of Robert earl of Orkney, ancestor of the lord Sinclair, by her had

had two sons, Andrew, his successor; and William; and six daughters. He died in 1612, and was succeeded by his eldest son,

Andrew, eighth lord Gray, who was fined 1500 l. for his adherence to the cause of king Charles I. He was lieutenant to the Gens d'Arms in France, under James duke of York, their captain; and having married Jane, countess dowager of Buchan, sister of James Ogilvy, earl of Finlater, by her had an only daughter, Ann, who being married to

William, the son of Sir William Gray of Pittendrum, descended from Andrew Gray of Mureton, above-mentioned, he, in her right, became master of Gray; and dying in 1660, he left by the said lady Ann, his wife, three sons, Patrick, William, and Charles; and

Patrick, the eldest, succeeding his grandfather, was ninth lord, and married Barbara, daughter of Andrew lord Balvaird, sister of David viscount Stormont, and by her had Marjory, his daughter and heir, mistress of Gray; who marrying John Gray of Crichie, grandson of Sir William Gray of Pittendrum, the said John became tenth lord Gray, upon the decease of his father-in-law, in 1711; and by his said wife had three sons, John, William, and Alexander; and three daughters, Barbara, Catharine, and Elizabeth. He died in 1724, and was succeeded by his eldest son,

John, eleventh lord, who married Helen, daughter of Alexander lord Blantyre, and by her had two sons and one daughter; John, master of Gray; Charles; and Anne, wife of William Gray of Balegarno, Esq; and dying in 1738, was succeeded by his eldest son,

John, twelfth and present lord Gray, who in 1741, married Miss Blair, heiress of Kinfauns, near Perth, by whom he has issue three sons, Andrew, master of Gray; Charles and William; John; and seven daughters, Jane, Helen, Margaret, Barbara, Elizabeth, Anne, and Mary.

TITLES.] The right honourable John Gray, lord Gray.

CREATION.] So created by king James II.

ARMS.] Ruby, a lion rampant, within a border ingrailed, pearl.

CREST.] On a wreath, an anchor in pale, topaz.

SUPPORTERS] Two lions gardant, ruby.

MOTTO.] Anchor fast anchor.

CHIEF SEATS.] At the castle of Gray; and at Foulis, in the Carse of Gowry.

CATHCART; Lord CATHCART.

THE surname of this ancient family is local, and taken from their lands and barony of Kethcart, in Renfrewshire, of which was Reynald de Kethcart, who in 1178, was witness to a charter of Allan, the son of Walter Dapifer; and William de Kethcart, his son, was one of those barons who swore allegiance to king Edward I. of England. To him succeeded his son, Sir Allan, a faithful adherer to the interest of king Robert I. and he marrying the sister and coheir of Sir Duncan Wallace of Sundrum, in Airshire, with her had that barony; and they had a son, Sir Allan, and he a son and successor, Sir Allan, whose son, Allan, had a son, Sir Allan, who succeeded him, in 1446.

Which Sir Allan was dignified with the title of lord Cathcart by king James II. in the year 1442. He was also in great favour with king James III. who appointed him warden of the west marches towards England in 1481, and for his services, rewarded him with a grant of the barony of Dundonald, and the lands of Tarbath, in King's Kyle, and made him master of the artillery. He married Janet, a daughter of the family of Maxwell, and had six sons; Allan, the eldest, dying before him, left a son,

John, second lord, who succeeded his grandfather; and marrying Margaret, daughter of John Kennedy of Blairquhan, had

Allan, his heir apparent, who was slain at the battle of Floddon in 1513. He married Margaret, daughter of Patrick Maxwell of Newark, and by her had

Allan, third lord, who succeeded his grandfather; but he losing his life at the battle of Pinkie, in 1547, left by Helen, his wife, daughter of William lord Semple,

Allan, fourth lord Cathcart, who was a hearty promoter of the reformation from popery, and one of the first peers who took arms in defence of the young king James VI. against the earl of Bothwell, who had married the queen. In recompence whereof, when his majesty came to the crown, he made him master of the houshold, with several beneficial grants. He married Margaret, daughter of John Wallace of Craigy, and heir to Wallace of Sundrum, and had a son,

Allan, who dying before him, left by Isabel his wife, daughter of Thomas Kennedy of Bargany,

Allan, fifth lord, who succeeded his grandfather in 1618; and marrying two wives, first, lady Margaret, daughter of Francis earl of Bothwell; and secondly, Jane, daughter of Sir Alexander Colquhoun of Luss; by the last, who afterwards married Sir George Hamilton, third son of James, the first earl of Abercorn, left an infant son,

Allan, sixth lord, who succeeded his father. He married Marian, daughter of David Boswell of Auchinleck; and dying in 1709, in the 81st year of his age, left issue *(inter alia)*

Allan, seventh lord, who married Elizabeth Dalrymple, daughter of James viscount Stair, and had three sons, Allan, Charles,

Charles, and James; and a daughter, Margaret, who was married to Sir Adam Whitford of Blairquhan, Bart. and the said Allan, lord Cathcart, died in 1732, aged 85; and Allan, the eldest son, having perished at sea going to Holland, he was succeeded by his second son,

Charles, eighth lord, who was first groom, and afterwards gentleman of the bedchamber to king George II. He was one of the sixteen peers for Scotland in the eighth parliament from the union, colonel of a regiment of horse in Ireland, and governor of Duncannon; but commanding the land forces, in chief, on an expedition with admiral Vernon, against the Spaniards, in the West Indies, he died at Dominica in 1740, and brigadier Thomas Wentworth succeeded in the command. He married first, Margaret, daughter of Sir John Schaw of Greenock, Bart. and had issue by her a son and heir, Charles; and two daughters, Eleonora, married to Sir John Houston of that ilk, Bart. and Mary-Anne, to the Hon. William, master of Napier, son and heir of the lord Napier, in December 1754. He married secondly, in 1739, Mrs. Sabine, widow of Joseph Sabine of Tring, in Hertfordshire, Esq; but without issue; and her lord dying as aforesaid, she married, to her third husband, lieutenant colonel Hugh Macguire. He was succeeded by his only son,

Charles Schaw, ninth lord Cathcart, who in the year 1745, received his commission as lieutenant colonel, and is now a lieutenant general, and governor of Dunbarton castle. In 1748, he was one of the hostages for the delivery of Cape Breton to the king of France, by virtue of the treaty of Aix la Chapelle. He was chosen one of the sixteen peers for Scotland, upon the death of the duke of Gordon, in 1752, and re-chosen in the last and present parliaments. In May 1756, he was appointed his majesty's high commissioner to the general assembly in Scotland, in which he was continued for several succeeding years, and is adjutant general for Scotland, first commissioner of the police, and a knight of the thistle. He married, July 24, 1753, Jane, daughter of lord Archibald Hamilton, and sister of the countess Brooke and of Warwick, by whom he has issue, William, master of Cathcart; Charles-Allan, George, Jane, Mary, and Louisa.

TITLES.] The right honourable Charles Cathcart, lord Cathcart.

CREATION.} So created by king James II. in 1442.

ARMS.] Quarterly, 1st and 4th sapphire, three cross croslets fitchy, issuing out of as many crescents, pearl, for Cathcart; 2d and 3d ruby, a lion rampant, pearl, for Wallace, as marrying that heiress.

CREST.] On a wreath, a dexter hand couped above the wrist, and erect, proper, grasping a crescent, as in the arms.

SUPPORTERS.]

SUPPORTERS.] Two parrots, proper.
MOTTO.] I hope to speed.
CHIEF SEAT.] At Sundrum, in Airshire.

SOMERVILLE, Lord SOMERVILLE.

THE first of this name on record is Sir Walter de Somerville, lord of Wichnore, in the county of Stafford, who came into England with William the Norman, and was progenitor of all the Somervilles in Great Britain. His second son, William de Somerville, was a frequent witness to the grants of king David I. and had a grant of the lands and barony of Carnwath from that prince.

About the beginning of the reign of king William, in 1170, the Somervilles were possessed of a fair estate in the county of Lanerk, and elsewhere; and at the marriage of Alexander II. who began his reign in the year 1214, William de Somerville, lineally descended of the said Sir Walter, was one of the barons appointed by that king to exercise in a tournament at the castle of Roxburgh. He had a son, Sir William, who had a son, Sir Thomas, and he a son, Sir Walter, whose eldest son, Sir James, lost his life at the battle of Durham in 1346, and was succeeded by his brother, Sir Thomas, who was a steady friend to king David Bruce, and was succeeded in 1370, by his eldest son, Sir William, whose eldest son, Sir Thomas, was one of the hostages for the ransom of king James I. from his captivity in England, and was created a baron by king James II. in 1424. He married Janet, daughter of Alexander Stewart, lord Darnley, with whom he got the lands and barony of Cambusnethan. He was succeeded by his eldest son,

William, second lord Somerville, who was succeeded, in 1456, by his eldest son, John, third lord, whose eldest son, William, master of Somerville, left two sons,

John, fourth lord, who died without issue in 1526, and was succeeded by his brother,

Hugh, fifth lord, who was a great favourite of James V. and by his great hospitality and generosity, much impaired his estate; and being prisoner in England after the battle of Solway, much ingratiated himself with Henry VIII. He died in 1549, and was succeeded by his eldest son, James, sixth lord, who was a fast friend to queen Mary. He was succeeded, in 1570, by his eldest son,

Hugh, seventh lord Somerville, who marrying Eleanor, daughter of George lord Seton, by her had William, who died young; John; Gilbert, his heir; Hugh Somerville of Drum; and four daughters. He was succeeded, in 1597, by his third son,

Gilbert, eighth lord, who having, by excess of living, wasted

his

his estate, and leaving no issue, the honour, in 1618, descended to his younger brother,

Hugh, ninth lord, then page of the bedchamber to king James VI. who had nothing to support the dignity: wherefore the title from thence lay dormant till the year 1722, when, at the election of the sixteen peers,

James Somerville of Drum, the twenty-fifth in a lineal male descent from the aforesaid Sir Walter, who came into England with king William I. putting in his claim, his vote and claim were allowed by the court of session. He was son of James, son of James, son of James, son of James, son of Hugh, fourth son of Hugh, seventh lord Somerville, and the first three may be stiled the tenth, eleventh, and twelfth lords.

Which James, now thirteenth lord Somerville, was chosen one of the sixteen peers to the ninth parliament of Great Britain, and is now a lord of police, a commissioner of the board of trade, and for forfeited estates. He married the only daughter of Henry Bayntun-Rolt of Spypark, in Wiltshire, Esq; and by her, who died in May 1755, had issue two sons, James, master of Somerville, and Hugh, both officers in the army; and a daughter, Anne-Wichnour, wife of George Burgess, Esq; who has by her a son and a daughter. He married secondly, in 1736, Frances, daughter and coheir of John Rotheram, Esq; by whom he had a daughter, who died in her infancy.

TITLES.] The right honourable James Somerville, lord Somerville.

CREATION.] So created by king James II.

ARMS.] Sapphire, three stars, topaz, accompanied with seven cross croslets fitchy, pearl, three in chief, one in fess, two in the flanks, and the last in base.

CREST.] On a wreath, a wheel, topaz, surmounted of a wyvern, emerald, spouting fire.

SUPPORTERS.] Two greyhounds, proper, each gorged with a plain collar, ruby.

MOTTO.] Fear God in life.

CHIEF SEAT.] At Drum, in Mid-Lothian, near Edinburgh.

DOUGLAS, Lord MORDINGTON.

WILLIAM, tenth earl of Angus, by his wife Elizabeth, daughter of Laurence lord Oliphant, by lady Margaret Hay, daughter of George, seventh earl of Errol, amongst other children, had issue William, afterwards marquis of Douglas; and Sir James, ancestor of this family. Which Sir James was created lord Mordington, with the precedency of lord Oliphant, by Charles I. He married Ann, daughter and heir of Laurence, fifth lord Oliphant, and by her had two sons,

James, who died before his father; and William; and one daughter, Anne, married to Robert lord Semple. His eldest son,

William, who succeeded as second lord, married Elizabeth, daughter of Hugh lord Semple, by whom he had a son,

James, third lord, who marrying Jane, daughter of Alexander, first viscount Kingston, by her had issue,

George, fourth lord Mordington, who married Katharine, daughter of Dr. Robert Lauder, rector of Shenley, in Hertfordshire, by whom he had issue a son, Charles; and two daughters, Mary and Cambelina; and dying in 1741, was succeeded by his son,

Charles, fifth lord, who, in September 1746, was arraigned at Carlisle for the rebellion, and pleaded his peerage as lord Mordington; which at first was opposed by all the king's council, but allowed afterwards. Dying some years after, in him ended the male line of the family, but the title is in abeyance between the two aforesaid daughters of George lord Mordington, Mary and Cambelina.

TITLES.] The right honourable —— Douglas, lord Mordington.

CREATION.] So created by king James IV. with precedency as lord Oliphant, in 1458.

ARMS.] Quarterly, 1st and 4th, pearl, a man's heart, ruby, ensigned with an imperial crown, proper, on a chief sapphire, three stars of the first, for Douglas; 2d and 3d, ruby, three crescents, pearl, for Oliphant.

CREST.] On a cap of dignity, a salamander in flames, regardant, emerald.

SUPPORTERS.] On the dexter side, a savage; and on the sinister, a stag, both proper; the first armed with a batoon, and wreathed about his head and middle with laurel; and the second collared and chained with leaves of the last.

MOTTO.} Forward.

SEMPLE, Lord SEMPLE.

THIS family is of great antiquity in the west of Scotland, and there had great possessions and offices, as stewards and bailiffs, under the lord high stewards of Scotland, who were superiors of Renfrewshire, before they came to the crown.

Robert de Sempill flourished in the reign of Alexander II. who ascended the throne in 1214, and died in 1249. He had a son, Robert, who had two sons, Robert, and Thomas, a firm friend of king Robert Bruce. He was succeeded by Robert, his eldest son, who was also a great patriot; and dying in 1330, was succeeded by his son, William, who was stiled baron of Eliotstoun. He had a son, Thomas, who was father of Sir John, who had issue a son, John, and a daughter, Jane, married to Sir John Stewart, ancestor of the earl of Bute. He

obtained

obtained from John Stewart, earl of Carrick, the lands and barony of Glasfford, in Cliddesdale, in which he was succeeded by John, his son and heir, who was particularly employed in transacting the redemption of king James I. in 1421. Sir Robert, his son, succeeding him, was knighted by king James II. and had a grant from that king of the lands of Southennin, in which, and his ancient patrimony of Eliotstoun, he was succeeded by Sir William, his heir, who was made sheriff of Renfrew by king James III. To him succeeded his son, Sir Thomas, who, at the battle of Bannockburn in 1488, lost his life with his royal master, and was succeeded by his son,

Sir John, who being much in favour with James IV. was by him created lord Semple in 1488; but attending his majesty to the battle of Floddon in 1513, he there, with his royal master, lost his life, and his body was buried in the collegiate church of Semple, which he had founded. He married Margaret, daughter of Sir Robert Colvill of Ochiltree, in Airshire, and by her had two sons, William, his heir; and Gabriel, ancestor of the Semples of Cathcart.

William, his eldest son, second lord, was by James V. made one of his privy council, and married three wives, but had issue only by the first, lady Margaret, daughter of Hugh, first earl of Eglington, by whom he had issue Robert, his heir; and David, ancestor of the Semples of Craigbetts, a branch of which settled in Spain 100 years ago, and flourish there to this day; and two daughters, Helen, married to Allan, third lord Cathcart; and Mary, to Sir John Stirling of Keir. He died in 1548, and was succeeded by his eldest son,

Robert, third lord, who signalized his valour at the battle of Pinkey, or Musselburgh, where he had the misfortune to be taken prisoner; and being sent to England, there remained till peace was concluded between the two kingdoms. He married first, Isabel, daughter of Sir William Hamilton of Sanquhar, by whom he had issue Robert, master of Semple; Andrew, ancestor of the Semples of Bruntshiel and Millbank; Grisel, wife of James Hamilton of Stanhouse; Margaret, first, of John Hamilton of Broomhill, ancestor of lord Bellhaven; and secondly, of John Whiteford of that ilk; Janet, of Hugh Montgomery of Harlehead; and ———, of Alexander Fleming of Barrochan. By his second wife, Elizabeth Carlyle, a daughter of the family of Torthorald, he had one son, John, ancestor of the Semples of Belltrees; and three daughters, Jane, married to James, third lord Rofs; Grifel, to John Blair of that ilk; and Dorothy, to Sir Robert Montgomery of Skelmorley. He died in 1571, and his eldest son, Robert, master of Semple, dying in his life-time, in 1569, leaving issue by his wife Barbara, daughter of Archibald Preston of Valleyfield, a son,

Robert, he succeeded his grandfather, and was fourth lord Semple,

Semple, who by king James VI. was sent ambassador to Spain. He married first, lady Agnes, daughter of Hugh, third earl of Eglington, by whom he had issue Hugh, his heir; and four daughters; Anne, wife of Sir Archibald Stewart of Castlemilk; Barbara, of Sir Colin Lawmont of Inneryne; Grisel, of John Logan of Raiss; and Margaret, of Robert Brisbane of Bishoptoun. His second wife was Joanna de Evieland, a Flemish lady, by whom he had a son, Sir William Semple of Letterkeny, who settled in Ireland; and had a daughter, ———, married to Sir Francis Hamilton, Knt. His lordship died in 1611, and was succeeded by his eldest son,

Hugh, fifth lord, who married two wives, first, lady Anne, daughter of James, earl of Abercorn; by whom he had a daughter, Marian, wife of Sir George Preston, of Valleyfield. And secondly, lady Elizabeth, daughter of Francis, ninth earl of Errol, and had issue by her, four sons, Francis, Robert, Archibald, and James, and two daughters, Elizabeth, married to William Douglas, second lord Mordington, and Jane, to William Menzies of Pitfoddils.

Francis the eldest son succeeded, and was 6th lord, who dying without issue in 1644, was succeeded by his brother,

Robert, seventh lord, who marrying Ann, daughter of James lord Mordington, had issue two sons and two daughters, viz. Robert, master of Semple, who died in his youth; Francis; Anne, of whom hereafter; and Jane, wife of Alexander Sinclair of Roslin. He died in 1675, and was succeeded by his only surviving son,

Francis, eighth lord Semple, who being, by the care of his noble relations, educated in the Protestant religion, took his place in parliament at the end of the reign of Charles II. where his ancestors, being all Roman Catholics, had never sat from the time of the Reformation. He married Grisel, daughter of Sir Archibald Primrose of Dalmeny, but dying without issue in 1684, his estate and title devolved on his eldest sister, Anne, as heir of line, who married Francis Abercromby of Fetternein, Esq; who was honoured by king James VII. with the title of lord Glasford, for life, in regard that the title of Semple was to descend to his lady's heirs. By her he had issue five sons and one daughter; Francis; captain Robert, killed abroad; John, of whom hereafter; Alexander, who died an infant; and Hugh, of whom afterwards. The daughter, Jane, died unmarried. The baroness, their mother, died in 1691; and was succeeded by her eldest son,

Francis, ninth lord Semple, who was a great opposer of the union. He died unmarried, and was succeeded by his brother,

John, tenth lord, who dying also without issue, was succeeded by his next surviving brother,

Hugh, the eleventh lord, who served with great reputation

In queen Anne's wars, both in Flanders and Spain. In 1718, he was major of the 26th regiment, and in 1740, was appointed colonel of the 42d, with which, in the year 1743, he acquired great glory in Flanders. In 1745, being in Flanders, he was appointed colonel of the 25th regiment; at the battle of Culloden, in 1746, he commanded the left wing of the king's army, acting as brigadier general, and behaved with remarkable bravery and conduct. Afterwards he commanded in Aberdeen, where he lost his life in December 1746, by the tendon of his arm being pricked in letting him blood. He married Sarah, daughter and coheir of —— Gaskall, Esq; by whom he had issue five sons and six daughters, viz. John, now lord Semple; George and Hugh, officers in the army; Philip and Ralph, deceased; Sarah, wife of Patrick Crawford of Auchinames, who died in 1750; Jane; Betty, who died young; Anne, wife of Dr. Adam Austin, physician of Edinburgh; Marian and Rebecca. He was succeeded by his eldest son,

John, twelfth and present lord, who married Janet, daughter and heir of —— Dunlop of Bishoptoun, by whom he has issue a son, Hugh, master of Semple; and a daughter.

TITLES.] The right honourable John Semple, lord Semple.
CREATION.] So created in 1488, by James IV.
ARMS.] Pearl, a chevron cheque, ruby, and of the first, between three buglehorns, diamond, garnished of the 2d.
CREST.] On a wreath, a stag's head, proper, attired, pearl.
SUPPORTERS.] Two greyhounds, pearl, each having a plain collar, ruby.
MOTTO.] Keep tryste.
CHIEF SEAT.] At Semple House, in Renfrewshire.

ELPHINSTONE, Lord ELPHINSTONE.

JOHN de Elphinstone, immediate ancestor of this noble family, was possessed of the lands and barony of Elphinstone, in the reigns of Alexander II. and III. and dying in the year 1263, was succeeded by his son Alexander, who was succeeded by his eldest son, Sir John, who was one of those great men that swore fealty to Edward I. of England, in 1296. He had a son, Alexander, whose son, Alexander, was succeeded, in 1399, by his eldest son, Sir William, whose eldest son, Sir Alexander, was slain at the battle of Piperden, 1437, where the Scots obtained a victory over the English: and leaving an only daughter, Agnes, who was married to Sir Gilbert, son of Sir Adam Johnston of that ilk, he, in her right, had the lands and barony of Elphinstone, in Lothian; but the estate in Stirlingshire came by arbitration, in 1471, to Henry Elphinstone, who was brother of the said Sir Alexander, and from him the family hath continued in a direct line to the present time. Henry

died

died in 1496, and his son James dying before him, was succeeded by his grandson, Sir John Elphinstone, who was succeeded by his son and heir,

Sir Alexander, who was created a baron, and made one of the privy council. He married Elizabeth Barlow, an English lady, then maid of honour to queen Margaret, the wife of king James IV. and with her had the lands of Kildrummy, in Aberdeenshire; and in September 1513, was slain with the said king at the battle of Floddon, in Northumberland, leaving issue Alexander his heir, and three daughters, viz. Isabel, wife of David Lindsay of Dunrod, and afterwards of Robert Maxwell of Calderwood; ———, of John Bruce of Cultmalindie; and Elizabeth, of Sir David Somerville of Plain. He was succeeded by his only son,

Alexander, second lord, who married Katharine, daughter of John lord Erskine, by whom he had five sons, Robert, John, James, Sir Michael, and William; and of those, the fourth was master of the houshold to king James VI. The daughters were, Isabel, wife of James Hamilton of Haggs; Margery, of Sir Robert Drummond of Carnock; and Margaret, of Alexander Livingston of Dunipace. He was killed at the battle of Pinkie in 1547, and was succeeded by his eldest son,

Robert, third lord, who married Margaret, daughter of Sir John Drummond of Innerpeffry, and had issue by her three sons and four daughters; Alexander, master of Elphinstone; George, a clergyman; Sir James, ancestor of the lords Balmerino: ———, wife of Walter lord Deskford, ancestor of the earl of Finlater; Jane, of Walter Barclay of Towie; Elizabeth, of Sir Robert Innes of that ilk; and Margaret, of John Cunningham of Drumquhassel. He died in 1602, and was succeeded by his eldest son,

Alexander, fourth lord, who was made one of the privy council to king James VI. and lord treasurer of Scotland. He married Jane, daughter of William lord Livingston, and had issue by her four sons, Alexander, master of Elphinstone; James, of whom hereafter; John, and Michael; and five daughters; Anne, wife of John earl of Sutherland; Jane, of Arthur lord Forbes; Elizabeth, of Sir John Bruce of Airth; Christian, of Sir Thomas Urquhart of Cromarty; and Helen, of Sir William Cockburn of Langton, and afterwards of Henry Rollo of Woodside. He died in 1648, and was succeeded by his eldest son,

Alexander, fifth lord, who married Elizabeth, daughter of Patrick, the third lord Drummond, and had a daughter named Lilias; but having no male issue, his honour descended to his nephew, Alexander, the son of his brother James: Which

Alexander, sixth lord, marrying the said Lilias, his uncle's only daughter, whereby the heirs male, and of line, were

united,

united, by her had issue two sons, Alexander and John; and a daughter, Ann, married to Walter Sandilands, lord Torphichen. He died in 1655.

Alexander, his eldest son, succeeded, and was seventh lord; who dying without issue in 1669, his estate and dignity descended to his brother,

John, eighth lord, who married lady Isabel Maitland, daughter of Charles earl of Lauderdale, and had issue by her three sons and three daughters, viz. Charles; John, who died unmarried; captain William, killed at Preston in 1715; Elizabeth, wife of John Campbell of Mammore, second son of Archibald, the ninth earl of Argyll, and father of John the present duke; Margaret, of George, count Lesley, of Balquhain, and after, of Sir James Gordon of Park; and Mary, of Mr. Thomas Buchan, advocate. He was succeeded by his eldest son,

Charles, ninth lord, who married Elizabeth, daughter of Sir William Primrose of Carrington, Bart. sister of James, first viscount Primrose, and had issue four sons, John, who married Marjory, daughter of Sir Gilbert Fleming of Farm, and died without issue; James, who died unmarried; Charles, the present lord; and Archibald, who died in the expedition against Carthagena, in 1741: also two daughters, Grisel, wife of captain Woodroofe Gascoigne; and Primrose, of Alexander earl of Home. His lordship dying in February 1757, was succeeded by his son,

Charles, the tenth and present lord, who married lady Clementina, only surviving daughter and heir of John earl of Wigton, by lady Mary Keith, eldest daughter of William, ninth earl Marshal, by whom he has issue four sons and four daughters, viz. John, master of Elphinstone, an officer in the army, and wounded in the battle of Quebec; Charles, a gallant youth, who lost his life in the Prince George, of ninety guns, burnt at sea in 1758; William, in the service of the East India company; Keith, in the navy: Mary, Eleanor, Primrose, and Clementina.

TITLES.] The right honourable Charles Elphinstone, lord Elphinstone.

CREATION.] Baron Elphinstone, in the county of Stirling, by king James IV. 1509.

ARMS.] Pearl, a chevron, diamond, between three boars heads erazed, ruby.

CREST.] On a wreath, a lady from the girdle richly attired, holding a castle in her right hand, and in her left a branch of laurel.

SUPPORTERS.] Two savages, proper, each wreathed about his head and middle with laurel, and holding in his outer hand a dart, proper.

P MOTTO.]

MOTTO.] Caufe cauſit, or chance produced it.
CHIEF SEAT.] At Elphinſtone caſtle, in the county of Stirling.

OLIPHANT, Lord OLIPHANT.

NOT to trouble my reader with the various traditional accounts of this family, I ſhall obſerve, that David de Oliphant, immediate anceſtor of this family, was one of thoſe barons who, in 1142, accompanied king David I. into England with an army, to aſſiſt his niece the empreſs Maud againſt king Stephen; but after raiſing the ſiege of Winchefter, the ſaid king David was ſo cloſely purſued, that had it not been for the ſingular conduct and courage of this David de Oliphant, the king had then been taken priſoner. He was alſo a witneſs to ſeveral donations of that prince to religious places, and particularly to the priory of Coldingham, whereto his ſeal is appending, being three creſcents, which clearly proves him to be the anceſtor of this family, whoſe armorial bearings are the ſame to this day. David his ſon ſucceeded, and was greatly in the favour of king Malcolm IV. and his brother king William. Sir Walter, ſon of this David, was one of the hoſtages for the ranſom of the ſaid king William, who was taken priſoner by the Engliſh at the battle of Alnwick, 1173. He married Chriſtian, daughter of Ferchard earl of Strathern, by whom he left iſſue another Walter, who ſucceeded him. He was ſucceeded by his ſon Sir William, who in 1297, was one of thoſe barons of Scotland whom king Edward I. required to attend him in perſon, with men, horſe, and arms, into France, in order to recover his province of Gaſcony; after which, in 1303, he was governor of Stirling caſtle, which he defended againſt the Engliſh for the ſpace of three months, but for want of proviſion, was compelled to ſurrender. He married Iſabel, a daughter of the family of Douglas, by whom he had a ſon,

Sir William, his heir, who had a grant from king Robert I. of the lands of Newtill and Kelſpindie, and was afterwards a ſubſcriber to the letter which, in 1320, was ſent from the barons of Scotland to the Pope, aſſerting the independency of their country. Sir Walter, his ſon, ſucceeded him, and marrying lady Elizabeth Bruce, daughter of king Robert I. and ſiſter of David II. had a ſon, Walter, who obtained from king Robert II. a grant of the lands of Kelly and Piterie ; and marrying Mary, daughter of Sir Robert Erſkine of that ilk, had two ſons, by the eldeſt of whom, John, he was ſucceeded, who married a daughter of Sir William Borthwick of that ilk, anceſtor of lord Borthwick, by whom he had his ſucceſſor,

Sir William, one of the hoſtages for the ranſom of king James I. in 1424, who was a priſoner in England. He
married

LORD OLIPHANT.

married Ifabel, daughter of Sir John Stewart of Innermeath, lord of Lorn, and had iffue Sir John, who was flain at the battle of Arbroath in 1455. He married Ifabel, daughter of Sir Walter Ogilvy of Auchterhoufe, and left two fons, Laurence and Thomas.

Laurence, the eldeft, fucceeding, was, by king James III. made a lord of feffion, one of the privy council, and fheriff of Perthfhire. He was alfo of the privy council to king James IV. by whom he was created a baron. He married the lady Ifabel Hay, daughter of William the fifth earl of Errol, and had three fons, John; William, anceftor of the Oliphants of Gafk; and George, of Balmaiton. He died in 1500, and was fucceeded by his eldeft fon,

John, second lord, who marrying lady Elizabeth, daughter of Colin earl of Argyll, had iffue two fons, Colin; and Laurence, abbot of Inchaffry, flain at the battle of Floddon. He died in 1516, and was fucceeded by his grandfon, Laurence, fon of his eldeft fon, Colin, who was killed alfo at the battle of Floddon, by his wife, lady Elizabeth Keith, daughter of William earl Marfhal.

Which Laurence, third lord, married Margaret, daughter of Sir James Sandilands of Calder, and had iffue by her two fons and four daughters, viz. Laurence; Peter, anceftor of the Oliphants of Langton: Catharine, wife of Alexander Oliphant of Kelly, and fecondly, of George Dundas of that ilk; Margaret, of William Murray of Abercairny, and fecondly, of James Clephane of Carflogie, in Fife; Jane, of William Moncrief of that ilk; and Lilias, of Robert Lindfay of Balgony. He died in 1566, and was fucceeded by his eldeft fon,

Laurence, fourth lord, who married lady Margaret, daughter of George, feventh earl of Errol, by whom he had two fons, Laurence, his heir apparent; and John, of whom hereafter: and three daughters, Elizabeth, wife of William, tenth earl of Angus; Jane, of Alexander Bruce of Cultmalindie; and Margaret, of Sir James Johnfton of Wefterhall. He died in 1592, and

Laurence, his heir apparent, dying before his father, left by his wife, lady Chriftian, daughter of William earl of Moreton, who afterwards married James earl of Home, a fon, Laurence; and a daughter, Ann, who was married to Robert lord Lindfay, anceftor of the earl of Crawford; and his faid fon,

Laurence, fucceeded his grandfather, and was fifth lord; marrying Lilias, daughter of James Drummond, lord Maderty, anceftor of the vifcount Strathallan, he had an only daughter, Ann, who married Sir James Douglas of Mordington; but having no male iffue, the title defcended to Patrick Oliphant, the fon of John, his father's brother.

Which Patrick, sixth lord, marrying firft, Elizabeth, daughter of Sir Patrick Cheyne of Effemont, had iffue a daughter, Lilias, married to Sir Laurence Oliphant of Gafk; and fecondly, Mary, daughter of Sir James Crichton of Frendraught, by whom he had issue three sons, Charles, William, and Francis; whereof the youngest was a captain, the second a colonel; and was succeeded by his eldest son,

Charles, seventh lord, who married Mary, a daughter of the Ogilvy family, and had issue,

Patrick, eighth lord, who dying in 1721, without issue, the honour descended to his uncle William, ninth lord; but he dying without issue, Francis Oliphant, said to be the next heir-male, assumed the title, and was tenth lord. He married Mrs. Linley, of York, but dying without issue, the title was claimed by William, son of Charles Oliphant, Esq; one of the clerks of session, who became the eleventh lord; but he dying also without issue, in 1751, David Oliphant of Bachilton, Esq; claimed the honour, which has been allowed him, and is the twelfth lord Oliphant.

TITLES.] The right honourable David Oliphant, lord Oliphant.

CREATION.] So created by king James IV.

ARMS.] Ruby, three crescents, pearl.

CREST.] On a wreath, a unicorn's head, couped, pearl, armed and maned, topaz.

SUPPORTERS.] Two elephants, proper.

MOTTO.] A tout pourvoir.

CHIEF SEATS.] At Don, in the county of Inverness; and at Pittindrek, near the town of Elgin.

SANDILANDS, Lord TORPHICHEN.

THE immediate ancestor of this noble family was Sir James Sandilands, who in the reign of David II. was laird of Sandilands; and marrying Eleanor, sister of William, first earl of Douglas, with her had the barony of West-Calder, called Calder Comitis; and by the said lady he had issue,

Sir James, his heir, who was knighted by king Robert II. who gave him the lady Jane, his second daughter, in marriage, by whom he had issue a son,

Sir James, who was one of the hostages for the ransom of king James I. when he was released from his captivity in England. To him succeeded Sir John, his son, the father of another Sir John, and he of Sir James, who married Margaret, a daughter of the family of Ker of Cefsford, and had two sons, Sir John and Sir James. The eldest dying before his father, left issue Sir James, who succeeded his grandfather, and married Marian, daughter of Archibald Forrester of Corstorphin, ancestor of the lord Forrester, and by her had issue John, of whom hereafter; and Sir James, afterwards lord St. John:

And

And two daughters, Alison, wife of Sir John Cockburn of Ormiston; and Margaret, of William Wauchop of Niddry.

Sir James Sandilands, the second son, having a learned education, was by Sir Walter Lindsay, lord of St. John, recommended to the great master of the knights of Malta, as a person well qualified to be his successor in the preceptory of Torphichen. On the death of the said Sir Walter, in 1543, Sir James Sandilands, who before had been received by the prior of the hospital, and his chapter, to be one of the knights of the military order of Malta, was fully invested with the title, power, and jurisdiction, as lord St. John of Jerusalem in Scotland, as also in the possession of the revenue thereof, which at that time was very great, and spread throughout the kingdom. He was often employed by king James V. and queen Mary, as ambassador to England and France; and at the time of the reformation, renouncing popery, and resigning the lordship of St. John into the hands of the said queen Mary, her majesty was pleased to grant it again, with the preceptory, to him, his heirs and assigns, and erected his lands into the lordship of Torphichen. He married Janet, a daughter of Murray of Polmais, but dying without issue, his estate and honour of lord Torphichen descended to James, his great nephew, grandson of John, his elder brother.

Which James Sandilands of Calder, second lord, married Elizabeth, daughter of James Heriot of Trabrown, and had three sons, James, John, and Walter; and a daughter, Isabel, wife of Hugh Wallace of Ellerstie.

James, the eldest, succeeding, was third lord; and dying unmarried, in 1622, was succeeded by his brother,

John, fourth lord; and he marrying Isabel, daughter of Sir Walter Dundas of that ilk, had two sons and two daughters, viz. John and Walter; ———, wife of Sir Thomas Kilpatrick of Closeburn; and Margaret, of Thomas Marjoribanks of that ilk. He died in 1637, and was succeeded by his eldest son,

John, fifth lord; but he dying without issue, was succeeded by his brother,

Walter, sixth lord, who married four wives, viz. Jane, daughter of Alexander Lindsay of Edzell; Catharine, daughter of William lord Alexander, and sister of William, the second earl of Stirling; Anne, daughter of Alexander, sixth lord Elphinstone; and Christian, daughter and sole heir of James Primrose, brother of Sir Archibald Primrose of Dalmenie, ancestor of the earl of Roseberry. By the first and third he had no issue; by the second, he had two daughters, Anne, wife of Robert, eldest son and heir of Sir Alexander Menzies of that ilk; and Catharine, of David Drummond of Cultmalindie. By his fourth, he had three sons and two daughters, Walter, who died young; James; and John, who died young: Christian,

stian, wife of Robert Pringle, Esq; and Magdalen, who died unmarried. He died in 1696, and was succeeded by his only surviving son,

James, seventh lord, who being a lieutenant colonel, served abroad in queen Ann's wars, and bravely commanded Ker's regiment at the battle of Dunblaine, in 1715. He quitted the army in 1722, and was appointed a lord of police, in which he continued till his death. He married lady Jane Hume, daughter of Patrick earl of Marchmont, lord chancellor of Scotland, and had issue by her eight sons and three daughters, viz. James, master of Torphichen, who at the battle of Preston-pans, in the year 1745, being a captain in the army, received twenty dangerous wounds, which brought on a consumption, and he died three years after, in his father's lifetime, unmarried; Walter, the present lord; Patrick, captain of a ship in the service of the East-India Company, who perished in a storm at sea, leaving no issue; Alexander, who died young; Andrew, major of the Scotch Fuzileers, who was shot through the thigh at the battle of Fontenoy, in 1745, which obliged him to retire from service, after the peace was concluded; George, who died young; Charles, a lieutenant in the army, who lost his life at the siege of Carthagena, in America; and Robert, now an officer in the army: Grisel, Christiana, and Wilhelmina Carolina. His lordship dying in 1752, was succeeded by his son,

Walter, the eighth and present lord, sheriff depute of the county of Edinburgh, who married Elizabeth, only daughter and heir of Dr. Alexander Sandilands, a cadet of the family, by whom he has issue James, master of Torphichen; Alexander, and Walter.

TITLES.] The right honourable Walter Sandilands, lord Torphichen.

CREATION.] So created by queen Mary, in 1563.

ARMS.] Quarterly, 1st and 4th, party per fess, sapphire and topaz; on the first a crown, and on the second a thistle, both proper, being a coat of augmentation; for as Sir James Sandilands, lord of St. John, was great prior of Malta in Scotland, the crown and thistle is borne by his family as a badge of that office; the 2d and 3d quarters are counter-quartered, 1st and 4th, pearl, a bend, sapphire, for the name of Sandilands; the 2d and 3d are the arms of Douglas, which they bear as arms of patronage.

CREST] On a wreath, an eagle displayed, topaz.

SUPPORTERS.] Two savages, each wreathed about his head and middle with laurel, and holding in his outer hand a batoon, all proper.

MOTTO.] Spero meliora.

CHIEF SEATS.]

LORD LINDORES. 215

CHIEF SEATS.] At Calder-houfe, in Mid Lothian; and the caſtle of Torphichen, in Weſt Lothian.

LESLY, Lord LINDORES.

ANDREW, the fifth earl of Rothes, by his firſt wife, Jane, daughter of Sir John Hamilton of Evandale, had two ſons, James, his ſucceſſor; and Sir Patrick, of Pitcairly, who being in great favour with James VI. was a gentleman of his bedchamber, and created baron of Lindores. He married lady Jane Stewart, daughter of Robert earl of Orkney, one of the natural ſons of king James V. and had by her five ſons and five daughters, Margaret, married to John Drummond, lord Maderty, anceſtor of the viſcounts Strathallan; Elizabeth, to Sir William Sinclair of May; Jane, to George Leſly of that ilk, and after, to John Forbes of Leſly; Janet, to Sir John Cunningham of Broomhill; and Mary, to Sir David Barclay of Culcarny. The ſons were, Patrick, who died vita patris; James, Robert, Ludowick, and David, created lord Newark. He was ſucceeded by his ſon,

James, ſecond lord. He married Mary, daughter of Patrick, the ſeventh lord Grey, and had iſſue, John, maſter of Lindores. By a ſecond wife, an Engliſh lady, of the name of Clepburn, he had a daughter, Jane, wife, firſt, of John Stewart of Innernytie, and ſecondly, of John Bruce of Blairhall. He was ſucceeded by his ſon,

John, third lord, who married lady Mary, daughter of James, ſecond earl of Airly; and dying in 1706, was ſucceeded by his only ſon,

David, fourth lord Lindores; but he dying without iſſue, was ſucceeded by

Alexander, fifth lord, lineally deſcended of Sir John Leſly of Newton, ſecond ſon of the third marriage of Andrew, fifth earl of Rothes, according to the entail, being ſon of David, ſon of Andrew, ſon of the ſaid Sir John. Which Alexander, fifth lord, was, on the 20th of September 1745, preferred to the rank of a lieutenant colonel, and in 1760, to that of a major general in the army, and was colonel of a regiment of invalids. He married Jane, daughter of Colin Campbell, late a commiſſioner of the cuſtoms, and brother of Sir James Campbell of Aberuchil, by whom he had iſſue a ſon,

Francis-James, the ſixth and preſent lord, who is an officer in the army, and unmarried.

TITLES.] The right honourable Francis-James Leſly, lord Lindores.

CREATION.] So created, 25 December 1600, by James VI.

ARMS.] Quarterly, 1ſt and 4th, pearl, on a bend, ſapphire, three buckles, topaz, for Leſly; 2d and 3d, topaz, a lion rampant,

pant, ruby, debruised with a ribbon, diamond, for Abernetty; and on a surtout, an escutcheon, ruby, charged with a castle, pearl, masoned, diamond, for the title of Lindores.

CREST.] On a wreath, a demi-angel winged, topaz, holding in his dexter hand a griffon's head erazed, proper.

SUPPORTERS.] Two griffons, pearl, winged, topaz.

MOTTO.] Stat promissa fides.

CHIEF SEAT.] At Lindores abby, near the Tay, in Fifeshire.

STEWART, Lord BLANTYRE.

I HAVE recited, in my account of the family of the earl of Galloway, that Sir William Stewart had issue, Sir Alexander, his successor, ancestor of the earls of Galloway; Sir Thomas Stewart of Minto, who was ancestor of the lords Blantyre; (see p. 119.) and Sir Walter, ancestor of the earls of Blessington.

Sir Thomas, the said second son, married Isabel, daughter and coheir of Sir Walter Stewart of Arthurlie, and with her had large possessions in the shires of Renfrew and Cliddesdale, and therein was succeeded by Sir John, their son, who married Janet, daughter of David, son and heir apparent of Robert lord Fleming, ancestor of the earl of Wigton. He lost his life at the battle of Floddon, with his royal master James IV. in 1513. He was succeeded by his only son, Sir Robert, who married Janet Murray, a daughter of the family of Polmais, by whom he had issue Sir John; Robert, prior of Whitehorn; Malcolm and Walter; and a daughter, Elizabeth, the wife of John Maxwell of Calderwood. He died in 1554, and was succeeded by his eldest son,

Sir John Stewart, who assisted at the coronation of king James VI. and in the year 1578, was provost of the town, and governor of the castle of Glasgow. By his first wife, Janet Hepburn, a daughter of the family of Bothwell, he had a son, Sir Matthew, whose male line is now extinct; and by his second, Margaret, daughter and coheir of Sir James Stewart of Cardonald, a son, Sir Walter, and four daughters, Janet, wife of Sir Archibald Stewart of Castlemilk; Agnes, of John Wallace of Achens and Dundonald; Marian, of William Cleland of that ilk; and ———, of Alexander Baillie of Carphin. Sir Walter, his only son by his second wife, was commendator of Blantyre, and bred up with James VI. under the famous George Buchanan. By that king he was made keeper of the privy seal, gentleman of his bedchamber, lord treasurer of Scotland, and created lord Blantyre; and dying in 1616, left by Nicola his wife, daughter of Sir James Somerville of Cambusnethan, in Cliddesdale, three sons and one daughter, viz. Sir James Stewart, knight of the Bath, killed in a duel with Sir

George

George Wharton, in 1609, in the life-time of his father; William, master of Blantyre; Walter Stewart, M. D. father of Frances, duchess of Lennox and Richmond, and of Sophia, the wife of Henry Bulkley, Esq; master of the houshold to Charles II. His daughter, Margaret, was married to George lord Salton. His lordship died in the year 1616, and was succeeded by his eldest surviving son,

William, second lord, who married Helen, daughter of Sir William Scott of Ardross, by whom he had issue two sons and one daughter, viz. Walter, Alexander, and ———, wife of Sir John Swinton of that ilk. He died in 1638, and was succeeded by his eldest son,

Walter, third lord, who dying without issue in 1641, was succeeded by his brother,

Alexander, fourth lord, who married Margaret, daughter of Sir John Schaw of Greenock, Bart. and had issue a son, Alexander, and a daughter, Helen, wife of James Muirhead of Broadsholm. He was succeeded by his said son,

Alexander, fifth lord, who married first, Margaret, daughter of Sir John Henderson of Fordel, by whom he had no issue; and secondly, Ann, daughter of Sir Robert Hamilton of Presmanen, one of the senators of the college of justice; and dying in 1704, left five sons, Walter, Robert, John, James, and Hugh; and four daughters, Marian, wife of James Stirling of Keir; Frances, of Sir James Hamilton of Rosehaugh; Helen, of John lord Gray; and Anne, of Alexander Hay of Drumelzier, Esq; He died in the year 1704, and was succeeded by his eldest son,

Walter, sixth lord, who was in 1710 elected one of the sixteen peers for Scotland, to serve in the parliament of Great Britain; but dying in June 1713, unmarried, the title and estate devolved on his brother,

Robert, seventh lord, who married first, lady Helen Lyon, daughter of John earl of Strathmore, by whom he had a son, Alexander, who died young; and secondly, Margaret, daughter of William Hay of Drumelzier, Esq; by whom he had six sons and four daughters; Walter, William, Alexander, John, James, and Charles; Margaret; Helen, wife of Oliver Colt of Auldhame, Esq; Marian; and Elizabeth, wife of William Colquhoun of Garscaden, Esq; He died in December 1743, and was succeeded by his eldest son,

Walter, eighth lord Blantyre, who died at Paris in May 1751, unmarried, and was succeeded by his brother,

William, ninth and present lord, then a colonel in the service of the States General.

TITLES.] The right honourable William Stewart, lord Blantyre, in the county of Lanerk.

CREATION.] Lord Blantyre, 20 July 1606, by James VI.

ARMS.]

ARMS.] Topaz, a fess cheque, pearl and sapphire, surmounted of a bend ingrailed, and in chief a rose, ruby.

CREST.] On a wreath, a dove with an olive leaf in its mouth.

SUPPORTERS.] On the dexter side, a savage, wreathed about his head and middle with laurel, and holding over his shoulder a batoon, all proper. On the sinister, a lion, ruby.

MOTTO.] Sola juvat virtus.

CHIEF SEATS.] At Erskine, in Renfrewshire; Cardonnel castle, in the same county; at Leithington, in East Lothian; and at the Craig of Blantyre, in Cliddesdale.

CRANSTON, Lord CRANSTON.

THIS family took their name from the lands and barony of Cranston, in Mid Lothian, of which was Elfric de Cranston, who lived after the year 1250, and was father of Thomas Cranston, whose son, Andreas, had a son, Hugh, one of the Scotch barons that swore fealty to Edward I. of England, in 1296. He was succeeded by his son Andreas, and he by his son Rodolphus de Cranston, whose son John was father of Thomas, who in the reign of David II. 1329, obtained a charter of the lands of his name, and was father of another Thomas, in great favour with James I. and his ambassador to Denmark in 1426. He was succeeded by his son, Sir Thomas, who dying about the year 1470, was succeeded by his eldest son, Sir William, a great favourite of king James II. who living to a great age, died in 1515, and was succeeded by his eldest son, John Cranston, who was father of another Sir William, who was succeeded by his only son, Sir John, who married Margaret, daughter of Nichol Ramsay of Dalhousie, and by her had Sarah, of whom hereafter, besides other daughters; and a son, John, who died before his father, and left issue a son, John de Cranston, who died also before his grandfather, without issue; whereupon the estate came to Sarah, his aunt, above-mentioned, who married Sir William Cranston, son of Sir John Cranston of Moriston, a cadet of her own family, by Barbara, a daughter of the family of Grey; which Sir William was by king James VI. made captain of the guard, and created lord Cranston, in 1611. They had issue John; James, of whom hereafter; Henry and Thomas; and a daughter, Margaret, wife of —— Edgar of Wedderlie. He died in 1627, and was succeeded by his eldest son,

John, second lord, who married two wives, Elizabeth, daughter of Walter Scot, lord Buccleugh; and Helen, daughter of James Lindsay; but dying without issue, the honour descended to his nephew,

William, third lord, son of his brother James, by his wife, lady

lady Elizabeth Stewart, daughter of Francis earl of Bothwell; and the said lord attending king Charles II. to the battle of Worcester, in 1651, was there taken prisoner, and sent to the Tower of London, where he remained several years, his estate being sequestered, and himself excepted out of Cromwell's indemnity, in 1654. He married lady Mary Lesly, daughter of Alexander earl of Leven, by whom he had a son,

James, fourth lord, who married Ann, daughter of Sir Alexander Don of Newton, Bart. by whom he had two sons, William, his heir; and Alexander, who died without issue.

His eldest son, William, fifth lord, who succeeded him, marrying lady Jane Ker, daughter of William, second marquis of Lothian, by her had issue James, his heir; William, who died young; Archibald, Alexander, and William-Henry, an officer in lord Mark Ker's regiment, who died at Dunkirk in January 1753; Charles, George; Jane, who died young; Anne, wife of —— Selby, Esq; Elizabeth, Jane, and Mary: and his lordship was succeeded by his eldest son,

James, now sixth lord Cranston, who married Sophia, daughter of —— Brown, an English lady, by whom he has four sons, viz. William, master of Cranston; Brown, James, and Charles.

TITLES.] The right honourable James Cranston, lord Cranston.

CREATION.] Baron Cranston, in the county of Edinburgh, 19 November 1611, by king James VI.

ARMS.] Ruby, three cranes, pearl.

CREST.] On a wreath, a crane sleeping, with its head under its wing, and holding up a stone with the right foot.

SUPPORTERS.] On the dexter side, a lady richly apparelled, holding a branch of strawberries towards a stag, proper, on the sinister.

MOTTO.] Thou shalt want, ere I want.

CHIEF SEAT.] At Creling, in the county of Roxburgh.

NAPIER, Lord NAPIER.

THE immediate ancestor of this noble family was John de Napier, who lived in 1280, and whose son, William, was father of John, and he father of another William, who was governor of the castle of Edinburgh in 1401. His son Alexander made a great figure in the reign of James I. and was provost of Edinburgh in 1437, and obtained the lands of Merchiston, afterwards the chief title of his family. He was succeeded by his son,

Sir Alexander Napier of Merchiston, who was made comptroller of Scotland by king James II. and vice admiral of Scotland

land by king James III. and marrying Elizabeth, a daughter of Laudre of Hatton, by her had a son,

John, who was provost of Edinburgh, and made a noble and beneficial alliance, by his marriage with Elizabeth Menteith, who was heir to the line of Menteith, earls of Lennox, by whom he had two sons, Sir Archibald and John.

Sir Archibald, who succeeded, marrying Katharine, a daughter of Douglas of Lochleven, by her had, *inter alia*, a son,

Sir Alexander, who in September 1513, lost his life at the battle of Floddon with king James IV. He married Janet, daughter of Edmund Chisholm of Cromlix, and by her had a son, Alexander; and two daughters, Eleanor, married to Sir John Melvil of Raith, ancestor of the earl of Melvil; and Janet, to Archibald Bruce of Pitfouls. He was succeeded by his eldest son,

Alexander, who married Margaret, daughter of Sir Duncan Campbell of Glenurchie, ancestor of the earl of Breadalbane, and had three sons, Sir Archibald, his heir; Alexander, whose son, Sir Robert Napier of Luton-Hoo, in the county of Bedford, Knt. was created a baronet in 1611, ancestor of the present Sir John Napier, Bart. from the same family also descended Sir Gerrard Napier of Middlemershal, Dorset, created a baronet in 1641, ancestor of Sir William Napier, Bart. and others of that name in Somersetshire and Oxfordshire; and Andrew. He was slain in the battle of Pinkie in 1547, and succeeded by his eldest son,

Sir Archibald, who was knighted by king James VI. and made master of the Mint, in 1587; and marrying first, Janet, daughter of Francis Bothwell, one of the senators of the college of justice, had a son, John; and by his second, Elizabeth, a daughter of the family of Mowbray, had a son, Sir Alexander, a senator of the college of justice in the reign of Charles I. and two daughters, Margaret, married to James lord Ogilvy; and Agnes, to Sir Patrick Gray of Innergowrie. He died in 1608, and was succeeded by his eldest son,

John, who being inclined to study, arrived to very great knowledge in several useful branches of literature, so that few equalled him in that age; and his great experience and abilities in mathematical learning rendered him so eminent, especially his logarithmic tables, that they will ever be esteemed as the masterly product of a great genius.

This gentleman, who died in 1617, in the 67th year of his age, marrying first, Margaret, daughter of Sir James Stirling of Keir, by her had issue Sir Archibald, his heir: and by his second, Agnes, daughter of Sir James Chisholm of Cromlix, he had issue five sons and five daughters, viz. John Napier of Easter Torrie; Robert, ancestor of the Napiers of Kilcroick; Alexander, of Gillets; William, ancestor of the Napiers of Craiganet;

Craiganet; and Adam, of the Napiers of Blackston: Margaret, wife of James Stewart of Rosythe; Jane, of James Hamilton of Kilbrackmot; Elizabeth, of William Cunninghame of Craigends; Agnes, of George Drummond of Balloch; and Helen, of the Rev. Matthew Brisbane, an eminent divine. He was succeeded by his eldest son,

Sir Archibald, who was by king James VI. made one of the privy council, treasurer depute, lord justice clerk, and one of the judges in the court of session; and by king Charles I. was for some time continued in the treasurer's office, and as one of the extraordinary lords of session. On the 2d of March 1626, he was created a baronet; and on May 4, 1627, advanced to the title of lord Napier of Merchiston. He married lady Margaret Graham, daughter of John earl of Montrose; and dying in 1645, left Archibald, his heir; and a daughter, Elizabeth, wife of Sir George Stirling of Keir.

Archibald, his son, second lord, was heartily engaged in the royal cause, during the time of the civil war, and at the end thereof went to Holland, where he died, in 1660. He married lady Elizabeth Erskine, daughter of John earl of Mar, by whom he had issue two sons, Archibald; and John, killed in the sea-fight with the Dutch, in 1672: and three daughters, Jane, married to Sir Thomas Nicholson of Carnock, Bart. Margaret, of whom hereafter; and Mary, who died unmarried. He was succeeded by his eldest son,

Archibald, third lord, who obtained a new patent, dated February 7, 1677, from king Charles II. whereby his honour was to remain to the heirs of his own body; and failing thereof, to the heirs of the bodies of his sisters successively; and dying in 1683, unmarried, the dignity of lord Napier descended to

Sir Thomas Nicolson, his nephew, by his sister Jane, aforesaid, who, according to the aforesaid patent, took the name and arms of Napier, and was fourth lord; but dying under age, and without issue, his honour descended to

Margaret, the second sister, who by John Brisbane, Esq; secretary to the navy, &c. &c. her husband, had a son, John, who was a lieutenant in the royal navy, and died at sea in 1704, unmarried; and the honour descended to his only sister, Elizabeth, who married Sir William Scot, son and heir of Sir Francis Scot of Thirlestane, by whom she had a son, Francis, now fifth lord Napier, great grandson of the second lord, of whose paternal descent we shall therefore speak.

In the reign of James V. Robert Scot of Thirlestane, great grandson of Robert Scot of Eskdale, who was warden of the western borders, marrying a daughter of the family of Johnston of that ilk, now dignified with the title of marquis of Annandale, by her had John Scot of Thirlestane, their heir, who for his loyalty and ready service to the said king before the route at
Solway,

LORD NAPIER.

Solway, or Solan Mofs, 1542, was by him honoured with a part of the royal enfigns, and other fuitable marks, for his armorial bearing, as by the following ordinance is expreffed.

'WE James, by the grace of God, king of Scots, confideran the faith and good fervis of right traift friend, John Scot of Thirleftan, quha commed to our hoft at Sautre Edge, with threefcore and ten lanciers on horfeback, of his friends and followers; and bean willing to gang with us into England, when all our nobles and others refufed, he was ready to ftake all at our bidding: for which caufe, it is our will, and we do command our lyon herald, and his deputis for the time bean, to give the faid John Scot a border of flower de liffes about his coat of arms, fike as is our royal banner, and alfwae an bundle of lances above his helmet, with thir words, Ready, Ay Ready, that he and all his aftercomers may bruick the fame, as a pledge and taiken of our goodwill and kindnefs for his trew worthinefs. Given at Fala-muir, under our hand and privy cafket, the 27 day of July, 1542.'

Thomas Erfkine, Sec.

Robert, his fon and heir, was warden depute of the weft borders; and marrying Margaret, fifter of Walter Scot, the firft lord Buccleugh, by her was father of Walter, and he of Patrick; who marrying Ifabel, daughter of Sir John Murray of Blackbarony, Bart. had a fon, Sir Francis, who in 1660 was created a baronet; and marrying lady Henrietta Ker, daughter of William, the third earl of Lothian, had a fon, Sir William Scot, who married Elizabeth, daughter of Margaret lady Napier, above-mentioned, and took the name of Napier; and dying on the 13th of October 1725, left

Francis, now lord Napier, as before recited; who married firft, lady Henrietta Hope, daughter of Charles earl of Hopeton, by whom, who died in February 1744-5. he had a fon, William, mafter of Napier, who in December 1754, married Mary-Anne, daughter of Charles, eighth lord Cathcart; and Charles, a captain in the navy in 1754; Francis, a captain of marines; John, a lieutenant in the 25th regiment of foot, who died in Germany the day after the battle of Minden; Mark, a captain of foot: and a daughter, Henrietta, who died an infant. His lordfhip married fecondly, Mary, daughter of major George Johnfton, in April 1750, by whom he had iffue, George; James, who died in 1760; Patrick; James-John: Elizabeth, who died in infancy; Efther and Mary. His lordfhip is a lord of the police.

TITLES.] The right honourable Francis Napier, lord Napier of Merchifton.

CREATIONS.] Lord Napier, 4 May 1627, by king Charles I. alfo a baronet, 22 Auguft 1680.

ARMS.]

ARMS.] Quarterly, 1st and 4th, pearl, a saltire ingrailed, between four roses, ruby, for Napier; 2d and 3d, topaz, on a bend, sapphire, a star between two crescents of the first, within a double tressure, counterflory with fleurs de lis of the 2d, for Scot of Thirlestane.

CREST.] On a wreath, a right arm couped below the elbow, and erect, grasping a crescent.

SUPPORTERS.] On the dexter side, an eagle, proper. On the sinister, a chevalier in a coat of mail, holding a launce with a penon, all proper; and below the shield, by way of compartment, a mural crown, pearl, masoned, diamond, out of which issue six launces disposed in saltire, as the former.

MOTTO.] Ready, Ay Ready.

CHIEF SEATS.] At Ballenton, in Perthshire; Thirlestane, Berwickshire; and Edinbillie, in Stirlingshire.

FAIRFAX, Lord FAIRFAX.

RICHARD Fairfax, in the sixth year of king John, of England, 1205, was possessed of the lands of Ascham, near York. His son, William, had another William, bailiff of York in 1249, whose son, Thomas, died in the twelfth year of Edward I. and was succeeded by his eldest son, John, whose son, Thomas, was succeeded by his son, William, and he by his eldest son, Thomas, who was living in 1350, and was succeeded by his eldest son, William Fairfax of Walton, Esq; whose eldest son, Thomas, died in 1415, and Richard, his eldest son, flourished in the reigns of Henry IV. V. and VI. He was chief justice of England after the year 1442; and by his wife, Anastasia, daughter and coheir of John Calthorp of Calthorp, Esq; had issue six sons and three daughters, viz. William, ancestor of the viscount Fairfax of Ireland; Bryan Fairfax, L.L.D. who died without issue; Sir Guy, of whom hereafter; Richard, a priest; Sir Nicholas, a knight of Rhodes; Miles: Margaret, Anne, and Elein.

Sir Guy, third son, being bred to the law, was attorney general, and afterwards justice of the king's bench, in the reigns of Edward IV. Richard III. and Henry VII. He built Steeton castle, in the county of York, which afterwards became the seat of his family. He married Isabel, daughter of Sir William Rither of Rither, and by her had Sir William, his heir; Thomas, serjeant at law; Guy and Nicholas: and two daughters.

Sir William, who succeeded, was by king Henry VIII. made justice of the common pleas; and marrying Elizabeth, eldest daughter of Sir Robert Manners, ancestor of the duke of Rutland, by her had Sir William, his heir, and four daughters.

Sir William, who succeeded in 1514, being sheriff of Yorkshire the 26th and 31st of Henry VIII. that king sent him two

letters,

letters, directed, To our trusty and well beloved Sir William Fairfax, Knt. which are still in the possession of the family. He obtained the castle and manor of Denton by Isabel, his wife, daughter and heir of John Thwaits, lord thereof; and died the 31st of October, 1557. He had five sons and five daughters; Sir Thomas, Francis, Edward, Henry, and Gabriel, who was seated at Streton, which his father gave him on disinheriting his eldest son, Sir Thomas, with whom he was highly offended for accompanying the duke of Bourbon, at the sacking of Rome, at the beginning of the Reformation. The five daughters all lived to be married. He died in 1557, and was succeeded by his eldest son, Sir Thomas, of Denton, sheriff of York in 157', and knighted by queen Elizabeth in 1579. By his wife Dorothy, daughter of George Gale of Acham-Grange, Esq; treasurer of the Mint at York, he had five sons and two daughters, viz. Sir Thomas; Edward, an excellent poet in the reign of Charles I. Henry and Ferdinando, who died young; and Sir Charles, colonel of 3000 soldiers at the siege of Ostend, in which he was killed: Ursula, wife of Sir Henry Bellassise, Bart. and mother of Thomas, viscount Falconberg; and Christian, of John Aske, of Aughton, Esq; He died in 1599, and was succeeded by his eldest son,

Sir Thomas, who accompanying the earl of Essex into France, in 1591, who was then general of the English army, sent by queen Elizabeth to the assistance of Henry IV. against the Spaniards and Popish league, was there knighted by the said general in the camp before Roan, in Normandy, for his bravery in that service, and was created lord Fairfax by king Charles I. He married Helen, daughter of Robert Ask, of Aughton, Esq; and dying in May 1540, in the 80th year of his age, he had issue five sons and two daughters, viz. Ferdinando; Henry, of whom more presently; major William, killed in 1621 at Frankendale, in the palatinate of which he was one of the defenders; colonel Charles, ancestor of the family of Menston; John; Peregrine, killed in the defence of Rochelle, in France; Thomas, slain in Turkey, in 1621: Dorothy, married to Sir William Constable, Bart. and Anne, to Sir George Wentworth of Wolley, Knt. He was succeeded by his eldest son,

Ferdinando, second lord, who was knighted in 1589, and at the beginning of the civil war, was the parliament's general for the associated county of York. In December 1642, being intrenched at Tadcaster, he was attacked by the earl of Newcastle, whom he vigorously repulsed, and obliged him to retreat with loss. In January 1643, he routed lord Byron, with his Irish forces, at Namptwich, in Cheshire, most of whom he killed, and took prisoner colonel George Monk. In April 1644, he defeated lord Bellassise, at Selby, and took him prisoner, with sixteen hundred of his men. In July

July following he commanded the main battle with the earl of Leven at Marston Moor, where the king's army, under prince Rupert, was defeated, and thereupon took possession of York as governor. He married lady Mary Sheffield, daughter of Edmund, the first earl of Mulgrave, ancestor of the late duke of Buckingham, by whom he had issue three sons and six daughters, viz. Sir Thomas; Charles, colonel of horse, slain at Marston-moor on July 23, 1644; John, who died young: Ursula, who died unmarried; Elizabeth, wife of Sir William Constable of Linchwick, in Worcestershire, Bart. Eleanor, of Sir William Selby of Twisdale, in Northumberland, Bart. Frances, of Sir Thomas Widdrington of Chiburn Grange, in the county of Northumberland, serjeant at law; Mary, of Henry Arthlington of Arthlington, Esq; and Dorothy, of Edward Hutton of Poppleton, Esq; He married secondly, Rhoda, daughter and heir of Thomas Chapman of Strafford, Esq; by whom he had a daughter, Ursula, married to William Cartwright of Aynho, in Northamptonshire, Esq; whose daughter, Rhoda, was wife of Henry, second son of William duke of Devonshire. He died in 1646, and was succeeded in his title, estates, and posts, by his son,

Thomas, third lord, who in January 1642, took the town of Leeds from Sir William Savil, and made five hundred men prisoners. In July 1644, he commanded the right wing of the parliament army at Marston-moor, which gained a complete victory over the royalists; having also, in the preceding April, joined his father in the fight with lord Bellassise. In 1645, the 34th year of his age, he was made general in chief of the parliament armies, which he commanded with great success; for in that year he fought and totally routed the king at Naseby, retook Leicester, beat colonel Goring, took Bridgewater, Dartmouth, Bristol, beat the lord Hopton, forced the prince of Wales to retire into Scilly, and thence to France; and then reducing all the west, drove the king from Oxford in May 1646. At this time he led the Presbyterian party in the house, and the next year waited on the king, when he was brought to the army, which he led to London, and was made governor of the Tower. In 1646, he succeeded his father as before observed, and in August following, reduced Colchester for the parliament; but the Independents now getting uppermost in the parliament, as well as army, he had no share in their violent resolutions; and as he had no hand in the death of the king, he had no power to prevent it. In 1649, he was continued general of the army; but being dissatisfied at the parliament's war with Scotland, he resigned his commission in 1650, and was succeeded by Oliver Cromwell. In 1659, he entered into measures with general Monk, to whom he gave considerable assistance in the restoration of king Charles II. and was one of the commissioners sent by the parliament to the king upon that great occasion; when arriving at the Hague, he was received by his majesty with singular favour and goodness, which was continued to the end of his life. Soon after the king was restored, he was elected knight of the shire for the county of York, but lived retired in the country, where he passed the remainder of his days, highly esteemed for his many heroic and virtuous qualities, for which he was justly celebrated by the greatest pens of that age; all parties agreeing in the due praise of his merit. He married Ann, daughter and coheir of Sir Horatio Vere, who in 1620 commanded the small body of English forces in the Palatinate, by whom he had a daughter, Mary, married to George Villiers, the second duke of Buckingham of that name, but died without issue; and Elizabeth, who died young: And the said lord dying in 1671, without male issue, the honour descended to Henry Fairfax of Oglethorp, Esq; son of Henry, the second son of Thomas, first lord Fairfax. Which

Henry, fourth lord, was also knight of the shire for the county of York, and married Frances, daughter and heir of Sir Robert Barwick of Tolston, and had four sons and five daughters, Dorothy, married first, to Robert Stapylton, Esq; and secondly, to Bennet Sherrard, Esq; and was mother of Philip earl of Harborough; Frances, to Mr. Rymer; Anne, to Ralph Ker, son of Sir Ralph Ker of Durham; and Ursula and Mary, who died unmarried. The sons were, Thomas; Henry, sometime sheriff of York; Bryan and Barwick. He died in 1680, and was succeeded by his eldest son,

Thomas, fifth lord, who was a colonel in the guards, and a brigadier general, and several times before the union, knight of the shire for the county of York, which seat he was obliged to give up, on becoming a peer of Great Britain. He married Catharine, only daughter and heir of Thomas lord Colepeper, and dying in 1710, left three sons, Thomas, his heir; Henry; and Robert, a major in the guards, and member in the present parliament for Kent, and lieutenant colonel of the western battalion of the militia of that county. He married the daughter of Anthony Collins of Baddow, in the county of Essex, Esq; by whom he had a son and heir, born in January 1743, and other children since. His lordship had also four daughters, Margaret, wife of Dr. David Wilkins, late archdeacon of Suffolk; Catharine, Frances and Mary, who all died unmarried. His lordship died in 1709, and was succeeded by his eldest son,

Thomas, sixth lord, who dying in 1738, was succeeded by his brother,

Henry, now seventh lord Fairfax.

TITLES.] The right honourable Henry Fairfax, lord Fairfax of Cameron.

CREATION.]

CREATION.] Lord Fairfax, 4 May 1627, by king Charles I.

ARMS.] Topaz, three bars gemel, ruby, surmounted of a lion rampant, diamond. His lordship also quarters the arms of Colepeper, pearl, a bend ingrailed, ruby.

CREST.] On a wreath, a lion passant gardant of the last.

SUPPORTERS.] On the dexter side, a lion gardant, diamond; on the sinister, a bay horse.

MOTTO.] Fare Fac.

CHIEF SEAT.] At Leeds castle, in Kent.

MACKAY, Lord REAY.

ALEXANDER Forbes flourished in the reign of Alexander II. who was father of Magnus, father of Morgan, father of Donald, who lived in the reign of David Bruce; father of Jye More, whose son was called Mack Jye, whence *Mackay*. Donald, son of Mack Jye, was father of Angus Mackay, who lived in 1410, and died in 1428, being succeeded by his son Neil, whose son, Angus Dou Mackay of Farre, was a brave soldier, who in 1443 was burnt to death in the church of Tarbet, by the Ross men, whom he had often molested; and was succeeded by his eldest son, John, who endeavouring to revenge his father's death, was slain by the Ross men, in 1479. He was succeeded by his brother, Jye Roy, or Odo Mackay, who from James IV. got a charter of lands in the county of Inverness, wherein he was succeeded by his son Donald, who married a daughter of the family of Sinclair, by whom he had Hutcheon, his heir, who married lady Elizabeth, daughter of George, fourth earl of Caithness, and had a son, Hugh, or Hutcheon, who married lady Jane, daughter of Alexander earl of Sutherland, and in 1614, was succeeded by his eldest son,

Donald, who by a warrant from king Charles I. in 1625, carried over to Germany a regiment of 1500 men, of his own name and followers, to the assistance of the king of Bohemia; and afterwards entered into the service of the kings of Denmark and Sweden, where he served with great reputation. In 1626, he returning to his native country, was first knighted, and soon after created lord Reay. In the civil war he joined the royal party, was taken prisoner at the surrender of Newcastle to the Scotch army, and sent to the castle of Edinburgh, in order to be tried; but being relieved by the marquis of Montrose, he retired to Denmark, where he died. He married first, Barbara Mackenzie, sister of Colin, the first earl of Seaforth, and by her had John, his heir; and Mary, wife of Henry Monro of Clynes, only brother of Sir Robert Monro of Foulis: and secondly, dame Rachael Harrison, by whom he had Robert and Hugh. He was succeeded by his eldest son,

John,

John, second lord, who marrying Barbara, daughter of Donald Mackay of Scaury, had three sons, Donald, brigadier general Æneas, and colonel Robert.

Donald, who was his heir apparent, marrying Ann, daughter of Sir George Munro of Culcairn, and dying before his father, left

George, third lord, who succeeded his grandfather, and was a fellow of the royal society. He married first, Margaret, daughter of that brave officer, lieutenant general Hugh Mackay, who was unfortunately killed at the battle of Steenkirk, 1692; and had a son, Donald. His second wife was Janet, daughter of John Sinclair of Ulbster, by whom he had colonel Hugh Mackay of Bighouse; and Anne, wife of John Watson of Muirhouse, Esq; By his third, who was Mary, daughter of John Dowel, Esq; he had two sons and four daughters; George, of Skibo; colonel Alexander: Mary; Harriot; Christian, wife of John Erskine, jun. of Carnock; and Marian. Dying in the year 1748, he was succeeded by his eldest son,

Donald, fourth lord Reay, who testified his loyalty during the rebellion 1745, by arming his tenants in defence of the government and royal family; and dying in August 1761, was succeeded by his only son,

George, fifth lord, who married first, Marian, daughter of colonel Hugh Mackay of Bighouse, by whom he left no issue; and secondly, a daughter of —— Fairly of that ilk, by whom he had one daughter, Jane. He died in 1765, and was succeeded by Donald, the present lord, though I cannot find by what relation.

TITLES.] The right honourable Donald Mackay, lord Reay, and baronet.

CREATIONS.] Baronet of New Scotland, 18 March 1626; and baron Reay, in the county of Caithness, 20 June 1628, by king Charles I.

ARMS.] Sapphire, on a chevron, topaz, between three bears heads couped, pearl, and muzzled, ruby, a roebuck's head erazed of the last, between two hands holding daggers, all proper.

CREST.] On a wreath, a right hand couped and erect, grasping a dagger as those in the arms.

SUPPORTERS.] Two men in a military dress, with muskets, in a centinel's posture, all proper.

MOTTO.] Manu Forti.

CHIEF SEAT.] At Tong, in Strathnaver, in the county of Sutherland.

ASTON,

ASTON, Lord ASTON.

THIS family is of English extraction. Ralph de Aston, of the county of Stafford, flourished in the reign of Henry III. to whose son, Roger, in the same reign, 1260, Roger de Moland, bishop of Litchfield, gave the keeping of the game in Cankwood, in that county, which office hath continued to his posterity ever since. To the said Roger, whose wife was Sibyl, daughter of James de Landa, succeeded Sir John, their son, who in the 7th of Edward III. was knight of the shire for the county of Stafford, as in the 18th and 32d, was Roger, his son, who was father of Sir John, and he of Sir Thomas, the last of whom often served in parliament for that county, and in the 10th of Henry IV. was sheriff thereof. He married Elizabeth, sister and heir of Reginald de Leigh, son of Richard, son of Reginald, lord of Parkhall, with whom he had a great estate.

Sir Roger, their son, in the 12th of Henry VI. was one of the prime gentry returned by the commissioners for the county; and marrying Joice, sister and coheir of Baldwin de Frevil, whose ancestors had been barons of parliament, and were heirs general to the noble families of Marmion and Montfort of Beaudesert, by her had

Roger, his heir, who marrying Isabel, daughter of Sir William Brereton, of the county of Chester, had a son,

John, who in the time of king Edward IV. and Richard III. was sheriff of Staffordshire; and marrying Elizabeth, daughter of John Delves of Doddington, Esq; by her was father of

Sir John Aston, who at the marriage of prince Arthur, eldest son of king Henry VII. was created a knight of the Bath. In the 4th of Henry VIII. he went in the expedition into Britany, and assisted that king in the siege of Terouaine and Tournay, as also at the battle of Spurs, 1513, when, for his conduct and bravery, he was made a knight bannaret in the open field; and marrying Joan, daughter of Sir William Littleton, by Helen his wife, daughter and coheir of Robert Welsh, lord of Wanlip, in the county of Leicester, he by that marriage possessed the said manor of Wanlip, and the lordship of Tixhall, in the county of Stafford, the latter being purchased by the Littletons. He had two sons, Sir Edward, his heir, and William.

Sir Edward, who had been several times sheriff for his own county, dying in 1568, left by Joan his wife, daughter of Sir Thomas Bowles, baron of the exchequer, Sir Walter, his heir; and three daughters, Katharine, married first, to Stephen Stanley, Esq; secondly, to Sir William Chetwynd of Ingstree, in the county of Stafford; and thirdly, to Sir Edward Cope of Cannons-

Cannons-Ashby, in Northamptonshire; Mary, to Simon Harcourt of Stanton Harcourt, in the county of Oxford, ancestor of the earl of that name; and Frances, to Robert Needham of Shenton, in the county of Leicester, ancestor of the viscount Kilmorey, in Ireland.

Sir Walter, who succeeded his father, dying in 1589, left, by Elizabeth his wife, daughter of Sir James Levison, Sir Edward, his heir; and Margery, married to Thomas Astley of Pateshul, in the county of Stafford, Esq;

Sir Edward was sheriff of Staffordshire, an office which all his ancestors had served from the time of king Edward III. and marrying Anne, daughter of Sir Thomas Lucy, Kt. by her had a daughter, Ann, married to Ambrose Elton, of the Halse, in the county of Hereford, Esq; and Sir Walter. who succeeded him, and at the coronation of king James I. of England, was made a knight of the Bath, and in 1611, created a baronet. In 1622, being then in a publick character at the court of Madrid, he was commissioned, with John Digby, earl of Bristol, to conclude a marriage treaty between Charles prince of Wales, and the eldest daughter of that crown; and to support the glory of his country, he spent there the greatest part of his estate. But though that marriage was defeated, the said Sir Walter, after his return, was by Charles I. for his good services, created lord Aston. He married Gertrude, daughter of Sir Ralph Sadler of Standon, in the county of Hertford; and dying in 1639, was succeeded by his eldest son,

Walter, second lord, who during the civil war, at the siege of Litchfield, being joined in commission with Sir Thomas Tildesly, the governor, they sent a trusty servant with a letter to the king at Newcastle, which being delivered safe, he returned with the following answer.

Newcastle, 6 June, 1646.

My lord Aston, and Tildesly,

' THE greatest of my misfortunes is, that I cannot reward
' such gallant and loyal subjects as you are, as I ought,
' or would. For the present I must deal freely with you,
' which is, that I can give you no relief; but I desire you
' to hold out till Oxford be surrendered, which will be ranked
' among the rest of the good services done by you to

' Your assured friend,

' CHARLES R.'

Oxford being surrendered in June, and no conditions made for them, they made the best they could for themselves, which was only a permission to go home and compound for their estates.

Tildesly,

Tildesly and lord Widrington were killed in the fight with colonel Lilburn, 1651, when he routed the earl of Derby in Wigan Lane: but the lord Aston living retired till the king's restoration, he then succeeded to the estate at Standon, aforesaid; which estate, with his majesty's grant to him and his heirs for a weekly market, and two several fairs every year in the town of Standon, each to continue for two days, without an account to be rendered in the exchequer, was all the reward for his services, loyalty, and sufferings. He married lady Mary Weston, daughter of Richard earl of Portland, lord treasurer of England, by whom he had Walter, his heir; and several daughters, whereof Frances was the second wife of Sir Edward Gage of Hangrave, in Suffolk, Bart. He was succeeded by his said son,

Walter, third lord, who dying in November 1714, left by Eleanor his wife, daughter of Sir Walter Blount of Soddington, in the county of Worcester, Bart. widow of Robert Knightley of Off-Church, in the county of Warwick, Esq; one son,

Walter, fourth lord, who married lady Mary Howard, sister of Thomas duke of Norfolk, and by her, who died in 1723, had several children. In 1727, one of his daughters married Robert Weld, Esq; whom she sued for insufficiency; but not obtaining a divorce, they were persuaded to live together; and the said Walter, lord Aston, dying in 1746, was succeeded by his son,

James, fifth lord, who married lady Barbara Talbot, daughter of George, late earl of Shrewsbury, who died at Paris in October 1759; and his lordship dying in August 1751, leaving only two daughters, the title descended to the next heir,

Philip, sixth lord Aston, who died 29 April 1755, upon which the title devolved on the next heir,

Walter, the seventh and present lord Aston.

TITLES] The right honourable Walter Aston, lord Aston of Forfar, in the county of Forfar.

CREATIONS.] Lord Aston of Forfar, in the county of Forfar, 8 November 1628; and baronet, 22 May 1611.

ARMS.] Pearl, a fess, and in chief, three lozenges, diamond.

CREST.] On a wreath, a bull's head couped, of the last.

SUPPORTERS.] Two Roman knights completely armed, their faces, hands, and knees, bare.

MOTTO.] Numini et Patriæ Asto.

CHIEF SEATS.] At Standon, in the county of Hertford; and at Tixhall, near Stafford.

MACLELLAN, Lord KIRCUDBRIGHT.

SIR Patrick Maclellan of Bomby had a son, Sir Patrick Maclellan of Bomby, who happening to take part with his near kinsman, lord Herries, against the earl of Douglas, he was besieged in his own castle of Raeberry by that earl, and put to death: whereupon his relations, without warrant or authority, making great depredations on the Douglas lands in Galloway, their office of sheriff, and barony of Bomby, was forfeited to the crown; and the said office, which was erected into the sheriffalry of Wigton and Kirkudbright, was given to other families; but the barony was recovered in the following manner:

In the reign of the same king James II. a company of gypsies coming from Ireland, and infesting the county of Galloway, that king issued a proclamation, that whoever would disperse them, and bring their captain dead or alive, should have a considerable reward; and in this attempt, Sir William, son of Sir Patrick, before-mentioned, being the fortunate person that slew him, brought his head to the king on the point of his sword; from whence, to perpetuate the memory of that brave action, he took the same figure for his crest, with the motto, Think on. The king also restored to him the barony of Bomby. He had issue,

Sir Thomas Maclellan of Bomby, who in the reign of kings James III. and IV. was very serviceable to the crown on several occasions; and marrying Agnes, daughter of Sir James Dunbar of Mochrum, by her had three sons, Sir William; Gilbert, of whom hereafter; and John, whose male line is extinct. He was succeeded by his eldest son,

Sir William, who obtained many lands in Galloway from James IV. and married Elizabeth, a daughter of the family of Muir. Being slain at the battle of Floddon in 1513, with the said king James, he left issue,

Sir Thomas, his heir, who was killed in a feud in the high street of Edinburgh, by the barons of Drumlanrig and Lochinvar, leaving issue,

Sir Thomas, who had a charter of all his lands from queen Mary; and married Helen, daughter of Sir James Gordon of Lochinvar, by whom he had a son,

Sir Thomas, who married Grisel, daughter of John Maxwell, lord Herries, by whom he had issue three sons, Sir Robert; William, of Glenshannoch, of whom hereafter; and John, of whom also here: . He died in 1607, and was succeeded by his eldest son,

Sir Robert, who was knighted by king James VI. to whom, and king Charles I. he was gentleman of the bedchamber, and by the latter was created a baronet, and a baron, May 25, 1633; but dying without male issue in 1641, the honour descended to his nephew, Thomas,

LORD KIRCUDBRIGHT.

Thomas, second lord, the son of his brother William, of Glenshannoch, before-mentioned, who marrying lady Jane Douglas, daughter of William the first earl of Queensbery, and dying without issue in 1648, the title descended to his cousin-german, and heir male,

John Maclellan, of Burg, third lord, son of John, younger brother of the first lord; and this worthy person, in the time of the civil war, raised a regiment of foot at his own charge for the service of king Charles II. whose train he helped to support at his coronation at Scoon in 1651. He married Ann, daughter of Sir Robert Maxwel of Orcardtoun; and dying in 1664, left a son, an infant,

William, fourth lord, who dying five years after unmarried, the dignity, for want of support, lay dormant till 1722; when, at the election of sixteen peers, James Maclellan, nephew of John, the third lord, succeeded as fifth lord of Kircudbright; but he dying without male issue, the representation devolved on William Maclellan, of Bournels, lineally descended of Sir Gilbert, second son of Sir Thomas, by Agnes Dunbar, as before recited.

Which William, sixth and present lord, making his claim and voting, was entered on the parliament rolls by the title as above, in 1734. He married Margaret Murray, by whom he has a son, John, master of Kircudbright, an officer in the army.

TITLE.] The right honourable William Maclellan, lord Kircudbright.

CREATION.] Lord Kircudbright, 25 May 1633, by king Charles I.

ARMS.] Topaz, two chevrons diamond.

CREST.] On a wreath, a right arm erect, the hand grasping a dagger with a moor's head on the point thereof couped, proper.

SUPPORTERS.] On the dexter side, a chevalier in armour, holding in his outer hand a batoon. On the sinister, a horse pearl, furnish'd ruby.

MOTTO.] Think on.

CHIEF SEAT.] At Kircudbright, the capital of that county.

OGILVIE, Lord BANFF.

THE descent of this family will be found under that of the earl of Finlater, and that Sir Walter Ogilvie, of Finlater and Deskford, in the reign of James II. had two sons, Sir James and Sir Walter; Sir Walter the second had two sons also, Sir George, and Sir Walter, ancestor of the family of Banff, whose eldest son, Sir George, was, in 1612, succeeded by his eldest son, Sir Walter, whose eldest son, Sir George, was created a baronet by king Charles I. July 10, 1627, in whose

whose behalf he was very zealous during the civil war, and who, in 1642, created him a baron. He married first, Helen, daughter of Sir Alexander Irvine of Drum, by whom he had a daughter Helen, married to James, earl of Airly; and by his second, Mary, daughter of Sir Alexander Sutherland of Duffus, he had a son, George, his heir, and two daughters, Mary, wife of Walter Innes, of Auchluncart, and —— of —— Gordon, of Badinscott. He was succeeded in 1663, by his son,

George, second lord, who marrying Agnes, daughter of Alexander, lord Halkerton, had two sons, George his heir, and Sir Alexander, who in the reign of queen Ann was created a baronet, and appointed one of the judges of session, of whom hereafter: also four daughters, Agnes, wife of Francis Gordon, of Craig; Mary, of John Forbes of Ballfluig; Helen, of Sir Robert Lauder of Bielmouth; and Janet, of John Leith of Leith-hall. He was succeeded by his eldest son,

George, third lord, who marrying the lady Jane, daughter of William, earl marshal, by her had a son, and a daughter, Mary, wife of John Joice of Collonaird. He was succeeded by his son,

George, fourth lord, who married Helen, daughter of Sir John Lauder of Fountain-Hall, one of the senators of the college of justice, by whom he had John-George, his heir, and Alexander.

John, the eldest, fifth lord, being drowned by bathing in the sea, in 1738, and leaving no issue, was succeeded by his brother,

Alexander, sixth lord, who for some years was a captain in the royal navy; but dying unmarried at Lisbon in 1747, the title devolved on Alexander, his cousin, grandson of Sir Alexander of Forglan, second son of George, second lord Banff.

Which Sir Alexander, by his wife Mary, daughter of Sir John Allardice of that ilk, had four sons and three daughters, viz. George, who died without issue; Alexander, father of the present lord; John, and Peter; Agnes, wife of Sir Alexander Reid of Barra; Mary, of Andrew Hay, of Mountblairie; and Helen, of —— Smollett, son and heir of Sir James Smollett of Bonhill.

Alexander, his second son, married Jane, daughter of —— Friend, Esq; by whom he had one daughter, and a son,

Alexander, seventh and present lord Banff, who married Jane, daughter of William Nesbit of Dirleton, Esq; by whom he has issue three sons and three daughters; Alexander, master of Banff; William, Archibald; Jane, Sophia, and Janet.

TITLE.] The right honourable Alexander Ogilvie, lord Banff in the county of Banff.

CREATION,

LORD BANFF.

CREATIONS.] Lord Banff, by Charles I. 30 August 1642, and baronet in 1627.

ARMS.] Quarterly, 1st and 4th pearl, a lion passant gardant ruby, crowned with an imperial crown proper, for Ogilvie; 2d and 3d pearl, three parrots emerald, for Hume of Fastcastle.

CREST.] On a wreath, a lion's head erazed ruby.

SUPPORTERS.] On the dexter side, a man in armour with a target in his right hand. On the sinister, a lion ruby.

MOTTO.] Fideliter.

CHIEF SEAT.] At Insdreur in the county of Banff.

MURRAY, Lord ELIBANK.

THIS noble family sprung from the house of Blackbarony, the head or chief of an honourable tribe of the name of Murray, which flourished in the south of Scotland for many centuries.

Sir Gideon Murray, knighted by king James VI. by whom he was made treasurer depute, was third son of Andrew Murray, of Blackbarony, by Grisel his wife, daughter of Sir John Bethune, of Creich.

This Sir Gideon, during the six years of his treasurership, managed that office with such advantage to the crown, that beside the charge of the government, he also repaired and enlarged the palaces of Holyrood, Falkland, Lithgow, and Dumferlin, with the castles of Dunbriton and Edinburgh: and in 1617, at the king's coming to Scotland, had the treasury so full, that his majesty appeared with as much splendor as at Whitehall. He married Margaret Pentland, and had two sons, Sir Patrick his heir, and Walter; and a daughter, wife of Sir William Scott, of Harden.

Sir Patrick, the eldest son, in respect of his loyalty to king Charles I. was on the 16th of May, 1628, created a baronet, and in 1643, advanced to the title of lord Elibank: he married, first, Elizabeth, daughter of Sir James Dundas of Arniston, by whom he had issue, Patrick, and —— Murray of Spot, and a daughter Elizabeth, wife of Sir Archibald Stirling of Carden; and secondly, Helen, daughter of Sir James Lindsay, by whom he had issue two sons and two daughters, Walter, who settled in Ireland, and was ancestor of the Murrays of Ravigny, and others; George, lieutenant-colonel in the troop of life-guards; ——, wife of —— Auchmoutie of Gosford; and ——, of Sir William Murray of Newton. He died in 1650, and was succeeded by his eldest son,

Patrick, second lord, who married lady Elizabeth, daughter of John earl of Traquair, and had issue by her two sons and one daughter, viz. Patrick; John, a captain in the army, killed at the battle of Antrim, in Ireland; and Elizabeth, wife of John Auchmoutie of Gosford. He died in 1658, and was succeeded by his eldest son,

Patrick, third lord, one of the privy-council of James VII. but laid aside for opposing the repeal of the penal laws, in 1687. He married Ann, daughter of Alexander Burnet, archbishop of St. Andrews, and had Alexander his heir, and three daughters; Mary, married to John earl of Cromartie; Helen, to Sir John Mackenzie of Coul, and Elizabeth, who died unmarried. He was succeeded by his son,

Alexander, fourth lord Elibank, who married Elizabeth, daughter of Mr. George Stirling of Edinburgh, by whom he had five sons, and six daughters; Barbara, married to Sir James Johnston of Westerhall, Bart. Elizabeth, who died unmarried; Anne, to James Ferguson of Pitfour, Advocate; Janet, to major Robert Murray; Mary, and Helen, married to Sir John Stewart of Gairntully, bart. The sons were, Patrick; George, a rear-admiral in the British navy, who married lady Isabel Mackenzie, daughter of George late earl of Cromartie, by whom he has a daughter; Gideon, a clergyman; Alexander, an officer in the army, who incurred the resentment of the honourable House of Commons for his behaviour at the Westminster election, on a vacancy for a member of parliament, in 1750; for which offence, refusing to beg pardon of the House, he was committed to Newgate, and there closely confined during the whole session 1751; James, a major-general, and late governor of Canada. His lordship died in 1735, and was succeeded by his eldest son,

Patrick, now fifth lord Elibank, who was a lieutenant-colonel in the army on the expedition to Carthagena. He married Maria Margaretta, lady dowager North, relict of William lord North and Grey, and daughter of Mynheer Elmeet, receiver-general of the United Provinces, by whom he has issue.

TITLE.] The right honourable Patrick Murray, lord Elibank.

CREATIONS.] Baron Elibank, by king Charles I. in 1643, and baronet of New Scotland in 1628.

ARMS.] Sapphire, three stars within a double tressure counterflory with fleurs de lis pearl, and in the centre a martlet topaz.

CREST.] On a wreath, a lion rampant ruby, holding between his paws a battle-axe, proper.

SUPPORTERS.] Two horses pearl, bridled, ruby.

MOTTO.] Virtute Fideque.

CHIEF SEATS.] At Ballencrief, in East Lothian; and at Newark House, in the county of Selkirk.

FALCONER, Lord HALKERTON.

THE first of this family on record is Walter de Loncorp, whose son Ranulph being falconer to king William the lion, obtained a charter of the lands of Luthra and Balbegno, in the county of Kincardin, which from his office were named Halkerton, or Hawkerton, and the family called Falconer, which for many years was honoured with knighthood. He left issue Walter, who was succeeded by his son Robert, and he by a son, ———, whose son, David, was succeeded by his son, Andrew, living in 1380. He was father of Alexander, and he of David, who flourished in the reigns of James II. and III. David was succeeded by his son, Alexander, and he by his son, Sir George Falconer of Halkerton, whose son, David, was succeeded by his eldest son, Sir Alexander, in 1540, who by Elizabeth his wife, daughter of Sir Archibald Douglas of Glenbervie, ancestor of the dukes of Douglas, had four sons and one daughter, viz. Sir Alexander; Archibald, ancestor of the Falconers of Phesdo; Samuel, of Kincorth; William, father of Colin, first bishop of Argyll; and Catharine, wife of Hugh Rose of Kilravock. He was succeeded by his eldest son,

Sir Alexander, who married Isabel, daughter of Patrick lord Gray, by whom he had three sons; Sir Alexander; Patrick, of Newton, of whom James Falconer of Monkton, Esq; is the representative; and James, of Middlehaugh. He was succeeded by his eldest son,

Sir Alexander, who married Agnes, daughter of Sir David Carnegie of Colathie, ancestor of the earls of Southesk, by whom he had four sons, Sir Alexander, his heir; Sir David, ancestor of the present lord; Sir John, of Balmakellie, master of the Mint to Charles II. and James, of Coatfield. He was succeeded by his eldest son,

Sir Alexander, who being a gentleman of great knowledge in the laws, was by king Charles I. made one of the privy council, and created a peer in 1647; and marrying Ann, daughter of John lord Lindsay, ancestor of the earl of Crawfurd, by her had Alexander, his heir; and a daughter, Agnes, married to George Ogilvie, second lord Banff. He was succeeded by his son,

Alexander, second lord, who married lady Margaret, daughter of James, second earl of Airly; and dying in 1684, by her left a son,

David, third lord, who dying unmarried, was succeeded by David Falconer of Newton, son of Sir David Falconer, lord president of session in 1682, who was second son of Sir David Falconer of Glenfarcar, second brother to the first lord Halkerton.

Which David, fourth lord, succeeded to the estate of Glenfarcar, some little time before the death of the preceding lord.

He

LORD HALKERTON.

He married lady Catharine Keith, daughter of William, second earl of Kintore, by whom he had five sons and four daughters, viz. Alexander; William; David; John; and George, a captain in the navy: Catharine, who died unmarried; Jane, wife of James Falconer of Monkton, Esq; Mary; and Marjory, wife of George Norvill of Boghall, Esq; He was succeeded by his eldest son,

Alexander, fifth lord, who married Frances, daughter of Herbert Mackworth of Glamorganshire, in Wales, Esq; and dying in November 1762, was succeeded by his brother,

William, sixth and present lord Halkerton.

TITLE.] The right honourable Alexander Falconer, lord Halkerton.

CREATION.] Baron Halkerton of Halkerton, in the county of Kincardin, by king Charles I. 29 July 1647.

ARMS.] Sapphire, a falcon displayed, pearl, crowned with a ducal crown, topaz, and charged on the breast with a man's heart, ruby, between three stars of the second. The stars and heart shew his descent from Douglas by the mother's side.

CREST.] On a wreath, an angel in a praying posture, within an orle of laurel.

SUPPORTERS.] Two falcons, proper.

MOTTO.] Vive ut vivas.

CHIEF SEATS.] At Halkerton and Glenfarquar, in the county of Kincardine.

HAMILTON, Lord BELHAVEN.

THE descent of this noble family may be seen under the title of Duke of Hamilton; and that James, first lord Hamilton, had a second son, Andrew, ancestor of the lords Belhaven, whose eldest son, John, having no male issue, was succeeded by his brother Robert, and he by his son John, who was succeeded by his son, another John, whose son, Sir James, was father of Sir John Hamilton of Broomhill, who during the civil war, taking up arms in defence of king Charles I. was thereupon created lord Belhaven and Straton, December 18, 1647. He married Margaret, natural daughter of James marquis of Hamilton, and had issue by her three daughters; Margaret, wife of Sir Samuel Baillie of Lamington; Anne, of whom hereafter; and Elizabeth, married to Alexander Seton, viscount Kingston. Having no male issue, he was succeeded by his cousin, Sir John Hamilton of Biel, who had married his grand-daughter, according to a new patent obtained for that purpose in 1675. For

The second daughter, Anne, above-mentioned, having married Sir Robert Hamilton of Silvertounhill, a cadet of the family, had by him an only daughter, Margaret, married to the
said

said Sir John Hamilton of Biel, the second lord, as above, who having signalized himself at the Revolution in 1688, by raising a troop of horse for the prince and princess of Orange, was, soon after their accession to the throne, made one of the privy council, and a commissioner of the exchequer. He also assisted in restoring the Presbyterian government, and the establishment of the Scots African Company. In the parliament 1700, he most zealously promoted the act to prevent the growth of Popery; and in 1704, was appointed one of the lords of the treasury. In 1706, when the union came to be debated, he joined with those who opposed it; and on this subject made several long and learned speeches, containing his reasons for opposing it. Dying in June 1708, in the 52d year of his age, he left issue by Margaret his wife, above-mentioned, two sons, John, his heir; and James, who died in 1732, without issue. He was succeeded by his eldest son,

John, third lord, who was elected one of the sixteen peers for North Britain in 1715, and the same year was appointed a gentleman of the bedchamber to George prince of Wales, afterwards George II. In 1721, he was appointed governor of Barbadoes, but was lost in the Royal Ann galley, near the Lizard Point, on the 10th of November that year; the ship having struck on the Stag rocks, was staved to pieces, and of 240 persons, only two men and a boy were saved. Lord Belhaven's body was taken up near Falmouth, being known by a diamond ring on his finger, and the letter-mark on his shirt; for he was in bed, as were most of the passengers, when the first dreadful shock surprized them. He married Mary, daughter of Andrew Bruce, merchant in Edinburgh, by whom he had four sons and one daughter, viz. John, now lord; Andrew, an officer in the army, who died unmarried; James, advocate, sheriff-depute of Haddingtonshire; Robert, major in the army; and Margaret, wife of Alexander Baird, Esq; son of Sir William Baird of Newbeath. He was succeeded by his eldest son,

John, fourth and present lord Belhaven, who is one of the commissioners for encouraging fisheries, and high sheriff of the county of Haddington.

TITLE.] The right honourable James Hamilton, lord Belhaven.

CREATION.] Baron Belhaven, in the county of Haddington, in 1648, by king Charles I.

ARMS.] Ruby, a sword erect in pale, proper, the pomel and hilt topaz, between three cinquefoils, pearl.

CREST.] On a wreath, a nag's head couped of the last, and bridled of the first.

SUPPORTERS.] Two horses, pearl, bridled as the crest.

MOTTO.]

MOTTO.] Ride through.
CHIEF SEATS.] At Biel, near Dunbar; and at Prefmanan, in Eaft Lothian.

ROLLO, Lord ROLLO.

OF this antient family, which is of Norman extraction, and which hath long been feated in Perthfhire, was John Rollo, who in the reign of Robert II. had a grant from David Stewart, earl of Strathern, of the lands of Duncrib, Findony, Pitirclethy, and feveral others, and therein was fucceeded by his fon, Duncan, the father of Robert, whofe fon, Robert, was father of William, who had a charter from king James IV. for erecting his lands into the barony of Duncrib. He married a daughter of the family of Oliphant, and had Robert, his heir, who married Jane, daughter of William lord Graham, by whom he was father of Andrew, who marrying Marjory, daughter and coheir of Sir David Rollo of Ballachie, by her had four fons and two daughters; George, who died without iffue; James, fucceffor to his brother, who married Agnes, daughter of Robert Collice of Bonymon; William, and Sir Walter: Marjory, wife, firft, of George Graham of Mohbraco; and fecondly, of John Graham of Balgowan; and Mary, of Laurence Oliphant of Gafk. He died in 1560; and was fucceeded by Sir Andrew, his grandfon, fon of James, his fecond fon.

Which Andrew was knighted by James VI. and created a baron by Charles II. and marrying Katharine, daughter of James Drummond, lord Maderty, anceftor of the vifcount Strathallan, had five fons and four daughters; Sir James; Sir John; Laurence, of Roffie; Andrew, parfon of Dunning; Sir William, who was beheaded at Glafgow, for adhering to the caufe of king Charles I. in 1645, being taken prifoner, with the marquis of Montrofe, at the battle of Philliphaugh: Margaret, wife of Sir John Drummond of Carnock; Jane, firft, of John Rollo of Powhoufe; and fecondly, of John Drummond of Pitkellony; Anne, of William Mercer of Elwedge; and Ifabel, of William Halliday of Tilliboke. He died in 1659, and was fucceeded by his eldeft fon,

Sir James, fecond lord, who married to his fecond wife, lady Mary, daughter of Archibald, feventh earl of Argyll, by whom he had iffue two fons, Andrew, his heir, and major Archibald; and a daughter, Margaret, wife of Sir George Oliphant of Newton. He died in 1671, and was fucceeded by his eldeft fon,

Andrew, third lord, who married Margaret, daughter of Robert Balfour, lord Burleigh, and had iffue John, mafter of Rollo, killed in a private quarrel in 1691, without iffue; Robert: and three daughters, Emilia, wife of William Irvine of
Bonfhaw;

Barshaw; Isabella, of Robert Johnson of Wamfrey; Susan, of Robert Gillespie of Cherryvally, in Ireland, Esq; and Jane, who died unmarried. He died March 1, 1700, and was succeeded by his only surviving son,

Robert, fourth lord Rollo, who married Mary, the eldest daughter of Sir Henry Rollo of Woodside. He joined in the rebellion against king George I. in which being disappointed, he, and the marquis of Huntley, surrendered themselves in April 1716, to brigadier Grant, in the north of Scotland, and were committed to Edinburgh castle. The marquis was pardoned, and lord Rollo was cleared by his majesty's act of grace in 1717. He had four sons, Andrew, his heir; Harry, an officer in the army, and married Anne, sister of James lord Rutherford, without issue; John, who married Cicely, daughter of James Johnston, merchant in Edinburgh, and had issue; and Clement, who married Maria-Æmilia, eldest daughter of John Irvine of Bonshaw, Esq; and had issue: Also three daughters; Mary, wife of David Drummond of Pitkellony, Esq; Janet, of captain Robert Johnston of Wamphrey; and Isabel, of John Aytoun of Inchdairny, Esq; and all had issue. His lordship died in 1758, and was succeeded by his eldest son,

Andrew, fifth lord Rollo. On the first of June 1750, he was made major of colonel O Farrel's regiment of foot, and was a colonel by brevet. Among many other eminent services done his country during the course of the late war in America, his lordship, in conjunction with Sir James Douglas, took the island of Dominica in June 1761. He married first, Catharine, daughter and coheir of lord James Murray of Dowally, third son of John, marquis of Athol, by whom he had a son, the Hon. captain John Rollo, a brave officer, who died at Martinico in June 1762. He had other children, who all died young. His second wife was Miss Murray, daughter of —— Murray of Abercairny, Esq; to whom he was married a few months before his decease. His lordship departing this life in 1765, on his journey to Scotland, was succeeded by his next surviving brother,

John, sixth and present lord Rollo, of whose issue I cannot procure the names; but the eldest son, ———, master of Rollo, was married in 1766, to Miss —— Ayton, daughter of —— Ayton, Esq;

TITLES.] The right honourable John Rollo, lord Rollo.

CREATION.] Baron Rollo of Duncrib, in the county of Perth, by king Charles II. 10 January 1650.

ARMS.] Topaz, a chevron between three boars heads erazed, sapphire.

CREST.] On a wreath, a stag's head couped, proper.

SUPPORTERS.] Two stags of the last.

MOTTO.] La fortune passe par tout.

CHIEF SEAT.] At Duncrib, in the county of Perth.

COLVILE,

COLVILE, Lord COLVILE.

THIS family came originally from Normandy, with William the conqueror, in 1066, and from England with king David I. who succeeded to the crown of Scotland in 1124.

Robert Colvile, who was created lord Colvile in 1609, married Isabel, daughter of Patrick lord Ruthven, by whom he had two sons and one daughter; James, who died before his father, unmarried; Robert, master of Colvile; and Jane, wife of Sir James Campbell of Lawers, by whom she had John, earl of Loudoun, lord high chancellor of Scotland, *temp. Car. I.* He died in 1620, and was succeeded by his grandson, James, second lord, son of Robert, master of Colvile, who dying without issue, was succeeded in 1722, by

John, third lord, eldest son of Alexander, eldest son of Dr. Alexander, eldest son of John, eldest son of Alexander, second lawful son of Sir James Colvile of Easter-Wemyss, commendator of Culross, brother-german of the first lord. Which John, third lord, married Miss Johnston, of the kingdom of Ireland, by whom he had issue five sons and two daughters, viz. Alexander, the present lord; George, who died in the West-Indies, without issue; John and Charles, officers in the army; James, captain of a ship of war, who died in the East-Indies: Margaret, wife of captain Castlemain; and Elizabeth, who died unmarried. His lordship died in the expedition to Carthagena, in the year 1740, and was succeeded by his eldest son,

Alexander, fourth lord Colvile, who on the 6th of March 1743, was made a captain in the royal navy, and is rear admiral of the white squadron of his majesty's fleet; and at Nova-Scotia, had the command of the squadron there stationed, till 1766.

TITLES.] The right honourable Alexander Colvile, lord Colvile.

CREATION.] Lord Colvile, by king Charles II. before the Restoration.

ARMS.] Quarterly, 1st and 4th, pearl, a cross moline, diamond; 2d and 3d, ruby, a fess cheque, pearl and sapphire.

CREST.] On a wreath, a hind's head, proper.

SUPPORTERS.] On the dexter side, a rhinoceros of the latter. On the sinister, a savage covered with a lion's skin, holding on his exterior shoulder a batoon.

MOTTO.] Oublier ne Puis.

RUTHVEN,

RUTHVEN, Lord RUTHVEN.

WILLIAM, second lord Ruthven, the thirteenth generation of the illustrious house of Gourie, in the direct male line, married Janet Haliburton, daughter and coheir of Patrick, lord Haliburton, of Dirleton, by whom he had issue two sons and seven daughters. Of the sons, Patrick was father of William, first earl of Gowrie, and Alexander was progenitor of the family I am treating of.

Which Alexander, by his wife Isabel, a daughter of —— Fotheringham of Powrie, had issue two sons and three daughters; William, his heir; Alexander: Jane, wife of —— Mercer of Clevige; Barbara, of Henry Rattray of that ilk; and Isabel, of baron Reid, in Stratherdale. He died in the year 1600, and was succeeded by his eldest son, William, who by his wife Elizabeth, daughter of Sir William Moncrief of that ilk, had a son, Sir Thomas; and two daughters, Mary, married to George Hay of Naughton; and Elizabeth, to Sir David Macgill of Rankeilor. He died of the plague in 1608, and was succeeded by his son,

Sir Thomas Ruthven of Freeland, who was one of the commissioners for the treaty of Rippon in 1641, and in 1644, colonel of one of the regiments sent against the earl of Huntley. In 1649, he was made a commissioner of the exchequer. Notwithstanding king Charles II. thought so highly of his attachment to him and his family, that he was pleased to raise him to the dignity of the peerage, by the title of lord Ruthven of Freeland, in the year 1651. He married Isabel, daughter of Robert lord Burleigh, by whom he had issue a son, David; and three daughters, Anne, married first, to Sir William Cunningham of Cunninghamhead; and secondly, to William Cunningham, jun. of Craigends; Elizabeth, of whom hereafter; and Jane, who died without issue. His lordship deceased in 1674, and was succeeded by his son,

David, second lord, who was in great favour with king William, and one of the lords of the treasury; but dying without issue in 1701, and his eldest sister, Anne, having no surviving issue,

Isabel, the only surviving daughter of his second sister, Elizabeth, by her spouse, Sir Francis Ruthven of Reidcastle, became baroness Ruthven, and was summoned as such to the coronations of king George I. and king George II. She married colonel James Johnston of Gratney, a cadet of the most noble family of Annandale, by whom she had issue a son, James; and a daughter, Anne, married first, to Henry Rollo, Esq; second son of Robert, fourth lord Rollo; and secondly, to Frederick Bruce of Bunzean, Esq; but without issue by either. The baroness died in 1732, and was succeeded by her son,

James, third lord Ruthven, who married two wives; 1. Janet, daughter of William Nisbet of Dirleton, Esq; by whom he had two sons, James, master of Ruthven; and William, who died unmarried. 2. Lady Anne, daughter of James earl of Bute, by whom he had two sons and eight daughters, viz. Stewart, who died young; John, a commander in the navy: Anne, wife of captain Elphingston; Isabel, wife of captain John MacDougal; Wortley-Montague; Elizabeth, wife of captain Lawrie; Jane, who died young; Grace, who also died young; Janet, and Crawford; which last died in her infancy.

James, master of Ruthven, is an officer in the army.

TITLES.] James Ruthven, lord Ruthven, of Freeland.
CREATION.] Lord Ruthven, as above, in 1651, by Charles II.
ARMS.] Pallee of six, sapphire and ruby.
CREST.] A ram's head, couped.
SUPPORTERS.] On the dexter side, a ram; on the sinister, a goat, both proper.
MOTTO.] Deed shaw.
CHIEF SEAT.] At Ruthven-house, in Perthshire.

LESLY, Lord NEWARK.

PATRICK, first lord Lindores, second son of Andrew, fifth earl of Rothes, had a fifth son, David (see the family of Rothes and Lindores) who was a colonel of horse under the king of Sweden, in the wars of Germany. In the reign of Charles I. when the civil war broke out, he returning to his native country, entered into the service of the parliament of Scotland, who had taken the covenant, and raised an army in defence of their liberties and religion. He was made one of their generals, and so continued till the defeat at Worcester. In 1645, the Scotch army under the earl of Leven, being then in the centre of England, as allies to the parliament, this David Lesly, after the battle of Naseby, was detached, with his whole party of horse, to oppose the marquis of Montrose, who having deserted his old friends, was grown very formidable, and with an army of Irish and Highland Scots, was marching into England to reinforce the king. The general met him at Philiphaw, near Selkirk, where, on 13 September 1645, the marquis was defeated with very great loss, and forced to retire abroad: and when the marquis returned, in the year 1650, to make an insurrection for king Charles II. this David was commissioned with a good body of forces to reduce him; but colonel Strahan making a quick march with six or seven troops of horse, the marquis was routed before the king's friends could join him, and being soon after taken prisoner, general Lesly sent him to Edinburgh. In 1650, the independents in England having got the supreme power, resolved to exclude all the royal family. The Scotch parliament, who never joined in the covenant with such intention, immediately declared for the king, under certain limitations. Hereupon an army, commanded by Oliver Cromwell, was ordered to act against Scotland; for general Fairfax having refused all concern in this affair, Cromwell was made general in his room. In July the forces landed in Scotland, where general Lesly had an army of 27,000 men. The English not being able to draw the Scots from their intrenchments, lost many of their men by skirmishing, and for want of provision and forage, their army was reduced to 12,000. Whereupon Cromwell retiring towards Dunbar, prepared to embark his infantry, and return with his horse into England. General Lesly perceiving this motion, left his camp, and followed the enemy close, not doubting of a sure and easy victory; but Cromwell making a stand, took a bold resolution to attack the Scots an hour before day, on the third of September, when after a vigorous dispute, Lesly was utterly defeated, losing all his cannon, and more than half his army were killed, wounded, or taken; but the fate of the times was such, that no good general, even with an excess of numbers, could withstand the mighty Cromwell. The next year, being 1651, after king Charles II. was crowned at Scoon, a new army was formed of about 20,000 men, to try the king's fortune in England. The third of September was again favourable to Oliver, for the royal army was intirely vanquished at Worcester, three thousand were slain, and ten thousand made prisoners. The king fled, lieutenant general duke Hamilton died of his wounds, general Lesly was taken prisoner, with major general Massey, as were seven Scotch eers, three English peers, and 640 officers, besides losing the oyal standard, and 158 colours.

This worthy gentleman being committed to the Tower of London, was there confined till the Restoration; when, as a return for his fidelity and service, the king was pleased to create him a peer, by the title of baron Newark, in the county of Fife; and he sent him also a letter, in these words:

'Although we have on all occasions been fully satisfied with
' your conduct in our service, and in consideration of the same,
' we have given you the title and dignity of a lord, with other
' marks of our esteem; yet, since malice and slander do not
' cease to persecute you, we have thought fit to declare under
' our hand, that while you was general of our army in Scot-
' land, you did, both there and in England, behave with as
' much conduct, reputation, and honesty, as any person in

' that

' that truft; and as we told you, fo we now repeat it, that if
' we had occafion to levy an army for ourfelf to command, we
' would not fail to give you an employment in it.'

He had alfo a penfion from his Majefty of 500 pounds a
year; and marrying Jane, daughter of Sir John York, knt.
had David his heir, and three daughters; Elizabeth, wife of
Sir Archibald Kennedy, of Culcairn, bart. Mary, of Sir
Francis Kinloch, of Gilmerton, bart. and Margaret, of colonel James Campbell, fourth fon of Archibald, ninth earl of
Argyll: and by reafon the honour of lord Newark was limited
to the male heirs of his body, he refigned his eftate and honour
unto his Majefty in favour of his fon the faid David, and his
heirs general, which his Majefty was pleafed to confirm. He
died in 1682, and was fucceeded by his faid fon,

David, fecond lord, who dying in 1694, left by Elizabeth
his wife, daughter of Sir Thomas Stewart of Grantully, five
daughters, viz. Jane; Mary, who died unmarried; Chriftian,
wife of Thomas Graham, of Balgowan, Efq; Grifel, of
Thomas Drummond, of Logyalmond, Efq; and Elizabeth,
who died unmarried.

Jane, the eldeft daughter, fucceeded as baronefs of Newark,
and marrying Sir Alexander Anftruther, bart. of that ilk, an
antient family in the county of Fife, by him had three fons,
and fix daughters, viz. William, David, Alexander, who is
married, and has iffue; Chriftian, Helen, wife of the rev. Mr.
John Chalmers; Jane, Catherine, Margaret, and Joanna.
Her ladyfhip dying in 1740, the eftate and honour devolved
on her eldeft fon,

William, third lord, who is an officer in the army, and
who taking the name and arms of Lefley, fucceeded as lord
Newark, and voted for one of the fixteen peers to fucceed
John earl of Crawford, who died in 1749, and at every election fince.

TITLES.] The right honourable William Lefly, lord
Newark.

CREATIONS] Baron Newark in the county of Fife, 31 Auguft 1660, by Charles II.

ARMS.] Quarterly, 1ft and 4th pearl, on a bend fapphire,
three buckles topaz, for Lefly; 2d topaz, a lion rampant
ruby, debruifed with a ribband diamond, for Abernetty; 3d
pearl, three piles iffuing from the chief diamond, for Anftruther; and by way of furtout an efcutcheon ruby, charged with
a three-towered caftle pearl, mafoned diamond, for Lindores.

CREST.] On a wreath, a demi-angel winged, topaz, holding
in his right-hand a griffon's head, proper.

SUPPORTERS.] Two griffons pearl, beaked, winged, and
armed, topaz.

MOTTO.]

LORD RUTHERFOORD.

MOTTO.] Periiſſem ni Periiſſem.
CHIEF SEAT.] At Newark in Fife.

RUTHERFOORD, Lord RUTHERFOORD.

ANDREW Rutherfoord, a cadet of the family of Hunthill, ſon of William Rutherfoord of Quarryholes, by his wife Iſabel Stewart, of the noble family of Traquair, went young into the French ſervice, where attaining ſeveral degrees of military preferment, he came at laſt to be a lieutenant-general in that kingdom. At the reſtoration in 1660, he came over to England with a very honourable teſtimony from the king of France, and for his ſingular ſervice and fidelity to the crown, king Charles II. was pleaſed to create him a baron, and ſoon after, for his management in the ſale of Dunkirk, of which he was governor, in 1663, earl of Teviot, to him and the heirs male of his body; but being made governor of Tangier, he was unfortunately ſlain by the Moors without iſſue in 1664, and the title of earl died with him; but that of Lord Rutherfoord, according to the grant of the patent, deſcended to

Sir Thomas Rutherfoord of Hunthill, who accordingly took his ſeat in parliament, as ſecond lord Rutherfoord; and dying in 1668, without iſſue, was ſucceeded in the title by his brother,

Archibald, third lord Rutherfoord, who alſo dying without iſſue, in 1685, was ſucceeded by his youngeſt brother,

Robert, fourth lord Rutherfoord, after whoſe death, in 1724, alſo without iſſue, the title deſcended to

John Rutherfoord, Eſq; heir of the family of Hunthill, and captain of an independent company in North-Britain, who was fifth lord Rutherfoord; but he dying in February 1744, was ſucceeded by

Alexander, his ſon, who claimed the title of Rutherfoord, as ſixth and preſent lord, and was a captain of marines. Another claimant ſtarted up, viz. George Durie, of Grange in Fifeſhire, Eſq; who aſſumed the ſurname and arms of Rutherfoord, but his claim was ſet aſide.

TITLES.] The right honourable David Rutherfoord, lord Rutherfoord of Hunthill in the county of Roxburgh.

CREATION.] Lord Rutherfoord, by king Charles II. 19 January 1660.

ARMS.] Pearl, an orle ruby, and in chief three martlet diamond.

CREST.] On a wreath, a martlet as in the coat.
SUPPORTERS.] Two horſes, proper.
MOTTO.] Nec Sorte nec Fato.
CHIEF SEAT.] At Grange in the county of Fife.

BALLENDEN,

BALLENDEN, Lord BALLENDEN.

THIS family had its rise in the time of king James IV. when Patrick Ballenden got the lands of Auchinoul from John earl of Morton, for which he obtained a charter from that prince, March 29, 1499. His son, Thomas Ballenden, of Auchinoul, Esq; was lord justice-clerk and director of the Chancery to James V. and he dying in 1546, left his son and heir, Sir John Ballenden, who was also lord justice-clerk in the reigns of queen Mary and her son king James VI. and marrying, first, Barbara, daughter of Sir Hugh Kennedy, had two sons, Sir Lewis his heir, and Adam, who became bishop of Aberdeen; and secondly, Janet, daughter of ⸺ Seton, of Touch, by whom he had three daughters; Elizabeth, first the wife of Sir James Lawson, of Hambie, and afterwards of Sir John Cockburn, of Ormistoun, lord justice-clerk; Margaret, of William Stewart, writer, in Edinburgh, and mother of Sir Lewis Stewart, of Kirkhill; and Marion, of John Ramsay, of Dalhousie. Sir Lewis, the eldest son, was one of the senators of the college of justice, and lord justice-clerk; and by Margaret his wife, daughter of William lord Levingston, sister of Alexander earl of Lithgow, had a son Sir James; who marrying Margaret, daughter of Sir William Ker of Cesford, and sister of Robert the first earl of Roxburgh, by her had Sir William his heir, and a daughter Margaret, who married Henry Erskine lord Cardross, ancestor of the earl of Buchan.

Sir William, the son, who succeeded, having given many proofs of his loyalty to king Charles II. was, in recompence thereof, after the restoration, made treasurer depute, one of the privy-council, and created a peer, by the title of lord Ballenden of Broughton, June 10, 1661, and was appointed heretable usher of the Exchequer in Scotland, by charter, to him, his heirs, or assigns whatever, dated Dec. 12, 1663. Having never married, he made a conveyance of his estate and honour to

John Ker, his cousin, fourth son of William, second earl of Roxburgh, who thereupon changed his name to Ballenden, and took the arms of that family, and became second lord; and marrying Mary, widow of William Ramsay, third earl of Dalhousie, and daughter of Henry Moor, earl of Drogheda in Ireland, by Alice his wife, daughter of William lord Spencer, sister of Henry earl of Sunderland, by her, who married thirdly, Samuel Collins, M.D. had five sons and four daughters, viz. John, master of Ballenden; Ker, of whom hereafter; Robert, William, and Sir Henry, gentleman-usher of the House of Lords; Margaret, who died unmarried; ⸺⸺, wife of
Ephraim

Ephraim Miller, of Hertingfordbury, Esq; Mary, of the Hon. John Campbell of Mammore, now duke of Argyll; and Diana, of John Bulteel of Fleet, in Devonshire, Esq; He was succeeded by his eldest son,

John, third lord; but he dying in 1741, without issue, was succeeded by his next brother,

Ker, fourth lord Ballenden, who was an officer in the royal navy, and in 1750, married a daughter of Mr. George Campbell, storekeeper at Woolwich, by whom he left a son,

John, now fifth lord Ballenden, hereditary usher of the exchequer, &c. &c. who is in his minority.

TITLE.] The right honourable John Ballenden, lord Ballenden, hereditary usher of the exchequer.

CREATION.] Baron of Ballenden, in the county of Selkirk, by king Charles II. 10 June 1661.

ARMS.] Ruby, a hart's head couped, attired with ten tynes, between three cross croslets fitchy, topaz, all within a double tressure, counterflory with fleurs de lis of the last.

SUPPORTERS.] On the dexter side, a lady holding in her right hand a sword erect, and a pair of scales pendant, both proper; on the sinister, another such lady holding in her left hand a branch of palm.

MOTTO.] Sic itur ad astra.

CHIEF SEAT.] At Broughton-house, in Mid-Lothian.

KINNAIRD, Lord KINNAIRD.

THE firname of this family is local, (says Douglas) and was assumed by the proprietors of the lands and barony of Kinnaird, in Perthshire, as soon as firnames began to be used in Scotland.

In the reign of king William, 1170, Radulph Rufus obtained from that prince a charter of the said lands, which continued in his family till the time of king Charles I. He had a son, Richard Kinnaird of that ilk, whose son and successor, Radulphus, was succeeded by his eldest son, Richard, father of another Radulphus, who was succeeded by his son, Richard; and his son, Sir Richard Kinnaird, left issue two sons, Thomas, and Reginald, of whom hereafter. Thomas married Giles, daughter and heir of Walter Murray of Cowbine, and had two sons, Allan, and Walter, of Cowbine, whose issue is now extinct. Alan's descendants continued till the reign of Charles I. and then became extinct. We therefore return to Reginald Kinnaird, second son of Sir Richard, above-mentioned, who by his wife Margery, daughter and heir of Sir John Kirkcaldy, got the lands of Inchture, from which his issue was afterwards called, and quartered the arms of Kirkcaldy with their own.

He

He had a son, Walter, whose son, Reginald, left issue a son, John, and he a son, George, whose eldest son, George, dying without issue, the estate devolved on his brother, Patrick, whose son, Patrick, was father of another Patrick, who married Eupheme, daughter and coheir of Gilbert Gray of Ballindoran, son of lord Gray, and by her had George, his heir; and a daughter, Margaret, who married Sir Andrew Hay, father of John, the twelfth earl of Errol. He was slain by William Ogilvie in 1590, and was succeeded by his said son, George, whose son, Patrick, was succeeded by his son,

George, who being of great service to king Charles II. during the usurpation of Oliver Cromwell, was by that king, at his restoration, made one of the privy council, and created lord Kinnaird of Inchture. He married Margaret, daughter of James Crichton of Ruthven, by whom he had six sons; Patrick; John; James; Alexander, and Charles, who died without issue; and George, of whom hereafter. He died December 29, 1689, and was succeeded by his eldest son,

Patrick, second lord, who married Ann, daughter of Hugh lord Lovat, and had issue three sons and one daughter; George, master of Kinnaird, who died without issue; Patrick, his successor; and Charles, of whom hereafter. The daughter, Anne, was the wife of Thomas Drummond of Lagiealmond, Esq; Dying in 1701, he was succeeded by his eldest surviving son,

Patrick, third lord, who married first, lady Henrietta Murray, daughter of Charles earl of Dunmore; and secondly, lady Elizabeth Lyon, daughter of Patrick earl of Strathmore, and widow of Charles Gordon, the second earl of Aboyn; and by her had issue a son,

Patrick, fourth lord, who in October 1727 succeeded him; but dying unmarried, was succeeded by

Charles, his uncle, fifth lord, third son of Patrick, the second lord, who married Magdalen, daughter of William Browne, merchant in Edinburgh; but dying without issue, in 1758, his estate and honours devolved upon his cousin and heir-male, Charles, son of George, son of George, sixth son of George, the first lord. Which Charles, sixth and present lord Kinnaird, married Barbara, daughter of Sir James Johnston of Westerhall, Bart. by whom he has issue two sons and three daughters, viz. George, master of Kinnaird; Patrick: Elizabeth, Helen, and Margaret.

TITLE.] The right honourable Charles lord Kinnaird, of Inchture.

CREATION.] Lord Kinnaird, 28 December 1682, by Charles II.

ARMS.] Quarterly, 1st and 4th, topaz, a fess wavey, between

tween three stars, ruby, for Kirkcaldy; 2d and 3d, ruby, a saltire between four crescents, topaz, for Kinnaird.

CREST.] On a wreath, a crescent rising from a cloud, with a star between its horns, all within two branches of palm, displayed orle wise.

SUPPORTERS.] Two savages, each wreathed about his head and middle with oak leaves, and their hands that support the shield in chains, hanging down to their feet, their other hands holding each a garland of laurel.

MOTTO.] Patitur qui vincit.

CHIEF SEAT.] At Drimmie, in the Carse of Gowrie.

SECOND TITLES;

Of Dukes, Marquisses, and Earls; by which, in Courtesy, their eldest Sons are generally distinguished.

A

Berdour lord, eldest son of the earl of Moreton.
Ancram earl of, eldest son of the marquis of Lothian.
Angus earl of, eldest son of the duke of Douglas.

B

Balgony lord, eldest son of the earl of Leven.
Berindale lord, eldest son of the earl of Caithness.
Binny lord, eldest son of the earl of Haddington.
Bowmont marquis of, eldest son of the duke of Roxburgh.
Boyd lord, eldest son of the earl of Kilmarnock.
Boyle lord, eldest son of the earl of Glasgow.
Bruce lord, eldest son of the earl of Kincardin.

C

Cardross lord, eldest son of the earl of Buchan.
Carmichael lord, eldest son of the earl of Hyndford.
Carnegy lord, eldest son of the earl of Southesk.
Cochran lord, eldest son of the earl of Dundonald.
Clairmont lord, eldest son of the earl of Middleton.
Cliddesdale marquis of, eldest son of the duke of Hamilton.
Crichton lord, eldest son of the earl of Dumfries.
Cummerlard, eldest son of the earl of Balcarras.

D

Dair lord, eldest son of the earl of Selkirk.
Dalkeith earl of, eldest son of the duke of Buccleugh.
Dalmeny lord, eldest son of the earl of Roseberry.
Dalrymple lord, eldest son of the earl of Stair.
Dalziel lord, eldest son of the earl of Carnwath.
Darnley earl of, eldest son of the duke of Lennox.
Deskford lord, eldest son of the earl of Finlater.

Down lord, eldest son of the earl of Murray.
Drumlanrig earl of, eldest son of the duke of Queensberry.
Drummond lord, eldest son of the earl of Perth.
Dunglas lord, eldest son of the earl of Hume.
Dupplin viscount, eldest son of the earl of Kinnoul.

E

Elcho lord, eldest son of the earl of Wemys.
Erskine lord, eldest son of the earl of Mar.

F

Fleming lord, eldest son of the earl of Wigton.
Fenton viscount, eldest son of the earl of Kelly.

G

Garlies lord, eldest son of the earl of Galloway.
Garnock viscount, eldest son of the earl of Crawford, formerly Lindsay.
Glamis lord, eldest son of the earl of Strathmore.
Gordon lord, eldest son of the earl of Aboyn.
Glenorchy viscount, eldest son of the earl of Breadalbane.
Graham marquis of, eldest son of the duke of Montrose.

H

Haddo lord, eldest son of the earl of Aberdeen.
Hay lord, eldest son of the earl of Errol.
Hope lord, eldest son of the earl of Hopeton.
Huntingtour lord, eldest son of the earl of Dysart.
Huntley marquis of, eldest son of the duke of Gordon.

J

Johnston lord, eldest son of the marquis of Annandale.

K

Keith lord, eldest son of the earl of Kintore.
Kelburn viscount, eldest son of the earl of Glasgow.
Kennedy lord, eldest son of the earl of Cassils.
Kilmaurs lord, eldest son of the earl of Glencairn.
Kintail lord, eldest son of the earl of Seaforth.
Kirkwall lord, eldest son of the earl of Orkney.

L

Lesley lord, eldest son of the earl of Rothes.
Lindsay lord, eldest son of the earl of Crawford.
Linton lord, eldest son of the earl of Traquair.
Lorn marquis of, eldest son of the duke of Argyll.

M

Mackenzie lord, eldest son of the earl of Seaforth.
Macleod lord, eldest son of the earl of Cromerty.
Maitland lord, eldest son of the earl of Lauderdale.
Mauchlane lord, eldest son of the earl of Loudoun.
Maxwell lord, eldest son of the earl of Nithsdale.
Milsington viscount, eldest son of the earl of Portmore.
Montgomery lord, eldest son of the earl of Eglington.
Mountstuart lord, eldest son of the earl of Bute.

Nidpath

N
Nidpath lord, eldeſt ſon of the earl of March.
O
Ogilvy lord, eldeſt ſon of the earl of Airly.
P
Paiſley lord, eldeſt ſon of the earl of Abercorn.
Polwarth lord, eldeſt ſon of the earl of Marchmont.
R
Ramſay lord, eldeſt ſon of the earl of Dalhouſie.
Roſehill lord, eldeſt ſon of the earl of Northeſk.
S
Seton lord, eldeſt ſon of the earl of Winton.
Strathnavern lord, eldeſt ſon of the earl of Sutherland.
T
Tullibairden marquis of, eldeſt ſon of the duke of Athol.
Y
Yeſter lord, eldeſt ſon of the marquis of Tweeddale.

A Liſt of thoſe Scots Peers who have been ſucceſſively returned to all the Parliaments of Great Britain ſince the Union, which took Place May 1, 1707.

Firſt Parliament ſummoned to meet the 23d of October, 1707.

JAMES Douglas, duke of Queensberry.
James Graham, duke of Montroſe.
John Ker, duke of Roxburgh.
John Hay, marquis of Tweeddale.
William Ker, marquis of Lothian.
John Lindſay, earl of Crawford.
John Sutherland, earl of Sutherland.
John Erſkine, earl of Mar.
Hugh Campbell, earl of Loudoun.
David Wemys, earl of Wemys.
David Leſley, earl of Leven and Melvil.
James Ogilvy, earl of Seafield.
John Dalrymple, earl of Stair.
Archibald Primroſe, earl of Roſeberry.
David Boyle, earl of Glaſgow.
Archibald Campbell, earl of Ila.

SECOND PARLIAMENT,
8 July, 1708.

James Hamilton, duke of Hamilton.
James Graham, duke of Montrofe.
John Ker, duke of Roxburgh.
William Ker, marquis of Lothian.
John Lindfay, earl of Crawford.
John Erfkine, earl of Mar.
John Lefley, earl of Rothes.
Hugh Campbell, earl of Loudoun.
David Wemys, earl of Wemys.
David Carnegy, earl of Northefk.
David Lefley, earl of Leven and Melvil.
George Hamilton, earl of Orkney.
James Ogilvy, earl of Seafield.
Archibald Primrofe, earl of Rofeberry.
David Boyle, earl of Glafgow.
Archibald Campbell, earl of Ila.

THIRD PARLIAMENT.
25 November, 1710.

James Hamilton, duke of Hamilton, *killed in a duel.*
John Murray, duke of Athol.
William Johnfton, marquis of Annandale.
William Keith, earl Marfhal, *died.*
John Erfkine, earl of Mar.
Alexander Montgomery, earl of Eglingtòn.
Alexander Hume, earl of Hume.
Hugh Campbell, earl of Loudoun.
Thomas Hay, earl of Kinnoul.
David Carnegy, earl of Northefk.
George Hamilton, earl of Orkney.
Archibald Primrofe, earl of Rofeberry.
Archibald Campbell, earl of Ila.
William Levingfton, vifcount Kilfyth.
John Elphingfton, lord Balmerino.
Walter Stewart, lord Blantyre.

Returned for thofe deceafed.

James Levingfton, earl of Linlithgow and Callender.
James Ogilvy, earl of Finlater and Seafield.

FOURTH

SIXTEEN PEERS.

FOURTH PARLIAMENT.
12 November, 1713.

JOHN Murray, duke of Athol.
John Erskine, earl of Mar.
Alexander Montgomery, earl of Eglington.
James Levingston, earl of Linlithgow and Callender.
Hugh Campbell, earl of Loudoun.
Thomas Hay, earl of Kinnoul.
Charles Hamilton, earl of Selkirk.
David Carnegy, earl of Northesk.
John Cochran, earl of Dundonald.
James Campbell, earl of Breadalbane.
John Murray, earl of Dunmore.
George Hamilton, earl of Orkney.
Archibald Primrose, earl of Roseberry.
David Colyear, earl of Portmore.
William Levingston, viscount Kilsyth.
John Elphingston, lord Balmerino.

FIFTH PARLIAMENT.
17 March, 1714-15.

JAMES Graham, duke of Montrose.
John Ker, duke of Roxburgh.
Charles Hay, marquis of Tweeddale, *died*.
William Ker, marquis of Lothian, *died, no new election*.
William Johnston, marquis of Annandale, *died*.
John Sutherland, earl of Sutherland.
John Lesley, earl of Rothes.
David Erskine, earl of Buchan.
Hugh Campbell, earl of Loudoun.
George Hamilton, earl of Orkney.
John Dalrymple, earl of Stair.
James Stewart, earl of Bute.
Henry Scot, earl of Deloraine.
Archibald Campbell, earl of Ila.
William Ross, lord Ross.
John Hamilton, lord Belhaven, *drowned*.

Returned for the deceased peers.

Thomas Hamilton, earl of Haddington.
William Gordon, earl of Aberdeen.
James Ogilvy, earl of Finlater and Seafield.

SIXTH PARLIAMENT.
10 May, 1722.

JAMES Graham, duke of Montrose.
John Ker, duke of Roxburgh.
John Hay, marquis of Tweeddale.
John Sutherland, earl of Sutherland.
John Lesley, earl of Rothes, *died.*
David Erskine, earl of Buchan.
Thomas Hamilton, earl of Haddington.
Hugh Campbell, earl of Loudoun.
Charles Hamilton, earl of Selkirk.
William Gordon, earl of Aberdeen.
George Hamilton, earl of Orkney.
John Dalrymple, earl of Stair.
James Stewart, earl of Bute.
Charles Hope, earl of Hopeton.
Henry Scot, earl of Delorain.
Archibald Campbell, earl of Ila.

Returned for the peer who died.
James Ogilvy, earl of Finlater and Seafield.

SEVENTH PARLIAMENT.
28 November, 1727.

JAMES Graham, duke of Montrose.
John Hay, marquis of Tweeddale.
John Sutherland, earl of Sutherland.
John Lesley, earl of Rothes, *died.*
David Erskine, earl of Buchan.
Thomas Hamilton, earl of Haddington.
Hugh Campbell, earl of Loudoun.
James Ogilvy, earl of Finlater and Seafield.
Charles Hamilton, earl of Selkirk.
John Murray, earl of Dunmore.
George Hamilton, earl of Orkney.
John Dalrymple, earl of Stair.
Alexander Hume, earl of Marchmont.
Charles Hope, earl of Hopeton.
Henry Scot, earl of Delorain.
Archibald Campbell, earl of Ila.

Returned for the earl of Rothes.
James Ogilvy, earl of Finlater and Seafield.

EIGHTH PARLIAMENT.
13 June, 1734.

FRANCIS Scot, duke of Buccleugh.
James Murray, duke of Athol.
William Ker, marquis of Lothian.
John Lindsay, earl of Crawford.
William Sutherland, earl of Sutherland.
George Douglas, earl of Moreton, *died*.
John Campbell, earl of Loudoun.
James Ogilvy, earl of Finlater and Seafield.
Charles Hamilton, earl of Selkirk, *died*.
Alexander Lindsay, earl of Balcarras, *died*.
John Murray, earl of Dunmore.
George Hamilton, earl of Orkney, *died*.
Charles Hope, earl of Hopeton.
Charles Colyear, earl of Portmore.
Archibald Campbell, earl of Ila.
Charles Cathcart, lord Cathcart.

Returned for the peers who died,

John Campbell, earl of Breadalbane.
John Stewart, earl of Bute.
John Carmichael, earl of Hyndford.
James Douglas, earl of Moreton.

NINTH PARLIAMENT.
25 June, 1741.

WILLIAM Ker, marquis of Lothian.
John Lindsay, earl of Crawford.
William Sutherland, earl of Sutherland.
James Douglas, earl of Moreton.
James Stewart, earl of Murray.
William Hume, earl of Hume.
Charles Maitland, earl of Lauderdale, *died* *.
John Campbell, earl of Loudoun.
James Ogilvy, earl of Finlater and Seafield.
John Campbell, earl of Breadalbane.
John Murray, earl of Dunmore.
John Carmichael, earl of Hyndford.
Charles Hope, earl of Hopeton, *died* †.
Charles Colyear, earl of Portmore.
Archibald Campbell, earl of Ila.
James Somerville, lord Somerville.

In the room of those deceased,

* John Hay, marquis of Tweeddale.
† John Dalrymple, earl of Stair.

TENTH PARLIAMENT.
14 August, 1747.

COSMO George Gordon, duke of Gordon, *died* §.
Archibald Campbell, duke of Argyll.
John Hay, marquis of Tweeddale.
William Ker, marquis of Lothian.
John Lindsay, earl of Crawford, *died* †.
John Lesley, earl of Rothes.
James Douglas, earl of Moreton.
James Stewart, earl of Murray.
William Hume, earl of Hume.
James Maitland, earl of Lauderdale.
John Campbell, earl of Loudoun.
James Ogilvy, earl of Finlater and Seafield.
Alexander Lesley, earl of Leven and Melvil.
George Gordon, earl of Aberdeen.
John Murray, earl of Dunmore, *died* ‖.
John Carmichael, earl of Hyndford.

In the room of those who died.

§ Hugh Hume, earl of Marchmont.
† John Campbell, earl of Breadalbane.
‖ Charles Cathcart, lord Cathcart.

ELEVENTH PARLIAMENT.
31 May, 1754.

ARCHIBALD Campbell, duke of Argyll.
John Hay, marquis of Tweeddale.
William Ker, marquis of Lothian.
John Lesley, earl of Rothes.
James Douglas, earl of Moreton.
James Stewart, earl of Murray.
William Hume, earl of Hume.
James Maitland, earl of Lauderdale.
John Campbell, earl of Loudoun.
James Ogilvy, earl of Finlater and Seafield.
Alexander Lesley, earl of Leven and Melvil, *died* †.
John Campbell, earl of Breadalbane.
George Gordon, earl of Aberdeen.

Hugh

Hugh Hume, earl of Marchmont.
John Carmichael, earl of Hyndford.
David Murray, viscount Stormont.

Returned for the peer who died.
† Charles Cathcart, lord Cathcart.

TWELFTH PARLIAMENT.
5 May, 1761.

JOHN Campbell, duke of Argyll.
John Hay, marquis of Tweeddale, *died* †.
John Lesley, earl of Rothes.
James Douglas, earl of Morton.
Alexander Montgomery, earl of Eglington.
James Stewart, earl of Murray.
William Hume, earl of Hume, *died* ‖.
James Hamilton, earl of Abercorn.
John Campbell, earl of Loudoun.
John Campbell, earl of Breadalbane.
William Murray, earl of Dunmore.
James Douglas, earl of March.
Hugh Hume, earl of Marchmont.
John Stewart, earl of Bute.
David Murray, viscount Stormont.
Charles Cathcart, lord Cathcart.

In the room of those who died.
† William Sutherland, earl of Sutherland, who died in 1766, and John Murray, duke of Athol, was elected in his room.
‖ John Carmichael, earl of Hyndford.

SCOTS PEERS,
Whose Titles are forfeited by Attainder.

ERSKINE, Earl of MAR.

IN the reign of Alexander II. 1226, lived Henry de Erskine, who was a witness to a gift which Amelick, brother of Maldwin earl of Lennox, made to the canons of Paisly: and to him succeeded Sir John Erskine, the father of another Sir John, the father of a third Sir John, whose son, Sir William, succeeded him in the barony of Erskine, and was a firm adherent of king Robert Bruce. To him succeeded his eldest son, Sir Robert, and his second son, Sir Alan, was ancestor of the Erskines of Inchmartin. Sir Robert was, after the return of king David from France, appointed constable and keeper of the castle of Stirling for life, and in 1348, after the unfortunate battle of Durham, was sent as one of the ambassadors to negotiate king David's liberty. After that king's return to Scotland, he was made justice general of the North, lord chamberlain to the king, ambassador to France, sheriff of the county of Stirling, and governor of that castle, and the castles of Edinburgh and Dumbarton, of all which he was possessed at the king's death; and then declaring for king Robert II. first of the name of Stewart, he contributed much to the bringing him peaceably to the throne. He married first, Beatrix, daughter of Sir David Lindsay; and secondly, Christian, the widow of Sir Edward Keith; and dying in 1385, left issue three sons, Sir Thomas, his heir; Sir Nicholas Erskine of Kinnoul, in Perthshire; whose family subsisted, in the male line, till the reign of James II. when Christian, only daughter of Sir John Erskine of Kinnoul, married Sir Robert Crichton of Sanquhar, ancestor of the earl of Dumfries; and Sir Alan: Also two daughters, Mariota, wife of Sir Maurice Drummond of Concraig; and Elizabeth, of Sir Walter Oliphant of Aberdalgie, ancestor of lord Oliphant. He was succeeded by his eldest son,

Thomas, seventh lord Erskine, who was knighted by the said king Robert, and afterwards sent ambassador to England, as he was again by Robert III. and marrying Janet, daughter of Sir Edward Keith, by her had issue Robert, the eighth lord Erskine; John, ancestor of the Erskines of Dun, and of Pittodrie; and two daughters, Elizabeth, wife of Duncan Wemyss of Luchars; and Christian, of Sir John Haldane of Gleneagles.

Robert, eighth lord Erskine, who in imitation of his noble ancestors, signalized his loyalty to king James I. when a prisoner in England, was one of the hostages for his ransom; and in 1436, upon the death of Alexander earl of Mar,

laid

laid claim to the half of that earldom, and assumed the title on account of the aforesaid marriage, his mother being heir of Sir John Menteith, by Helen, daughter of Gratney earl of Mar; but the crown interfering, it was not ended in his days. He marrying a daughter of Robert Stewart, lord Lorn, and dying in 1453, left issue Thomas, his heir; and a daughter, Elizabeth, married to Sir Henry Douglas of Lochleven.

Thomas, who succeeded as ninth lord Erskine, prosecuting his father's claim to the earldom of Mar, in 1457, had a decree of the committee of estates given in his favour. He married lady Janet, daughter of James earl of Moreton, by whom he had issue Alexander, his heir; and three daughters, Elizabeth, married to Sir Alexander Seton of Touch; Mary, to William Livingston of Kilsyth; and Mariota, to the second earl Marshal.

Alexander, his son, second earl, succeeded him, and was made governor of Dumbarton castle, and one of the privy council to James IV. with whom he was in great favour. He married Christian, daughter of Sir Robert Crichton of Sanquhar; and his second wife was Helen, daughter of Alexander, first lord Home, by whom he had three sons and two daughters; Robert, Alexander, and Walter; lady Christian, wife of Sir David Stewart of Rosyth; and lady Agnes, of Sir William Menteith of Carse. He died before the year 1510, and was succeeded by his eldest son,

Robert, third earl, who married Elizabeth, daughter of Sir George Campbell of Loudoun, ancestor of the earls of Loudoun; and being with his majesty, was slain at the battle of Floddon in 1513, and left issue five sons and four daughters, viz. Robert, who died unmarried, before his father; John; James, ancestor of the Erskines of Balgony; Alexander, William: lady Catharine, wife of Alexander, second lord Elphinstone; lady Margaret, first, of John Haldane of Gleneagles; and secondly, of George Home of Lawndies; lady Elizabeth, of Sir James Forbes of Torwood; and lady Janet, of John Murray of Touchaddam. He was succeeded by his eldest surviving son,

John, fourth earl, who being a nobleman of great honour and probity, had the care and tuition of the young king James V. in the castle of Stirling, of which he was governor. In the year 1534, when the king came of age, he was sent ambassador to France to propose a match between his Majesty and the princess Magdalen de Valois, daughter of Francis I. which he having performed to the king's satisfaction, he afterwards sent him in the same quality to Henry VIII. of England; and in 1537 he was one of those peers who attended his master into France, where he espoused the said princess. In 1542, upon the death of the king, young queen Mary was also committed to his care in Stirling castle; and that great trust his lordship discharged with the same fidelity he had done in her father's minority; for in 1548, notwithstanding the endeavours of king Henry VIII. of England, and the party that was for him in Scotland to get her out of his hands, he carried her safe into France. He married lady Margaret, eldest daughter of Archibald, second earl of Argyll, and had issue by her six sons and two daughters; lady Elizabeth, wife of Walter Seton of Touch; and lady Margaret, mother of James, prior of St. Andrews, and earl of Murray, by king James V. and afterwards wife of Sir Robert Douglas of Lochleven, ancestor of the earl of Morton. The sons were, Robert, who married lady Margaret, eldest daughter of William earl of Montrose, and was slain at the battle of Pinkey, without issue; Thomas, who thereupon became heir apparent, and being a nobleman of great capacity, was employed in several embassies in England, where he acquired great reputation by faithfully serving his country, but also died without issue; John; Sir Alexander of Gogar, ancestor of the earls of Kelly; Sir George, of Innerteel, a senator of the college of justice; and Sir James of Tillybody. His lordship deceased in 1552, and was succeeded by his eldest surviving son,

John, fifth earl. He was a person of such a noble generous nature, and other bright qualities, as rendered him very capable of sustaining the part of a consummate statesman, which he did afterwards in the highest and most eminent stations. On the demise of his father, though he was then very young, the queen regent in 1553 appointed him governor of Edinburgh castle; after which he was one of her majesty's privy council, and obtained a grant of the abbey of Insmaconock, with divers other lands; and then renewing his claim to the earldom of Mar, it was finally allowed and ratified by an act of parliament, in 1563. When her majesty was happily delivered of the young prince, afterwards king James VI. she committed him to the guardianship of the earl of Mar, in the castle of Edinburgh; which great trust he so well discharged, that when the earl of Bothwell had married the queen, they could not prevail with the lord Mar, either by promises or menaces, to deliver up the young prince to them, till he had solemnly set the crown upon his majesty's head. This noble earl dying at Stirling in November 1572, left behind him an excellent reputation; for notwithstanding their mutual heats, he was acknowledged by both parties to be a person of great judgment and integrity: And having been elected regent of Scotland in 1571, during the minority of the said king James VI. he, in the time of his sickness, when his son was a minor, appointed the laird of Tullibairden, and his own brother, Alexander Erskine, to be governors of his majesty, and keepers of Stirling castle.

castle. He married Annabella, daughter of William lord Murray of Tullibairden, ancestor of the duke of Athol, and by her had issue John, his successor; and lady Margaret, the wife of Archibald earl of Angus.

John, sixth earl, who succeeded his father, was also in great favour with king James VI. (with whom he was educated) who committed to his care the tuition of his young son, prince Henry. In 1601, he was sent ambassador to queen Elizabeth, where, in his negotiation, he deported himself with such prudence and conduct, that his majesty gratefully owned his peaceable accession to the crown of England, next to the goodness of God, owing to the earl of Mar; and thereupon made him knight of the most noble order of the garter, one of his privy council in England, and lord high treasurer of Scotland, which office he held for fifteen years. He married first, Ann, daughter of David lord Drummond, ancestor of the earls of Perth, by whom he had issue John, his heir; and secondly, lady Mary Stewart, daughter of Esme duke of Lennox, by whom he had issue seven sons and four daughters; Sir James, who marrying Christian, daughter and sole heir of Robert Douglas earl of Buchan, he in her right became earl thereof, the king bestowing the title by patent upon him and his heirs male; Henry, who was created lord Cardross, and was commendator of Dryburgh, from whom is descended the present earl of Buchan; Sir Alexander, senator of the college of justice, who was blown up at Dunglass-house in 1640, without issue; Sir Charles, of Alva; Sir John, of Otterstown; Sir Arthur, of Scotscraig; and William, cupbearer to Charles II. and master of the charter-house, London: lady Mary, wife, first, of William sixth earl Marshal; and secondly, of Patrick earl of Panmure; lady Anne, of John earl of Rothes; lady Margaret, of John earl of Kinghorn, ancestor of the earl of Strathmore; and lady Catharine, of Thomas, second earl of Haddington. His lordship deceased in 1634, and was succeeded by his eldest son,

John, seventh earl, who was made knight of the Bath in 1610, at the creation of Henry prince of Wales, and afterwards one of his majesty's privy council, one of the judges in the court of session, and governor of Edinburgh castle; and when the civil war broke out in the reign of Charles I. he applied himself with great resolution and fidelity to promote his majesty's cause; for which he was reckoned among the first rank of malignants, and suffered accordingly in his estate. He married the lady Christian, daughter of Francis, ninth earl of Errol, and by her had issue three sons and two daughters, viz. John, Sir Francis, and William; the two last of which died without issue: lady Elizabeth, wife of Alexander lord

Napier; and lady Mary, who died unmarried. He died in 1654, and was succeeded by his eldest son,

John, eighth earl, who was strongly attached to the king, during the whole course of the civil war. He married first, lady Mary, daughter of Walter earl of Buccleugh, by whom he had no issue; but by his second wife, lady Mary, daughter of George earl of Seaforth, he had issue Charles, his heir; George who died young; and three daughters, lady Barbara, married to James marquis of Douglas; lady Jane, to John Coningham, earl of Glencairn; and lady Sophia, to Alexander lord Pitsligo, who all left issue. He died in 1664, and was succeeded by his eldest son,

Charles, ninth earl, who was one of the privy council to king Charles II. and James VII. during whose reign he was colonel of a regiment of foot, which he raised, and commanded till his death, since known by the name of the Scotch Fusileers. He came heartily into the revolution, but dying in 1689, left issue by lady Mary, daughter of George earl of Panmure, who afterwards married Sir John Erskine of Alva, Bart. one daughter, lady Jane, who married Sir Hugh Paterson of Bannockburn, and had issue, but died in October 1763; and three sons, of which colonel Henry, the youngest, was killed at the battle of Almanza in Spain in 1707; James, the second, was promoted by queen Anne to be one of the senators of the college of justice, and lord justice clerk; but upon passing the act for disabling the judges of Scotland to sit in parliament, he made a formal resignation of his office, and was elected representative in parliament for the shire of Clackmannan. In 1715, he was returned to parliament for the burghs of Aberdeen, &c. in 1734, for the shire of Clackmannan; in 1741, for the burghs of Inverskeithing, &c. and was secretary to the late prince of Wales for Scottish affairs. He was succeeded by his eldest son,

John, tenth earl of Mar, who was by queen Anne made colonel of a regiment of foot, knight of the thistle, and in 1705 secretary of state; and the next year was one of the commissioners for the treaty of union between the two nations; which being concluded, he was elected one of the sixteen peers to parliament, and in 1713 he was again made secretary of state for Scotland. He was likewise one of the sixteen peers in the three succeeding parliaments of queen Anne. Upon the accession of king George I. he was deprived of all his offices; and in the year 1715, retired to his estates in the north, where being joined by several noblemen and gentlemen, with their followers, to the number of 600, and setting up his standard, and proclaiming the Pretender at Kirkmichael, in Perthshire, on Sept. 11, and his forces increasing to 6 or 7000 men, he marched to Sheriffmuir, near Dumblane, where being met by the king's army, commanded by the duke of Argyll, he was defeated,

defeated, after having behaved like an able and gallant commander. He afterwards made his escape beyond sea, and in the year 1716, was attainted with the duke of Ormond and lord Bolingbroke, whereby his estate and honours were forfeited to the crown. He went to Rome, and was in the Pretender's service until the year 1721; from thence repairing to Paris, he continued there till 1729, and from thence, on account of his ill state of health, went to Aix la Chapelle, where he died in May 1732. His estate was sold by the commissioners of forfeited estates, and bought by his brother, James Erskine of Grange, Esq; for the benefit of his nephew, lord Erskine, to whom he conveyed it in 1739. He married first, lady Margaret, daughter of Thomas earl of Kinnoul, by whom he had two sons, John, who died in his infancy; and Thomas lord Erskine: and secondly, lady Frances, daughter of Evelyn duke of Kingston, by whom he had a daughter, lady Frances, who had settled upon her, by king George I. the same fortune she was intitled to by her mother's marriage settlement, out of her father's estate. The king also granted to her mother her jointure out of the said estate. Lady Frances was married to her cousin, James Erskine, Esq; son of the above Mr. Erskine of Grange, and has issue two sons, John-Francis, and James-Francis, both officers in the army. Thomas lord Erskine, who has the estate, as before observed, married lady Charlotte, daughter of Charles earl of Hopetoun, by whom he has issue. In 1727, he was elected member to parliament for the burghs of Inverkeithing, &c. in 1746-7, for the shire of Stirling; and in 1747, for the shire of Clackmannan.

TITLES.] The right honourable John Erskine, earl of Mar, and lord Erskine of Alloa.

CREATIONS.] Created or confirmed earl of Mar, and lord Erskine of Alloa, or Alloway, in the county of Clackmannan, 1436, by king James II.

ARMS.] Quarterly, 1st and 4th sapphire, a bend between six cross croslets fitchy, topaz, for the title of Mar; 2d and 3d pearl, a pale diamond, for Erskine.

CREST.] On a wreath, a dexter hand, couped above the wrist, holding a dagger out, proper, the pomel and hilt, topaz.

SUPPORTERS.] Two griphons, pearl, beaked, winged, and armed, topaz.

MOTTO.] Je pense plus.

CHIEF SEATS.] Alloa; castle of Kildrimmie; Castletown of Mar; at Stirling, &c.

MAXWELL, Earl of NITHSDALE.

THE firname of Maxwell is as antient as the firſt uſe of firnames in Scotland; but not to perplex my reader with traditionary and dark accounts of the origin of this family, I ſhall begin with Sir Hubert de Makſwell, lord of Carlavarock, who was a man of great honour and abilities, and one of the *Magnates Scotiæ*, who was forced to ſwear fealty to Edward I. of England, for lands lying in different counties, in 1296. He left iſſue Sir John, his heir; Sir Herbert, of whom preſently; and Alexander. Sir John, the eldeſt ſon and ſucceſſor, died without iſſue, and was ſucceeded by his brother Sir Herbert, and he by his ſon Sir Euſtace, who was a firm adherent to king Robert Bruce. His ſon and ſucceſſor, Sir John Maxwell of Carlaverock, was ſucceeded by his ſon, another Sir John, and he by his ſon Sir Robert, who made a great figure in the reigns of Robert II. and III. and was knighted by the former. He died about the year 1420, and was ſucceeded by his eldeſt ſon, Sir Herbert, who was one of the hoſtages for king James the firſt's ranſom in 1423, and was created lord Maxwell of Carlaverock in 1424. He had two ſons, whereof Euſtace, the youngeſt, was anceſtor of the Maxwells of Tealing, in Forfar, and the eldeſt, Robert, dying in his life-time, his ſon Herbert, ſecond lord, ſucceeded his grandfather. Herbert had by his firſt wife, a daughter of Sir Herbert Herries, two ſons and a daughter, viz. Robert; Sir Edward, anceſtor of the Maxwells of Tinwald, Monreith, &c. and Agnes, wife of Gilbert lord Kennedy. By his ſecond wife, Iſabel, daughter of William lord Seton, he had iſſue George, anceſtor of the Maxwells of Garnſalloch; David: Adam, progenitor of the Maxwells of Southbar, &c. in Renfrewſhire; John; William; Janet and Marriotte. He died in 1452, and was ſucceeded by his eldeſt ſon,

Robert, third lord, who by his wife lady Janet, daughter of George earl of Caithneſs, had iſſue John; George, of Barnton; Thomas, anceſtor of the Maxwells of Kirkconnel; and Janet, the wife of William lord Carlile of Torthorald. He was ſucceeded by his eldeſt ſon,

John, fourth lord, who loſt his life at the battle of Floddon in 1513, leaving iſſue by Agnes his wife, daughter of Sir Alexander Stewart of Gairlies, Robert, his heir; Herbert, anceſtor of the Maxwells of Cloudon; Henry: Mary, wife of Sir John Johnſtone of that ilk; Agnes, of —— Charteris of Amsfield; and Elizabeth, of —— Jardine of Applegirth. He was ſucceeded by his eldeſt ſon,

Robert, fifth lord, who was in great favour with king James V. by whom he was made captain and governor of Lochmaben, and colonel of his guard. He was alſo by that king

king sent ambassador to the court of France, to treat of a marriage between his majesty and Mary of Lorrain, daughter of the duke of Guise; which being concluded, he espoused the lady in his master's name, and brought her to Scotland: In recompense whereof, and other public services, the king bestowed on him the lands of Eskdale and Wachopdale; and made him gentleman of his bedchamber. He married first, Janet, daughter of Sir William Douglas of Drumlanrig, ancestor of the duke of Queensberry, by whom he had two sons, Robert; and Sir John, of whom hereafter: Also a daughter, Margaret, wife, first, of Archibald earl of Angus; and secondly, of Sir William Baillie of Lamington. By his second wife, lady Agnes, daughter of James earl of Buchan, he had no issue; and dying in 1546, was succeeded by his eldest son,

Robert, sixth lord, who married lady Beatrix, sister of David earl of Douglas and Angus, and daughter of James earl of Moreton, and by her had a posthumous son,

John, seventh lord, who was by king James VI. made warden of the west marches; but upon a new turn at court, was dismissed his office, and succeeded by the laird of Johnston; upon which a great quarrel arose between the two families, and in a scuffle among a party of his own friends and the Johnstons, he was killed, in December 1593. He married lady Elizabeth, daughter of David earl of Douglas and Angus, and by her left two sons and three daughters; Elizabeth, married to William lord Herries; Agnes, to William Douglas of Panrie; and Margaret, to Hugh Wallace of Craigie: The sons were, John, and Robert, successively lords, &c. He was succeeded by his eldest son,

John, eighth lord, who married lady Margaret, daughter of John marquis of Hamilton, without issue; but he having killed the laird of Johnston, in revenge of Johnston's killing his father, was in 1613 beheaded at the cross of Edinburgh, and his honour forfeited; but in the year 1618, by the favour of his majesty,

Robert, his brother, ninth lord, was restored to the lordship of Maxwell, created earl of Nithsdale in 1620, and suffered much by sequestration and imprisonment, for his loyalty to king Charles I. He married Elizabeth, daughter of Sir Francis Beaumont, a near relation of George Villiers, the great duke of Buckingham; and dying in 1647, by her left issue,

Robert, second earl; but he dying unmarried in 1667, his estate and honour descended to his cousin and heir male, John, lord Herries, son of John lord Herries, son of Sir John Maxwell of Terregles, (second son of Robert, fifth lord Maxwell) who by his wife Agnes, eldest daughter and coheir of William lord Herries, became lord Herries.

Which John, lord Herries, third earl of Nithsdale, by Elizabeth

zabeth his wife, daughter of Sir Robert Gordon of Lochinver, ancestor to the viscount Kenmure, had issue,

Robert, fourth earl, who married the lady Lucy, daughter of William marquis of Douglas, and by her had a son, William; and a daughter, lady Mary, wife of Charles Stewart, earl of Traquair; and dying in 1695, was succeeded by his only son,

William, fifth earl, who in January 1715-16, being brought prisoner from Preston to London, for appearing in rebellion against king George I. was tried, and condemned to be beheaded on the 24th of February following, with the lords Derwentwater and Kenmure; but the night before execution, he made his escape out of the Tower, and in the year 1744, died in his exile at Rome. He married Winifred, fifth and youngest daughter of William Herbert, marquis of Powis, by Elizabeth his wife, youngest daughter of Edward Somerset, marquis of Worcester, and by her left issue,

William, lord Maxwell, who, had not his father been attainted, would have been sixth earl of Nithsdale. He married his cousin german, lady Catharine Stewart, daughter of Charles earl of Traquair, by whom he had issue two daughters, Mary, who died young; and Winifred, wife of William Constable of Effringame, Esq; by whom she has two sons and a daughter; Marmaduke-William, William, and Catharine: Also a daughter, lady Ann, married to John lord Bellew, of the kingdom of Ireland.

TITLES.] The right honourable William Maxwell, earl of Nithsdale, lord Maxwell and Herries.

CREATION.] Earl of Nithsdale, October 29, 1581, 16 James VI.

ARMS.] Pearl, an imperial eagle displayed, diamond, beaked and membered, ruby; surmounted of a shield of the 1st, charged with a saltire of the 2d, and thereon a hedge-hog, topaz.

CREST.] On a wreath, a mount and holly-bush, and a stag lodged or couchant, all proper.

SUPPORTERS.] Two stags, proper, attired, pearl.

MOTTO.] Revirefco.

CHIEF SEATS were.] At Terregles; and Carlavarock, in Dumfriesshire.

SEATON, Earl of WINTON.

THIS family is one of the noblest in North Britain, and many illustrious families are descended from it. The name is derived from their antient lands of Seton, in East Lothian, the first whereof was Dowgal Seaton, who lived in the reign of king Edgar, and Alexander I. who succeeded to

the

the crown in 1107, and was succeeded by Secher, his son, who also inherited the lands of Winton and Winsburgh, and was father of Alexander, whose son, Philip, had issue Sir Alexander, his heir, who married Margaret, daughter of Walter Barclay, chancellor to king William the lion, and was succeeded by his son, Sir Serlo, or Secher, and he by Sir Alexander, his eldest son, whose eldest son and successor, Sir Christopher, in the reign of Robert I. bravely stood for the freedom of his country against the English usurpation; and was one of those worthies who, at the battle of Methwen, near Perth, in 1306, rescued the king from the English party; whereupon, for that singular piece of service, the king gave him in marriage his sister, the lady Christian Bruce; but at last he had the ill fortune to be taken by the English, and carried to London, where, with his brother John Seaton, and Nigel Bruce, the king's brother, he was put to death by order of king Edward I. for the said revolt. He had issue Sir Alexander, his heir. Which Sir Alexander, who succeeded, made a great figure during the reign of his uncle, king Robert, from whom he obtained sundry grants of lands, and a charter under the great seal, for erecting his lands of Seaton into a free barony; and, on account of maternal descent and merit, had his three crescents surrounded with the double tressure; which, with the coat of augmentation given to his father, being ruby, a sword supporting an imperial crown, hath remained in the family ever since He married lady Isabel, daughter of Duncan earl of Fife, and by her had Sir Alexander, his heir; who marrying Christian, daughter of —— Cheyne of Straloch, by her had four sons, Alexander; William; Thomas; and Sir John, ancestor of the Seatons of Porbroath, Lathrisk, &c. William and Thomas were cruelly put to death by king Edward I. upon their father's bravely holding out the town of Berwick against him, in their father's sight, who bore it with amazing fortitude, not willing to forfeit his honour, and his country's cause, to save their lives. Alexander, the eldest son, succeeded, and married Margaret, sister of William Murray, captain and governor of Edinburgh castle, and by her had Sir William Seaton, who married Katharine, daughter of Sir William Sinclair of Herdmanston, by whom he had two sons, Sir John; and Sir Alexander, who married Elizabeth, daughter and heir of Adam lord Gordon, of whom the dukes of Gordon, and the Seatons of Touch, Meldrum, &c. are descended: and four daughters, Margaret, wife of John lord Kennedy, ancestor of the earl of Cassilis; Marian, of Sir John Ogilvy, progenitor of the earl of Airly; Jane, of John lord Lisle; and Katharine, of Bernard Haldane of Gleneagles. He was succeeded by his eldest son,

Sir John, who was one of the hostages for the ransom of king James I. to whom he was afterwards master of the houshold, and was the first lord Seaton. He attended the princess Margaret, that king's daughter, into France, in order to her marriage with Louis the Dauphin, eldest son of Charles VII. of that realm, and married lady Janet, daughter of George Dunbar, earl of March, by whom he had Sir William, his successor; and two daughters, Janet, married to Robert master of Keith, son of William earl Marshal of Scotland; and Christian, to Norman, lord Lesley of Rothes. He died in 1441, and his only son, Sir William, who was slain in 1424, at the battle of Vernuil, in France, leaving a son, George, he succeeded his grandfather. He had also two daughters, viz. Catharine, wife, first, of Sir Alan Stewart of Darnley, ancestor of the royal family; and secondly, of Herbert lord Maxwell; and Janet, wife or John, second lord Haliburton.

Which George, second lord, married lady Jane Stewart, only daughter and heir of John earl of Buchan, by whom he had a son, John, his heir; and secondly, Christian ——, by whom he had a daughter, wife of Hugh Douglas of Borgue. He died about the year 1470, and his son, John, who died before him, having married Mary, daughter of John lord Lindsay, ancestor of the earl of Crawford, by her had George, successor to his grandfather.

Which George, third lord Seaton, married the lady Isabel, daughter of Colin Campbell, earl of Argyll, and by her left issue a daughter, Martha, married to William Maitland, ancestor of the earl of Lauderdale; and two sons, George, his heir; and John, ancestor of the Seatons of Northrig. He died in 1507, and was succeeded by his eldest son,

George, fourth lord, who being slain at the battle of Floddon with king James IV. left by Janet his wife, daughter of Patrick Hepburn, earl of Bothwell, George, his heir; and a daughter, Marian, married to Hugh Montgomery, the second earl of Eglington. He was succeeded by his said son,

George, fifth lord, who married Elizabeth, daughter of John Hay, lord Yester, ancestor of the marquis of Tweeddale, by whom he had two sons, George, his heir; John, ancestor of the Seatons of Carristoun, and four daughters, Marian, wife of John, fourth earl of Menteith; Margaret, of Sir Robert Logan of Restalrig; Eleanor, of Hugh, seventh lord Somerville; and Beatrix, of Sir George Ogilvie of Dunluglas, ancestor of lord Banff. By a second wife, Mary Paris, a French lady, he had also a son, Robert. He deceased in 1545, and was succeeded by his eldest son,

George, sixth lord, who being governor of Edinburgh castle during the regency of queen Mary of Lorrain, was in 1557 commissioned by the estates of Scotland, to treat with the

French

French king about the marriage of queen Mary with Francis the Dauphin; and by the bounty of Henry II. had a penfion for his fervice to that crown. After his return to Scotland, he was made one of her majefty's privy council, and by James VI. in 1583, was again fent ambaffador to France; but dying foon after his return, left iffue by Ifabel his wife, daughter of Sir William Hamilton of Sanquhar, four fons and one daughter; Margaret, married to Claud Hamilton, lord Paifley, anceftor of the earl of Abercorn. The fons were, Robert, his heir; John, anceftor of the Seatons of Barns; Alexander, created earl of Dumferlin; and Sir William, who had one fon, but he died without iffue.

Robert, the eldeft fon, feventh lord, being much efteemed by king James VI. his majefty, on the 10th of November 1600, raifed him to the honours of earl of Winton, &c. and he marrying lady Margaret, daughter of Hugh Montgomery, third earl of Eglington, by her had five fons and one daughter, viz. Robert, who died without iffue, before his father; George; Sir Alexander, who changed his name to Montgomery, and became the fixth earl of Eglington, purfuant to the entail made by his coufin german, Hugh, the fifth earl of Eglington; Sir Thomas, anceftor of the Seatons of Oliveftob; and Sir John. The daughter, lady Elizabeth, married James Drummond, the firft earl of Perth; and fecondly, Francis Stewart, fon of Francis earl of Bothwell. He died in 1608, and was fucceeded by his eldeft furviving fon,

George, fecond earl, who was one of the privy council. He was alfo one of the privy council to Charles I. whom, with his whole retinue, in the king's progrefs to Scotland, he entertained at his houfe at Seaton with great fplendor and magnificence, and was very faithful to that prince during the time of the civil war. He married firft, lady Ann, daughter of Francis Hay, earl of Errol, by whom he had two fons, George; and Alexander, vifcount Kingftoun: and a daughter, Elizabeth, married to William Keith, fixth earl Marfhal. The faid Alexander, the youngeft fon, was created vifcount Kingftoun; and George lord Seaton, the eldeft, dying in his father's lifetime, left by lady Henrietta, daughter of George Gordon, fecond marquis of Huntley, who after his deceafe, married John earl of Traquair, George, who fucceeded his grandfather: and the faid George, the fecond earl, marrying to his fecond wife, Elizabeth, daughter of John Maxwell, lord Herries, by her had two fons and three daughters, viz. Sir John, of Garleton; Sir Robert, of Windygowl: lady Ifabel, married to Francis lord Semple; lady Ann, to John earl of Traquair; and lady Mary, to James earl of Carnwath.

George, third earl, who in 1650 fucceeded his grandfather, married firft, lady Mary, daughter of Hugh, feventh earl of Eglington,

Eglington, by whom he had no surviving issue; and secondly, Christian, daughter and coheir of John Hepburn of Aldiston, by whom he had two sons, George and Christopher. He died in 1704, and was succeeded by his eldest son,

George, fourth earl, who being unhappily engaged in the rebellion in 1715, was brought prisoner to London from Preston in Lancashire, and committed to the Tower. In March following being tried, he was found guilty of high treason, and received sentence of death, which was pronounced by lord chancellor Cowper, the lord high steward; but in August following, by some secret management, he made his escape, and ended his days at Rome, in 1749, without issue. The representation of this family is now vested in Sir George Seaton of Garleton, son of Sir George, son of Sir John, third son of George, second earl of Winton. Which Sir George, but for the attainder and forfeiture of George the fourth earl, would now have been fifth earl of Winton. He resides in France, and is unmarried.

TITLE.] The right honourable George Seaton, earl of Winton, and lord Seaton of Tranent, in the county of Haddington.

CREATION.] Earl of Winton, 10 November 1600, the 31st of James VI. as king of Scotland.

ARMS.] Quarterly, 1st and 4th topaz, three crescents within a double tressure, flowered and counterflowered with fleurs de lis ruby, for Seaton; 2d and 3d sapphire, three garbs, topaz, the arms of Buchan, as having pretension to that earldom. And over all, by way of surtout, an escutcheon party per pale, ruby and sapphire; the first charged with a sword in pale, proper, pomelled and hilted, topaz, supporting an imperial crown with a double tressure of the last, given by king Robert Bruce, for their bravery and loyalty; and the 2d is charged with a star of 12 points, pearl, for the title of Winton.

CREST.] In a ducal coronet, topaz, a dragon emerald, spouting fire, his wings elevated.

SUPPORTERS.] Two foxes, proper, collared and chained, topaz, each collar charged with three crescents, ruby; and upon a scroll coming behind the shield, and passing over the middle of the supporters, are these words, Intaminatis fulget honoribus, relative to the surtout.

MOTTO.] Invia virtuti via nulla.

CHIEF SEATS were] At Seaton, in East Lothian; at Winton, two miles from the former; and a fine house in Edinburgh.

LIVINGSTON, Earl of LINLITHGOW.

THE firſt of the name of Livingſton is ſaid to be one of the gentlemen who accompanied queen Margaret, wife of king Malcolm Canmore, to Scotland; where, in the reign of king David I. he got lands in Weſt Lothian, which he called Livingſton, after his own name; and was ſucceeded therein by his ſon Thurſtan, the father of Alexander, whoſe poſterity enjoyed the barony of Livingſton above 400 years, which was till the reign of James IV. when Bartholomew Livingſton dying without iſſue male, with him that family became extinct; and of his three daughters and coheirs, Agnes, the eldeſt, was the wife of —— Learmont. Others, with more reaſon, ſuppoſe Livingſton to be rather a modern Scotch name, both from the termination, which is ſo common in North Britain, and Levin, which is the name of a town, lake, and river, in Fifeſhire, Perthſhire, and Lenos. In the reign of David II. Sir William Livingſton, the immediate anceſtor of this noble family, marrying Chriſtian, daughter and heir of Patrick de Callender, lord of Callender, in the county of Stirling, with her had that barony; and afterwards obtained a royal grant, to him and his heirs, of the lands of Kilſyth, lying weſt of Callender, then in the king's hands. In 1346, he was one of the commanders at the battle of Durham, where he was taken priſoner with the king; but afterwards being releaſed, he was commiſſioned to treat with the Engliſh about the redemption of his royal maſter; which being happily agreed to, on the payment of 100,000 merks, he delivered Sir William, his ſon and heir, as one of the hoſtages for the ſecurity thereof.

Sir William, who ſucceeded his father, had a ſon, Sir John, who being ſlain in 1402, at the battle of Homildon-hill, againſt the Piercies, left by his firſt wife, a daughter of Menteith of Carſe, Sir Alexander, his heir; and a younger ſon, Robert, from whom ſprung the Livingſtons of Weſt Quarter, and of Kinnaird, progenitors of the earls of Newburgh; and by his ſecond wife, Agnes, daughter of Sir James Douglas of Dalkeith, he had Sir William Livingſton, firſt of the branch of Kilſyth.

Sir Alexander, his eldeſt ſon, was one of the hoſtages for the ranſom of king James I. when he was relieved from his captivity in England; and upon the deceaſe of his maſter, was made choice of by the three eſtates of Scotland, to be governor to the young king James II. till he was fourteen years of age; but ſoon after, the earl of Douglas being the principal favourite at court, and bearing no good will to Sir Alexander, or any of the former miniſtry, prevailed ſo far with the king as to call a parliament, which met at Perth, where he and others of his party were summoned to answer to such accusations as should be exhibited against them; and Sir Alexander being accused of having alienated the crown lands, wasted the royal revenues, seized upon the king's jewels, and the furniture of his houses, and what else he could divert to his own private use, was declared a rebel, his estate confiscated, and he sent prisoner to the castle of Dunbarton; but after some time of imprisonment, the king was pleased to restore Sir Alexander to his estate, and made him one of his privy council, and justice general of Scotland. He married a daughter of Dundas of that ilk, by whom he had issue James; Alexander, ancestor of the Livingstons of Dunipace; Janet, wife of James, first lord Hamilton; and Elizabeth, of James Dundas of that ilk. He was succeeded by his eldest son,

James, who was created lord Livingston, and for his great prudence and ability, was made captain of Stirling castle, where he had the custody of the young king committed to him by his father, when he was the king's governor; which great trust he faithfully discharged, and was afterwards appointed master of the houshold, one of the privy council, and high chamberlain of Scotland; and dying in 1467, by Marian, his wife, had issue two sons; James, his successor; Alexander, of whom hereafter: and two daughters, Elizabeth, wife of John earl of Ross; and Eupheme, of Sir Malcolm Fleming, son and heir of Robert lord Fleming. He was succeeded by his eldest son,

James, second lord, who dying without issue, his estate and honour fell to his nephew,

Sir John Livingston, the son of his brother Alexander, who became third lord; and marrying Elizabeth, daughter of Robert lord Fleming, by her had William, his heir; and by his second wife, a daughter of Sir John Houstoun of that ilk, a son, Alexander, ancestor of the Livingstons of Glentyran, whose male line is extinct. He died in 1510, and was succeeded by his eldest son,

William, fourth lord, who married Agnes, daughter of Adam Hepburn, lord Hailes, and by her had Alexander, his successor; and two daughters, Margaret, married to John Hay, lord Yester, ancestor of the marquis of Tweeddale; and Isabel, to Nicholas Ramsay of Dalhousie, ancestor of the earl of Dalhousie. He was succeeded by his son,

Alexander, fifth lord, who had the tuition of queen Mary committed to him in her nonage; and he afterwards accompanied her majesty into France, where he died, leaving issue by Agnes his second wife, daughter of John, second earl of Moreton, three sons and four daughters, viz. John, master of Livingston, who was killed in the life-time of his father, at the battle of Pinkie, without issue; William, his successor; Thomas,

mas, anceſtor of the Livingſtons of Haining; Elizabeth, wife of John Buchanan of that ilk; Janet, of Sir Alexander Bruce of Airth; Magdalen, firſt, of Arthur Erſkine of Grange; and ſecondly, of John Scrimgeor of Glaſtre; and Mary, wife of John Semple of Belltree, ſon of lord Semple. He died in the year 1550, and was ſucceeded by his ſon,

William, ſixth lord, who was in great favour with the aforeſaid queen Mary, to whom he continued loyal and ſerviceable to the end of the civil war; and marrying Agnes, daughter of Malcolm lord Fleming, anceſtor of the earl of Wigton, by her had Alexander, his heir; John and Henry, who both died young; Sir George, of Ogleface, anceſtor of the Livingſtons of Bedlamorlie; Sir William: and two daughters, Janet, married to Alexander, fourth lord Elphingſton; and Margaret, wife, firſt, of Sir Lewis Ballantyne of Broughton; and ſecondly, of Patrick Stewart, earl of Orkney. He was ſucceeded by his eldeſt ſon,

Alexander, ſeventh lord, who was much eſteemed by king James VI. who, in recompence of his care in the education of his daughter, the princeſs Elizabeth, afterwards queen of Bohemia, created him earl of Linlithgow; and in 1603, when his majeſty ſucceeded to the crown of England, his lordſhip carried the princeſs from Linlithgow to London, with a retinue, upon his own charge, ſuitable to her birth and dignity. He married lady Eleanor, daughter of Andrew Hay, the eighth earl of Errol; and dying in 1622, left two ſons and one daughter; Margaret, married to John Fleming, earl of Wigton. The ſons were, Alexander; and Sir James, who acquiring honours and riches in the wars abroad, was, after his return, by king Charles I. in 1633, created lord Almond, and in 1641, earl of Callendar. He married Margaret, daughter of James lord Yeſter, anceſtor of the marquis of Tweeddale, widow of Alexander Seton, earl of Dumferlin. He was ſucceeded by the eldeſt ſon,

Alexander, ſecond earl, who married firſt, the lady Elizabeth, daughter of George marquis of Huntley, by whom he had George, his heir; and by his ſecond wife, lady Mary, daughter of William, the tenth earl of Angus, he had two daughters, lady Margaret, wife, firſt, of Sir Thomas Nicholſon of Carnock; ſecondly, of Sir George Stirling of Keir; and thirdly, of Sir John Stirling of Keir: and lady Eleanor, who died unmarried: and a ſon, Alexander, to whom his uncle, James earl of Callendar, dying without iſſue, left his eſtate and honours, whereby he became ſecond earl of Callendar, &c. He was ſucceeded by his eldeſt ſon,

George, third earl, who in the time of the civil war firmly adhered to the cauſe of king Charles I. and ſuffered much for it; but after the reſtoration, was made one of his majeſty's privy

privy council, captain of the royal regiment of foot guards, and justice general of Scotland. He married lady Elizabeth, daughter of Patrick Maul, first earl of Panmure, and widow of John Lyon, earl of Kinghorn; and dying in 1690, left issue by her two sons, and a daughter, Henrietta, married to Robert Macgill, viscount Oxenford. The sons were, George; and Alexander, who was third earl of Callendar. The eldest, George, succeeded his father, and was fourth earl. He was one of the privy council to king William III. by whom he was also made one of the commissioners of the treasury. He married Henrietta, daughter of Alexander Sutherland, lord Duffus; but dying in 1695, without issue, his estate and honour devolved on his nephew,

James, the fourth earl of Callendar, son of his brother Alexander, fifth earl of Linlithgow, and one of the sixteen peers of Scotland, by the titles of earl of Linlithgow and Callendar, in 1710 and 1713, the third and fourth parliaments of Great Britain. He married lady Margaret, daughter of John Hay, twelfth earl of Errol, by whom he had a son of his name, who died in 1715; and a daughter, lady Ann, who became his sole heir, and married William, fourth earl of Kilmarnock, whose eldest son is now earl of Errol. (See that title.)

James, the abovesaid earl, was attainted, and his estates and honours forfeited to the crown, for his concern in the rebellion in 1715.

TITLES.] The right honourable James Livingston, earl of Linlithgow and Callendar, and lord Almond.

CREATIONS.] Earl of Lithgow, or Linlithgow, in West Lothian, 15 November 1600, by James VI. lord Almond, in 1633; and earl of Callendar, 1641, both in the county of Stirling, by Charles I.

ARMS.] Quarterly, 1st and 4th, pearl, three cinquefoils, ruby, within a double tressure, flowered and counterflowered with fleurs de lis, emerald, for the name of Livingston; 2d and 3d diamond, a bend between six billets, topaz, for Callendar; and over all, by way of surtout, in an escutcheon, sapphire, an oak growing out of the base, topaz, within a border, pearl, charged with eight julyflowers, ruby, as a coat of augmentation, for the title of earl of Linlithgow.

CREST.] On a wreath, a demi-savage, wreathed about the temples and waist with laurel, proper, holding in his right hand a batoon erect, and in the left a serpent, which is twisted about his arm.

SUPPORTERS.] Two savages, proper, wreathed as the crest, each holding on his exterior shoulder a batoon, topaz.

MOTTO.] Si je puis.

CHIEF SEATS were.] Callendar-castle, in Stirlingshire; and at Brighouse, near Lithgow.

DRUMMOND,

DRUMMOND, Earl of PERTH.

SIR Malcolm Drymen, or Drummond, flourished in the reign of king William, which commenced in 1165, and ended in 1214. He was succeeded by his eldest son, Malcolm de Drummond, who married Ada, daughter of Maldurn, third earl of Lenox, by Beatrix, daughter of Walter, lord high steward of Scotland, and was succeeded by his eldest son, Malcolm Drummond, and he by his eldest son, Sir John, whose eldest son, Sir Malcolm, was succeeeded by his son, another Sir Malcolm, who being probably killed at the battle of Durham, in 1346, was succeded by his eldest son, Sir John, who maintained a long and troublesome dispute with the house of Menteith, which came to an open rupture, and being disputed in the field, wherein Menteith lost three sons, the king obliged both parties to go no farther in the quarrel; and, to compleat the agreement, appointed a meeting of the great men of the kingdom. The earls of Douglas, Angus, Arran, and the lord Robert, nephew to king Robert Bruce, being guardians for the performance of articles, their hands and seals are still to be seen in the deed of treaty, wherein lord Robert, the king's nephew, owns himself related to both families. Drummond, having by an article in the treaty, lost the lands which he held in the sheriffdom of Lennox, retired into Perthshire, where he took to wife Mary, eldest daughter and coheir of Sir William de Montefax, lord treasurer of Scotland, with whom he had divers lands in the said county, beside the baronies of Scrobbal and Cargil, near Perth; and by his said wife had issue four sons and four daughters; Sir Malcolm; Sir John; William, ancestor of the Drummonds of Carnock and Hawthornden; and Dougal, bishop of Dunblain: Annabella, married to Robert III. king of Scotland, and mother of king James I. Margaret, wife of Sir Colin Campbell, ancestor of the duke of Argyll; Jane, of —— Stewart of Dowallie; and Mary, of —— Macdonald, lord of the Isles.

Sir Malcolm, the eldest son, succeeding his father, and marrying lady Isabel Douglas, daughter of William earl of Douglas, by Margaret his wife, countess of Mar, sister and sole heir of Thomas earl of Mar, he in her right was stiled lord of Mar; and at the battle of Otterburn, or Chevy Chace, in 1388, joining his own men with his brother-in-law, James earl of Douglas, to fight the English, he there took prisoner Sir Ralph Piercy, brother of Henry lord Piercy, called Hotspur, who in the same rencounter had killed earl Douglas: but dying without issue by his lady, the estate reverted to herself, and his hereditary fortune descended to his next brother,

Sir John Drummond, who married lady Elizabeth, daughter of Henry earl of Orkney, ancestor of the earl of Caithness, a person of great eminence both in Denmark and Scotland; and by this lady he had three sons and two daughters; Elizabeth, wife of Sir Archibald Kinnaird; and ——, of John Lockhart of Bar, in Airshire. The sons were, Sir Walter, Robert, and John; which last settled in the Madeira islands, where his posterity made a considerable figure; and Robert married the heiress of Barnbougle, and changed his name to Mowbray.

Sir Walter, the eldest, who was knighted by James II. succeeded his father. He married Margaret, daughter of Sir William Ruthven of that ilk, and by her had three sons; Walter, the youngest, was baron of Liderief, from whom descended the family of Blair Drummond, which produced the two other branches of Newton and Gairdrum; John, the second, was dean of Dumblain; and Sir Malcolm, the eldest, marrying Mariotte, daughter of Sir David Murray of Tullibairden, ancestor of the duke of Athol, had by her six sons; Sir John; Walter, dean of Dunblain, and clerk register to James IV. James, ancestor of the Drummonds of Corrievechter, &c. Thomas, who was laird of Drummerinock, ancestor of those of Innermay, Cultmalindri, Culdee, &c. William and Andrew.

Sir John, the eldest, succeeded his father, and was made steward of Strathern, justice general of Scotland, and created lord Drummond by king James III. He married the lady Elizabeth Lindsay, daughter of David earl of Crawford, who was duke of Montrose for life; and being justice general, which in those days was the best post in the kingdom, he purchased all the estate which his kinsman the baron of Concraig was possessed of, in the sheriffdom of Strathern, and likewise, with the king's approbation, the heretable jurisdiction of Strathern. He likewise did great service to king James IV. having routed the earl of Lennox, and the lord Lisle, as they were upon their march to join the earl Marshal and lord Gordon, in order to seize the king and the administration, under pretence of revenging the death of king James III. after which he was sent ambassador into England, to conclude a peace with king Richard III. but after the death of the king of Scotland, he forfeited all his offices and estate, for giving a box on the ear to Lyon King at Arms, who was sent to summon him before the parliament, to give an account of the queen's marriage with the earl of Lennox; but by the queen's interest, and the intercession of some great men, he was soon after restored to his honour and estate. He had issue by his said lady, William, master of Drummond, who died before his father; William, his heir apparent; Sir John, ancestor of the Drummonds of Innerpeffry, Riccarton, &c. and five daughters, whereof Margaret, the eldest, was privately married to king James IV. by whom

whom she had a daughter, lady Margaret, who was married to John lord Gordon, eldest son of Alexander earl of Huntley; and a son, James, who was earl of Murray; Elizabeth, married to George, master of Angus, whose grand-daughter, lady Margaret Douglas, was mother of Henry lord Darnley, father of king James IV. Beatrix, wife of James lord Hamilton, and earl of Arran, nephew of James III. Annabella, of William earl of Montrose; and Eupheme, of John lord Fleming, ancestor of the earls of Wigton. He died in 1519.

William, who was heir apparent, married lady Isabel Campbell, daughter of Colin, the first earl of Argyll, and by her had two sons; Walter; and Andrew, ancestor of the Drummonds of Bellyclone; but the said William and his family being in open defiance with that of Murray, among other feuds between them, there were several gentlemen of the house of Murray barbarously burnt in a church, by some of Drummond's party; for which crime, notwithstanding he pleaded innocence, yet being out of favour with the king, he was condemned to lose his head, and the sentence was executed accordingly, in 1511. Walter Drummond, his eldest son, marrying lady Elizabeth, daughter of William earl of Montrose, and dying before his grandfather, by her left an only son,

David, who in 1519 succeeded his great grandfather, and was second lord; and married lady Margaret Stewart, daughter of Alexander duke of Albany, by whom he had only one daughter, Sibilla, married to Sir Gilbert Ogilvie of that ilk; and by his second wife, Lillias, daughter of William lord Ruthven, he had two sons and five daughters; Jane, married to John Graham, earl of Montrose, chancellor of Scotland; Ann, to John, seventh earl of Mar, lord treasurer of Scotland; Lillias, to David lord Lindsay, eighth earl of Crawford; Katharine, to John Murray, earl of Tullibairden; and Mary, to Sir James Stirling of Keir. The sons were, Patrick and James; the latter, in the year 1607, was created lord Maderty by James VI. and from him descended the viscounts Strathallan.

Patrick, the eldest, was third lord Drummond, and married lady Elizabeth, daughter of David earl of Crawfurd, by whom he had two sons, James, his heir; John: and five daughters, Katharine, married to James lord Lesley, eldest son of Andrew earl of Rothes; Lillias, to Alexander earl of Dumferlin, by whom she was mother of the countesses of Seaforth, Lauderdale, and Kelly, and of the lady Lindsay, mother of the earl of Balcarras; Jane, to Robert Ker, the first earl of Roxburgh, and governor to the children of king Charles I. Elizabeth, to Alexander lord Elphingston; and Anne, first, to Peter Barclay of Towie; and secondly, to Andrew Fraser of Murchhill, ancestor of lord Fraser. By a second wife, Agnes, daughter and coheir of John Drummond of Innerpeffry, he had no issue.

issue. He deceased before the year 1600, and was succeeded by his eldest son,

James, who being much in favour with king James VI. was by him sent with Charles Howard, earl of Nottingham, ambassador to Spain, and after his return, was created earl of Perth, March 4, 1605; and marrying lady Elizabeth, daughter of Robert, first earl of Winton, by her had a daughter, lady Jane, who was married to John earl of Sutherland; but having no male issue, his honour and estate descended to his brother,

John, second earl of Perth, who married lady Jane, daughter of Robert earl of Roxburgh, and had issue by her four sons and two daughters; lady Jane, married to John earl of Wigton; and lady Lillias, to James earl of Tullibardin. The sons were, Henry, who died in infancy; James; Sir John, of Logiealmond, grandfather of John Drummond of Logiealmond, Esq; and of Dr. Thomas Drummond; Sir William, who became earl of Roxburgh, by marrying the lady Jane Ker, eldest daughter of Henry lord Ker, only son of Robert earl of Roxburgh, and from him also descended the lord Bellenden. He died in 1662, and was succeeded by his son,

James, third earl, who married lady Ann Gordon, daughter of George, third marquis of Huntley, by whom he had two sons, and a daughter, lady Anne, who was married to John, earl of Errol, lord high constable of Scotland. The sons were, James and John, the latter of whom was created earl of Melfort by king James VII. and by him made secretary of state for Scotland. He married to his first wife the heiress of Lundy, by whom he had three sons, and as many daughters; lady Ann, married to the laird of Houston; lady Elizabeth, to William viscount Strathallan; and lady Mary. The sons were, James, Robert, and Charles, the eldest of whom was called baron of Lundy, in Forfarshire. To his second wife, the said earl of Melfort married Eupheme, daughter of Thomas Wallace, baron of Craig, the chief of a very ancient family, and by her had six sons and three daughters; which sons were, John, laird of Torth; Thomas, William, Andrew, Reynald, and Philip: and the daughters were, Katharine, Teresa, and Mary. In the Scots parliament, July 1695, this John earl of Melfort, and Charles earl of Middleton, were outlawed by an act of attainder. James, third earl, died in 1675, and was succeeded by his eldest son,

James, fourth earl, who by king Charles II. in 1678, was made one of the privy council; in 1682, justice general; and in 1684, lord chancellor of Scotland; in which station he was continued by king James VII. till the revolution in 1688, and then following that prince into France, was by him made a duke, and knight of the garter, but was also outlawed in parliament,

liament. This noble lord, who died at St. Germains, in France, in the year 1716, and the 68th of his age, married to his first wife, lady Jane, daughter of William marquis of Douglas, by whom he had James lord Drummond; and two daughters, lady Mary, married to William Keith, the ninth earl Marshal; and lady Anne, who died unmarried. He married, secondly, Lillias, daughter of Sir James Drummond of Machany, by whom he had two sons, John, who married the heirefs of Dalgerno; and Charles: And thirdly, lady Mary Gordon, daughter of Lewis marquis of Huntley, by whom he had a son, Edward; and a daughter, lady Terefa.

James, his eldest son and heir apparent, was master of the horse to Mary, queen dowager of king James VII. and dying in his father's life-time, left by lady Jane his wife, daughter of George duke of Gordon, two sons, James and John; and two daughters, ladies Mary and Henrietta.

James, the eldest son, would have succeeded as earl of Perth, were it not for the outlawry. Both these brothers were in the rebellion in 1745; and next year, at the battle of Culloden, John commanded the centre, and James the left wing; but the latter being mortally wounded, died in his passage to France; John, the youngest, would have succeeded to the estate, which his brother had enjoyed; but it was forfeited by his attainder. As neither of them left issue, the representative of the family was John, eldest son of their grandfather's second marriage; but he dying without issue in 1757, Edward, the only son of the chancellor's third marriage, became the representative; but he also died without issue in 1760, and the chief of the family is now James, grandson and heir of John earl of Melfort, before mentioned, second son of James, third earl of Perth. He married lady Rachael Bruce, daughter of Thomas, seventh earl of Kincardin, by whom he has issue Thomas, James, and a daughter, Rachael.

TITLES *were.*] Right honourable James Drummond, earl of Perth, and lord Drummond, and hereditary steward of Strathern and Menteith.

CREATIONS.] Lord Drummond, by James III. earl of Perth, March 14, 1604, 35 James VI. and I. of England.

ARMS.] Topaz, three clolets wavey, ruby.

CREST.] On a ducal coronet, topaz, a greyhound, pearl, collared and leashed, proper.

SUPPORTERS.] Two savages, bound about the temples and waists with oak leaves, each holding on the outer shoulder a batoon, all proper; both standing on a green hill, semee of caltropps.

MOTTO.] Gang warily.

CHIEF SEAT *was.*] At Drummond castle, in Perthshire.

MACKENZIE,

MACKENZIE, Earl of SEAFORTH.

THE immediate ancestor of this family was a son of the Fitzgeralds, earls of Desmond, Kildare, &c. in Ireland. His name was Calinus, and upon some discontent, he left Ireland, and with a number of followers, settled in Scotland, about the year 1261, where he was kindly and hospitably received by Alexander III. whom he faithfully served as long as he lived. This prince made him a grant of the whole lands of Kintail, in Invernessshire, which were erected into a free barony, to him and his heirs for ever, by the royal charter, dated January 9, 1266. Having killed a stag, that was in full career at the king, on that account he had a stag's head, &c. assigned him for his armorial bearing. He was succeeded in the barony by his son Kenneth, and he by another Kenneth, who was a firm friend to king Robert Bruce. He was succeeded by his son, a third Kenneth, he by his son, Murdoch, and he by his son, another Murdoch, who was succeeded by his son, Alexander, who married two wives, first, lady Agnes, daughter of Colin, first earl of Argyle, by whom he had his successor, Sir Kenneth: and secondly, —— M'Dowal, of the family of Lorn, by whom he had Duncan, ancestor of the Mackenzies of Logie, Hiltoun, &c. and Hector, of those of Garloch, &c. He died in 1488. Sir Kenneth, his successor, was knighted by James IV. and by Agnes, daughter of Hugh, second lord Lovat, had John, his heir; Alexander, ancestor of the Mackenzies of Davachmaluack; Roderic, of those of Achiltry, Fairbourn, &c. Kenneth, of those of Suddy, Ord, Corrovielzier, Highfield, Inverlal, Little Findon, Scatwell, &c. Agnes, wife of Roderick Macleod of Lewis; and Katharine, of Hector Monro of Foulis. John, his eldest son and successor, behaved gallantly in the field of Floddon, in 1513, and was of the privy council to James V. a faithful subject of queen Mary, and fought valiantly at the battle of Pinkey (tho' then an old man) in 1547. He was succeeded by his only son, Kenneth, who by his wife lady Elizabeth, daughter of John, second earl of Athol, had issue, Colin; Roderick, ancestor of the Mackenzies of Redcastle, Kincraig, Rosend, &c. and five daughters. His eldest son, Colin, succeeded him, who was a brave man, and of the privy council to James VI. By his first wife, Barbara, daughter of James Grant of that ilk, he had issue Kenneth, afterwards lord Kintail; Sir Roderick, of Tarbat, ancestor of the earls of Cromartie; Colin, ancestor of the families of Kennock and Pitlundie; Alexander, of those of Kilcoy, &c. and three daughters. By his second wife, Mary, eldest daughter of Rorie Mackenzie of Devamaluack, he had Alexander, ancestor of the Mackenzies of Applecross, Coul, Delvin, Affint, &c. Kenneth, his eldest son, was created lord Mackenzie of

Kintail,

Kintail, Nov. 19, 1609. He married first, Anne, daughter of George Ross of Balnagowan, by whom he had issue, Colin; John, of Lochflyne, who had no male issue, but whose daughter was wife of Sir Norman Macleod, ancestor, by her, of Macleod of Mureavenside; Barbara, wife of Donald lord Reay; Janet, of Sir Donald M'Donald of Slate. He married secondly, Elizabeth, daughter of Sir Gilbert Ogilvie of Pourie, by whom he had issue George, earl of Seaforth; Thomas, of Pluscarthy, a great loyalist; Simon, of Lochflyne; and Sibilla, wife of John M'Leod of that ilk. He died in 1611, and was succeeded by his eldest son,

Colin, second lord Kintail, a great favourite of king James VI. who on December 3, 1623, raised him to the dignity of earl of Seaforth. He married lady Margaret, daughter of Alexander earl of Dunfermlin, by whom he had two daughters; lady Margaret, first the wife of John lord Berrendale, by whom she had George, fifth earl of Caithness; and secondly, of Alexander lord Duffus; and lady Anne, married first, to Alexander, the second earl of Balcarras, and afterwards was the second wife of Archibald, the ninth earl of Argyll; but the said earl, their father, having no male issue, his estate and honour descended to

George, his half-brother, second earl, who for his adherence to king Charles I. had his estate sequestered, was himself excommunicated, and forced to leave the kingdom; and repairing to king Charles II. in Holland, was very graciously received, and made secretary of state for Scotland. He married Barbara, daughter of Arthur lord Forbes; and dying in 1651, left two sons, Kenneth, his heir; Dr. George Mackenzie, the famous biographer: and a daughter, lady Mary, married to John Erskine, the ninth earl of Mar. He was succeeded by his eldest son,

Kenneth, third earl, who was an eminent loyalist to the aforesaid king during the usurpation, for which he suffered a long imprisonment, and was not relieved till the king was restored. He married Isabel, daughter of Sir John Mackenzie of Tarbat, Bart. ancestor of the earls of Cromartie, by whom he had three sons, Kenneth, John, and colonel Alexander; and four daughters, lady Margaret, married to James lord Duffus; lady Anne; lady Isabel, wife of Roderick Macleod of that ilk, and afterwards of Sir Duncan Campbell of Lochnell; and lady Mary, of Alexander M'Donald of Glengary. He died in 1678, and was succeeded by his eldest son,

Kenneth, fourth earl, who in 1678, by king James VII. was made one of the privy council. He was also by that king made knight of the thistle, which his majesty was pleased to revive in 1687; and at the revolution, when the said king retired into France, and thence into Ireland, he following him thither,

thither, was created a marquis, though that honour was not allowed here. He married the lady Frances Herbert, daughter of William marquis of Powis, in England, by the lady Elizabeth his wife, younger daughter of Edward Somerset, marquis of Worcester; and dying in 1701, left by her, who died at Paris in 1732, aged 98, a daughter, Mary, wife of ―― Caryl, Esq; and

William, fifth earl, who in 1715 married Mary, only daughter and heir of Nicholas Kennet of Coxhow, in Northumberland, Esq; and by her, who died in France in 1739, had three sons, Kenneth, lord Fortrose; Ronald, who died unmarried; and Nicol Mackenzie, Esq; and a daughter, lady Frances, married to John, representative of the family of Kenmure. His lordship being a party in the rebellion in 1715, against king George I. he, with many lords and others, was summoned by proclamation to surrender at Edinburgh; but he made his escape, and in April 1719, landed in the north-west of Scotland, with the marquis of Tullibairden, the earl Marshal, and some Spanish forces, to carry on a second rebellion; but they were soon defeated at Glensheil by major general Wightman. He was attainted in June 1716, with the earls of Mar, Southesk, Lithgow, Marshal, and Panmure; but through the king's great clemency in 1726, he obtained a pardon, and returned home, where he remained in a quiet retirement till his death, in the year 1740.

Kenneth, lord Fortrose, his eldest son, was elected member of parliament for the burghs of Fortrose, &c. in 1741, and for the shire of Ross in 1747, 1754, and 1761. He married lady Mary Stewart, daughter of Alexander earl of Galloway, by whom he had issue, Kenneth; Margaret, Mary, Agnes, Catharine, Frances, Euphemia. He died in 1762, and was succeeded by his son,

Kenneth, who has been created (October 28, 1766) viscount Fortrose, of the kingdom of Ireland, who will consequently be treated of in the peerage of that kingdom, which is preparing by the same editors.

TITLES.] William Mackenzie, earl of Seaforth, &c.
CREATIONS.] As before.
ARMS.] Sapphire, a stag's head caboshed, topaz.
CREST.] On a wreath, a mountain inflamed, proper.
SUPPORTERS.] Two savages, wreathed about their temples and middles with laurel; each holding in his exterior hand a batoon erect, with fire issuing out of the top of it, all proper.
MOTTO.] Luceo non uro.
CHIEF SEATS.] At the island of Donan, in Invernessshire; and at the castles of Fortrose and Brahan, in Rossshire.

WEMYSS,

WEMYSS, Earl of WEMYSS.

THIS family name is local, and was first assumed by the proprietors of lands called (of old) Wemyss-shire, containing all that track lying between the lower part of the water of Ore and the sea. They are descended of Hugo, second son of Gillimichael, fourth earl of Fife, and great grandson of Macduff, the first earl. The said Hugo had a son, Hugo, who was succeeded by his son, Sir John, who first assumed the sirname of Wemyss. His son, Michael, had a son, another Sir John, who was succeeded by his eldest son, another Sir Michael, who was sent on an embassy to Norway, to bring home the princess Margaret of Norway, undoubted heir of the crown of Scotland, after the death of Alexander III. This embassy was in the year 1290; but on their return with the princess, to the universal misfortune of the nation, she died at the Orkneys; and thereupon happened the fatal competition between Bruce and Baliol, about the right of succeeding, which was at length settled upon the latter. His successor, Sir David, in the time of king Robert I. was one of those great men of the kingdom, who wrote that letter to the Pope, asserting the independency of their country; so rare a piece of antiquity, that it deserves to be wrote in characters of gold, and preserved to all posterity: And this David obtaining from that king, by charter, the lands of Glasnock, was therein succeeded by Sir Michael, his son.

Which Sir Michael obtained a grant from Duncan earl of Fife, of the lands of Easter Monikie, and Wester Dron; and had three sons, of whom the second, Sir John, was of Rires and Kincaldrum, of whom hereafter: his eldest son, David, was succeeded by his son, Sir David, who having issue only one daughter, gave his estate to Sir John Wemyss, his undoubted heir male, grandson of the above Sir John of Rires, his uncle. His daughter was wife of Sir John de Inchmartin; and the said Sir John marrying Isabel, daughter and coheir of Sir Allen Erskine of Inchmartin, by which marriage the lines, male and female, of this noble family, were united, by her had Sir David, his heir; Duncan; and Alexander, ancestor of Wemyss of Lathocker: and two daughters, Elizabeth, married to Sir Andrew Gray of Foulis, ancestor of the lord Gray; and Eupheme, to Sir William Livingston of Drumray.

Sir David, his successor, married Christian, daughter of Sir William Douglas of Lochleven, and by her had Sir John Wemyss, whose wife was Margaret, daughter of Sir Robert Livingston of Drumray, and by her he had issue Sir John, his heir, who by Christian his wife, a daughter of the family of Abernethy, was father of Sir David Wemyss, who in 1511 obtained a charter from king James IV. for erecting his lands

into

into the barony of Wemyss; and being slain with the said king at the battle of Floddon, in Northumberland, left a son, Sir David, who succeeded him, and married Catharine, daughter of Henry lord Sinclair, by whom he had Sir John, his successor; and James Wemyss of Caskbierry; and the said Sir John marrying Margaret, daughter of Sir David Otterburn of Redhall, by her had Sir David, his heir; and four daughters, of whom Eupheme was married to Sir David Carnegie of Coluthie, ancestor of the earl of Southesk. He married secondly, Janet, daughter of Alexander Trail of Blebo, by whom he had Gavin Wemyss of Powguild, who married Catharine Wemyss, heiress of Winthank, of whom the Wemyss's, now of Winthank, are descended.

Sir David, the eldest son, who in 1571 succeeded his father, married Cecil, daughter of William, second lord Ruthven, and by her had five sons and five daughters, viz. Sir John; Sir James, of Bogie, ancestor of the Wemyss's of Bogie, and those in Ireland; David, ancestor of the Wemyss's of Fingask; Henry, of the Wemyss's of Foodie; Patrick, of those of Rumgay, Craighall, &c. Margaret, wife of James Bethune of Creich; Cecilia, of —— Kinnynmouth of that ilk; Jane, of James Macgill of Rankeillor; Elizabeth, of Alexander Wood of Lamyletham; and Isabel, of John Auchmoutie of that ilk. He died in 1591, and was succeeded by his eldest son,

Sir John, who by his second wife, Anne Stewart, daughter of James lord Down, had issue David, his heir; Sir John, after earl of Wemyss; and four daughters, Cecilia, married to William, second earl of Tullibardin; Janet, to Robert lord Colvil; Isabel, to Hugh Fraser, eighth lord Lovat; and Catharine, to John Haldane of Gleneagles. He died in 1616, and was succeeded by his second son, John; his eldest son, David, who died before him, by lady Elizabeth, daughter of Andrew, earl of Rothes, having no issue.

The said Sir John being in great favour with king Charles I. was by him, in May 1625, created a baronet, and afterwards, in 1628, lord Elcho, and earl of Wemyss, in 1633. He married Jane, daughter of Patrick, seventh lord Gray; and dying in 1653, by her left David, his successor; and five daughters, lady Mary, married to John, the sixth lord Sinclair; lady Ann, to Sir Mungo Murray, viscount Stormont; and lady Jane, to Harry Maule, second son of Patrick, the first earl of Panmure, in Scotland; lady Elizabeth, to Sir John Ayton of that ilk; and lady Catharine, of Sir David Carnegie of Craig. He died in 1649, and was succeeded by his son,

David, second earl, who married first, Jane, daughter of Robert Balfour, lord Burleigh, by whom he had lady Jane, who was married first, to Archibald earl of Angus; and secondly, to George earl of Sutherland. He married secondly, lady
Eleanora,

Eleanora, daughter of John earl of Wigton, without issue; and thirdly, lady Margaret, daughter of John earl of Rothes, widow first, of Alexander lord Balgony; and secondly, of Francis Scot, earl of Buccleugh; and had another daughter, lady Margaret, who in 1680 became countess of Wemyss, as successor to her father, but the title of baronet ceased.

Which lady Margaret continued the honour; and marrying Sir James Wemyss, descended from James Wemyss of Caskbierry, before-mentioned, he, by the favour of king Charles II. was honoured with the title of lord Bruntisland, in Fife, during life; and dying in 1685, left by the said countess his wife, David, their heir; and two daughters, lady Ann, married to David Lesley, earl of Leven and Melvil; and lady Margaret, to David Carnegie, earl of Northesk. The countess died in 1705, and was succeeded by her son,

David, third earl, who was one of the privy council to queen Anne, by whom he was constituted lord admiral of Scotland, as also one of the commissioners for the treaty of union with England. He was elected to represent the peerage of Scotland in the first and second British parliaments; and married first, lady Anne, daughter of William duke of Queensberry, by whom he had issue David, lord Elcho, who died in the 17th year of his age, unmarried; and James, late earl. His second wife was Mary, daughter of Sir John Robertson of Farringwood, in Northamptonshire, Bart. but by her had no issue. His third wife was Elizabeth, daughter of Henry lord Sinclair, by whom he had two daughters, lady Elizabeth, wife of William earl of Sutherland, mother of the late earl; and lady Margaret, of James earl of Murray. He deceased in 1720, and was succeeded by his only surviving son,

James, fourth earl of Wemyss, who married Janet, daughter and heir of colonel Francis Charteris of Amisfield, by whom he had issue three sons and four daughters, viz. 1. David, lord Elcho, who having engaged in the rebellion of 1745, was attainted of treason, but escaped to France; 2. Francis-Charteris, who succeeded to his grandfather's estate at Amisfield, &c. and married lady Catharine, daughter of Alexander duke of Gordon, by whom he has issue one son; 3. James, who now represents the family. The four daughters were, lady Frances, wife of Sir James Stewart of Goodtrees, Bart. lady Walpole, of ———; lady Anne, of John Hamilton of Bargeny, Esq; and lady Helen, of Hugh Dalrymple of Fordel, Esq; David lord Elcho, on account of his attainder, being incapable of succeeding, his lordship made a conveyance of his estate in favour of his third son, James, in which he was succeeded by him in 1756.

Which James Wemyss, now of Wemyss, Esq; is member in the present parliament for Fifeshire, &c. and married lady
Elizabeth,

Elizabeth, daughter of William earl of Sutherland, by whom he has issue three sons, James, William, and David.

TITLES *were.*] James Wemyss, earl of Wemyss, lord Elcho, &c.

CREATIONS.] Lord Elcho, April 1, 1628; earl of Wemyss, May 25, 1633.

ARMS.] Topaz, a lion rampant, ruby, armed and langued, sapphire.

CREST.] On a wreath, a swan, proper.

SUPPORTERS.] Two swans, as the crest.

MOTTO.] Je pense.

CHIEF SEATS.] Wemyss, in Fifeshire; and Elcho, near Perth.

CARNEGIE, Earl of SOUTHESK.

THIS noble family were anciently proprietors of the lands of Carnegie, in the county of Forfar, which were long possessed by them. John, ancestor of this family, lived in the reign of Alexander III. From the said John descended Duthac de Carnegie, who in the year 1409, by a charter from Robert duke of Albany, got part of the lands of Kinnaird; and eight years after purchasing the remainder, was therein succeeded by his son Walter, who joining the earl of Huntley against the Lindsays, in behalf of king James II. at the battle of Brechin, in 1452, had thereupon his house burnt, with all his writs and evidences; and dying in 1478, was succeeded by his son and heir John, who died in 1508, and was succeeded by his son John, who being slain at the battle of Floddon, in Northumberland, in 1513, with king James IV. left a son, Sir Robert; and a daughter, Janet, married to William Maul, son of Sir Thomas Maul of Panmure. Sir Robert, the son, was promoted by the regent, James Hamilton, duke of Chatelherault, first to be one of the judges in the court of session, then ambassador to England, and after his return was knighted. He was also sent ambassador to France by the said regent in 1551, and dying in 1565, left issue by Margaret his wife, a daughter of the family of Guthry, six sons and seven daughters, viz. Sir John, who succeeded his father; David, of Coluthie, who carried on the line of the family; William, of Leuchland; Robert; James, ancestor of the Carnegies of Balmackie; Alexander, of Cookston: Margaret, wife of Sir James Scrimgeor of Dudhope; Helen, first, of William Lundie of Benholm, and secondly, of Robert Turren of Foveran; Elizabeth, of Andrew Arbuthnot of that ilk; Catharine, of David Ramsay of Balmain; Isabel, of —— Gordon of Glenbucket; Jane, of ———; Mary, of —— Strachan of Carmylie. He was succeeded, in 1565, by his eldest son, (as before

fore observed) Sir John, who being a hearty friend to queen Mary in the time of her misfortunes, her majesty had so great an esteem for his fidelity and prudence, that in 1570, when a cessation was obtained by the bishop of Ross, she wrote to the said John, craving his advice therein. He married first, Agnes, daughter of David Wood of Craig, and secondly, Margaret Keith; but having no son, his estate descended to Sir David, his next brother, who being bred to the law, and a person of great reputation, was by king James VI. made one of the lords of session, one of his privy council, and a commissioner of the treasury. He married first, Elizabeth, daughter and heir of William Ramsay of Coluthie, and by her had three daughters, Catharine, wife of Sir John Ayton of Kinnaldie; Margaret, of William Dundas of Fingask; and Elizabeth, of John Inglis of Tarvat; which last only had issue; and her daughter, Catharine, was mother of Mr. George Martin of Clermont, the learned antiquary. His second wife was Eupheme, daughter of Sir David Wemyss, ancestor of the earl of Wemyss, by whom he had four sons and three daughters; Agnes, married to Alexander Falconer of Halkerton, whose son was created lord Halkerton; Jane, to James Carmichael of Balmedie, and afterwards to Archibald Dundas of Fingask; and Eupheme, to Robert Graham of Morphy, who all left issue. The sons were, David; Sir John, first of the family of Northesk, which vide; Sir Robert; and Alexander, ancestor of the Carnegies of Balnamoon.

David, the eldest son, succeeded, and was created a baron and earl. He married Margaret, daughter of Sir David Lindsay of Edzal, and by her had issue four sons and six daughters; lady Margaret, married to William earl of Dalhousie; lady Agnes, to James lord Abercromby; lady Katharine, to John Stewart, earl of Traquair; lady Margery, to Robert viscount Arbuthnot; lady Elizabeth, to Sir Andrew Murray, ancestor of viscount Stormont; and lady Magdalen, to James, the great marquis of Montrose: and of the sons, David, the eldest, who died in his father's life-time, having married lady Margaret, daughter of Thomas Hamilton, earl of Haddington, by her had issue two daughters, Margaret, married to Gavin Dalziel, earl of Carnwath; and Magdalen, to Sir John Crawford of Kilberney, ancestor of the earls of Crawford; but the said David having no male issue, his next brother, Sir James Carnegie, became heir to his father, and succeeded to the honours. Sir John, of Craig, the third son, had a son, who died without issue; and Sir Alexander, the youngest, was the first of the family of Pittarro.

Which Sir James, second earl, was one of the privy council to king Charles II. by whom he was also made sheriff of Forfar. By his wife, lady Isabel, he had issue, Robert; lady Elizabeth,

Elizabeth, wife, first, of James Murray, earl of Annandale; and secondly, of David, viscount Stormont; and lady Katharine, of Gilbert, eleventh earl of Errol. He was succeeded, in 1669, by his son,

Robert, third earl, who was a fine gentleman, and captain of the guards to Lewis XIV. king of France. By his wife, lady Anne, daughter of William, second duke of Hamilton, he had issue two sons, Charles lord Carnegie; and William, killed at Paris by William Talmash, son of the dutchess of Lauderdale, in 1681. He died in 1688, and was succeeded by his eldest son,

Charles, fourth earl, who by lady Mary, daughter of Charles earl of Lauderdale, had issue,

James, fifth earl, who married lady Margaret, daughter of James earl of Galloway, by whom he had a son and a daughter, who both died young; and engaging in the rebellion of 1715, he was attainted, and his estate and honours forfeited to the crown. However, he made his escape, and died in France in 1729, and in him ended the male line of James, second earl of Southesk. Whereupon the representation of the family devolved upon Sir James Carnegie of Pitarro, Bart. lineally descended of Sir Alexander, fourth son of David, first earl of Southesk, and brother of James the second earl, who was member in the last parliament for the shire of Kincardine. He married Christian, eldest daughter of David Doig of Cookston, by whom he has four sons and two daughters, viz. David, James, John, and George; Mary and Elizabeth.

TITLES.] The right honourable James Carnegie, earl of Southesk, and lord Carnegie.

CREATIONS.] Lord Carnegie of Kinnaird, in the county of Forfar, 24 April 1616, by James VI. and earl of Southesk, in the same county, 22 June 1613, by Charles I.

ARMS.] Topaz, an eagle displayed, sapphire, beaked and membered, ruby.

CREST.] On a wreath, a right hand, couped at the wrist, and erect, holding a thunderbolt, inflamed at both ends, all proper, shafted saltire, and winged in fess, topaz.

SUPPORTERS.] Two greyhounds, pearl, each gorged with a plain collar, ruby.

MOTTO.] Deum timete.

CHIEF SEATS were.] Kinnaird, in the county of Angus; and the castle of Leuchars, in Fifeshire.

OGILVIE, Earl of AIRLY.

THIS noble family descended from Gilbert, second son of Gilibred, and brother of Gilchrist earl of Angus, a man of great distinction in the reign of king William the lion, between 1165 and 1214. Gilbert assumed his sirname from his lands and barony of Ogilvie. He had a son, Alexander, and he a son, Patrick, whose son, Sir Patrick, had two sons, Alexander, and Patrick, first of the family of Auchterhouse. Alexander succeeded, and was succeeded by his son, Sir Patrick Ogilvie, of whom the Ogilvies of that ilk, and of Easter Pourie, descended. Patrick, second son of Sir Patrick, abovementioned, was succeeded by his son, Walter, and he by his eldest son, Sir Walter, who was killed in 1391, by Duncan Stewart, natural son of the earl of Buchan, with his brother, and 60 of his followers. He had issue three sons, Sir Alexander; Sir Walter, of Lintrethan; and Sir John; and was succeeded by the eldest, Sir Alexander, whose grandson, Sir Alexander, dying without male issue, was succeeded by the next heir male, descended of Sir Walter of Lintrethan, abovementioned. Which Sir Walter had issue, Sir John; and Sir Walter, ancestor of the earls of Findlater. Sir John, the eldest, had issue three daughters, and Sir James, his successor, who was created lord Ogilvie by king James IV. He married Elizabeth, a daughter of the family of Kennedy, and by her had issue,

John, second lord, who married Jane, daughter of William lord Graham, by whom he had two sons, James and Anthony.

James, the eldest, third lord, succeeding, married lady Elizabeth Lindsay, daughter of David earl of Crawford, and had three sons, James, John, and Archibald.

James, his heir, fourth lord, marrying Helen, daughter of Henry lord Sinclair, by her had five sons, James, John, David, William, and Archibald; and four daughters, of whom Marian was married to Patrick lord Gray; and Margaret, to David Graham of Fintrie.

James, the eldest son, fifth lord, succeeding his father, married Katharine, daughter of Sir John Campbell of Calder; and dying in 1564, was succeeded by his only son,

James, sixth lord, who firmly adhering to queen Mary during her troubles, suffered a long imprisonment; but when king James VI. took the government on himself, he was released, and sent ambassador to Denmark. He married Jane, daughter of William lord Forbes, by whom he had six sons, and a daughter, Margaret, who was wife of George Keith, earl Marshal. The sons were, James, his heir; Sir John, of Craig; David, of Pitmouis; Peter, ancestor of the Ogilvies of Clunie; George, of Fernault; and Sir Francis, of Grange. He died in 1606, and was succeeded by his eldest son,

James, seventh lord, who marrying lady Jane, daughter of William earl of Gowry, by her was father of

James, eighth lord, who was created earl of Airly. He married lady Isabel Hamilton, daughter of Thomas earl of Haddington,

Haddington, and had issue by her three sons, James, lord Ogilvie; Sir Thomas, a man of great honour and courage, killed at the battle of Inverlochie; and Sir David, of Clova: Also one daughter, lady Helen, wife of Sir John Carnegie of Balnamoon. He was succeeded by his eldest son,

James, second earl, who being also very zealous in the royal cause, he at length was taken prisoner at the battle of Philiphaugh, in 1645, when Montrose was defeated. He was condemned by the parliament to be executed, but escaping the night before in his sister's habit, he engaged again in the same service. He married Helen, daughter of George Ogilvie, lord Banff, and had a son, David; and four daughters, lady Marion, married to John Lesley, lord Lindores; lady Margaret, to Alexander lord Halkerton; lady Helen, to Sir John Gordon of Park; and lady Mary, to Sir John Wood of Bonnytoun.

David, their brother, third earl, marrying lady Grisel, daughter of Patrick Lyon, the third earl of Strathmore, by her had two sons, James and John; whereof James, when he was lord Ogilvie, about twenty years of age, was attainted for joining in the rebellion 1715; the estate not being in his person, was saved, and went to his brother John. Some time after this, he obtained a pardon for his life, came home, and married Ann, daughter of David Erskine of Dun, Esq; one of the senators of the college of justice; but dying about a month after the marriage, was succeeded by

John, his brother, who now represents the family, and possesses the estate. He married Margaret, heir of —— Ogilvie of Clunie, by whom he had two sons, David; and Walter, advocate: and two daughters, Elizabeth, and Helen, wife of Roger Robertson of Ladykirk, Esq;

In the year 1745, David, the eldest son, came over from France, and joined with the rebels in Scotland. He made his escape after the battle of Culloden, and was attainted by the act of parliament 1746. He commands a regiment in the French service, called Ogilvie's regiment. He married Margaret, daughter of Sir James Johnston of Westerhall, Bart. by whom he has one son, David, commonly called master of Ogilvie; and two daughters, Margaret and Joanna.

TITLES were.] James Ogilvie, earl of Airly; lord Ogilvie, &c. &c.

CREATIONS.] Lord Ogilvie, by James IV. in 1495; earl of Airly, April 2. 1639, by Charles I.

ARMS.] Pearl, a lion passant guardant, ruby, crowned with an imperial crown, proper, and gorged with a ducal crown, topaz.

CREST.] In an earl's coronet of the last, a woman from her waist upwards, holding a portcullis.

SUPPORTERS.]

SUPPORTERS.] Two bulls, diamond, each gorged with a garland of flowers.

MOTTO.] A Fin.

CHIEF SEAT.] Airly castle, in Forfarshire.

DALZIEL, Earl of CARNWATH.

THIS noble family is of great antiquity in the shire of Lanerk, and intermarried with many worthy families there, before they moved to the county of Dumfries, where they settled; and Mr. Nisbet, the noted herald, gives the following story concerning the origin of their sirname. In the reign of Kenneth II. a near kinsman and favourite of that king being hung up by the Picts, it so exceedingly grieved his majesty, that he offered a great reward to any of his subjects that would venture to rescue his corpse; but none would undertake that dangerous enterprize. At last a certain gentleman came to the king, and said, *dal zell*, which in the Irish or old Scots language is, I DARE; and he effectually performing it to the king's satisfaction, his posterity took for their sirname the word Dalziel; and for their armorial ensign, that remarkable bearing, which has been continued to the present time.

In the year 1365, Sir Robert Dalziel, who faithfully adhered to king David Bruce during his captivity in England, obtained a grant of the barony of Selkirk; and Sir William Dalziel, his successor, having a gift from king Robert III. of the revenue belonging to St. Leonard's hospital, within the town of Lanerk, was therein succeeded by George, his son, from whom, after several generations, descended Sir Robert Dalziel of that ilk, who firmly adhered to queen Mary in all her troubles. He was succeeded by his son,

Sir Robert, who was knighted by king James VI. and by Charles I. created lord Dalziel, and earl of Carnwath. He married Margaret, daughter of Sir Robert Crichton of Clunie, and had two sons, Robert, his heir; and Sir John Dalziel of Glenay, Bart. and a daughter, lady Mary, wife of Sir James Muirhead of Lachop. He was succeeded by his eldest son,

Robert, second earl, who raising both horse and foot for his majesty's service in the time of the civil war, in which he was a commander, suffered very much thereby, both by sequestration and other ways; and in 1651, attending king Charles II. to the battle of Worcester, was taken prisoner, and kept divers years confined. He married Christian, daughter of Sir William Douglas of Drumlanrig, ancestor of the duke of Queensberry, and by her had

Gavin, third earl, who married first, Margaret, daughter of David lord Carnegie, by whom he had two sons, James and John; and a daughter, lady Jane, wife of Claud Muirhead of Wauchop;

Wauchop; and secondly, lady Mary Erskine, daughter of Alexander, the third earl of Kelly, but by her had no issue.

James, the eldest son, was fourth earl; and marrying lady Mary Seaton, daughter of George earl of Winton, by her had a daughter, lady Elizabeth, married to the lord John Hay, son of John marquis of Tweeddale; but having no male issue, his brother,

John, became fifth earl; and he dying a batchelor in 1702, his estate and honour descended to

Sir Robert, son of Sir John Dalziel of Glenay, Bart. son of Sir Robert, son of Sir John Dalziel of Glenay, second son of the first earl of Carnwath. Which Sir Robert, sixth earl, in January 1715, being brought prisoner to London from Preston in Lancashire, where he was taken in rebellion against king George I. he and six other lords were condemned for high treason on the 9th of February following; only two of them were executed, and the earl afterwards got a pardon for his life. He married first, lady Grace, daughter of Alexander earl of Eglingtoun, by whom he had a daughter, lady Margaret; and secondly, Grizel, daughter of Alexander Urquhart of Newhall, Esq; by whom he had a son, Alexander. His third wife was Margaret, daughter of John Hamilton of Bangower, Esq; by whom he had a daughter, who died young. His fourth wife was Margaret Vincent, a Yorkshire lady, by whom he had a son, Robert. His eldest son, Alexander, but for the forfeiture, would have been seventh earl of Carnwath; and married Miss Elizabeth Jackson, an English lady, by whom he has issue.

TITLES.] The right honourable Robert Dalziel, earl of Carnwath, and lord Dalziel.

CREATION.] Lord Dalziel, in 1628; and earl of Carnwath, in the county of Dumfries, 1639, by Charles I.

ARMS.] Diamond, a naked man, with his arms extended, pearl.

CREST.] On a wreath, a dagger erect, the pomel and hilt topaz.

SUPPORTERS.] Two chevaliers in complete armour, each having a target on his exterior arm, proper.

MOTTO.] I dare.

CHIEF SEAT.] At Kirkmichael, in Annandale.

MAULE, Earl PANMURE.

THIS very ancient and noble family is originally French, and derive their firname from the town and lordship of Maule, in France, eight leagues from Paris, upon the confines of Normandy. Ansold, lord of Maule, made a donation to the priory of St. Martin des Champs at Paris, in 1015, and his
son,

son, Guarin, is mentioned in a charter of Robert king of France, before 1030; and was succeeded by another Anfold, and he by Peter, lord of Maule, who in 1078 founded a priory of Benedictines at his town of Maule, and was general of the French army against the king of England, 1098, and had issue Anfold, his successor; and Guarin de Maule, who came into England with William the conqueror, besides several other children.

Anfold of Maule was famous in the wars of Italy and Greece, and one of the chief of the Norman and French captains under Robert duke of Normandy, and was so great at home, that he had his barons and knights, whom he caused to swear fealty, and do homage to his son, before his death. He married Odeline, daughter to Raoul, lord of Rony, and was succeeded by his son, Peter, lord of Maule, who was one of the generals of the French army at the battle of Breneville, in 1119, and went, with forty knights in his retinue, to the siege of Bretteuill, in 1138. He married Ade, daughter of the earl of Guisnes, by his wife, sister to the lord of Montmorency, by whom he had Robert, lord of Maule, who married Idoin, daughter of the viscount of Chamount. His son Robert went to the Holy Land with Louis king of France, where he was taken prisoner by the Saracens, and upon his return, founded the priory of St. Leonard at the castle of Panmore. This family continued to flourish in France, till another Robert, last lord of Maule there, whose arms are still remaining in the church of Maule, being the very same the earls of Panmure carry for their paternal coat to this day. He was killed in Hungary, in the war against the Turks in 1398, leaving issue one daughter, his sole heir, who carried the lordship of Maule, and many other seigneuries, to her husband, Simon de Meranvilliers, lord of Flacourt, steward to the Dauphin of France.

Having done with the eldest branch, we return to Guarin de Maule, younger son of Peter lord of Maule, the direct ancestor of this noble family. Which Guarin came into England with William the Conqueror, amongst the names of whose followers Maule is always found, particularly in Holingshed, and got the lordship of Hatton de Cliveland, out of which Robert de Maule, his son, made a donation to the Abbay de Whiteby, in the reign of Henry I. from whom descended Serlo de Maule, who was a baron of England in the reign of king John.

Of this same family was William de Maule, who sided with David I. king of Scotland, in the battle of the standard, in 1138; and continuing to follow that king's fortune, obtained from him the lordship of Fowlis, out of which he made donations to the priory of St. Andrews, and is witness to some of the charters made by king David, and his son prince Henry, before the year 1152. He dying without issue male, Sir Richard de Maule,

Maule, his nephew, carried on the line of the family, and was succeeded by his son, Sir Peter Maule. Which Sir Peter, about the year 1224, in the reign of Alexander II. obtained the barony of Panmure, by the marriage of Christian, daughter and sole heir of William de Valoignes, lord of Panmure, and great chamberlain of Scotland; and dying in 1254, by the said Christian his wife, left issue, Sir William, his successor; Sir Thomas, who was governor of Brechin castle, which he defended forty days against king Edward I. and was there slain in 1303. Which William, baron of Panmure, was high sheriff of the county of Forfar at the death of king Alexander III. and one of the barons of Scotland who did homage to king Edward I. for his lands which he had of the crown in 1292. He married Echam, daughter of John de Vaus, lord of Dirleton, high sheriff of the county of Edinburgh, by whom he left issue Henry, his son and heir. Which Sir Henry de Maule was knighted by king Robert Bruce, whom he served in the wars against England; and married Margaret, daughter of William Hay of Locherrat, ancestor of the marquis of Tweeddale, by whom he had Walter de Maule, baron of Panmure, who was governor of Kildrimmy in the beginning of the reign of king David Bruce, and had Sir William, his son and successor.

Which Sir William married Marion, only daughter of Sir David Fleming of Biggar, ancestor of the earl of Wigton, by Jane his wife, daughter of David Barclay, lord Brechin, and by her had Thomas, his son and successor. Which Thomas de Maule, baron of Panmure, was knighted by king Robert III. and was one of the commanders of the governor of Scotland's army at the battle of Hairlan, where he was slain, with many of his followers, in 1411, leaving issue by Elizabeth his wife, daughter of Sir Andrew Gray of Foulis, ancestor of the lord Gray, a son born after his death, named Thomas, who preserved the family, that otherways would have been extinguished. Which Thomas, baron of Panmure, was knighted by king James I. and upon the death of Walter earl of Athol, who was executed for the murder of king James I. in 1437, laid claim to the lordship of Brechin, in right of his great grandmother, daughter of David lord Brechin, and obtained some parts of the estate of that family, but was kept out of the barony by the ministry of king James II. which after some time returned to the family of Panmure. He married Margaret, daughter of Sir Thomas Abercromby of that ilk, in the county of Fife, and left issue Sir Thomas, his son and successor. Which Sir Thomas was also knighted, and was very powerful in the reign of king James III. and stiled in records the noble and puissant lord, Thomas de Maule, lord of Panmure. He married the lady Elizabeth Lindsay, daughter of Alexander earl of Crawfurd, and grandchild of the lady Jane, daughter

of

of king Robert II. by whom he had a son, Alexander, who died in his life-time, leaving issue by Elizabeth his wife, daughter of Sir David Guthrie of that ilk, Knt. lord high treasurer of Scotland, Thomas, who succeeded his grandfather. Which Thomas was bailiff of Barrie, and knighted by king James IV. and married first, Elizabeth, eldest daughter and coheir of Sir David Rollo of Ballachie, by Elizabeth his wife, daughter of Andrew lord Gray; and after her death, Christian, daughter of William lord Graham, ancestor of the duke of Montrose. He was killed, with his master king James IV. at the fatal field of Floddon, in 1513, and was succeeded by his eldest son of the first marriage, Robert, baron of Panmure, who was some time high sheriff of the county of Forfar, and bailiff of Barrie, had a licence from king James V. exempting him from parliaments, was at the battle of Lithgow bridge, with the earl of Lennox, for that king's liberty, in 1526, and in queen Mary's reign, with the lord Gray, storm'd the town of Perth, which held out against the queen's authority; and after the battle of Pinkeycleugh, was besieged in his castle of Panmure by the English, wounded, and carried prisoner to the Tower of London. He married first, Isabel, daughter of Sir Laurence Mercer of Aldie, in the county of Perth; secondly, Isabel, daughter of Sir Robert Arbuthnot, ancestor of the lord viscount Arbuthnot, and was succeeded by Thomas, his eldest son of the first marriage.

Which Thomas went over with cardinal Beaton, ambassador to France, in 1538; and upon his return, was taken prisoner at the fight of Haldenrig; and being released, was again with the earl of Angus in the van of the Scots army, at the bloody battle of Pinkeycleugh, in 1547, where he escaped with great difficulty, having many of his followers killed. He was also amongst the Scots nobility, who entered into that memorable association for the defence of king James VI. upon his inauguration. He married first, Elizabeth, daughter of David earl of Crawford; and secondly, Margaret, daughter of Sir George Haliburton of Pitcur; by the last he had one son, Patrick, who succeeded him. Which Patrick was by king James VI. made hereditary bailiff of Barrie; and dying in 1605, left issue by Margaret his wife, daughter of Sir John Erskine of Dun, (privy counsellor, and one of the ambassadors to France at the marriage of queen Mary) Patrick, his only son and heir.

Which Patrick was a gentleman of the bedchamber to king James VI. and king Charles I. keeper of the king's house and park at Eltham; high sheriff and vice admiral of the county of Forfar; and created lord Brechin and Navarre, and earl of Panmure, and to the heirs male of his body for ever. This earl was with king Charles in all the battles in which his royal person was engaged, and attended his majesty in all his removes, after he was delivered up by the Scots army to the English commissioners; and staid with him till he was made prisoner in Carisbroke castle, that all his old servants were forbid, upon their peril, to come near him; and after the king's murder, Oliver Cromwell imposed a fine of ten thousand pounds sterling on him for his loyalty. This noble earl married first, Frances, daughter of Sir Edward Stanhope, lord president of the North, and elder brother of the lord Stanhope, by whom he had George lord Brechin, his successor. His second wife was Mary Waldrum, maid of honour to queen Henrietta, and a near cousin to the great duke of Buckingham: and his third wife was Mary, daughter of John earl of Mar, lord high treasurer of Scotland, and widow of William earl Marshal.

George, earl of Panmure, was colonel of a regiment of horse for the king, during the civil wars, with which he was present at the battles of Dunbar and Innerkeithing; and after the defeat at Worcester, commanded the remains of the king's army in Scotland, but was forced to surrender to Cromwell the year following. He married Jane, eldest daughter of John earl of Loudoun, lord high chancellor of Scotland, and by her had George lord Maule, his successor; James Maule of Balcembie; and Harie Maule of Kellie. George was one of the privy council to king Charles II. and James VII. He married Jane, only daughter of John earl of Wigton, but died without surviving issue, and was succeeded by James his brother. Which James, earl of Panmure, was also of the privy council to king James VII. He married the lady Margaret, third daughter of William and Ann, duke and dutchess of Hamilton; but he dying without issue also, in the year 1723, the honour would have devolved upon Harie, the youngest brother, had it not been for the forfeiture of the said James, who was concerned in the rebellion with his nephew the earl of Mar, in 1715.

This Harie married first, the lady Mary, only daughter of William Fleming, earl of Wigton, by whom he had James, who died in the life-time of his father; and William, who succeeded him: and a daughter, Jane, who was married to George lord Ramsay, eldest son of William earl of Dalhousie. And by his second wife, Ann, sister of John, lord viscount of Garnock, he had a son, John, and a daughter, Margaret, who died unmarried. Which John was chosen member of parliament for the burghs of Aberdeen, Montrose, &c. in the year 1739, and in the year 1748, constituted one of the barons of his majesty's court of exchequer in Scotland.

William, now earl Panmure, who entered into the king's service in the life-time of his eldest brother, was chosen to represent the shire of Forfar in parliament, in the year 1735.

had

had the command of a company of foot guards in the year 1741; served in Germany and Flanders the whole course of the last war; and upon the death of the earl of Crawford, in 1747, got the command of a regiment of foot; is now colonel of the Royal North British Fuzileers, and a lieutenant general of his majesty's forces. He was created a peer of Ireland, by his majesty's privy seal at St. James's, 6th April, and by patent at Dublin, on the 2d May 1743, by the titles of earl Panmure of Forth, and viscount Maule of Whitechurch, the honours being limited to the heirs male of his own body, and his brother John's.

TITLES were before the forfeiture.] Earl of Panmure, lord Maule of Navarre and Brechin, hereditable justice of Southesk and Northesk, and bailiff of Barry.

CREATIONS.] Baron of Panmure, in Scotland, by tenure, in the reign of king Alexander II. Claimed the lordship and barony of Brechin, by female descent, 1437. Created lord Brechin and Navarre, and earl of Panmure, in the county of Forfar, 3d of August 1646, by king Charles I. and lord Maule by king Charles II.

ARMS.] Quarterly, 1st, party per pale, pearl and ruby, on a border, eight escallops, all counterchanged, for the name of Maule; 2d pearl, three pellets wavey, ruby, for Valoignes, as married to the heiress of that family; 3d quarter counterquartered, 1st and 4th sapphire, a chevron between three crosses patees, topaz, for Barclay, lord of Brechin; 2d and 3d pearl, three piles issuing from the chief, conjoined by the points, ruby, for Brechin lord Brechin; 4th quarter as the first.

CREST.] On a wreath, a wyvern, emerald, spouting fire before and behind.

SUPPORTERS.] Two greyhounds, proper, each gorged with a collar, ruby, charged with three escallop shells, pearl.

MOTTO.] Clementia et animis.

CHIEF SEATS.] At Panmure, in the county of Forfar; and at the castle of Brechin, in the same county.

MIDDLETON, Earl of MIDDLETON.

THE immediate ancestor of this noble family was Kenneth, who lived in the reigns of Malcolm IV. and his successor, William, and was father of Malcolm, ancestor of all the Middletons in Scotland. He was succeeded by Humfridus, whose son, Humfridus de Middleton, was one of the Scots barons that swore fealty to Edward I. of England, in 1296. His son Gilbert succeeded him, and was succeeded by his son, Laurence, as he was by his son, another Gilbert, whose son, John, was succeeded by his grandson, John Middleton

ton of Cadham, whose son, John Middleton, Esq; was a colonel belonging to the royal party; and in 1648, attended duke Hamilton into England, when he brought the army to Preston, which was defeated by Cromwell with less than half the number. At the battle of Worcester, 1651, he commanded as lieutenant general of horse, when he and most of the principal officers were made prisoners; but he had the good fortune, in a short time, to escape out of the Tower. Soon after the restoration, he was appointed the king's high commissioner in Scotland, and general of his forces in that kingdom. He was a great enemy to the marquis of Argyll, and the chief instrument of his ruin, not without hopes to get part of his estate; and to procure that lord's condemnation, the letters which the marquis formerly wrote to general Monk, approving the commonwealth system, were now on his trial made high treason, which letters Monk himself sent down, in order to betray him. This John earl of Middleton had two daughters, lady Helen, married to Patrick Lyon, earl of Strathmore; and lady Grisel, to William earl of Morton: also a son,

Charles, second earl, who was secretary of state for Scotland from the year 1684, to the revolution, when he followed king James into France. He was attainted by the Scots parliament in July 1695, with John Drummond earl of Melfort, it having been enacted treason to continue in France after the first of August 1693. They were both zealous managers at the French court for the projected invasion of 1696, and the assassination of king William. He married lady Katharine, daughter of Robert earl of Cardigan, by whom he had two sons, John lord Clairmont, and Charles Middleton, Esq; and two daughters, lady Elizabeth, married to Edward, commonly called lord Edward, son of James earl of Perth; and lady Mary, to Sir John Giffard, Knt. The sons were both taken at sea by admiral Byng, in the descent which the French intended to make in Scotland in 1708; but by the queen's order, they were soon released; after which they returned to France, and died without issue. Who therefore now represents the family, I cannot say.

TITLES *were*.] The right honourable Charles Middleton, baron Clairmont, and earl of Middleton.

CREATIONS.] So created in 165 , by king Charles II.

ARMS.] Party per fess, diamond and ruby, a lion rampant, within a double tressure, flowered and counterflowered with fleurs de lis, all counterchanged.

CREST.] A tower embattled, ruby, and on the top of it a lion rampant,

SUPPORTERS.] Two eagles, ruby.

MOTTO.] Fortis in arduis.

CHIEF SEAT *was*.] At Montrose, in the county of Forfar.

BOYD, Earl of KILMARNOCK.

THE first of the firname of Boyd is said to be Robert, the son of Simon, third son of Alan, second lord steward of Scotland. The name is derived from Boydh, a Gallic or Celtic word, *fair* or *yellow*, the said Robert being called so from his fair complexion. His son was Sir Robert Boyd, who in 1263 signalized his valour at the battle of Largis, in Coningham, against the Norwegians, and had thereupon a grant of several lands in that district, wherein he was succeeded by another Sir Robert, and he by a third Sir Robert, who in the second of king Robert I. for his loyalty and merit, was rewarded with the lands of Kilmarnock. To him succeeded his son, Sir Thomas, the father of another Sir Thomas, whose wife being one of the daughters and coheirs of Sir John Gifford of Yester, in East Lothian, he thereby had part of those lands: and Sir Thomas, their son, who was one of the hostages for the ransom of king James I. marrying Jane, a daughter of the family of Montgomery, by her had a son, Sir Thomas, who was father of Sir Robert, lord Boyd of Kilmarnock, and Sir Alexander Boyd of Duncow.

Sir Robert, the eldest, married Mariota, daughter of Sir Robert Maxwell of Calderwood, by whom he had three sons, Thomas; Alexander; Archibald, first of the Boyds of Bonshaw: and a daughter, Elizabeth, married to Archibald, earl of Douglas and Angus, and regent of Scotland in the minority of king James III. He was created lord Boyd in 1459, and marrying his son Thomas to the princess Mary Stewart, king James the IIId's eldest sister, the said Thomas was thereupon created earl of Arran, and afterwards sent ambassador to Denmark, to treat of a marriage between his brother-in-law, the young king, and the princess Margaret of that crown; but while he was absent, his enemies contrived the ruin of his family, by representing their ambition as too dangerous for the condition of subjects; and so far prevailed with the king, that he called a parliament, before whom the lord Boyd, his son, the earl of Arran, and his brother, Sir Alexander Boyd, being summoned, to give an account of their administration, the old lord fearing the power of his enemies, fled into England; but Sir Alexander was condemned for high treason, and executed. The earl of Arran arriving with the queen at Leith, and being informed of these melancholy circumstances, immediately retired into Denmark with his lady, from thence into France; and dying at Antwerp in 1471, was honourably interred by Charles duke of Burgundy, who erected a handsome monument, with an inscription, to his memory. By his said lady (who in 1474 was arbitrarily divorced, and married to James lord Hamilton) he left a son, James; and a daughter, Margaret, who was first married to Alexander, fourth lord Forbes; and secondly, to David earl of Cassils; but had no issue by either.

James, third lord, and second earl of Arran, dying without issue, the title of earl of Arran became extinct; but his uncle, Alexander, the second son of Robert lord Boyd, continued the line. He married Jane, daughter of Sir Robert Colvil of Ochiltree, and had three sons, Thomas; Adam; and Robert, the eldest, who was restored to the honours and estates of lord Boyd, in 1536, by James V. He married Helen, daughter of Sir John Somerville of Camnethan, and had issue,

Robert, fourth lord, who marrying Margaret, daughter and sole heir of George Colquhoun of Glins, had issue Robert, who died before him; Thomas, his heir; William; and Giles, wife of Hugh earl of Eglingtoun; Agnes, of Sir John Colquhoun of Luss; Christian, of Sir James Hamilton of Evandale; and Elizabeth, of Sir John Cunningham of Drumquhassel. He was succeeded by his son,

Thomas, fifth lord, who marrying Margaret, daughter of Sir Matthew Campbell, ancestor of the earl of Loudoun, had four sons, Robert, Sir Thomas, Adam, and John; and three daughters, Mariana, married to James earl of Abercorn; Isabel, to John Blair of that ilk; and Agnes, to Sir Gilbert Elphingston of Blythswood. Robert, the eldest son, dying before his father, left by his wife, the lady Jane Ker, daughter of Mark earl of Lothian, two sons, Robert and James; and

Robert, the eldest, succeeding his grandfather, was sixth lord; who married lady Christian, daughter of Thomas earl of Haddington; and dying in 1628, left issue Robert, his heir; and four daughters, Jane, wife of Alexander Morrison of Preston-grange; Isabel, of John Sinclair of Stevenson; Christian, of Sir William Scot of Harden; and Marian, of Sir James Dundas of Arniston. He died in 1628, and was succeeded by his only son,

Robert, seventh lord, who marrying lady Anne, daughter of John earl of Wigton, by her, who afterwards married George Ramsay, earl of Dalhousie, left no issue, and the estate and honour devolved on his uncle,

James, eighth lord, who married Katharine, daughter of John Craik, of the city of York, Esq; and had issue William, master of Boyd; and Eva, wife of Sir David Cunninghame of Robertland. He died in 1654, and was succeeded by his son,

William, ninth lord, who was created earl of Kilmarnock by king Charles II. He married lady Jane Coningham, daughter of William earl of Glencairn; and dying in 1692, left four sons, William, James, Charles, and Robert; and two daughters, lady Mary, wife of Sir Alexander M'Laine; and
lady

lady Catharine, of Alexander Porterfield of that ilk. His eldest son,

William, lord Boyd, succeeded, and was second earl; but dying in the same year as his father, left by Lettice his wife, daughter and heir of Thomas Boyd, of the city of Dublin, merchant, by Mary, daughter of Sir Adam Loftus, William, the third earl of Kilmarnock, and Thomas Boyd, Esq; advocate.

William, third earl, married Eupheme, daughter of William lord Ross; and dying in 1717, left issue by her,

William, fourth earl, who married lady Anne, daughter and sole heir of James, earl of Linlithgow and Calendar, by whom he had issue, James, Charles, and William. Unfortunately engaging in the rebellion of 1745, this lord was taken prisoner at the battle of Culloden, tried, condemned, and beheaded on Towerhill, Aug. 18, 1746, for high treason, and his titles and estate thereby forfeited to the crown. His eldest son, James, is now earl of Errol. (See that title.)

TITLES were.] The right honourable William Boyd, earl of Kilmarnock, and lord Boyd.

CREATION.] Earl of Kilmarnock, in Coningham of Airshire, 27 August 1661, by Charles II.

ARMS.] Sapphire, a fess cheque, pearl and ruby.

CREST.] On a wreath, a dexter hand, couped at the wrist, and erect, pointing with the thumb and the two next fingers, the other turning down.

SUPPORTERS.] Two squirrels, proper.

MOTTO.] Confido.

CHIEF SEAT was.] At Kilmarnock, in the county of Air.

DRUMMOND, Earl of MELFORT.

THE descent of this family has been already deduced under the title of Drummond, earl of Perth; and that

John, second son of James, third earl of Perth, was created earl of Melfort, viscount Forth, lord Drummond of Riccarton, Castlemain and Gilston, by king James VII. in 1686, whose fortunes he followed upon the revolution, and was created by him a duke at St. Germains en laye; but not returning to Scotland in the time limited by law, was attainted, and his estate and honours forfeited to the crown. By his second wife, Eupheme, daughter of Sir Thomas Wallace of Craigie, Bart. the issue of which marriage only suffered by his attainder, he had six sons and five daughters, (commonly called lords and ladies) viz. John; Thomas, an officer in the Austrian service, who died unmarried; William, abbe prioral of Liege, deceased; Andrew, colonel of horse in the French service, whose issue are now in being in France; Bernard, who died young; Philip, who was an officer in the French service, and died of his wounds:

wounds: Henrietta, who died unmarried; Mary, married to the count Castle Blanco, a Spanish nobleman; Frances, who, by a dispensation from the pope, married the said count after her sister's death; Louisa and Theresa. He died in 1714, at St. Germains.

John, his eldest son, had three sons, Thomas; Lewis, major general in the French service, and late colonel of the Royal Scots; and John, major general in the Saxon service.

The eldest son, Thomas, has a considerable estate in Languedoc; and by Mary Berenger, his wife, has four sons and two daughters; James-Lewis, Charles-Edward, Henry-Benedict, Maurice; Maria-Cecilia-Henrietta, and Emilia-Felicitas.

MACKENZIE, Earl of CROMARTIE.

THE rise and descent of this noble family is set forth under the title of Seaforth, where we find that Sir Roderick, second son of Sir Colin Campbell of Kintail, was knighted by James VI. and his son, Sir John, was by Charles I. created a baronet in 1628, and died in 1654, to whom succeeded Sir George, his eldest son, a man of great learning, and well versed in the laws. He had a commission from king Charles II. then in exile, to raise what forces he could in order to promote his restoration; and for those his good services, when his majesty came to the crown, he was made a senator of the college of justice, clerk register, one of the privy council, and justice general; and by king James VII. created viscount Tarbat. In the reign of queen Ann he was constituted secretary of state, one of the privy council, created an earl, and continued in the post of justice general. He died in August 1714, in the 84th year of his age. He married first, Anne, daughter of Sir James Sinclair of May, and by her had three sons and four daughters; James, the youngest son, was created a baronet in 1704, and promoted to be one of the senators of the college of justice. The second son, Kenneth, was created a baronet on the same day as his brother, but with precedence according to his grandfather's patent, 1628; one of whose sons married lady Elizabeth, daughter of Charles Gordon, the first earl of Aboyn. The daughters were, lady Margaret, wife of David Bruce of Clackmannan; lady Elizabeth, of Sir George Brown of Coalston; lady Jane, of Sir Thomas Stewart of Balcaskie; and lady Anne, of John, brother of the earl of Caithness. By his second wife, Margaret, countess dowager of Wemyss, he had no issue. He was succeeded by his eldest son,

John, second earl, who married to his second wife, Mary, daughter of Alexander lord Elibank, by whom he had issue, George, lord Macleod; captain Roderick, of the army; William, an officer in the India service, who was lost in a storm in 1737; and Patrick, a merchant: lady Mary, who died young; and lady Anne. By his third wife, Anne, daughter of Hugh lord Lovat, he had three sons and one daughter; James, who died young; Norman, an officer in the Dutch service, who perished at sea; Hugh, an officer in the same service, but since in Montgomery's Highland battalion: and lady Emilia, wife of Archibald Lawmont of that ilk. By his first wife, lady Elizabeth, daughter of Charles earl of Aboyne, he had no issue. He died in 1731, and was succeeded by his eldest son,

George, third earl, who having engaged himself, with 400 of his men, in the last rebellion, 1745, was surprized and defeated by the earl of Sutherland's militia, near Dunrobin castle, in Sutherland, which happened on the 15th of April 1746, the day before the battle of Culloden. He, and his son, lord Macleod, being taken prisoners, were sent to Inverness, and from thence to London, where the earl was committed to the Tower. In August, he being tried, was condemned, and received sentence of death, and his estate and honours were forfeited to the crown; but by great intercession, he was pardoned, and permitted to reside in England. He married Isabel, daughter of Sir William Gordon of Invergordon, Bart. by whom he had two sons and seven daughters; his eldest son, lord Macleod, was likewise pardoned, and in 1750, had leave to accept of a commission in the service of Sweden, where he is major, and aid de camp to the king of Sweden; George, an officer in the British army: lady Elizabeth, wife of admiral George Murray; lady Mary, of Mr. Drayton; lady Anne, of Mr. Atkins; lady Caroline, of Mr. Drake; ladies Jane, Margaret, and Augusta. This unfortunate nobleman died in 1766.

TITLES *were*.] The right honourable George Mackenzie, earl of Cromartie, &c. &c.

CREATIONS.] Lord Macleod and viscount Tarbat, April 15, 1685, by James VII. earl of Cromartie, January 1, 1702, by queen Anne.

ARMS.] Quarterly, 1st topaz, a mountain inflamed, proper, for Macleod; 2d sapphire, a stag's head cabossed, topaz, for Mackenzie; 3d ruby, three legs of a man armed, proper, conjoined in the center at the upper part of the thighs, flexed in triangle, and the spurs topaz, formerly belonging to the Macleods, as old possessors of the Isle of Man; 4th pearl, on a pale, diamond, an imperial crown within a double tressure, counterflory, with fleurs de lis, ruby, for Erskine of Innerdale.

CREST.] On a wreath, the sun in its splendor.

SUPPORTERS.] Two savages, each wreathed about the head and middle with laurel, and holding a batoon over his shoulder, proper.

MOTTO.] Luceo non uro.

CHIEF SEATS were.] At Macleod castle, New Tarbat, and Castlehaven, all in the county of Cromartie.

GORDON, Viscount KENMURE.

IN the 10th of king Robert I. Sir Adam Gordon, in reward of his good services, obtained from that prince the barony of Stickel, in the county of Roxburgh, and was succeeded by his second son, William, in all his lands in the south, from whom descended Sir John Gordon of Lochinvar, who in the reign of James IV. marrying Annabella, daughter of Robert lord Boyd, had a son, Alexander; and by a second wife, Elizabeth Lindsay, had three sons, Sir Robert, his successor; William, of Crauchlaw, ancestor of the Gordons of Pulvenan, Grange, Balmig, &c. and John: also two daughters. His eldest son, Sir Alexander, who succeeded, was in great favour with James III. but being slain in the battle of Floddon, was succeeded by his brother,

Sir Robert, who marrying Marian, daughter and sole heir of John Accasarlan of Glenshyre-burn, had six sons and three daughters, whereof Sir James, his heir, by Margaret his wife, daughter and heir of Robert Crichton of Kilpatrick, had five sons and five daughters; Janet, married to William Coningham, earl of Glencairn; Margaret, to William, son of Sir James Douglas of Drumlanrig; Catharine, to Sir James Macculloch of Cardnets; Helen, to Sir Thomas Maclellan of Bombie; and Elizabeth, to William Grierson of Lag. The sons were, John; William, ancestor of the late lord; Robert, James, and Alexander. He was slain at the battle of Pinkie in 1547, and was succeeded by his eldest son,

John, who marrying to his first wife Juliana, daughter of Sir David Hume of Wedderburn, had one daughter, Margaret, married to Hugh lord Loudoun; and by his second wife, Elizabeth, daughter of John lord Herries, ancestor of the earl of Nithisdale, he had five sons, Sir Robert, his heir; William; John; James, of whom hereafter; and Alexander: and four daughters, Mary, married to Alexander Kennedy of Bargany; Janet, to John McDowal of Garthland; Elizabeth, to Alexander Stewart of Gairlies, ancestor of the earl of Galloway; and Grisel, to James lord Carlile of Torthorald. He was succeeded, in 1604, by his eldest son,

Sir Robert, who was knighted, and then created a baronet, and was a gentleman of the privy chamber to Henry prince of Wales, eldest son of king James VI. He married lady Elizabeth, daughter of John earl of Gowrie, and had two sons, Sir John and Robert; and two daughters, Elizabeth, married to John earl of Nithisdale; and Isabel, to Alexander Fraser, jun.

of Philorth, ancestor of lord Salton. He was succeeded by his eldest son,

Sir John, who was by king Charles I. created a baron and viscount. He married lady Jane Campbell, third daughter of Archibald, seventh earl of Argyll, and dying in 1634, was succeeded by his only son,

John, second viscount, who dying young, the title descended to

John, third viscount, his cousin-german, son of James, son of John, before mentioned; but he dying unmarried, his brother,

Robert, became fourth viscount; and dying in 1663, without issue, the title descended to

John, of Penygame, son of William, son of Alexander, son of John, son of William, second son of Sir James, before mentioned; but the said John, fifth viscount, dying without issue in 1662, was succeeded by his brother,

Alexander, sixth viscount, who married first, a daughter of the family of Gordon of Auchlauin, by whom he had a daughter, Agnes, wife, first, of William Maxwell of Kelton; and secondly, of John Lindsay of Wauchop. He married secondly, Marian, daughter of —— Macculloch of Ardwell, by whom he had William, his heir; and three daughters, Jane, wife of William Gordon of Skimmers; Marian, of Sir Alexander Gordon of Earlstoun; and Elizabeth, first, of Samuel Maxwell of Newlaw; and secondly, of Samuel Brown of Mollance. His third wife was lady Grisel, daughter of James earl of Galloway, and by her he had two sons and three daughters; Mary, married to Sir Patrick Maxwell of Springel, Bart. Isabel, to John Macgie of Balmagie; and Grisel, to Robert Gordon of Dundugh. The sons were, John, of Greenlaw; and James. Dying in 1698, he was succeeded by his eldest son,

William, seventh viscount, who being engaged in the rebellion 1715, against king George I. was taken prisoner at Preston in Lancashire, and from thence, in January, brought to London, where, on Friday the 24th of February following, he was beheaded on Towerhill, with James Radcliffe, earl of Derwentwater; but his corpse was carried by sea to Leith, where it was received by his relations in mourning, and conveyed to his burial-place at Kenmure. He married Mary, daughter of Sir John Dalziel of Glenae, and sister of Robert earl of Carnwath, who was condemned for the same rebellion, and had issue by her three sons, Robert, John, and James; and one daughter, wife of John Dalziel, Esq;

Robert, the eldest son, through his majesty's great indulgence, got possession of the estate by the care and management of lady Kenmure, but the title was forfeited; and he dying unmarried, was succeeded therein by his brother John, who now represents the family. He married lady Frances, daughter of William earl of Seaforth, by whom he has issue four sons and one daughter; William, John, Adam, Robert, and Frances.

TITLES.] The right honourable William Gordon, viscount Kenmure, baron of Lochinvar, and baronet.

CREATIONS.] Baron and viscount of Kenmure castle, in the county of Kirkcudbright, 18 May 1633, by king Charles I. and baronet, 1 May 1626.

ARMS.] Sapphire, three boars head erazed, topaz.

CREST.] On a wreath, a demi savage, proper, wreathed about his temples and middle with laurel.

SUPPORTERS.] Two savages, wreathed as the crest; each holding in his outer hand a batoon erect, proper.

MOTTO] Dread God.

CHIEF SEAT.] At Kenmure castle, in the county of Kirkcudbright.

LIVINGSTON, Viscount KILSYTH.

SIR William Livingston, son of Sir John of Callendar, a branch of the family of Linlithgow, was the ancestor of this family, and married Elizabeth, daughter of William de Caldecoat, and was succeeded by his eldest son, Edward, and he by his son, William, whose son, another William, was succeeded by his son, a third William, who lost his life at the battle of Flodden, 1513; and by his wife, Janet Bruce, had a son, William, whose eldest son, Sir William Livingston of Kilsyth, married lady Christian, daughter of William earl of Menteith, by whom he had Sir William, his successor, who by his first wife, Antonia de Board, had a son, Sir William; and a daughter: and by his second, Margaret, daughter of Sir John Houstoun of that ilk, Sir James, of whom presently; and a daughter. His eldest son, Sir William, died before his father; and by lady Anne, daughter of John earl of Wigton, had a son, William, heir to his grandfather, whose son, William, married Margaret, daughter of George lord Ramsay, by whom he had a son, William; and two daughters, Margaret, wife of Andrew Rutherford of Hunthill; and Christian, married to James Macgill, the first viscount Oxenford. The son, William, dying in his minority, was succeeded by Sir James Livingston, his grand uncle, as above mentioned, who by Charles II. for his faithful services during the rebellion, was created viscount Kilsyth, lord Campsie, &c. Aug. 17, 1661; and marrying Eupheme, daughter of Sir David Cunningham of Robertland, had issue James and William; and a daughter, Elizabeth, wife of major general Robert Montgomery, son of Alexander earl of Eglingtoun. He died in 1661, and was succeeded by his eldest son,

James,

James, second viscount, who dying unmarried in 1706, was succeeded by his brother,

William, third viscount, who married first, Jane, daughter of William lord Cochran, and had issue a son, William, who died in infancy; and secondly, Barbara, daughter of —— M'Dowgal of Mackerston, by whom he had a daughter, Barbara, who died young. He was elected one of the sixteen peers in the two last parliaments of queen Anne; but joining with the earl of Mar in the rebellion in 1715, and refusing to surrender, was attainted, and his estates and honours forfeited.

TITLES.] The right honourable William viscount Kilsyth, lord Campsie, &c.

CREATIONS.] As before.

ARMS.] Pearl, three gilliflowers slipped, ruby, within a double tressure, flowered and counterflowered with fleurs de lis, emerald.

CREST.] On a wreath, a demi savage wreathed about the temples and waist with laurel.

SUPPORTERS.] Two lions, proper.

MOTTO.] Spe expecto.

DRUMMOND, Viscount STRATHALLAN.

JAMES Drummond, commendator of Inchaffery, second son of David, second lord Drummond, ancestor of the earl of Perth, by Lillias his wife, daughter of William lord Ruthven, was created lord Maderty by king James VI. and marrying Jane, daughter of Sir James Chisholm of Cromlix, by her had John, his heir; Sir James Drummond of Machony, ancestor of the last viscount; and several daughters, whereof Lillias was married to Laurence lord Oliphant, and Katharine, to Andrew lord Rollo.

John, the eldest son, second lord, married Margaret, daughter of Patrick lord Lindores, and by her had David lord Maderty, his successor; and general William Drummond. David, third lord, dying without issue male, was succeeded by his brother,

William Drummond of Cromlix, who from his youth chusing a military life, was a lieutenant general in Muscovy; and upon his return home, was advanced for his merit to the like post in Scotland by king Charles I. In the time of the usurpation, being taken prisoner at the battle of Worcester, 1651, he made his escape; but seeing no farther hopes of serving his master, he went into the service of the king of Prussia, under whom he had some high commands. On the restoration of king Charles II. he was called home, and made major general of the forces, in which character he served the crown many years; and when king James VII. ascended the throne, he was made general of all the forces in Scotland, a commissioner of the treasury, and created a viscount. He married Elizabeth, daughter of Sir Archibald Johnston of Wariston, and dying in 1688, left William, his heir; and a daughter, Elizabeth, married to Thomas Hay, earl of Kinnoul. He died in 1688, and was succeeded by his son,

William, second viscount, who marrying lady Elizabeth, daughter of John earl of Melfort, by her had a son, James, third viscount, who dying a youth in 1711, the honour of viscount devolved on William Drummond of Machony, son of Sir John, son of Sir James, son of Sir James, second son of James, first lord Maderty, who became fourth viscount, and married Margaret, daughter of William lord Nairn; and bearing a part in the rebellion 1715, was taken prisoner at the battle of Dunblain, and committed to the castle of Edinburgh, but was discharged by the act of grace in 1717. He afterwards, with his eldest son, James Drummond, joining in the rebellion 1745, were both attainted by the act of parliament in 1746. The viscount, however, was slain in the battle of Culloden. His issue, by the said Elizabeth Nairn, were James, William, Robert, Henry; Margaret, Anne, Mary, and Æmilia.

James, the eldest, master of Strathallan, was, upon the death of his father, fifth viscount, but was attainted by the name of James Drummond, eldest son of William viscount Strathallan; and perhaps, on account of that misnomer, the attainder may hereafter be set aside. He married Eupheme, daughter of Peter Gordon of Abergeldy, Esq; by whom he had a son, James, and a numerous issue beside.

TITLES.] The right honourable William Drummond, baron and viscount Strathallan, and baron Maderty.

CREATIONS.] Baron Maderty, in 1607, by king James VI. and baron and viscount Strathallan, in the county of Perth, the 16th of August 1686, by king James VII.

ARMS.] Quarterly, 1st and 4th topaz, three closets wavey, ruby, for Drummond; 2d and 3d topaz, a lion's head erazed, within a double tressure counterflory with fleurs de lis, ruby, as a coat of augmentation.

CREST.] On a wreath, a falcon rising, proper, his bells topaz.

SUPPORTERS.] Two savages, each holding a batoon over his shoulder, proper, and wreathed about his temples and middle with laurel.

MOTTO.] Lord have mercy.

CHIEF SEAT was.] At Inchaffery and Machany, in the county of Perth.

GRAHAM,

GRAHAM, Viscount DUNDEE.

JOHN Graham of Claverhouse, a branch of the Montrose family, was created baron Graham and viscount Dundee, in the county of Forfar, by king James VII. after whose abdication he commanded a body of Highlanders, and other troops in that prince's interest, but was killed in the battle with general Mackay, at Killicranky, near Blair, on July 27, 1689. He married Jane, daughter of William, first earl of Dundonald, by whom he had a son, James, who died in his infancy; whereupon the honours devolved upon his brother,

David, second viscount, who being with his brother in the battle of Killicrankie, was outlawed and forfeited, in 1690. He died in 1700, in France, and but for the outlawry would have been succeeded by William Graham of Duntroon, son of his uncle, Walter, of Duntroon; whose posterity engaging in the rebellions of 1715 and 1745, when they were called viscounts Dundee, were attainted.

GRAHAM, Viscount PRESTON.

SIR John Graham of Kilbride, second son of Malise, earl of Strathern and Menteith, a branch of the illustrious house of Montrose, was the immediate ancestor of this noble family. John, his second son, settled, in the reign of James V. in the north of England, where he acquired a considerable estate, and of him was lineally descended Sir Richard Graham of Netherby and Plump, in Cumberland, gentleman of the horse to king Charles I. to whom, in all his troubles, he was a faithful servant, and by whom he was created a baronet, 29th March 1629. He married Katharine, daughter and coheir of Sir Thomas Musgrave of Cumeath, in Cumberland, Esq; by whom he had two sons, Sir George and Sir Richard; and four daughters, 1. Katharine, who died unmarried; 2. Mary, married to Sir Edward Musgrave of Hayton, in Cumberland, baronet of Nova Scotia; 3. Elizabeth, married to Sir Cuthbert Heron of Chipchase, in Northumberland, Bart. 4. Susan, to Reginald Carnaby of Hulton, in the same county, Esq; Sir Richard, the second son, was of Norton Conyers, in Yorkshire, and was created a baronet November 17, 1662, from whom descended Sir Reginald Graham, the present baronet.

Sir George, who succeeded his father, married lady Mary Johnston, daughter of James earl of Annandale, and had issue two sons, Sir Richard, and James, who was member to parliament for Appleby in 1702 and 1705, and in the five succeeding parliaments, for the county of Westmoreland. He was succeeded by his eldest son,

Sir Richard Graham, who was one of the commissioners of excise, and one of the council to her majesty Catharine, queen dowager, and member of parliament for Windsor in 1685. He was created baron of Esk, and viscount Preston, in the county of Haddington, in Scotland, by king Charles II. on May 12, 1681. By James VII. after his abdication, he was created baron Esk, in Cumberland, but the patent was rejected here by the house of lords. He was advanced to be secretary of state in 1688, in the room of Robert Spencer, earl of Sunderland. In 1690, he, and his brother, James Graham, with John Ashton, William Pen the Quaker, Dr. Turner, bishop of Ely, and Henry Hyde, earl of Clarendon, were apprehended for a treasonable conspiracy to restore king James. Lord Preston and Mr. Ashton were tried and condemned; the latter was executed, but the former had his life granted. He married lady Ann, daughter of Charles earl of Carlisle, and had issue a son,

Charles, who married Miss Cox, sister of the countess of Peterborough, and died in February 1738-9, leaving a son,

William Graham, now a clergyman of the church of England.

TITLES.] Richard Graham, viscount Preston, lord Esk, &c. &c.

CREATIONS.] As before.

ARMS.] Quarterly, 1st and 4th topaz, on a chief, diamond, three escallop shells of the field; 2d and 3d topaz, a fess, pearl and sapphire; on a chief, a chevron, ruby, for Stewart.

CREST.] On a wreath, pearl and sapphire, two wings conjoined.

SUPPORTERS.] On the dexter an eagle, on the sinister a lion, both ermine, and ducally crowned, topaz.

MOTTO.] Reason contents me.

SINCLAIR, Lord SINCLAIR.

THE descent of this ancient family may be seen under the title Earl of Caithness. William, earl of Orkney and Caithness, marrying to his first wife, lady Margaret, daughter of Archibald, fourth earl of Douglas, by her had a son and heir, William, from whom descended the lords Sinclair. William married lady Elizabeth Lesley, daughter of George earl of Rothes, and by her had a son,

Henry Sinclair of Dysart, who was created lord Sinclair by king James IV. and he marrying lady Margaret Hepburn, daughter of Patrick earl of Bothwell, by her had William, his heir; and three daughters, Katharine, married to Sir David Wemyss of that ilk; Helen, to James lord Ogilvy; and Jane, to Alexander, master of Crawfurd. He was in 1513 slain at the battle of Flodden, in Northumberland, and was succeeded by his son,

William, second lord, who married lady Elizabeth Keith, daughter of William earl Marshal, and by her had two sons, Henry and Magnus.

Henry, the eldest, third lord, married Elizabeth, daughter of William, seventh lord Forbes, by whom he had a son,

James, his heir apparent, who dying before him, left by Isabel his wife, daughter of Andrew Lesley, the fifth earl of Rothes, two sons,

James, fourth lord, who succeeded his grandfather; but dying without issue, the honour descended to his brother,

Patrick, fifth lord, who married Margaret, daughter of Sir John Cockburn of Ormiston, and had

John, sixth lord, who married lady Mary, daughter of John earl of Wemyss, by whom he had

Katharine, his only daughter, who married Sir John Sinclair of Hermanston, by whom she had a son,

Henry, seventh lord, who succeeded her in the honour, and married Grisel, daughter of Sir James Cockburn of that ilk, and had five sons and five daughters, viz. 1. John, the eldest, master of Sinclair, was returned to parliament in 1708, for the burghs of Dysart, Kinghorn, &c. but was voted incapable of sitting, as being the eldest son of a peer. He married first, Margaret, countess dowager of Southesk, daughter of James, the sixth earl of Galloway. He married secondly, in 1750, Amelia, daughter of lord George Murray, brother of the duke of Athol, and died the same year. He was attainted for his concern in the rebellion of 1715; 2. James was twice member of parliament for Sutherland, three times for the burghs of Dysart, Kinghorn, &c. and at last representative for the shire of Fife. He was made a lieutenant general of his majesty's forces June 4, 1745, and was colonel of the first British regiment of foot, commonly called the Royal, of two battalions, in which his younger brother, 3. William, was major; but he is deceased. 4. Henry; 5. Matthew; 6. Grisel; 7. Catharine, wife of Sir John Erskine of Alva; 8. Mary, of Sir William Baird of Newbyth; 9. Elizabeth, third wife of David earl of Wemyss; 10. Anne.

John, the master, was afterwards pardoned, and returned home, to whom his brother, the general, restored the estate for his life, which had been settled upon him by his father; and both of them dying without issue, and his other brothers having no children, the general settled the estate upon John Paterson, Esq; son of his eldest sister, Grisel, by John Paterson of Prestonhall, Esq; her husband, who accordingly succeeded the general therein in 1762, and is now the representative of the family.

TITLE.] The right honourable Henry Sinclair, lord Sinclair.

CREATION.] Lord Sinclair in 1489, the first of James IV.

ARMS.]

ARMS.] Quarterly, 1st and 4th sapphire, a ship at anchor, her oars erect, in saltire, within a double tressure, with fleurs de lis counterflory, topaz, for Orkney; 2d and 3d sapphire, a ship under sail, topaz, for Caithness: over all, by way of surtout, an escutcheon, pearl, charged with a cross ingrailed, diamond, for Sinclair.

CREST.] On a wreath, a swan, pearl, having a ducal collar and chain, topaz.

SUPPORTERS.] Two griffins, proper, armed and beaked, topaz.

MOTTO.] Fight.

CHIEF SEAT.] At Dysart, in Fifeshire.

FRASER, Lord LOVAT.

SIR Alexander Fraser, thane of Cowie, and lord chamberlain of Scotland, marrying lady Mary Bruce, sister of king Robert I. by her had five sons; from the second, Sir Simon, descended this family; and William, the third, was ancestor of the lords Salton. Sir Simon had a grant of the barony of Lovat, and many other possessions, by which he greatly increased his wealth and repute. His son, Hugh, had a son, Hugh Fraser of Lovat, who marrying Janet, sister and coheir of William Fenton of that ilk, had a son, Hugh, who succeeded him, and married lady Janet, daughter of Thomas earl of Murray, and by her had two sons and one daughter; Thomas; Alexander, ancestor of the Frasers of Farabrie; and Agnes, wife of Sir Kenneth M'Kenfie of Kintail. He died about 1494, and was succeeded by his eldest son,

Thomas, who in the reign of James IV. was created a baron, and made justice general in the north; and marrying first, Janet, daughter of Sir Alexander Gordon of Midmar, had two sons, Thomas, master of Lovat, who was slain at Floddon, in the life-time of his father; and Hugh. He married secondly, Jane, daughter of Andrew, third lord Gray, by whom he had a son, James, and a daughter, Janet, wife of John Crichton of Ruthven. He died in 1530, and was succeeded by his only surviving son,

Hugh, second lord, who by his first wife, Anne, daughter of John Grant of Freuchie, had a son, Hugh, master of Lovat, killed at Lochlochy in 1544, and by his second, Janet, daughter of Walter Rofs of Balnagoun, had two sons and one daughter; Alexander, his heir; and William, ancestor of the Frasers of Invernefsshire: Agnes, his daughter, was the wife of William Macleod of Dunvegan, and afterwards of Alexander Bayne of Tulloch. He was killed, with his eldest son, in 1544, and was succeeded by his eldest surviving son,

Alexander,

Alexander, third lord, who by Jane, daughter of Sir John Campbell of Calder, had four sons, Hugh; Thomas, ancestor of the Frasers of Strichen; James; and ———: and a daughter, Anne, wife of John Fraser of Dalcrofs. He died in 1558, and was succeeded by his eldest son,

Hugh, fourth lord, who married lady Elizabeth, daughter of John, fourth earl of Athol; and dying in 1576, left issue

Simon, fifth lord, who marrying first, Margaret, daughter of Sir Colin Mackenzie of Kintail, ancestor of the earl of Seaforth, by her had a son, Hugh; and by his second, who was Jane, daughter of James lord Down, he had two sons and one daughter; Sir Simon, ancestor of the Frasers of Inncolachy; and Sir James, of Brae. His daughter, Margaret, was the wife of Sir Robert Arbuthnot of that ilk, and afterwards of Sir John Haldane of Gleneagles. He died in 1633, and was succeeded by

Hugh, sixth lord, who married Isabel, daughter of Sir John Wemyss of that ilk, and had two sons, Hugh and Thomas; and three daughters, Anne, wife of John earl of Sutherland; Mary, of David Rofs of Balnagowan; and Catharine, of Robert viscount Arbuthnot.

Hugh, the eldest son, dying before his father, left by his wife lady Ann, daughter of Alexander, the first earl of Leven, a son,

Hugh, seventh lord, who succeeded his grandfather. He married Ann, daughter of Sir George Mackenzie of Tarbat, Bart, by whom he had Hugh, his heir; and three daughters, Ann, married to Patrick lord Kinnaird; Isabel, to Alexander Macdonald of Glengary; and Margaret, to colonel Andrew Monro. He died in 1672, and was succeeded by his eldest son,

Hugh, eighth lord, who marrying lady Amelia Murray, daughter of John marquis of Athol, had issue four daughters, Amelia, wife of Alexander Mackenzie of Preftonhall; Anne, of Norman Macleod of that ilk, and afterwards of Peter Fotheringhame of Pourie; Catharine, of Sir William Murray of Auchtertyre; and Margaret. After a long contest between the eldest daughter, Amelia, and Simon Frafer of Beaufort, fon of Thomas, fon of Hugh, sixth lord Lovat, which was at last determined in favour of the said

Simon, he thereupon became ninth lord, who married first, Janet, daughter of Ludovick Grant of that ilk, by whom he had two sons, Simon, master of Lovat; and Alexander, who was an officer in the army, and died in August 1762: and two daughters, Janet, married to Macpherfon of Cluny, chief of the Macpherfons, who was attainted for the rebellion in 1745; and Sibilla, who died unmarried. His second wife was ——— Primrofe, daughter of John Campbell of Mammore, father of the present duke of Argyll, by whom he had one son, Archibald, a merchant in London.

In

In the rebellion 1715, this Simon lord Lovat did the king great service, in securing the important town of Inverness, so suddenly, that Sir John Mackenzie, who kept it for the rebels, not expecting the Frasers to be his enemies, was forced to deliver it up: for as lord Lovat had always been in the other interest, his turning about on that critical occasion was a surprize to many. But though he seemed herein to desert his old friends, it was only to recommend himself to the king and court, that by a new acquisition of influence and power, he might thereafter labour more effectually to destroy the Protestant settlement in the royal family; for in the next rebellion he was deeply concerned, and employed all the interest of his own clan to render it successful. Having no command in the Pretender's army, he was not at the battle of Culloden; so that he was not taken till June 1746, when he was sent up to London. In the March following, he was tried as a British peer before the House of Lords, in Westminster-hall, where the lord chancellor Hardwicke sat as lord high steward. After seven days trial, he was unanimously found guilty, received sentence of death, and on the 9th of April 1747, was beheaded on Tower-hill, in the 80th year of his age, by which the title and estate were forfeited to the crown.

Simon, his eldest son, master of Lovat, was attainted, with many others, in the parliament of 1746; but it appearing that he was over-ruled and compelled by his father, he some time after obtained his majesty's free pardon; and in January 1757, was appointed lieutenant colonel of the second battalion of the two new Highland battalions sent to North America. In 1762, he was advanced to the rank of a colonel, and afterwards to that of brigadier general, in which capacity he bravely served under lord Loudoun in Portugal, as he had also done all along in the war in America; and in 1761, was elected member of parliament for Invernessshire.

TITLE.] The right honourable Simon Frafer, lord Lovat.
CREATION.] Lord Lovat, by king James IV.
ARMS.] Quarterly, 1st and 4th sapphire, three cinquefoils, pearl, for Frafer; 2d and 3d ruby, three Eastern crowns, pearl.
CREST.] On a wreath, a stag's head erazed, proper.
SUPPORTERS.] Two stags of the last.
MOTTO.] Je suis prest.
CHIEF SEATS are.] At Lovat and Beaufort, in the county of Inverness; and at Beauly, in the county of Ross.

ELPHINGSTON,

ELPHINGSTON, Lord BALMERINO.

SIR James Elphingston, youngest son of Robert, the third lord Elphingston, studying the law, became so highly esteemed for his abilities, that king James VI. made him one of the senators of the college of justice, secretary of state, a commissioner of the treasury, lord president of session, and created him lord Balmerino. He married first, Clara, daughter of Sir John Menteith of Carse, by whom he had John, his heir; and by his second, who was Margaret, daughter of Hugh Maxwell of Tealing, he had a son, James, who was created lord Coupar: also two daughters, Ann, married to Andrew lord Fraser; and Mary, to John Hamilton of Blair. He died in 1612, and was succeeded by his eldest son,

John, second lord, who marrying Ann, daughter of Sir Thomas Ker of Fernihersh, and sister of Robert Ker, earl of Somerset, by her had a son,

John, third lord, who dying in 1704, left by his wife lady Margaret, daughter of John, the first earl of Loudoun, a son,

John, fourth lord, who by queen Anne was made general of the mint, sheriff of the county of Edinburgh, and in the two last parliaments of her reign, was one of the sixteen peers for Scotland. He married first, lady Christian, daughter of Hugh earl of Eglington, by whom he had two sons, Hugh and James; and two daughters, Margaret, married to Sir John Preston, Bart. and Jane, to Francis Stewart, eighth earl of Murray. Of the sons, James succeeded his father; and the eldest, Hugh, was killed at the siege of Lisle, in Flanders, in 1708. His second wife was Ann Ross, daughter of Arthur, archbishop of St. Andrews, by whom he had two sons, Arthur; and Alexander, who died unmarried; and dying in 1736, was succeeded by his eldest surviving son,

James, fifth lord, who was many years one of the senators of the college of justice. He married lady Betty Carnegy, second daughter of David earl of Northesk; but dying without issue in January 1745-6, was succeeded in the honour by his half-brother,

Arthur, sixth lord, who was born in 1688, and chusing a military life, had a commission in a regiment of foot during the reign of queen Anne. In the rebellion 1715, disliking the service of king George, he resigned his captain's commission to the duke of Argyll, and immediately joined the earl of Mar; but that rebellion being suppressed, he had the good fortune to obtain a pardon, after which he went into the French service; and in the next rebellion, commanded a troop of horse at the battle of Culloden, in April 1746; where he was taken prisoner, and brought to the Tower of London, with the earls of Kilmarnock and Cromertie, in May following. They were all tried in Westminster-hall, before the House of Lords, in July, and on the first of August, received sentence of death from the lord high steward; on the 18th of which month, this lord, and the earl of Kilmarnock, were beheaded on Tower-hill. He married Margaret, daughter of captain Chalmers, by whom he left no issue. His majesty, in regard to her distress, was pleased to give orders that she might receive a yearly pension of 50 l. for life.

TITLE.] The right honourable Arthur Elphingston, lord Balmerino, in the county of Fife.

CREATION.] Lord Balmerino, 25 February 1603, by king James VI.

ARMS.] Pearl, on a chevron, diamond, between three boars heads erazed, ruby, as many buckles of the first.

CREST.] A dove, pearl, with a snake, proper, linked about its legs.

SUPPORTERS.] Two griffins, proper, beaked and armed, or.

MOTTO.] Prudentia fraudis nescia.

BALFOUR, Lord BURLEIGH.

OF this family, which originally took its firname from the barony and castle of Burleigh, in Fifeshire, was Michael de Balfour, in the said county, who lived after 1420. He was succeeded by his son, Sir John, who had two sons, Michael, and James, ancestor of the Balfours of Denmiln, Kinnaird, Forret, &c. Michael, the eldest, dying about 1490, left issue another Michael, whose son, David, had a son, Sir Michael, whose only daughter, Margaret, succeeded him in his estates, and married Sir James Balfour of Montwhannie, who was in great favour with, and a faithful servant of queen Mary. They had issue five sons and three daughters.

In Sir Michael, their heir, the two families became united; and the said Sir Michael being in great favour with king James VI. was by him sent ambassador to the dukes of Tuscany and Lorrain, and created lord Balfour of Burleigh.

This lord, whose honour was granted to his heirs general, marrying Margaret, a daughter of the family of Lundin, of that ilk, by her had an only daughter and sole heiress,

Margaret; which lady being married to Robert Arnot of Ferney, Esq; he, by the marriage articles, changed his name to Balfour, and in her right became second lord Burleigh. In 1641, he was elected president of the parliament, and by the said lady had John, his heir; and three daughters, Jane, married to David, the second earl of Wemyss; Margaret, to Sir James Crawford of Kilbirny; Isabel, to Thomas lord Ruthven; and ——, to —— Arnot of Ferney.

John,

John, who succeeded his father as third lord, marrying Isabel, daughter of Sir William Balfour of Pitcullo, who in the reign of king Charles I. was lieutenant of the Tower of London, by her had three sons, Robert; John, of Ferney; and Henry, of Dunbog: and six daughters, Margaret, married to Andrew lord Rollo; Isabel, who died unmarried; Emilia, wife of Sir John Malcolm of Inneshil; Jane, of —— Oliphant of Gask, and afterwards of Sir Robert Douglas of Kirkness; Susan, of Robert Douglas of Strathendry; and Anne, of captain Robert Sinclair. He died in 1688, and was succeeded by his eldest son,

Robert, fourth lord, who marrying lady Margaret, daughter of George earl of Melvil, by her had a son, Robert, master of Burleigh; and two daughters, Margaret, and Mary, wife of Alexander Bruce of Kennet, in Clackmannan, and had issue. He died in 1713; and

Robert, his son, being guilty of a cruel murder, was forced to abscond, and fly from his native country; after which, entering into the rebellion 1715, he was attainted, but by the interest and good management of his sisters, the estate was recovered. He died in 1757, without issue, and his sister, Margaret, represents the family; but if she dies without issue, the representation will devolve upon Robert Bruce of Kennet, Esq; son and heir of her sister Mary, now one of the lords of session.

TITLE.] The right honourable Robert Balfour, lord Burleigh, in the county of Fife.

CREATION.] Lord Burleigh, 16 July 1607, by king James VI.

ARMS.] Pearl, on a chevron, diamond, an otter's head erazed, of the first.

CREST] On a wreath, a rock, and thereon a lady, holding in her right hand the head of an otter, and in her left the head of a swan.

SUPPORTERS.] On the dexter side, an otter sejant, proper; on the sinister, a swan of the last.

MOTTO.] Omni solum forti patria.

CHIEF SEAT.] Castle of Burleigh, in Kinross-shire.

FORBES, Lord PITSLIGO.

SIR John Forbes of that ilk, ancestor of this branch of the family of Forbes, marrying Elizabeth Kennedy, of the family of Dunure, by her had three sons, who were all knights. Sir William, the second son, married Agnes, daughter and heir of Sir William Fraser of Philorth, ancestor of the lord Salton; and with her having the barony of Pitsligo, in Aberdeenshire, he quartered the arms of Fraser. Alexander, the heir of that marriage, had a son, Sir Alexander, and he a son, Sir John, whose son, John, was succeeded by Alexander, who whose sons were, Sir William, Alexander, John, Arthur, and Hector. Sir William, the eldest, succeeded, and having no male issue, was succeeded by Alexander, his brother, and he by Sir John, his son, who married Christian, daughter of Sir Walter Ogilvie of Deskford, ancestor of the earl of Finlater, and had four daughters, the eldest of which, Anne, married Alexander, tenth lord Forbes; and a son,

Alexander, who was created lord Forbes of Pitsligo; and married lady Jane Keith, daughter of William, the sixth earl Marshal, and had

Alexander, second lord, who marrying lady Mary, daughter of James earl of Buchan, had

Alexander, third lord; and he dying in 1691, left by lady Sophia his wife, daughter of John Erskine, ninth earl of Mar,

Alexander, fourth lord, who married Rebecca, daughter of John Norton, of London, merchant, by whom he had one son, John, master of Pitsligo. By a second wife, Elizabeth Allen, an English lady, he had no issue. In the last rebellion he unfortunately took up arms, with a view to overturn the Protestant settlement of Great Britain. The cause came soon to a final issue at the battle of Culloden, in April 1746; from the destruction of which day he had the luck to escape in a ship from his own country, on the coast of Buchan; but was attainted, with many others, in May following, and his estate and honours forfeited to the crown. He died very old, in December 1762. His eldest son, John, master of Pitsligo, married Rebecca Ogilvie, of the family of Auchincross, but has no issue.

TITLE.] The right honourable Alexander Forbes, lord Pitsligo.

CREATION.] Baron Pitsligo, in the county of Aberdeen, 24 July 1633, by Charles I.

ARMS.] Quarterly, 1st and 4th sapphire, three bears heads couped, pearl, and muzzled, ruby, for Forbes; 2d and 3d sapphire, three cinquefoils, pearl, for Fraser.

CREST.] On a wreath, a falcon, pearl.

SUPPORTERS.] Two bears, proper, muzzled, ruby.

MOTTO.] Altius ibunt qui ad summa nituntur.

CHIEF SEAT was.] At Pitsligo, in Aberdeenshire.

SUTHERLAND, Lord DUFFUS.

KENNETH, sixth earl of Sutherland, who in 1333 lost his life at the battle of Halidounhill, leaving two sons, from Nicholas, the youngest, descended the lord Duffus. Which Nicholas, by his brother's grant in 1360, having obtained the lands of Terboll, had the same confirmed by king David II. and marrying Jane, daughter and heir of Reynald de Cheyne,

Cheyne, lord of Duffus, by her had those lands and barony. Henry, his heir, was father of Alexander, who married the heiress of Chisholm, and by her had two sons and one daughter, viz. Alexander, and William, of Quarrelwood. The daughter, Isabel, was wife of Sir Alexander Dunbar of Westfield. Alexander, the eldest, succeeded, who having only one daughter, Christian, married to William Oliphant of Berindale, the barony of Duffus thereupon descended to William Sutherland of Quarrelwood, son of William, second son of Alexander, before mentioned; and he marrying Janet, daughter of Sir Alexander Innes of that ilk, by her had a son, William, whose son, William, of Duffus, was succeeded by his son, Alexander, who was created lord Duffus by king Charles II. December 8, 1650. He married to his third wife, lady Margaret, daughter of James earl of Murray, and had issue James, his heir; and a daughter, Henrietta, married to George Livingston, earl of Linlithgow.

James, who succeeded as second lord, marrying lady Margaret Mackenzie, daughter of Kenneth, third earl of Seaforth, had three sons, Kenneth, his heir; Sir James Sutherland, who, on marrying Mary, daughter and heir of Sir William Dunbar of Hemprigs, Bart. changed his name to Dunbar; and William Sutherland of Roscomen, who married Mary, daughter of William lord Forbes.

Kenneth, who in 1705 succeeded his father as third lord, was advanced by queen Anne to the command of the Advice, a 50 gun ship of war, in which character he served in several expeditions with good conduct and bravery; but being engaged in the rebellion in 1715, he made his escape, and was attainted by act of parliament: after which he was taken at Hamburg, brought to London, and committed prisoner to the Tower in 1716; but the next year being released by the act of grace, he withdrew to Russia, and became a flag officer in the navy of that empire. He married Charlotte, daughter of Eric, governor of Gottenburgh, in Sweden, by whom he had a son, Eric; and two daughters, married in Sweden.

Eric, his son, married Elizabeth, daughter of his uncle, Sir James Dunbar of Hemprigs, Bart. by whom he has two sons and three daughters; James, Axle; Elizabeth, Charlotte, and Anne.

TITLES.] The right honourable Kenneth Sutherland, lord Duffus.

CREATION.] Baron Duffus, in Elginshire, 8 Dec. 1650, by king Charles II.

ARMS.] Quarterly, 1st ruby, three stars, topaz, for Sutherland; 2d sapphire, three cross croslets, fitchy, pearl, for Cheyne; 3d sapphire, a bear's head erazed, pearl, for Chisholm; 4th as the first.

CREST.]

CREST.] On a wreath, a cat sejant, proper.

SUPPORTERS.] Two savages, proper, each wreathed about his head and middle with laurel, and armed with a batoon.

MOTTO.] Without fear.

CHIEF SEATS were.] Skelbo, in Caithness; and Elgin-house, in Elgin.

NAIRN, Lord NAIRN.

THE first of this name on record is Michael de Nairn, a witness to the grant which Robert duke of Albany made to Andrew de Hamilton, of the lands of Galyston; from whom descended Alexander Nairn, who in the reign of James II. was many years comptroller of the houshold. His son, John, was father of Alexander, whose second son, John, carried on the line of this family. He had a son, John, whose son, a third John, was succeeded by his son, Thomas, and he by his son, Robert, whose eldest son, Robert, in the reigns of James VI. and Charles I. raised a competent fortune by the practice of the law; and by Margaret, daughter of Patrick Græme of Inchbraco, had one daughter, Margaret. After the king's death, taking arms in defence of king Charles II. he was surprised by a party of the English, and committed prisoner to the Tower of London, where he remained ten years; but living to see his master restored, was, in reward of his merit, created lord Nairn in 1681. He died in 1683, and his daughter, Margaret, lady Nairn, was married to lord William Murray, brother of John, the first duke of Athol, who, in right of his wife, was lord Nairn; and by him had four sons and eight daughters, viz. John, master of Nairn; Robert, of Aldie, who married Jane Mercer, which name his son took up; William, a captain in the Swedish East-India service, who died without issue; James, an officer in the British army: Margaret, wife of William viscount Strathallan; Emilia, of Laurence Oliphant of Gask; Catharine, of William earl of Dunmore; Marjory, of Duncan Robertson of Drumaquhan, heir male of the family of Strowan; Charlotte, of John Robertson of Lude; Mary; Louisa, wife of David Græme of Orchil; and Henrietta. This lord being a party in the rebellion 1715, against king George I. was taken at the battle of Preston, in Lancashire, and being tried, received sentence of death; but his majesty being moved by his natural clemency and great compassion for the widow and children of the said lord Nairn, not only included him in the act of grace 1717, but gave back the estate. He died in 1725, and was succeeded by his eldest son,

John, third lord, who marrying lady Katharine, daughter of Charles Murray, earl of Dunmore, by her, who died at Versailles, failles, May 16, 1754, had issue John, master of Nairn, an officer in the army; Charles, an officer in the Dutch service; Thomas; Henry: and a daughter, Clementina.

Notwithstanding the aforesaid events of the year 1715, this lord engaged himself as a captain in the rebellion 1745, and his name was put in the general act of attainder; but he escaped to France, where, if living, he now resides.

TITLE.] The right honourable William Nairn, lord Nairn, of Nairn, in Perthshire.

CREATION.] Lord Nairn, by king Charles II. 27 January 1680.

ARMS.] Quarterly, 1st and 4th party per pale, diamond and pearl, a chaplet charged with four cinquefoils, all counterchanged, for Nairn; 2d sapphire, three stars, pearl, within a double tressure counterflory with fleurs de lis, topaz, for Murray; and the 3d is counterquartered, 1st and 4th pally of six, topaz and diamond, for Athol; 2d and 3d topaz, a fess cheque, pearl and sapphire, for Stewart earl of Athol.

CHIEF SEATS were.] At Nairn and Strathurd, in Perthshire.

KEITH, Earl MARISHAL.

⁎ *By an oversight, this family is improperly placed; for, according to the date of creation, it should have been put the first of the attainted peers.*

THE family of Keith is one of the most ancient and illustrious in Scotland. Robert, from whom they are derived, performed many glorious exploits against the Danes, in the reign of Malcolm II. and had for his reward the lands and barony of Keith, in East Lothian, from which his posterity assumed their sirname. Malcolm also appointed him hereditary great marshal of Scotland, which high office has continued in his family ever since. From him was lineally descended Hervicus de Keith, who flourished in the reign of David I. He was father of Malcolm, and he of Philip, whose son, Hervey, had a son, Sir John, and he a son, Sir William, who died before the year 1296, and was succeeded by his eldest son, Sir Robert, who was one of the *Magnates Scotiæ* who signed the famous letter to the pope in 1320. He was killed at the battle of Duplin in 1332, and was succeeded by his son, John, whose son, Sir Robert, was succeeded by his son, Sir Edward, as he was by his eldest son, Sir William, his heir, who was one of the commissioners on the part of Scotland, that in 1369 were appointed to treat with the English about a peace between the two realms, which they concluded. He married Margaret, daughter and heir of Sir John Fraser, with whom he had a very large estate in the county of Kincardin, and elsewhere;

and by her had a son, John, whose wife was daughter of king Robert II. but he dying before his father, by her left a son, Sir Robert, who was heir apparent to his grandfather, who dying without male issue, his estate and honour fell to Robert Keith, his uncle, a person in great favour with king James I. under whom he held several important offices; and marrying lady Elizabeth, daughter of David earl of Crawfurd, by her he had several sons and daughters, and was succeeded by Sir William, the eldest, who was highly esteemed by king James II. and was created lord Keith and earl Marishal. He married Margaret, daughter of James lord Hamilton, by whom he had, *inter alia*, a son,

William, second lord, who married Mariota, daughter of ⸺ lord Erskine, and by her had two sons, William and Robert.

William, the eldest, third earl, married lady Elizabeth, daughter of Alexander earl of Huntley, by whom he had four sons, Robert, William, Gilbert, and Alexander; and five daughters, lady Janet, married to William earl of Montrose; lady Elizabeth, to William lord Sinclair; lady Jane, to John lord Glammis; lady Agnes, to Sir Archibald Douglas of Glenbervy; and lady Beatrix, to Alexander Fraser of Philorth. He died in 1530. Robert, lord Keith, his eldest son, dying in his father's life-time, left issue by his wife lady Elizabeth, daughter of James earl of Morton, two sons and two daughters; the eldest, William, succeeded his grandfather as fourth earl Marishal, who married Margaret, daughter and co-heir of Sir William Keith of Innerugie, and by her had two sons and seven daughters; William, lord Keith; Robert, afterwards lord Altree: lady Anne, wife of James earl of Murray, regent of Scotland, and afterwards of Colin earl of Argyle; lady Elizabeth, of Sir Alexander Irvine of Drum; lady Alison, of Alexander lord Abernethy; lady Mary, of Sir John Campbell of Calder; lady Beatrix, of John Allardice of that ilk; lady Janet, of James Crichton of Fendraught; and lady Margaret, of Sir John Kennedy of Blairquhain. He died in 1581. William, his eldest son, dying before his father, left issue by lady Elizabeth, daughter of George earl of Errol, George, William, Robert, and John; Mary, wife of Sir Robert Arbuthnot of that ilk; Barbara, of Alexander Forbes of Pitsligo; and Margaret, of Sir William Keith of Ludquhairn. George, the eldest son, succeeded his grandfather, and was fifth earl Marishal, who was one of the privy council to king James VI. by whom he was sent ambassador to the court of Denmark, where, at his own expence, he espoused the princess Ann, a daughter of that crown, in the name of his majesty; and in the year 1593, founded the Marishal college, in the city of New Aberdeen. In 1609, he was high commissioner to the parliament;

parliament; and dying in 1623, left issue by Margaret his first wife, daughter of Alexander lord Hume, William, his heir; and two daughters, lady Ann, married to William earl of Morton; and lady Margaret, to Sir Robert Arbuthnot of that ilk. And by his second wife, who was Margaret, daughter of James lord Ogilvy, ancestor of the earl of Airly, he had Sir James Keith of Benholm, whose daughter, Elizabeth, married Sir Archibald Primrose, ancestor of the viscount Primrose, and the earl of Roseberry; and John. He died in 1623, and was succeeded by his eldest son,

William, sixth earl, who was one of the privy council to king Charles I. and dying in 1635, left issue by lady Margaret his wife, daughter of John Erskine, earl of Mar, three sons and two daughters; lady Mary, married to John lord Kilpont, son and heir of William earl of Menteith; and lady Jane, to Alexander Forbes, lord Pitsligo. The sons were, William, lord Keith; George; and Sir John, who was created earl of Kintore.

William succeeded his father as seventh earl. In the time of the civil war, he, at his own charge, levied a troop of horse for the king's service; but after being taken prisoner, and sent to the Tower of London, he remained there ten years; and then being released, was made one of the privy council to king Charles II. and lord privy seal. He married lady Elizabeth, daughter of George earl of Winton, by whom he had four daughters, lady Mary, wife of Sir James Hope, ancestor of the earl of Hopetoun; lady Elizabeth, of Robert viscount Arbuthnot; lady Jane, of George lord Banff; and lady Isabel, of Sir Edward Turner, an English baronet. Dying in 1661, without male issue, he was succeeded by his brother,

George, eighth earl; and he dying in 1694, left by the lady Mary Hay, daughter of George earl of Kinnoul,

William, ninth earl, who, in the reign of queen Anne, strenuously opposed the union of the two kingdoms, and before the conclusion thereof, entered a protestation in these words:

' I DO hereby protest, that whatever is contained in any
' article of the treaty of union between Scotland and Eng-
' land, shall in no manner derogate from, or be prejudicial to
' me or my successors, in our heretable office of great marshal
' of Scotland, or in the full and free possession of the whole
' rights, dignities, powers, and privileges thereto belonging,
' which my ancestors and I have exercised as rights of property
' these 700 years. And I do further protest, that the parlia-
' ment and constitution of Scotland may remain and continue
' as formerly, and desire that this my protestation may be re-
' corded in the books of parliament.'

But in 1710, he was elected one of the sixteen Scotch peers, to serve in the parliament of Great Britain; and dying in 1712, left by lady Mary his wife, daughter of James earl of Perth, two sons, George and James; and two daughters, lady Mary, married to John earl of Wigton; and lady Ann, to Alexander earl of Galloway: and of the sons,

George, the eldest, succeeded, and was tenth earl; and being a nobleman of a military genius, queen Anne gave him, while he was lord Keith, a troop of horse, and afterwards made him a colonel in her majesty's guards; but after the accession of king George I. to the crown, his lordship was removed; and in 1715, joining in the rebellion with the earl of Mar, his estate and honours were forfeited by an act of attainder, in 1716, with the earls of Mar, Southesk, Linlithgow, Panmure, and Seaforth. His lordship has been for many years in the service of the king of Prussia, and is now governor of Neuffchattel, in Switzerland; and being the next of kin to John earl of Kintore, who died without issue in December 1761, an act of parliament passed to enable his lordship to inherit the estate of Kintore, or any other estate that might devolve to him.

James, the late renowned Prussian field marshal, followed his brother's fortune; and after their disappointment in Scotland, engaged in the service of Peter the Great, emperor of Russia, who gave him the rank of brigadier general. He was afterwards raised to the rank of field marshal, and commanded the Russian army in the war which broke out between Russia and Sweden in 1740; after which war, he entered into the service of the king of Prussia, and after many signal services, was unfortunately killed, October 14, 1758, when the right wing of the Prussian army, where he commanded, was surprised at Hockirchen by the Austrians, under marshal Daun, who, after the action, buried marshal Keith with great military honours; but the king of Prussia had his corpse taken up, and sent to Berlin, where a superb monument is erected to his memory.

TITLES.] Right honourable George Keith, earl Marishal, lord Keith, &c. &c.

CREATION.] Earl Marishal, of Keith, in 1455, by James II.

ARMS.] Pearl, on a chief, ruby, three pallets, topaz.

CREST.] On a wreath, a stag's head erazed, proper, and attired with ten tynes, topaz.

SUPPORTERS.] Two stags proper, attired as the crest.

MOTTO.] Veritas vincit.

CHIEF SEATS were.] Dunotar castle, and Fatereffo, in Kincardinshire; Inverugy and Newburgh, in Aberdeenshire.

RADCLIFFE, Earl of NEWBURGH.

I HAVE purposely placed this family last, though, in order of creation, it should have preceded the earl of Kilmarnock, because I am not certain whether, from some legal impediment, the present possessor of the title has been placed upon the roll of parliament.

From Robert, second son of Sir John Livingston of Calendar, who lived in the reigns of king James I. and II. was lineally descended Sir John Livingston of Kinnaird, whose son and successor, Sir James Livingston of Kinnaird, being greatly in favour with king Charles I. that prince, on the 13th of November 1647, raised him to the dignity of viscount Newburgh, (See Livingston, earl of Linlithgow, p. 273.) After the restoration, he was constituted captain of the guards, and further honoured with the titles of earl of Newburgh, viscount Kinnaird, lord Livingston of Flancraig, &c. by patent, to his heirs whatsoever, dated December 31, 1660. He married lady Catharine, daughter of Theophilus, earl of Suffolk, by whom he had issue a son,

Charles, second earl, who succeeded in 1670, and married Frances, daughter of Francis lord Brudenel, son and heir apparent of Robert, and brother of George, earls of Cardigan, who after his decease, married secondly, Richard, third lord Bellew, of the kingdom of Ireland, and had issue. By her the earl had only one daughter and sole heiress,

Charlotte, countess of Newburgh, who succeeded to his honours and estates in 1694. She married first, Thomas, son and heir apparent of Hugh lord Clifford of Chudleigh, by whom she had issue two daughters, ladies Frances and Anne. She married secondly, the honourable Charles Radcliffe, second son of Francis earl of Derwentwater, by whom she had issue two sons and three daughters, all born in France, viz. James, James-Clement; ladies Charlotte, Barbara, and Mary.

Charles Radcliffe, her husband, being taken at sea, in a French ship, in the year 1745, was sent prisoner to the Tower of London, and upon a former sentence of death, for the rebellion in 1715, was beheaded upon Towerhill, Dec. 8, 1746. His countess dying in 1755,

James, his eldest son, took the title of earl of Newburgh, as third earl.

TITLE.] The right honourable James Radcliffe, earl and viscount of Newburgh, and lord Kinnaird.

CREATIONS.] As above recited.

ARMS.] Pearl, on a bend, between three juliflowers, ruby, an anchor of the first, all within a double tressure, flowered and counterflowered, emerald.

CREST.] A moor's head couped, proper, bended, ruby and pearl, with pendlets, pearl, at his ears.

SUPPORTERS.] On the dexter, a savage, proper, wreathed about the head and middle, emerald; and on the sinister, an horse, pearl, furnished, ruby.

MOTTO.] Si je puis.

CHIEF SEAT.] When the family resided in Scotland, was at Kinnaird.

EXTINCT

EXTINCT PEERS OF SCOTLAND,

In Alphabetical Order.

Abercrombie, Sandilands, lord, so created December 12, 1647, and his son died without issue.

Abernethy, Abernethy, lord, so created by Alexander III. His son, Alexander, having no heir male, the title became extinct about 1312. See *Lord Salton*.

Albany, Stewart, duke of, so created in 1399 by Robert III. His son, Murdoch, was executed, and forfeited for treason, in 1425.

Albany, Stewart, duke of, so created in 1452, and died without issue in 1536.

Albany, Henry lord Darnley, duke of, husband of queen Mary, and since his death, the title has been enjoyed by the royal families of Scotland and England.

Altree, Keith, lord, so created in 1587 by James IV. He died without issue, in 1612.

Ancrum, Robert Ker, earl of, so created in 1633 by Charles I. Upon the death of his son, Charles, the title devolved upon the family of Lothian.

Angus, Gilchrist, earl of, so created about 1220, and the title, after five descents, was carried to the Umfravilles by Matilda, only daughter and heir of Malcolm, the fifth earl. That family enjoyed the title for seven descents, and became extinct in 1437.

Angus, Stewart, earl of, so created in 1330 by king David Bruce. The title merged in 1377, in the family of the Douglas's, and on the death of the late duke, came to the duke of Hamilton.

Annandale, Murray, earl of, so created in 1624 by James VI. His son, James, died without issue in 1658.

Athol, Malcolm, earl of, so created by David I. His son, Henry, dying without issue male, the title was conferred by Alexander II. on Alanus de Londinus in 1223; and he dying without issue, it was conferred, in the same year, on Thomas of Galloway, whose son, Patrick, dying without issue, Sir David Hastings had the title bestowed upon him, which went with his daughter and heir to John de Strabolgie. It became extinct in that family, for want of heirs male, in 1375, and king Robert Bruce conferred it upon his nephew, Sir John Campbell of Moulin, but he died without issue. It was then conferred on William Douglas, lord of Liddesdale, in 1341, by David II. (see earl of Morton) but he having no male issue, Robert II. bestowed the title upon lord Walter Stewart, his second son, who was forfeited and executed for being concerned in the mur-

der

der of James I. James II. then conferred it upon his uterine brother, Sir John Stewart of Balveny, in 1457. The title returned to the crown, for want of issue male, in 1625.

Badenoch, Cumming, lord of, became extinct in 1306.

Bargeny, Hamilton, lord, so created in 1639 by Charles I. became extinct, for want of heirs male, in the person of James, fourth lord.

Belhaven, Douglas, viscount, so created by Charles I. in 1633, but died without issue male.

Bewlie, Hay, lord, so created by James VI. in 1609. For want of issue male, the title expired in 1660.

Bothwell, Moray, lord of. The title became extinct in 1366.

Bothwell, Ramsay, lord, so created in 1486 by James III. and forfeited at the beginning of the reign of James IV.

Bothwell, Hepburn, earl of, created in 1488 by James IV. forfeited by James V. (earl and duke of Orkney, second husband of queen Mary, in 1567.)

Bothwell, Stewart, earl of, created by James VI. between 1584 and 1587. Extinct in 1624.

Brechin, Brechin, lord, created by David I. David, fourth lord, was executed for high treason in 1321, whereupon the title went with his sister to Sir David Barclay of Cairns, but was forfeited by his great great grandson, Robert, third lord, a party in the murder of James I.

Bruntisland, Wemyss, lord. See *Earl of Wemyss.*

Buchan, Cummin, earl of, became possessor of that title by marriage with the daughter and heir of Fergus, earl of Buchan, in the reign of Alexander II. It was forfeited by John, fourth earl, about 1329, whose son died without issue. Robert II. afterwards bestowed it upon Alexander Stewart, his fourth son, in 1374, but he had no male issue; and James III. created Sir James Stewart, second son of the black knight of Lorn, earl of Buchan. It went by the grand-daughter and heir of earl John, in 1551, to Robert Douglas, second son of Sir Robert of Lochleven, and by his grand-daughter, Mary, to James Erskine, eldest son, by the second venter of John earl of Mar, in 1625; upon whose decease, according to the entail, it devolved upon David Erskine, lord Cardross, ancestor of the present earl.

Caithness, earl of. One Macwilliam held this title in 1129. In 1222, Magnus, son of Gilibred earl of Angus, had it, who was forfeited. In 1450, George Crichton was so created, who died five years after, without issue.

Carlyle, Carlyle, lord, created in 1471 by James III. Michael, fourth lord, leaving no surviving issue male, in 1580 the title expired. But the said Michael's daughter having a daughter, Elizabeth, who married Sir James Douglas

glas of Parkhead, the title, after a long dispute, was adjudged to their son, Sir James; but his son William, lord Carlyle of Torthorald, died without issue.

Carrick, earl of. King William the Lion conferred this title, about 1180, upon Duncan, son of Gilbert, lord of Galloway. By his grand-daughter, Margaret, in 1256, it went to her husband, Adam Kilconath, who died without issue. His countess married, secondly, Robert de Bruce, lord of Annandale, who thereby became earl of Carrick; and the title came to the crown by the death of earl Thomas, in 1344. It was only enjoyed by the royal family from thence to 1633, when it was conferred by Charles I. on John Stewart, lord Kincleven, and is now claimed in right of his grand-aunt, Margaret Heath, great grand-daughter of the said John, earl of Carrick, by lord Willoughby de Broke.

Colville of Ochiltree, Colville, lord, created by K. Charles II. in 1651. Robert, third lord, died without issue.

Coupar, Elphingston, lord, created in 1607 by James VI. but died without male issue in 1669. (See *Balmerino*.)

Cramond, Richardson, lord. Created in 1628 by Charles I. and expired in Elizabeth Beaumont, wife of Sir Thomas Richardson, who was the patentee.

Crawfurd, Crawfurd, lord, became extinct in 1248. (See earl of Crawfurd.)

Crichton, Crichton, lord, and viscount *Frendraught*. Created in 1445. Extinct in 1483.

Denniston, Denniston, lord. Created in 1375, became extinct in 1394.

Dingwall, Keith, lord. Created in 1584 by James IV. but extinct, for want of issue male in the patentee, about 1589.

Dingwall, Preston, lord. Created in 1607 by James VI. Became extinct in the person of James, late duke of Ormond, grandson of the heiress.

Dirleton, Maxwell, earl of. Created in 1646 by Charles I. but died without issue male.

Douglas, Douglas, duke of. Created by queen Anne in 1703. Extinct on the death of the late duke Archibald, in 1761; but his titles of marquis of Douglas and earl of Angus devolved on the duke of Hamilton. Which see.

Dunbar, Home, earl of. Created in 1605; became extinct, for want of issue male, about 1689.

Dunbar, Constable, viscount. Created in 1620 by James VI. Became extinct by the decease of William, fourth viscount, without issue. The representation of the family, however, is now in the Constables of Burton-constable, descended from Cecily, sister of the last viscount.

Dunbarton,

Dunbarton, Douglas, earl of. Created in 1675 by Charles II. His son, George, second earl, died without issue.

Dundee, Scrymgeour, earl of. Created viscount Dudhope in 1641, and earl of Dundee in 1661. John, the third viscount and first earl, died without issue in 1688.

Dunfermline, Seton, earl of. Created in 1605 by James VI. Became extinct, for want of issue, in 1694.

Dunkeld, Galloway, lord. Created in 1645 by Charles I. The title was forfeited after the battle of Killicrankie, but the family still subsists.

Elgin, Bruce, earl of. See *Kincardin*, earl of.

Eythen, King, lord. Created in 1642 by Charles I. The honour has never been claimed since the death of the patentee.

Forfar, Douglas, earl of. Created in 1651 by Charles II. The second earl was killed at the battle of Sheriff-muir in 1715, and left no issue.

Forrester, Forrester, lord. Created in 1633 by Charles I. William, the seventh lord, died without issue, in 1748.

Forth, Ruthven, earl of. Created in 1642 by Charles I. and earl of Brentford, in England, in 1645. He died in 1651, leaving only a daughter, who died without issue, by her husband, James, lord Forrester.

Fraser, Fraser, lord. Created in 1633 by Charles I. Charles, fourth lord, died without issue. See *Lovat*.

Fyfe, Macduff, earl of. Created in 1057 by Malcolm Canmore. Isabel, only daughter of Duncan, thirteenth earl, (who died in 1353) married Sir William Ramsay, who became earl in her right, but by him, and a second and third husband, left no issue.

Galloway, lords of. The hereditary sovereign lords of Galloway governed that country from 1165 to 1234. Their names being Fergus, Uchtred, Gilbert, Roland and Alan; Alan left a daughter, Dervegild, who was wife of John Baliol, king of Scotland, by whom she is said to have had a daughter, wife of John Cummin, lord of Badenoch, whose only daughter was wife of Archibald, tenth lord Douglas, ancestor of the late duke.

Glasford, Abercrombie, lord. Created in 1685 by James VII. See *Lord Semple*.

Gowrie, Ruthven, earl of. Created in 1581 by James V. John, third earl, was slain in the attempt upon the person of James VI. at Perth, in 1600, with his brother Alexander, and the honour forfeited.

Haddington, Ramsay, viscount. Created in 1606, the patentee tentes being Sir John Ramsay, who killed the earl of Gowrie in the above attempt. He died without issue in 1625.

Halyburton, Halyburton, lord. Created in 1440, or 1441, by James II. Patrick, sixth and last lord, died without issue male in 1506. Halyburton of Pitcur has a claim to the title, which he has not yet made.

Harries, Harries, lord. Created in 1493. John, the seventh lord, succeeding to the honours of earl of Nithisdale, &c. the title of Herries merged in that family.

Holyroodhouse, Bothwell, lord. Created in 1607 by James VI. John, the second lord, died unmarried.

Jedburgh, Ker, lord. Created in 1622 by James VI. Upon the death of Robert, third lord, the title merged in the family of Lothian.

Irvine, Campbell, earl of. Created in 1642 by Charles I. but the patentee died without issue.

Islay, Campbell, earl of. See *Duke of Argyle*.

Kingston, Seton, viscount. Created in 1650 by Charles II. James, the third viscount, died in 1726, without issue.

Lennox, earls of. The first who bore this ancient title was Mac Arkill, so created by king Malcolm IV. Donald, sixth earl, lineally descended from him, left an only daughter, Margaret, who married Walter, of Faslane. Her eldest son by him, Sir Duncan, was created earl of Lennox by Robert II. He was beheaded in 1425, for high crimes and misdemeanours; and leaving three daughters, Isabel, the eldest, conveyed the title, by marriage, and indenture of her father, to Murdoch, duke of Albany. After the death of her husband, she continued countess of Lennox till her death, in 1452, when Elizabeth, her next sister, who married Sir John Stewart of Darnley, her eldest son, Sir Alan, of Darnley, having a son, John, he was ancestor of the dukes and earls of Lennox, of the name of Stewart.

Lennox, Stewart, duke of. Succeeded as earl of Lennox about 1468; duke in 1581: and Charles, the sixth duke, dying without issue in 1672, the honours and estates of the family devolved on king Charles II. who gave the life-rent to his widow, and thereafter created his natural son, Charles, duke of Lennox, &c. See *Duke of Lennox*.

Lorn and *Innermeath*, Stewart, lord. Created about 1404. See *Duke of Athol*.

Lyle, Lyle, lord. Created in 1446 by James II. James, master of Lyle, only son of John, fourth lord, died without issue.

Maderty,

Maderty, Drummond, lord. Created in 1607 by James VI. See *Viscount Strathallan*.

March, Dunbar, earl of. Created about 1128. The title was forfeited about 1434.

March, Stewart, earl of. Created by James VI. but the patentee died without issue in 1586.

Menteth, Menteth, earl of. Created about 1248. Mary, daughter of earl Alan, married Robert duke of Albany, upon the death of whose son, the title expired.

Menteth, Graham, earl of. Created, or rather exchanged for the earldom of Strathern, in 1428. William, eighth earl, died without issue in 1694. His estate went to the family of Montrose.

Methven, Stewart, lord. Created in 1528. Henry, third lord, died without issue, about 1570.

Moneypenny, Moneypenny, lord. Created in 1450 by James II. Alexander, third lord, died without issue in 1495.

Murray, Randolph, earl of. Created about 1313 by Robert II. John, third earl, was killed at the battle of Durham in 1346, leaving no issue.

Murray, Dunbar, earl of. Created in 1372. James, fifth earl, forfeited in 1455.

Newburgh, Barret, lord. Created in 1627 by Charles I. but the patentee died without male issue.

Newhaven, Cheyne, viscount. Created in 1681 by Charles II. His son, William, second viscount, died without male issue, leaving an only daughter, wife of Sir Henry Monson, of Lincolnshire, Bart.

Ochiltree, Stewart, lord. Created, or rather exchanged for the lordship of Evandale, and confirmed by act of parliament in 1543. Andrew, the fourth lord, sold it to his cousin, Sir James Stewart of Killeth, and was created lord Castle-Stewart, of the kingdom of Ireland, in 1619; and that title became extinct by his grandson's dying without issue. William, grandson of the above Sir James of Killeth, second lord Ochiltree, died unmarried in 1675, by which the title expired.

Orkney, Sinclair, earl of. Created in 1379 by Haco, king of Norway, and confirmed the same year by Robert II. Surrendered by William, the third earl, in favour of king James III. and annexed to the crown. See *Earl of Caithness*, and *Lord Sinclair*.

Orkney, Hepburn, duke of. Created in 1567 by queen Mary, who married him. He died without issue, in exile, in 1577. See *Bothwell, before*.

Orkney, Stewart, earl of. Created in 1581 by James VI. The title returned to the crown in 1614.

Oxenford,

Oxenford, Macgill, viscount. Created in 1651 by Charles II. Robert, the third viscount, died without issue. Arthur Macgill of Kemback is now the representative of the family.

Panmure, Valoniis, lord of. Created about 1066. See *Earl of Panmure*.

Pittenweem, Stewart, lord. Created in 1609 by James VI. but the patentee died without male issue.

Primrose, Primrose, viscount. See *Roseberry, Earl of*.

Ross, Ross, earl of. Created by Malcolm IV. Eupheme, countess of Ross, died without issue.

Ross, Ross, lord. Created in 1489 by James IV. George, the twelfth lord, died without issue male.

Rothsay, duke of. David, prince of Scotland, eldest son of king Robert III. was created duke of Rothsay, earl of Carrick, &c. in 1398. Since his death in 1401, the eldest sons of the kings of Scotland are born dukes of Rothsay, earls of Carrick, lords of Renfrew, &c.

Ruglen, Hamilton, earl of. See *Earl of March*.

Salton, Abernethy, lord. Created in 1445 by James II. See *Lord Salton*.

Spynie, Lindsay, lord. Created in 1698 by James VII. George, the fourth lord, died without issue about 1676.

St. Colme, Stewart, lord. Created in 1511 by James VI. His son and successor died without issue.

Stair, Dalrymple, earl of. See *Earl of Dumfries and Stair*.

Strathern, earl of. Created in 1068 by Malcolm Canmore. Malise, seventh earl, died without issue.

Strathern, Stewart, earl of. Created in 1358. Malise, third earl, had that of Menteith in lieu of it, *temp. Jac. I*.

Tarras, Scot, earl of. Created in 1660 by Charles II. for life only.

Teviot, Rutherford, earl of. Created in 1661 by Charles II. The patentee was killed, leaving no issue, in 1664.

Teviot, Spencer, viscount. Created in 1686 by James VII. but died without issue.

Teviot, Livingston, viscount. Created in 1698 by William III. but died without issue in 1711.

Yester, Giffard, lord. Created by William the Lion. Hugh, sixth lord, died without issue.

ADDITIONS and CORRECTIONS,

Since the foregoing Sheets were worked off at Press.

P. 13. Lord Campbell Scott, only surviving brother of the duke of Buccleugh, died in August 1766.

P. 34. The marquis of Lorn, eldest son and heir apparent of the duke of Argyll, was, on Dec. 20, created a peer of Great Britain, by the title of baron Sundridge, of Coombank, in Kent, to him and his heirs male; which failing, to his brothers, lords Frederick and William, and their heirs male, successively.

P. 39, line 22, for *James*, read *John*.

P. 53. William lord Newbottle has issue a son, William, master of Newbottle.

P. 65. The earl of Errol's first lady dying in 1764. he married secondly, Miss Carr, daughter of William Carr of Etal, in Northumberland, Esq; by whom he has one daughter, lady Charlotte.

P. 70, line 6. For had issue *a son*, read, *a daughter, lady Katherine*, who, &c. Line 10. For *infant son*, read, *eldest daughter*. Line 19, read, Their remains were carried to Scotland, and interred in the Abbey Church, at Edinburgh.

P. 95, line 26. The viscount M'Duff succeeded as earl of Fife in 1763. Alexander, ninth earl of Caithness, died in 1766. His successor we do not yet know.

P. 105. It seems it has been determined by the house of lords, that Dr. Fleming has no right to the title of earl of Wigton.

P. 109. The earl of Strathmore married, Feb. 14, 1767, Miss Bowes, only daughter and heir of the late George Bowes of Gibside, in the county palatine of Durham, Esq; a lady of an immense fortune.

P. 114. Duddingston, one of the earl of Abercorn's seats, is in Mid-Lothian.

P. 115. Lady Anne, second daughter of the earl of Kelly, is the wife of Sir Robert Anstruther, Bart.

P. 120, line 6, from the bottom; *read*, and Keith, captain in the royal navy.

P. 124. The countess of Lauderdale was delivered of a fifth son, in August 1765. Line 22, for *Edinburgh or Mid-* read, *West-*.

P. 132. The earl of Dumfries and Stair married secondly, Anne, daughter of William Duff of Crombie, Esq; therefore dele, *His lordship is now a widower*.

P. 137. The countess of Elgin and Kincardin, in June 1766, was delivered of a son, ——, lord Bruce.

P. 137 et seq. for *Dalhatsie*, read *Dalhousie*.

P. 141. Charles, fifth earl of Traquair, dying in 1764, without issue, was succeeded by his brother, John, now sixth earl of Traquair.

P. 144, line 26. After John Ogilvie, Esq; add, who died in 1764. Line 31, after *issue*, read, His lordship dying in 1765, was succeeded by his only son, James, now sixth earl of Finlater, &c.

P. 151, line 19. For *Hamilton*, read *Douglas*.

P. 152, line ult. Read, Lady Elizabeth, married in 1766 to the Hon. James Hope, second son of the earl of Hopetoun, and lady Margaret.

P. 158, line 4. For Paisley, read, Culross; and for Renfrewshire, read Fifeshire; and dele Kilmarnock in Lenos.

P. 160, line 18. After Carolina, read, who died in 1766.

P. 163. The earl of Dunmore has likewise a son, George, lord Fincastle. Line 2 from the bottom, for William, read John.

P. 164, lines 23 and 24, read, At Dunmore Park, in the county of Stirling.

P. 166. The earl of March has also a seat at Barnton, in the county of Mid-Lothian.

P. 170, line 1. After Margaret, read, married to — Stuart, lieutenant colonel in the army. She died in 1765, without issue.

P. 175, line 30. Read, Lady Mary, who died young; and lady Dorothea, married to Adam Inglis, Esq; eldest son of Sir John Inglis of Cramond, Bart. Line 31, dele *who died young*: The present earl of Roseberry, in 1764, married Miss ———, only daughter and heir of Sir ——— ———, Bart.

P. 177, line 22. For *David*, read *John*.

P. 181, line 6, from the bottom. After James, read, who married lady Betty Carnegie, sister of the earl of Northesk.

P. 182, line 2. After Sophia, read, His lordship married secondly, Jane, daughter of Robert Oliphant of Rossie, Esq; by whom he has one son and two daughters. Line 3, dele *police and of*.

P. 187, line 7, from the bottom. After Bunace, read, (who died at Vienna in March 1766.)

P. 190. The viscountess Irvine was delivered of a daughter in May 1765, and of another in June 1766.

P. 199, line 31. Dele *and*. Line 32, read, *and* John. Line ib. after Jane, read, who married Francis lord Down, son and heir of the earl of Moray.

P. 202, line 3. After Airshire, read, and Sauchie, in Stirlingshire.

P. 203, line 25. After infancy, read, and his lordship dying in 1766, was succeeded by his eldest son, James, now fourth lord Somerville.

P. 209,

P. 209, line 32. After Quebec, read, who married Miss Anne Ruthven, eldest daughter of lord Ruthven, by whom he has issue.

P. 210, line 2. For Elphinstone castle, read, Cumbernauld.

P. 214. Walter, lord Torphichen, died in 1765, and was succeeded by his eldest son, James, now ninth lord.

P. 223, line 15. For Edinbellie, in Stirlingshire, read, Merchiston, in Mid-Lothian.

P. 228, line 25. For *he left no issue*, read, he had issue Donald, master of Reay. Line 28, after succeeded by, read, his son Donald, &c. and dele what follows *lord*; and add to that word, His lordship is married, and had a son and heir born in May 1766.

P. 231. Walter, the present lord Aston, married in 1767, Miss Anne Hutchinson.

P. 234. Lord Banff has four daughters, but the name of the youngest is not known to us. His third son, Archibald, is deceased.

P. 234. The dowager lady Halkerton married again in 1765, to the honourable Anthony Brown, son and heir of the viscount Montague.

P. 239. John, fourth lord Belhaven, died in 1763, and was succeeded by his brother James, fifth lord Belhaven.

P. 244, lines 9 and 10. For *who also died young*, read, wife of captain Caulfield.

P. 247, line 10 from the bottom. For David, read Alexander.

P. 284, line 30. After Mary, read, who is wife of Harry Howard, Esq;

INDEX.

A

Abercorn, Hamilton earl of page 109
Aberdeen, Gordon earl of 161
Aboyne, Gordon earl of 154
Airly, Ogilvie earl of 290
Annandale, Johnston marq. of 54
Arbuthnot, Arbuthnot visc. 188
Argyll, Campbell duke of 26
Aston, Aston lord 229
Athol, Murray duke of 35
Attainted Peers 260

B

Balcarras, Lindsay earl of 153
Ballenden, Ballenden lord 248
Balmerino, Elphingston lord 317
Banff, Ogilvie lord 233
Belhaven, Hamilton lord 238
Blantyre, Stewart lord 216
Borthwick, Borthwick lord 191
Breadalbine, Campbell E. of 159
Buccleugh, Scot duke of 10
Buchan, Erskine earl of 80
Burleigh, Balfour lord 318
Bute, Stuart earl of 177

C

Caithness, Sinclair earl of 94
Carnwath, Dalziel earl of 293
Cassilis, Kennedy earl of 91
Cathcart, Cathcart lord 109
Colvile, Colvile lord 242
Cranston, Cranston lord 218
Crawfurd, Crawfurd earl of 56
Cromartie, M'Kenfie earl of 304

D

Dalhousie, Ramsay earl of 137
Deloraine, Scot earl of 183
Duffus, Sutherland lord 320
Dumfries, Crichton earl of 130
Dunblain, Osborne viscount 190
Dundee, Graham viscount 311
Dundonald, Cochran earl of 155
Dunmore, Murray earl of 163
Dysart, Talmash earl of 148

E

Eglingtoun, Montgomery E. of 86
Elgin, Bruce earl of 135
Elibank, Murray lord 235
Elphinstone, Elphinstone lord 207
Errol, Hay earl of 61
Extinct peers, alphabetical list of 328

F

Fairfax, Fairfax lord 223
Falkland, Carey viscount 184
Finlater, Ogilvie earl of 142

Forbes, Forbes lord page 192

G

Galloway, Stuart earl 118
Glasgow, Boyle earl of 176
Glencairn, Cunningham E. of 82
Gordon, Gordon duke of 14
Gray, Gray lord 197

H

Haddington, Hamilton E. of 116
Halkerton, Falconer lord 237
Hamilton, Hamilton duke of 1
Home, Home earl of 98
Hopetoun, Hope earl of 180
Hyndford, Carmichael E. of 171

I

Irvine, Ingram viscount 189

K

Kelly, Erskine earl of 114
Kenmure, Gordon viscount 306
Kilmarnock, Boyd earl of 301
Kilsyth, Livingston viscount 308
Kinnaird, Kinnaird lord 249
Kinnoul, Hay earl of 127
Kintore, Keith earl of 158
Kircudbright, Maclellan lord 232

L

Lauderdale, Maitland earl of 121
Lennox, Lenox duke of 14
Leven, Lesley earl of 145
Lindores, Lesley lord 215
Linlithgow, Livingston E. of 273
Lothian, Ker marquis of 51
Lovat, Fraser lord 314
Loudon, Campbell earl of 124

M

Mar, Erskine earl of 260
March, Douglas earl of 165
Marchmont, Hume earl of 166
Marshal, Keith earl 323
Melfort, Drummond E. of p. 303
Middleton, Middleton earl 279
Montrose, Graham duke of 40
Mordington, Douglas lord 203
Morton, Douglas earl of 75
Murray, Stewart earl of 95

N

Nairn, Nairn lord 322
Napier, Napier lord 219
Newark, Lesly lord 244
Newburgh, Ratcliffe earl of 326
Nithsdale, Maxwell earl of 266
Northesk, Carnegie earl of 151

O

Oliphant, Oliphant lord 210
Orkney,

INDEX

Orkney, Obrien Ctſs. of p. 164
P
Panmore, Maule earl of 294
Perth, Drummond earl of 277
Pitſligo, Forbes lord 319
Portmore, Collier earl of 182
Preſton, Graham viſcount 311
Q
Queenſberry, Douglas D. of 20
R
Reay, Mackay lord 227
Rollo, Rollo lord 240
Roſeberry, Primroſe earl of 173
Rothes, Leſley earl of 70
Roxburgh, Ker duke of 45
Rutherfoord, Rutherfoord Ld. 247
Ruthven, Ruthven lord 243
S
Salton, Fraſer lord 195
Seaforth, Mackenzie earl of 282

Second titles of peers page 251
Selkirk, Douglas earl of 150
Semple, Semple lord 224
Sinclair, Sinclair lord 313
Sixteen peers ſince the union 253
Somerville, Somerville lord 202
Southeſk, Carnegie earl of 268
Stirling, Alexander earl of 135
Stormont, Murray viſcount 185
Strathallan, Drummond viſc. 309
Strathmore, Lyon earl of 106
Sutherland, Sutherland Ctſs. 60
T
Torphichen, Sandilands lord 212
Traquair, Stewart earl of 142
Tweeddale, Hay marquis of 48
W
Wemyſs, Wemyſs earl of 226
Wigton, Fleming earl of 101
Winton, Seaton earl of 268

INDEX to the ARMS.

Name.	Numb.	Name.	Numb.	Name.	Numb.
Abercorn	27	Elgin & Kincardin	35	Marchmont	52
Aberdeen	48	Elibank	86	Montroſe	8
Aboyne	45	Elphinſtone	75	Mordington	73
Annandale	12	Errol	14	Morton	17
Arbuthnot	62	Fairfax	81	Murray	23
Argyll	6	Falkland	60	Napier	80
Aſton	83	Finlater & Seafield	38	Newark	92
Athol	7	Forbes	67	Northeſk	42
Balcarras	43	Galloway	29	Oliphant	74
Ballenden	94	Glaſgow	55	Orkney	50
Banff	85	Glencairn	19	Portmore	58
Belhaven	88	Gordon	4	Queenſberry	5
Blantyre	78	Gray	69	Reay	82
Borthwick	66	Haddington	30	Rollo	89
Breadalbine	47	Halkerton	87	Roſeberry	54
Buccleugh	2	Hamilton	1	Rothes	16
Buchan	18	Home	24	Roxburgh	9
Bute	56	Hopetoun	57	Rutherfoord	93
Caithneſs	22	Hyndford	53	Ruthven	91
Caſſilis	21	Irvine	64	Salton	63
Cathcart	70	Kelly	28	Selkirk	41
Colvile	92	Kinnaird	95	Semple	77
Cranſton	79	Kinnoul	33	Somerville	71
Crawfurd & Lindſay	13	Kintore	96	Stirling	44
Dalhouſie	36	Kircudbright	81	Stormont	61
Deloraine	59	Lauderdale	31	Strathmore	26
Dumfries and Stair	34	Lennox	3	Sutherland	15
Dunblain	65	Leven	32	Torphichen	76
Dundonald	46	Lindores	77	Traquair	37
Dunmore	40	Lothian	11	Tweeddale	10
Dyſart	40	Loudon	32	Wigton	25
Eglingtoun	20	March and Ruglen	51		

www.ingramcontent.com/pod-product-compliance
Lightning Source LLC
Chambersburg PA
CBHW051728300426
44115CB00007B/516